3e

Statistics Unplugged

Sally Caldwell

Texas State University | SAN MARCOS

WADSWORTH
CENGAGE Learning™

Australia • Brazil • Canada • Mexico • Singapore • Spain • United Kingdom • United States

WADSWORTH
CENGAGE Learning™

Statistics Unplugged,
Third Edition
Sally Caldwell

Acquisitions Editor, Psychology:
Jane Potter

Assistant Editor: Rebecca
Rosenberg

Marketing Manager: Tierra
Morgan

Marketing Communications
Manager: Talia Wise

Content Project Management:
Pre-PressPMG

Creative Director: Rob Hugel

Art Director: Vernon Boes

Print Buyer: Karen Hunt

Rights Acquisitions Account
Manager, Text: Margaret
Chamberlain-Gaston

Production Service:
Pre-PressPMG

Cover Designer: Gia Giasullo

Cover Image: Corbis Images

Compositor: Pre-PressPMG

For product information and
technology assistance, contact us at **Cengage Learning
Customer & Sales Support, 1-800-354-9706.**

For permission to use material from this text or product,
submit all requests online at **www.cengage.com/permissions**.
Further permissions questions can be e-mailed to
permissionrequest@cengage.com.

Library of Congress Control Number: 2009930829

Student Edition:
ISBN-13: 978-0-495-60218-7

ISBN-10: 0-495-60218-3

Wadsworth
10 Davis Drive
Belmont, CA 94002-3098
USA

Cengage Learning is a leading provider of customized learning solutions with office locations around the globe, including Singapore, the United Kingdom, Australia, Mexico, Brazil, and Japan. Locate your local office at **www.cengage.com/global.**

Cengage Learning products are represented in Canada by Nelson Education, Ltd.

To learn more about Wadsworth, visit
www.cengage.com/wadsworth

Purchase any of our products at your local college store or at our preferred online store **www.ichapters.com.**

Printed in the United States of America
1 2 3 4 5 6 7 13 12 11 10 09

In memory of Geoff Wood,
whose mom wrote the book on friendship

About the Author

Sally Caldwell earned her Ph.D. in Sociology from the University of North Texas. The author of *Romantic Deception* (Adams Media, 2000), Caldwell focuses her primary research interest on the topic of deception in social relationships. Caldwell resides in a small village in the hill country of south central Texas and serves on the faculty of the Department of Sociology at Texas State University I San Marcos.

Brief Contents

Contents

3 *The Shape of Distributions* — 52

4 *The Normal Curve* — 71

5 *Four Fundamental Concepts* — 93

8 Hypothesis Testing With Two Samples (Mean Difference and Difference of Means) 178

9 Beyond the Null Hypothesis   203

Preface

The idea behind this book came from my students, after I watched countless semesters unfold in a predictable fashion. The scene repeats itself each year in a classroom largely populated with panic-stricken students facing their first formal encounter with the field of statistical analysis. I like to think that my passion for the subject matter allows me to *connect* with most of the students, but there are always some students who remain locked in the throes of fear. For those students, mere passion on my part won't get the job done. What's called for, I've discovered, is constant attention to the students' perspective—a willingness to respect the roadblocks (real or imaginary) that exist in their minds.

For some students, the roadblock is what I call the *fear of the formula* factor—the tendency to recoil at the mere mention of a mathematical formula. For other students, it's the *so what?* scenario—the tendency for many students to question the relevance of the subject matter and why they have to take the course in the first place. I believe there's a way to overcome these roadblocks, and that's the method I've attempted to present in *Statistics Unplugged*.

For those who are familiar with the second edition, I trust that you'll find the fundamental approach has remained the same in this third edition. I've maintained the emphasis on the *logic* behind statistical analysis and the focus on an *intuitive* understanding that I believe lies within virtually every student. I've also tried to keep the language simple and friendly—something that seems to work for the students.

Changes to the Third Edition

The changes that appear in this third edition fall into three categories. First, I've expanded the introductory material in most chapters. I've also expanded the discussion of some central concepts, largely as a result of student questions about those concepts. Finally, I've sprinkled in a few additional examples in an effort to increase student understanding of the material.

As an example of the first sort of modification, I've included a *Before We Begin* section as a prelude to most of the chapters. The *Before We Begin* sections have been designed to accomplish two things in your trek through the book: 1) Give you some perspective of where you have been; and 2) get you prepared for where you're going. Some are longer than others, but all are intended to set the stage for new material. I urge you to take the sections to heart.

As an example of the second sort of modification, the material regarding measures of variability or dispersion is a case in point. For example, the discussion of the standard deviation has been expanded significantly, largely in response to student questions.

As to the third sort of change, I'm a firm believer in the notion that repetition is an important ingredient in the learning process; thus I've included some new examples of concepts and calculations. It's difficult to imagine that examples can hinder the learning process, so I trust the new examples represent a positive addition.

Acknowledgments

Books never *just happen*. They take time and effort. And they usually require the contributions of a lot of people along the way. The third edition of *Unplugged* isn't any different. The changes that have found their way into this edition came from many sources, including different corners within the Cengage organization and a number of universities.

When it came to getting everything moving along on the right track, it was my editor, Jane Potter, whose direction helped me navigate the sometimes complicated revision process. Jane was patient, understanding, encouraging, and responsive. Moreover, she brought a critical mind to the project. Her assistance was invaluable. The same can be said about Vernon Boes who was in charge of art direction on the project.

As to contributions from the halls of academe, I'm extremely indebted to the reviewers who were willing to review painstakingly the second edition of *Unplugged* and make suggestions for revisions. Accordingly, my sincere appreciation is extended to the following: David J. Hard (Loyola Marymount University); Heather Gelhorn (University of Colorado, Boulder); Andrew Garner (University of Mississippi); Allan R. Barnes (University of Alaska, Anchorage); and Colleen Swain (University of Florida). Those individuals join a long list of others who made similar contributions to previous editions. By now, I think of this book as a truly collaboration, group effort, and those earlier contributions deserve recognition.

In the first edition, those reviewers were:

James Knapp, Southeastern Oklahoma State University
Paul Ansfield, University of Wisconsin, Oshkosh
Lora Schlewitt-Haynes, University of Northern Colorado
Ida Mirzaie, Ohio State University
Charles Harrington, University of Southern Indiana
Steve Weinert, Cuyamaca Community College

J. Oliver Williams, North Carolina State University
Holly Straub, University of South Dakota
Faye Plascak-Craig, Marian College
Michael Hurley, George Mason University
Susan Nolan, Seton Hall University

For the second edition I am most appreciative for the help from

Robert Abbey, Troy University
David Hardy, Loyola Marymount University, Los Angeles
Steven Scher, Eastern Illinois University
Allen Shoemaker, Calvin College
Beverley Whalen-Schmeller, Tennessee State University

For the third edition I would like to thank

David J. Hardy, Loyola Marymount University
Heather Gelhorn, University of Colorado, Boulder
Colleen Swain, University of Florida
Andrew Garner, University of Mississippi
Allan R. Barnes, University of Alaska, Anchorage

Within the halls of my institution there were several individuals who were willing to listen to my incessant requests to discuss various statistical concepts. Moreover, they were willing to offer suggestions as to how *Unplugged* might be improved. At the top of the list is Professor Kay Newling—someone who shares my passion for the field of statistics and someone who can always be counted on to offer a refreshing perspective. I also owe a debt of gratitude to Ms. Michelle Edwards and Mr. Francisco Carrejo—graduate students who were invaluable in this effort. Ms. Edwards, in her role as a statistics lab instructor, developed a true connection with the students. That, coupled with her superb communication skills, meant that I was in the position to constantly monitor how the book material was being received by students. As for Mr. Carrejo, his assistance in grading, organizing my classes, and organizing me, for that matter, made my life far less complicated. Mr. Carrejo also went beyond the call of duty in his willingness to listen to me muse out loud about this or that statistical concept.

And then there's that cadre of very special people who make my life a joy. They make me laugh; they give my life purpose; they keep me sane. And in that category there is Eric Groves, a very significant character in my life's journey. Eric is willing to tolerate almost any of my eccentricities, unless, of course, it's something that gets in the way of a football game. Then there are the likes of Susan Abughazaleh, John Friedli, and Steve Klepfer, friends from far and near. The mere thought of any one of them brightens my day. To be with them is pure pleasure. They are clever, witty, engaging people. And finally, there are my pals, Marilee Wood and Tevis Grinstead. I never quite know what to say about them. I lack the words to describe their generosity, just as I can't begin to express what their friendship has meant to me. When I think about Marilee and Tevis, I know I am blessed.

Introduction

Methods, Material, and Moments to Remember

*S*tatistics, *Quantitative Methods, Statistical Analysis*—words, phrases, and course titles that can shake the confidence of nearly any student. Let me put your mind at ease right away. Your experience with statistics doesn't have to be a horror story. In fact, your experience with statistics can be an enjoyable one—a venture into a new way of thinking and looking at the world. It's all a matter of how you approach the material.

Having taught statistics to legions of undergraduate students, I've spent a lot of time trying to understand how students react to the material and why they react the way they do. In the process, I've developed my own approach to the subject matter, and that's what I've tried to lay out in this book. As we get started, let me tell you a little more about what to expect as you work your way through this book.

First, let me explain my method. I'm committed to the idea that the subject matter of statistics can be made understandable, but I'm also convinced that it takes a method based on *repetition*. Important ideas and concepts can be introduced, but they have to be reintroduced and reemphasized if a student is to get the connection between one concept and the next. Repetition—that's the method I've used in this book, so you should be prepared for that.

At times you may wonder why you're rereading material that was emphasized at an earlier point. Indeed, you'll likely start muttering "not that again!" If that happens, enjoy the moment. It signals that you're beginning to develop a sense of familiarity with the central concepts.

I've also tried to incorporate *simplicity* into the method—particularly in the examples I've used. Some examples will probably strike you as extremely simplistic—particularly the examples that are based on just a few cases and the ones that involve numbers with small values. I trust that simplistic examples won't offend you. The goal here is to cement a learning process, not to master complicated mathematical operations.

My experience tells me that a reliance on friendly examples, as opposed to examples that can easily overwhelm, is often the best approach. When numbers and formulas take center stage, the logic behind the material can get lost. That point, as it turns out, brings us to the essence of the material you're about to encounter.

In the final analysis, it's often the logic behind statistics that proves to be the key to success or failure. You can be presented with formulas—simple or complex—and you can, with enough time and commitment, memorize a string of them. All of that is well and good, but your ability to grasp the logic behind the formulas is a different matter altogether. I'm convinced that it's impossible to truly understand what statistics is all about unless you understand the logic behind the procedures. Consequently, it's the *logic* that I've tried to emphasize in this book.

Indeed, it's safe to say that numbers and formulas have taken a back seat in this book. Of course you'll encounter some formulas and numbers, but that's not where the emphasis is. Make no mistake about it—the emphasis in this book is on the conceptual basis behind the calculations.

There's one other thing about the material that deserves comment. Like it or not, the traditional approach to learning new material may come up short when you want to learn about statistical analysis. The reason is a simple one: The field of statistics is very different from other subjects you've studied in the past.

If, for example, you were taking a course to learn a foreign language, you'd probably figure out the goal of the course fairly early. You'd quickly sense that you'd be learning the basics of grammar and vocabulary, trying to increase your command of both over time. I suspect you'd have a similar experience if you signed up for a history course. You'd quickly sense that you were being introduced to names, dates, places, and overall context with the goal of increasing your understanding of the how and why behind events.

Unfortunately, the field of statistical analysis doesn't fit that learning model very well. You may be able to immediately sense where you're going in a lot of courses, but that's not necessarily the case in the field of statistics. In fact, my guess is that a command of statistical analysis is probably best achieved when you're willing to go along for the ride without really knowing at first where you're going. A statement like that is close to heresy in the academic world, so let me explain.

There *is* an end game to statistical analysis. People use statistical analysis to describe information and to carry out research in an objective, quantifiable way. Indeed, the realm of statistical analysis is fundamental to scientific inquiry. But the eventual application of statistical analysis requires that you first have a firm grasp of some highly abstract concepts. You can't even begin to appreciate the very special way in which scientists pose research questions if you don't have the conceptual background.

For a lot of students (indeed, most students, I suspect), it's a bit much to tackle concepts and applications at the same time. The process has to be broken down into two parts—first the conceptual understanding, and then the applications. And that's the essence of my notion that you're better off if you don't focus at the outset on where you're going. Concentrate on the conceptual basis first. Allow yourself to become totally immersed in an abstract, conceptual world, without any thought about direct applications. In my judgment, that's the best way to conquer the field of statistical analysis.

If you're the sort of student who demands an immediate application of concepts—if you don't have much tolerance for abstract ideas—let me strongly suggest that you lighten up a bit. If you're going to master statistics—even at the introductory level—you'll have to open your mind to the world of abstract thinking.

Toward that end, let me tell you in advance that I'll occasionally ask you to take a moment to seriously think about one notion or another. Knowing students the way I do, I suspect there's a chance (if only a small chance) that you'll ignore my suggestion and just move ahead. Let me warn you. The approach of trying to get from Point A to Point B as quickly as possible usually doesn't work in the field of statistics. When the time comes to really think about a concept, take whatever time is necessary.

Indeed, many of my students eventually come to appreciate what I mean when I tell them that a particular concept or idea requires a "dark room moment." In short, some statistical concepts or ideas are best understood if contemplated in a room that is totally dark and void of any distractions. Those should become your moments to remember. I'm totally serious about that, so let me explain why.

Many statistical concepts are so abstract that a lot of very serious thought is required if you really want to understand them. Moreover, many of those abstract concepts turn out to be central to the statistical way of reasoning. Simply reading about the concepts and telling yourself that you'll remember what they're all about won't do it. And that's the purpose behind a dark room moment.

If I could give you a single key to the understanding of statistics, it would be this: Take the dark room moments seriously. Don't be impatient, and don't think a few dark room experiences are beneath your intellectual dignity. If I tell you that this concept or that idea may require a dark room moment, heed the warning. Head for a solitary environment—a private room, or even a closet. Turn out the lights, if need be, and undertake your contemplation in a world void of distractions. You may be amazed how it will help your understanding of the topic at hand.

Finally, I strongly urge you to deal with every table, illustration, and work problem that you encounter in this text. The illustrations and tables often contain information that can get you beyond a learning roadblock. And as to the work problems, there's no such thing as too much practice when it comes to statistical applications.

Now, having said all of that as background, it's time to get started. Welcome to the world of statistics—in this case, *Statistics Unplugged!*

1

The What and How of Statistics

We start our journey with a look at the question of what statisticians do and how they go about their work. In the process, we'll explore some of the fundamental elements involved in statistical analysis. We'll cover a lot of terms, and most of them will have very specific meanings. That's just the way it is in the field of statistics—specific terms with specific meanings. Most of the terms will come into play repeatedly as you work your way through this book, so a solid grasp of these first few concepts is essential.

Before We Begin

One question that seems to be on the mind of a lot of students has to do with *relevance*—the students want to know why they have to take a course in statistics in the first place. As we begin our journey, I'll try to answer that question with a few examples. Just to get started on our relevance mission, consider the following:

Let's say that you're applying for a job. Everything about the job is to your liking. You think that you're onto something. Then you encounter the last line of the job description: *Applicants must have a basic knowledge of statistics and data analysis.*

Perhaps you're thinking about applying to graduate school in your chosen field of study. You begin your research on various graduate programs across the nation and quickly discover that there's a common thread in program requirements: *Some background in undergraduate statistics or quantitative methods is required.*

Maybe you're starting an internship with a major news organization and your first assignment is to prepare a story about political races around the state. Your supervisor hands you a stack of recent political polls, and you hit the panic button. You realize that you really don't know what is meant by the phrase *margin of error*, even though you've heard that phrase hundreds of times. You have some idea of what it means, but you don't have a clue as to its technical meaning.

Finally, maybe it is something as simple as your employer telling you that you're to attend a company *year-end review* presentation and report back. All's well until you have to comprehend all of the data and measures that are discussed in the *year-end review*. You quickly realize that your lack of knowledge about statistics or quantitative analysis has put you in a rather embarrassing situation.

Those are just a few examples that I ask you to consider as we get started. I can't promise that your doubts about the relevance of statistics will immediately disappear, but I think it's a good way to start.

A World of Information

People who rely on statistical analysis in their work spend a lot of time dealing with different types of information. One person, for example, might collect information on levels of income or education in a certain community, while another collects information on how voters plan to vote in an upcoming election. A prison psychologist might collect information on levels of aggression in inmates, while a teacher might focus on his/her latest set of student test scores. There's really no limit to the type of information subjected to statistical analysis.

Though all these examples are different, all of them share something in common. In each case, someone is collecting information on a particular *variable*—level of income, level of education, voter preference, aggression level, test score. For our purposes, a **variable** is anything that can take on a different quality or quantity; it is anything that can *vary*. Other examples might include the age of students, attitudes toward a particular social issue, the number of hours people spend watching television each week, the crime rates, in different cities, the levels of air pollution in different locations, and so forth and so on. When it comes to statistical analysis, different people may study different variables, but all of them generally rely on the same set of statistical procedures and logic.

 LEARNING CHECK

Question: What is a variable?

Answer: A variable is anything that can vary; it's anything that can take on a different quality or quantity.

The information about different variables is referred to as **data,** a term that's at the center of statistical analysis. As Kachigan (1991) notes, the field of statistical analysis revolves around the "collection, organization, and interpretation of data according to well-defined procedures." When the data relative to some specific variables are assembled (and note that we say *data are* because the word *data* is actually plural), we refer to the collection or bundle of information as a **data set.** The individual pieces of information are referred to as **data points,** but taken together, the data points combine to form a data set. For example, let's say that you own a bookstore and you've collected information from 125 customers—information about each customer's age, income, occupation, marital status, and reading preferences. The entire bundle of information would be referred to as a data set. The data set would be based upon 125 cases or observations (two terms that are often used interchangeably), and it would include five variables for each case (i.e., the variables of age, income, occupation, marital status, and reading preferences). A specific piece of information—for example, the age of one customer or the educational level of one customer—would be a data point.

With that bit of knowledge about data, data sets, and data points behind you, let's consider one more context in which you're apt to see the term, *data.* Statisticians routinely refer to **data distributions.** There are many ways to think of or define a data distribution, but here's one that's keyed to the material that you've just covered. Think of a data distribution as a listing of the values or responses associated with a particular variable in a data set. With the previous example of data collected from 125 bookstore customers as a reference, imagine that you listed the age of each customer—125 ages listed in a column. The listing would constitute a data distribution. In some situations you might want to

Simple Listing of Data	Frequency Distribution		Grouped Frequency Distribution	
Age	Age	Frequency (f)	Age Category	Frequency (f)
15	15	8	15–17	24
21	16	4	18–20	46
25	17	12	21–23	50
18	18	9	24–26	20
23	19	21		
17	20	16		
19	21	14		
22	22	18	Shows different age categories	
16	23	18	and number of times (the fre-	
15	24	10	quency or f) an age within a	
19	25	10	specific category is represented	
24			in the distribution. For example,	
.			the distribution contains a total	
.		Shows each value and	of 46 cases that are within the	
.		number of times (the fre-	age category of 18–20.	
Continued listing		quency or f) that it occurs.		
of individual		For example, the value		
cases for a total		15 occurred 8 times in		
of 140 cases		the distribution; the value		
		20 occurred 16 times in		
		the distribution		

Figure 1-1   Examples of Data Distributions (Based on a Distribution of Ages Recorded for a Distribution Having 140 Cases)

develop what's referred to as a **frequency distribution**—a table or graph that indicates how many times a value or response appears in a data set of values or responses. Even if you developed age categories (e.g., Under 18, 18 through 29, 30 through 39, 40 through 49, etc.), and you wrote down the number of cases that fell into each category, you'd still be constructing a frequency distribution (although you would refer to it as a *grouped* frequency distribution). For some examples of the different ways that a data distribution might appear, take a look at Figure 1-1.

☑ LEARNING CHECK

Question: What is a data distribution?
Answer: A data distribution is a listing of values or responses associated with a particular variable in a data set.

Later on, you'll encounter a lot more information about data distributions—particularly, what you can learn about a distribution when you plot or graph the data, and what the shape of a distribution can tell you. For the moment, though, just remember the term *data,* along with *case* or *observation.* You'll see these terms over and over again.

Levels of Measurement

Closely related to variables is the concept of *levels of measurement.* Every variable is measured at a certain level, and some levels of measurement are, in a sense, more sophisticated than others. Here's an example to introduce you to the idea.

Let's say that you took a test along with 24 other students. Suppose the test scores were posted (a form of a data distribution) showing student rankings but not the actual test scores. In this case, you could determine how you did relative to the other students, but that's about all you could determine. You could easily see that you had, for example, the third highest score on the test. All you'd have to do is take a look at the list of rankings and look at your rank in comparison to the ranks of the other students. Someone would have the top or number one score, someone would have the second highest score, and so forth—right down to the person with the lowest rank (the 25th score). You'd know something about everyone's test performance—each person's rank—but you really wouldn't know much.

If, on the other hand, the actual test scores were posted, you'd have a lot more information. You might discover that you actually scored 74. The top score, for example might have been 95 and the next highest score might have been 80, so that your score of 74 was in fact the third highest. In this case, knowledge of the actual test score would tell you quite a lot.

In the first example (when all you knew were student ranks on the test), you were dealing with what's referred to as the *ordinal level of measurement.* In the second instance, you were dealing with a higher level of measurement, known as the *ratio level of measurement.* To better understand all of this, let's consider each level of measurement, from the simplest to the most complex.

The most fundamental or simplest level, **nominal level of measurement,** rests on a system of *categories.* A person's religious affiliation is an example of a nominal level variable, or a variable measured at the nominal level of measurement. If you were collecting data on that variable, you'd probably pose a fairly direct question to respondents about their religious affiliation, and you'd put their responses into different categories. You might rely on just five categories (Protestant, Catholic, Jewish, Muslim, Other), or you might use a more elaborate system of classification (maybe seven or even nine categories). How you go about setting up the system of categories is strictly up to you. There are just two requirements: The categories have to be mutually exclusive, and they must be collectively exhaustive. Let me translate.

First, it must be possible to place every case you're classifying into one category, but only one category. That's what it means to say that the categories are *mutually exclusive*. Returning to the question about religious affiliation, people could categorized as Protestant *or* Catholic *or* Jewish *or* Muslim *or* Other, depending on their responses, but they couldn't be placed into more than one category each.

Second, you have to have a category for every observation or case that you're classifying or recording. That's what it means to say that the categories are *collectively exhaustive*. In the process of classifying people according to their religious affiliations, for example, what would you do if someone said that he/she was an atheist? If you didn't have a category to handle that, then your system of categories wouldn't be collectively exhaustive. In many instances, a classification system includes the category Other for that very reason—to ensure that there's a category for every case being classified.

So much for the nominal level of measurement. Now let's look at the next level of measurement.

When you move to the **ordinal level of measurement,** an important element appears: the notion of *order.* For example, you might ask people to tell you something about their educational level. Let's say you give people the following response options: less than high school graduate, high school graduate, some college, college graduate, post–college graduate. In this instance, you can say that you've collected your data on the variable Level of Education at the ordinal level. You'll then have some notion of order to work with in your analysis. You'll know, for example, that the people who responded "some college" have less education than those who answered "college graduate." You won't know exactly how much less, but you will have some notion of order—of *more than* and *less than*.

If, on the other hand, you asked students in your class to tell you what time they usually awaken each morning, you'd be collecting data at the **interval level of measurement.** The key element in this level of measurement is the notion of *equal intervals*. For example, the difference between 9:15 AM and 9:30 AM is the same as the difference between 7:45 AM and 8:00 AM—15 minutes.

The final level of measurement—the **ratio level of measurement**—has all the properties of the interval level of measurement, along with one additional feature: The ratio level has a true or known *zero point*. It's a minor point, but one that you should understand.

To say that a variable is measured at the ratio level of measurement means that the variable could actually assume a value of 0 and that the value of 0 is, in a sense, legitimate. For example, if you asked students how much money they spent each week on entertainment, it is possible for some to say that they don't spend any money on entertainment. In other words, a response of 0 is possible. In this case, the 0 is "legitimate" because it really represents an absence of entertainment spending. In the process of research, it isn't necessary for you to actually have an observation in your distribution that is recorded as a 0 to say that you are working with data measured at the ratio level. All that's necessary is that a 0 response or observation be possible. When you're dealing with a scale of measurement that has the possibility of a value of 0, it is possible to speak in terms of ratios (and hence the phrase *ratio level of measurement*). For example, you can speak in terms of one value being twice as large as another value.

As a practical matter, the difference between the interval and ratio levels of measurement is of no consequence in the world of statistical analysis. The most sophisticated statistical techniques will work with interval level data. For that reason, some statistics textbooks don't even mention the ratio level of measurement. Others simply refer to the **interval/ratio level of measurement**—the practice we'll follow.

    LEARNING CHECK

Question: What are the different levels of measurement?
Answer: The different levels of measurement are nominal, ordinal,
             interval, and ratio. Some statisticians combine the last
             two levels and use the term *interval/ratio,* since there's no
             real practical difference between the two.

My guess is that you're still wondering what the real point of this discussion is. The answer will have more meaning down the road, but here's the answer anyway: It's very common for students to complete a course in statistics, only to discover that they never quite grasped how to determine which statistical procedure to use in what situation. Indeed, many students slug their way through a course, memorizing different formulas, never having the faintest idea why one statistical procedure is selected over another. The answer, as it turns out, often relates to the level of measurement of the variables being analyzed. Some statistical procedures work with nominal or ordinal data, but other procedures may require interval/ratio data. Other factors also come into play when you're deciding which statistical procedure to use, but the level of measurement is a major element.

All of this will become more apparent later on. For the moment, let's return to some more of the fundamental elements in statistical analysis.

Samples and Populations

Samples and *populations*—these terms go to the heart of statistical analysis. We'll start with the larger of the two and work from there. In the process, we'll encounter some of the other terms you've already met in the previous section.

Here's a straightforward way to think about the term *population:* A **population** (or **universe**) is all possible cases that meet certain criteria. It's the total collection of cases that you're interested in studying. Let's say you're interested in the attitudes of registered voters in your community. All of the registered voters (all possible cases) in your community would constitute the population or universe. If you were interested in the grade point averages of students enrolled for six hours or more at a particular university, then all the students who met the criteria (that is, all students enrolled for six hours or more at the university) would constitute the population.

When you think about it, of course, you'll realize that the population of registered voters is constantly changing, just as the population of students enrolled for six hours is apt to be constantly changing. Every day, more people may register to vote, and others may be removed from the voter rolls because they have died or moved to another community. By the same token, some students may drop a course or two (thus falling below the six-hour enrollment criterion), and some students may drop out of school altogether.

Once you begin to understand the idea that a population can change (or is potentially in a state of constant flux), you're on your way to understanding the fundamentally theoretical nature of statistical analysis. Think of it this way: You want to know something about a population, but there's a good chance that you can never get a totally accurate picture of the population simply because it is constantly changing. So, you can think of a population as a collection of all possible cases, recognizing the fact that what constitutes the population may be changing.

Not only are populations often in a constant state of flux, but practically speaking, you can't always have access to an entire population for study. Matters of time and cost often get in the way—so much so that it becomes impractical to work with a population. As a result, you're very apt to turn to a sample as a substitute for the entire population.

Unfortunately, a sample is one of those concepts that many people fail to truly grasp. Indeed, many people are inclined to dismiss any information gained from a sample as being totally useless. Cuzzort and Vrettos (1996), however, are quick to point out how the notion of a sample stacks up against knowledge in general:

> There is no need to apologize for the use of samples in statistics. To focus on the limitations of sampling as a criticism of statistical procedures is absurd. The reason is evident. All human knowledge, in one way or another, is knowledge derived from a sampling of the world around us.

A **sample** is simply a portion of a population. Let's say you know there are 4,329 registered voters in your community (at least there are 4,329 registered voters at a particular time). For a variety of reasons (such as time or cost), you may not be able to question all of them. Therefore, you're likely to question just a portion of them—for example, 125 registered voters. The 125 registered voters would then constitute your sample.

Maybe you want to take a snapshot look at student attitudes on a particular issue, and let's say you've defined your population as all the students enrolled for six hours or more. Even if you could freeze the population, so to speak, and just consider the students enrolled for six or more hours at a particular time (recognizing that the population could change at any moment), you might not be able to question all the students. Because time or the cost of a total canvass might stand in your way, you'd probably find yourself working with a portion of the population—a sample, let's say, of 300 students.

As you might suspect, a central notion about samples is the idea of their being representative. To say that a sample is representative is to say that the sample mirrors the population in important respects. For example, imagine a population that has a male/female split, or ratio, of 60%/40% (60% male and 40% female). If a sample of the population is representative, you'd expect it to have a male/female split very close to 60%/40%. Your sample may not reflect a perfect 60%/40% split, but it would probably be fairly close. You could, if you wanted to, take a lot of different samples, and each time you might get slightly different results, but most would be close to the 60%/40% split. Later on, you'll encounter a more in-depth discussion of the topic of sampling, and of this point in particular. For the moment, though, let's just focus on the basics with a few more examples.

Let's say you're an analyst for a fairly large corporation. Let's assume you have access to all the employee records, and you've been given the task of conducting a study of employee salaries. In that case, you could reasonably consider the situation as one of having the population on hand. In truth, there's always the possibility that workers may retire, quit, get fired, get hired, and so on. But let's assume that your task is to get a picture of the salary distribution on a particular day. In a case such as this, you'd have the population available, so you wouldn't need to work with just a sample.

To take a different example, let's say your task is to survey customer attitudes. Even if you define your population as all customers who'd made a purchase from your company in the last calendar year, it's highly unlikely that you could reach all the customers. Some customers may have died or moved, and not every customer is going to cooperate with your survey. There's also the matter of time and expense. Add all of those together, and you'd probably find yourself working with a sample. You'd have to be content with an analysis of a portion of the population, and you'd have to live with the hope that the sample was representative.

Assuming you've grasped the difference between a sample and a population, now it's time to look at the question of what statistical analysis is all about. We'll start with a look at the different reasons why people rely on statistical analysis. In the process, you'll begin to discover why the distinction between a sample and population is so important in statistical analysis.

 LEARNING CHECK

Question: What is a population?
Answer: A population is all possible cases that meet certain
             criteria; it is sometimes referred to as the universe.

LEARNING CHECK

Question: What is a sample?
Answer: A sample is a portion of the population or universe.

The Purposes of Statistical Analysis

Statisticians make a distinction between two broad categories of statistical analysis. Sometimes they operate in the world of *descriptive statistics;* other times they work in the world of *inferential statistics.* Statisticians make other distinctions between different varieties of statistical analysis, but for our purposes, this is the major one: descriptive statistics versus inferential statistics.

Descriptive Statistics

Whether you realize it or not, the world of descriptive statistics is a world you already know, at least to some extent. **Descriptive statistics** are used to *summarize* or *describe* data from samples and populations. A good example is one involving your scores in a class. Let's say you took a total of 10 different tests throughout a semester. To get an idea of your overall test performance, you'd really have a couple of choices.

You could create a data distribution—a listing of your 10 test scores—and just look at it with the idea of getting some intuitive picture of how you're doing. As an alternative, though, you could calculate the average. You could add the scores together and divide by 10, producing what statisticians refer to as the *mean* (or more technically, the arithmetic mean). The calculation of the mean would represent the use of descriptive statistics. The mean would allow you to summarize or describe your data.

Another example of descriptive statistics is what you encounter when the daily temperature is reported during the evening weather segment on local television. The weathercaster frequently reports the low and high temperature for the day. In other words, you're given the *range*—another descriptive statistic that summarizes the temperatures throughout the day. The range may not be a terribly sophisticated measure, but it's a summary measure, nonetheless. Just like the mean, the range is used to summarize or describe some data.

 LEARNING CHECK

Question: How are descriptive statistics used?
Answer: Descriptive statistics are used to describe or summarize data distributions.

Inferential Statistics

We'll cover more of the fundamentals of descriptive statistics a little later on, and my guess is that you'll find them to be far easier to digest than you may have anticipated. For the moment, though, let's turn to the world of inferential statistics. Since that's the branch of statistical analysis that usually presents the greatest problem for students, it's essential that you get a solid understanding. We'll ease into all of that with a discussion about the difference between *statistics* and *parameters*.

As it turns out, statisticians throw around the term *statistics* in a lot of different ways. Since the meaning of the term depends on how it's used, the situation is ripe for confusion. In some cases, the exact use of the term isn't all that important, but there's one case in which it is of major consequence. Let me explain.

Statisticians make a distinction between *sample statistics* and *population parameters*. Here's an example to illustrate the difference between the two ideas. Imagine for a moment that you've collected information from a sample of 2000 adults (defined as people age 18 or over) throughout the United States—men and women, people from all over the country. Let's also assume that you have *every* reason to believe it is representative of the total population of adults, in the sense that it accurately reflects the distribution of age and other important characteristics in the population.

Now suppose that, among other things, you have information on how many hours each person in the sample spent viewing television last week. It would be a simple matter to calculate an average for the sample (the average number of hours spent viewing television). Let's say you determined that the average for your sample was 15.4 hours per week. Once you did that, you would have calculated a summary characteristic of the sample—a summary measure (the average) that tells you something about the sample. And that is what statisticians mean when they use the expression *sample statistic*. In other words, a **statistic** is a characteristic of a sample. You could also calculate the range for your sample. Let's say the viewing habits range from 0 hours per week to 38.3 hours per week. Once again, the range—the range from 0 to 38.3—would be a summary characteristic of your sample. It would be a sample statistic.

Now let's think for a moment about the population from which the sample was taken. It's impossible to collect the information from each and every member of the population (millions of people age 18 or over), but there is, in fact, an average or mean television viewing time for that population. The fact that you can't get to all the people in the population to question them doesn't take away from the reality of the situation.

The average or mean number of hours spent viewing television for the entire population is a characteristic of the population. By the same token, there is a range for the population as a whole, and it too is a characteristic of the population. That's what statisticians mean when they use the expression *population parameter.* In other words, a **parameter** is a characteristic of the population.

This notion that there are characteristics of a population (such as the average or the range) that we can't get at directly is a notion that statisticians live with every day. In one research situation after another, statisticians are faced with the prospect of having to rely on sample data to make inferences about the population. And that's what the branch of statistics known as **inferential statistics** is all about—using sample statistics to make inferences about population parameters. If you have any doubt about that, simply think about all the research results that you hear reported on a routine basis.

It's hard to imagine, for example, that a political pollster is only interested in the results of a sample of 650 likely voters. He/she is obviously interested in generalizing about (making inferences to) a larger population. The same is true if a researcher studies the dating habits of a sample of 85 college students or looks at the purchasing habits of a sample of 125 customers. The researcher isn't interested in just the 85 students in the sample. Instead, the researcher is really interested in generalizing to a larger population—the population of college students in general. By the same token, the researcher is interested in far more than the responses of 125 customers. The 125 responses may be interesting, but the real interest has to do with the larger population of customers in general. All of this—plainly stated—is what inferential statistics are all about. They're the procedures we use to "make the leap" from a sample to a population.

 LEARNING CHECK

Question: How are inferential statistics used?

Answer: Inferential statistics are used to make statements about a population, based upon information from a sample; they're used to make inferences.

Question: What is the difference between a statistic and a parameter, and how does this difference relate to the topic of inferential statistics?

Answer: A statistic is a characteristic of a sample; a parameter is a characteristic of a population. Sample statistics are used to make inferences about population parameters.

As you'll soon discover, that's where the hitch comes in. As it turns out, you can't make a direct leap from a sample to a population. There's something that gets in the way—something that statisticians refer to as *sampling error*. For example, you can't calculate a mean value for a sample and automatically assume that the mean you calculated for your sample is equal to the mean of the population. After all, someone could come along right behind you, take a different sample, and get a different sample mean—right? It would be great if every sample taken from the same population yielded the same mean (or other statistic, for that matter)—but that's not the way the laws of probability work. Different samples are apt to yield different means.

We'll eventually get to a more in-depth consideration of sampling error and how it operates to inhibit a direct leap from sample to population. First, though, let's turn our attention to some of those summary measures that were mentioned earlier. For that, we'll go to the next chapter.

Chapter Summary

Whether you realize it or not, you've done far more than just dip your toe into the waters of statistical analysis. You've actually encountered some very important concepts—ideas such as data distributions, levels of measurement, samples, populations, statistics, parameters, description, and inference. That's quite a bit, so feel free to take a few minutes to think about the different ideas. Most of the ideas you just encountered will come into play time and time again on our statistical journey, so take the time to digest the material.

As a means to that end, let me suggest that you spend some of your free time thinking about different research ideas—things you might like to study, assuming you had the time and resources. Maybe you're interested in how the amount of time that students spend studying for a test relates to test performance. That's as good a place to start as any. Think about how you'd define your *population*. Mull over how you'd get a *sample* to study. Think about how you'd measure a *variable* such as time spent studying. Think about how you'd record the information on the variable of test performance. Would you record the actual test score (an interval/ratio *level of measurement*), or would you just record the letter grade—A, B, C, D, or F (an ordinal level of measurement)?

Later on, you might think about another research situation. Maybe there are questions you'd like to ask about voters or work environments or family structures or personality traits. Those are fine, too. All's fair in the world of research. Just let the ideas bubble to the surface. All you have to do is start looking at the world in a little different way—thinking in terms of variables and levels of measurement and samples and all the other notions you've just encountered. When you do that, you may be amazed at just how curious about the world you really are.

Some Other Things You Should Know

At the outset of your statistical education, you deserve to know something about the field of statistical analysis in general. Make no mistake about it; the field of statistical analysis constitutes a discipline unto itself. It would be impossible to cover the scope of statistics in one introductory text or course, just as it would be impossible to cover the sweep of western history or chemistry in one effort. Some people become fascinated with statistics to the point that they pursue graduate degrees in the field. Many people, with enough training and experience, carve out professional careers that revolve around the field of statistical analysis. In short, it is an area of significant opportunity.

Whether you take the longer statistical road remains to be seen. Right now, the focus should be on the immediate—your first encounter with the field. Fortunately, the resources to assist you are present in spades. For example, Cengage (the publisher of this text) has an excellent website available and easily accessible for your use. Let me encourage you to visit it at the following URL:

www.cengage.com/psychology/caldwell

Libraries and bookstores also have additional resources—other books you may want to consult if some topic grabs your attention or seems to be a stumbling block. My experience tells me that it pays to consider several sources on the same topic—particularly when the subject matter has to do with statistical analysis. The simple act of consulting several sources introduces you to the fact that you'll likely find different approaches to symbolic notation in the field of statistics, as well as different approaches to the presentation of formulas. Beyond that, one author's approach may not suit you, but another's may offer the words that unlock the door. There's hardly a lack of additional information available. What's needed is simply the will to make use of it when necessary. In the world of statistical analysis, there's a rule of thumb that never seems to fail: If a good resource is available, give it a look.

Key Terms

data
data distribution
data point
data set
descriptive statistics
frequency distribution
inferential statistics
interval level of measurement
interval/ratio level of measurement

nominal level of measurement
ordinal level of measurement
parameter
population
ratio level of measurement
sample
statistic
universe
variable

Chapter Problems

Fill in the blanks with the correct answer.

1. A researcher is trying to determine if there's a difference between the performance of liberal arts majors and business majors on a current events test. The variables the researcher is studying are _____ and _____. (Provide names for the variables.)

2. A researcher is studying whether or not men and women differ in their attitudes toward abortion. The variables the researcher is studying are _____ and _____. (Provide names for the variables.)

3. The level of measurement based upon mere categories—categories that are mutually exclusive and collectively exhaustive—is referred to as the *nominal* level of measurement.

4. The level of measurement that has all the properties of the nominal level of measurement, plus the notion of order is referred to as the *ordinal* level of measurement.

5. The level of measurement at which mathematical operations can be carried out is referred to as the _____ level of measurement.

6. A researcher collects information on the political party affiliation of people at a local community meeting. The information on party affiliation (Republican, Democrat, Independent, or Other) is said to be measured at the *Nominal* level of measurement.

7. A researcher collects information on the number of absences each worker has had over the past year. He/she has the exact number of days absent from work. That information would be an example of a variable (absences) measured at the *interval* level of measurement.

8. Participants in a research study have been classified as lower, middle, or upper class in terms of their socioeconomic status. We can say that the variable of social class has been measured at the *ordinal* level of measurement.

9. A researcher wants to make some statements about the 23,419 students at a large university and collects information from 500 students. The sample has *500* members, and the population has *23,419* members.

10. A statistic is a characteristic of a *sample*; a parameter is a characteristic of a *population*

11. In the world of inferential statistics, sample _____ are used to make inferences about population _____.

12. *Descriptive* statistics are used to describe or summarize data; *Inferential* statistics are used to make inferences about a population.

2

Describing Data and Distributions

This chapter has three goals. The first goal is to introduce you to the more common summary measures used to describe data. As we explore those measures, we'll key in on two important concepts: central tendency and variability or dispersion. The second goal follows from the first—namely, to get you comfortable with some of the symbols and formulas used to describe data. The third goal is a little more far-reaching: getting you to visualize different types of data distributions. The process of data visualization is something that you'll want to call upon throughout your journey. We'll start with some material that should be fairly familiar to you.

Before We Begin

Imagine the following scenario: Let's say that you're reading a report about health care in the United States. As the report unfolds, it reads like a general narrative—outlining the historical changes in leading causes of death, summarizing the general upward trend in the cost of health care, and so forth and so on. You tell yourself that you're doing fine—so far, so good. But before you know it, you're awash in a sea of terms and numbers. Some are terms that you've heard before, but you've never been really comfortable with them. Others are totally new to you. You get the idea of what the report is dealing with, but all the terms and numbers are just too much.

For someone else, it might be a report about crime (e.g., types of crime, length of sentence, characteristics of offenders, etc.), and packed with terms that are unfamiliar. And, just to consider another example, the scenario might involve a report on voter participation, with an emphasis on the last two presidential election cycles.

With any of those topics, it's easy to imagine the scenario. The report begins with a well-crafted narrative, but eventually it turns into a far more quantitative exposé on the subject at hand. What started out as a high level of reading comprehension on your part gives way to a sea of confusion. All too often, it's the reader's lack of solid grounding in basic statistical analysis that makes the report unintelligible.

It is against that background that the next chapter unfolds. You're going to be introduced to quite a few terms. Some of the terms may be very familiar to you, but others will likely take you into new territory. Allow me to throw in a cautionary note at the outset. If some of the terms or concepts are familiar to you, count yourself lucky. On the other hand, don't suspend your concentration on what you're reading. There's likely to be some new material to digest. Accordingly, let me urge you to take whatever time is necessary to develop a thorough understanding of the various concepts. In many ways, they represent essential building blocks in the field of statistics.

Measures of Central Tendency

To a statistician, the mean (or more correctly, the arithmetic mean) is only one of several measures of **central tendency.** The purpose behind any measure of central tendency is to get an idea about the *center,* or typicality, of a distribution. As it turns out, though, the idea of the center of a distribution and what that really reflects depends on several factors. That's why statisticians have several measures of central tendency.

The Mean

The one measure of central tendency that you're probably most familiar with is the one I mentioned earlier—namely, the mean. The **mean** is calculated by adding all the scores in a distribution and dividing the sum by the number of scores. If you've ever calculated your test average in a class (based on a number of test scores over the semester), you've calculated the mean. I doubt there is anything new to you about this, so let's move along without a lot of commentary.

Now let's have a look at the symbols that make up the formula for the mean. Remember: All that's involved is summing all the scores (or values) and then dividing the total by the number of scores (or values). In terms of statistical symbols, the mean is calculated as follows:

$$\text{Mean} = \frac{\Sigma X}{N}$$

In this formula, there are only three symbols to consider. The symbol Σ (the Greek uppercase sigma) represents *summation* or *addition*. Whenever you encounter the symbol Σ, expect that summation or addition is involved. As for the symbol X, it simply represents the individual scores or values. If you had five test scores, there would be five X values in the distribution. Each one is an individual score (something statisticians often refer to as a *raw score*). The N in the formula represents the number of test scores (cases or raw scores) that you're considering. We use the lowercase n to represent the number of cases in a sample; the uppercase N represents the number of cases in a population. If, for example, you were summing five test scores (and treating the five cases as a population), you would say that N equals five. Consider the examples in Table 2-1.

As you've no doubt discovered when you have calculated the mean of your test scores in a class, the value of the mean doesn't have to be a value that actually appears in the distribution. For example, let's say you've taken three tests

Table 2-1   Calculation of the Mean

Scores/Values ($N = 5$)	Scores/Values ($N = 7$)	Scores/Values ($N = 10$)
1	2	5
2	4	1
3	6	3
4	7	4
5	8	1
	9	4
$\Sigma X = 15$	13	3
$15/5 = 3$		5
Mean = 3	$\Sigma X = 49$	2
	$49/7 = 7$	2
	Mean = 7	
		$\Sigma X = 30$
		$30/10 = 3$
		Mean = 3

Table 2-2   Calculation of the Mean

Scores/Values (N = 3)	Scores/Values (N = 6)
80	1
84	2
86	3
	4
ΣX = 250	5
250/3 = 83.33	6
Mean = 83.33	
	ΣX = 21
	21/6 = 3.50
	Mean = 3.50

and your scores were 80, 84, and 86. The mean would be 83.33—clearly a value that doesn't appear in the distribution. Similar examples are shown in Table 2-2.

By the same token, consider three incomes: $32,000; $41,500; and $27,200. The mean income would be $33,566.67—a value that isn't found in the distribution.

 LEARNING CHECK

Question: What is the mean, and how is it calculated?
Answer: The mean is a measure of central tendency. It is calculated by adding all the scores in a distribution and dividing the sum by the number of cases in the distribution.

Now let's give some thought to what we've been looking at. The formula, at least the way I presented it to you, tells you how to calculate the mean. Now the question is, which mean are we really considering? Since the goal of inferential statistics is to use information from a sample to make statements about a population, it's essential to make it clear when you're referring to the mean of a sample and when you're referring to the mean of a population. Therefore, it shouldn't surprise you to learn that statisticians use different symbols to refer to the mean—one for a sample mean, and the other for a population mean. Just as there's a difference in the way we express the number of cases for a sample (n), as opposed to a population (N), we make a distinction between the mean of a sample and the mean of a population. Here's the difference:

$\overline{X}$ is the symbol for the mean of a sample (and n = number of cases)
μ is the symbol for the mean of a population (and N = number of cases)

So, the symbol for the mean of a sample is $\overline{X}$, and the symbol for the mean of the population is represented by μ. The symbol μ stands for *mu* (the Greek letter, pronounced "mew"). Technically, the term *mean* is used in reference to a sample, and **mu (μ)** is used in reference to a population. It's certainly OK to speak of the population mean, but you should always keep in mind that you are really speaking about mu. The formula essentially is the same for either the mean or mu, so you may be inclined to think this is a minor point—the fact that statisticians have different symbols for the sample mean and the population mean. Later on, you'll develop an appreciation for why the symbols are different. For the moment, just accept the notion that the distinction is an important one—something that you should take to heart. As a matter of fact, it's always a good idea to be clear in your thinking and speech when it comes to statistics. Use expressions such as *sample mean, population mean,* or *mu.* Unless you're making reference to the mean in general, don't just think or speak in terms of a mean without making it clear which mean you have in mind.

 LEARNING CHECK

Question: What is the symbol for the mean of a sample? What is the symbol for the mean of a population? What is another term for the mean of the population?

Answer: The symbol for the mean of a sample is $\overline{X}$; the mean of the population, which is also referred to as mu, is μ.

Let me make one last point about the mean—whether you're talking about a population mean (μ) or a sample mean ($\overline{X}$). One of the properties of the mean is that it is sensitive to extreme scores. In other words, the calculated value of the mean is very much affected by the presence of extreme scores in the distribution. This is something you already know, particularly if you've ever been in a situation in which just one horribly low test score wrecked your overall average.

Imagine, for example, that you have test scores of 80, 90, 80, and 90. So far, so good; everything seems to be going your way. But what if you took a final test, and your score turned out to be 10? You don't even have to calculate the mean to know what a score like that would do to your average. It would pull your average down, and that's just a straightforward way of saying that the mean is sensitive to extreme scores. The 10 would be an extreme score, and the mean would be pulled down accordingly. You shouldn't have to do the calculations; you should be able to feel the effect in your gut, so to speak. If you did take the time to calculate the mean under the two different scenarios, you'd see that it moved from a value of 85 (when you were basing it on the first four tests) to a value of 70 (when you added in the fifth test score of 10). The presence of that one extreme score (the score of 10) reduced the mean by 15 points (see Table 2-3)!

Table 2-3   Effect of an Extreme Score

Test Scores (N = 4)	Test Scores (N = 5)
80	80
90	90
80	80
90	90
	10
ΣX = 340	
340/4 = 85	ΣX = 350
Mean = 85	350/5 = 70
	Mean = 70

 LEARNING CHECK

Question: What does it mean to say that the mean is sensitive to extreme values?

Answer: The mean is sensitive to extreme values in the sense that an extremely high or extremely low score or value in a distribution will pull the value of the mean toward the extreme value.

The Median

Now we turn our attention to a second measure of central tendency—one referred to as the *median*. Unlike the mean, the median is not sensitive to extreme scores. In the simplest of terms, the **median** is the point in a distribution that divides the distribution into halves. It's sometimes said to be the midpoint of a distribution. In other words, one half of the scores in a distribution are going to be equal to or greater than the median, and one half of the scores are going to be equal to or less than the median. Like the mean, the median doesn't have to be a value that actually appears in the distribution.

As I introduce you to the formula for the median, let me emphasize one point. It is a positional formula; that is, it points you to the *position* of the median. Again, the formula yields the position of the median—not the value. Here's the formula for the position of the median:

$$\text{Median} = \frac{N + 1}{2}$$

Note the use of *N*, indicating the number of cases in a population. If we were determining the median for a sample, we would use *n* to represent the number of cases.

Before you apply the formula, there's one thing you should always remember: You have to arrange all the scores in your distribution in ascending or descending *order*. That's a must—otherwise, the formula won't work.

Table 2-4 Calculating the Median

- 13 scores
- Arrange the scores in ascending or descending order
- Formula for the Position of the Median $= \dfrac{N + 1}{2}$

$$\frac{N + 1}{2} = \frac{13 + 1}{2} = \frac{14}{2} = \text{7th Score}$$

- SCORES

  1, 1, 2, 4, 9, 11, 12, 21, 21, 24, 25, 25, 30

  ↑

  7th Score = Position of the Median

  Value of the Median = 12

Assuming you've arranged all the scores in ascending or descending order, (see Table 2-4), all you have to know is how many scores you have in the distribution. That's what the N in the formula is all about; it's the number of cases, scores, or observations. If there are 13 scores, the formula directs you to add 1 to 13 and then divide by 2. The result would be 14 divided by 2, or 7. The median would be the 7th score—that is, the score in the 7th *position*. Once again, the median would not have the value of 7. Rather, it would be the value of whatever score was in the 7th position (from either the top or the bottom of the distribution). The *value* of the median—of the score in the 7th position— is 12.

The nice thing about the formula for the position of the median is that it will work whether you have an odd or an even number of cases in the distribution. When you have an even number of cases, the formula will direct you to a position that falls halfway between the two middle cases. For example, consider a distribution with the following scores: 1, 2, 3, 12, 20, 24. With 6 scores in the distribution, the formula gives us (6 + 1)/2. The median, then, would be the 3.5th score. The halfway point between the third and fourth scores is found by calculating the mean of the two values: (3 + 12)/2 = 15/2 = 7.5. In other words, the *position* of the median would be the 3.5th score; the *value* would be 7.5. All of this should become more apparent when you look at the examples in Table 2-5.

The other nice thing about the formula for the position of the median is that it works for distributions with a small number or a large number of values. For example, in a distribution with 315 scores, the position of the median would be the 158th score (315 + 1)/2 = 158. In a distribution with 86,204 scores, the position of the median would be the 43,102.5th score (86,204 + 1)/2.

Table 2-5   Locating the Median

Scores/Values		Scores/Values	
1		1	
2		2	
4	← Median = 4	4	← Median = 4
8		8	
12		120	
Scores/Values		Scores/Values	
3		10	
5		15	
7	← Median = 6	25	← Median = 20
9		80	
Scores/Values		Scores/Values	
10		17	
10		27	
14		34	
23	← Median = 23	34	← Median = 34
23		34	
80		59	
100		62	

Once again, the formula determines the position of the median—not the value of the median. Also, the formula rests on the assumption that the scores in the distribution are in ascending or descending order.

 LEARNING CHECK

Question: What is the median, and how is it determined?
Answer: The median is a measure of central tendency; it is the score that cuts a distribution in half. The formula locates the position of the median in a distribution, provided the scores in distribution have been arranged in ascending or descending order.

The Mode

In addition to the mean and the median, there's another measure of central tendency to consider—namely, the mode. The **mode** is generally thought of as the score, value, or response that appears most frequently in a distribution. For example, a distribution containing the values 2, 3, 6, 1, 3, and 7 would produce a mode of 3. The value of 3 appears more frequently than any other value.

A distribution containing the values 2, 3, 6, 1, 3, 7, and 7 would be referred to as a **bimodal distribution** because it has two modes—3 and 7. Both values (3 and 7) appear an equal number of times, and both appear more frequently than any of the other values. A distribution with a single mode is called a **unimodal distribution.** A distribution in which each value appears the same number of times has no mode. Table 2-6 provides a few more examples to illustrate what the mode is all about.

☑ LEARNING CHECK

Question: What is the mode?
Answer: The mode is a measure of central tendency. It's the score
             or response that appears most frequently in a distribution.

As it turns out, there are some situations in which the mode is the only measure of central tendency that's available. Consider the case of a nominal level variable—for example, political party identification. Imagine that you've collected data from a sample of 100 voters, and they turn out to be distributed as follows: 50 Republicans, 40 Democrats, and 10 Independents. You couldn't calculate a mean or median in a situation like this, but you could report the modal response. In this example, the modal response would be Republican, because that was the

Table 2-6 Identifying the Mode

Scores/Values		Scores/Values	
1		1	
2		2	
2		2	
7		7	
9		7	
9	9 is the mode	7	Bimodal
9		9	modes = 7 and 9
21		9	
		9	
		25	
		29	

Scores/Values		Scores/Values	
200		20	
200	200 is the mode	22	
200		28	No mode
305		30	
309		36	
318		38	

most frequent response. If nothing else, this provides a good example of a point I made earlier about levels of measurement: Which measure of central tendency you use is often a function of the level of measurement that's involved.

In the long run, of course, the most widely used measure of central tendency is the mean, at least in inferential statistics. So, let's return to a brief discussion of the mean as a jumping-off point for our next discussion.

Assume for the moment that you're teaching two classes—Class A and Class B. Further assume that both classes took identical tests and both classes had mean test scores of 70. At first glance, you might be inclined to think the test performances were identical. They were, in terms of the mean scores. But does that indicate the classes really performed the same way? What if the scores in Class A ranged from 68 to 72, but the scores in Class B ranged from 40 to 100? You could hardly say the overall performances were equal, could you? And that brings us to our next topic—variability.

Measures of Variability or Dispersion

The last example carries an important message: If you really want to understand a distribution, you have to look beyond the mean. Indeed, two distributions can share the same mean, but can be very different in terms of the variability of individual scores. In one distribution, the scores may be widely dispersed or spread out (for example, ranging from 40 to 100); in another distribution, the scores may be narrowly dispersed or compact (for example, ranging from 68 to 72). Statisticians are routinely interested in this matter of **dispersion** or **variability**— the extent to which scores are spread out in a distribution.

Statisticians have several measures at their disposal when they want to make statements about the dispersion or variability of scores in a distribution. Even though a couple of the measures aren't of great utility in statistical analysis, you should follow along as we explore each one individually. By paying attention to each one, you're apt to get a better understanding of the big picture.

 LEARNING CHECK

Question: What is meant by dispersion?

Answer: Dispersion is another term for variability. It is an expression of the extent to which the scores are spread out in a distribution.

The Range

One of the least sophisticated measures of variability is the **range**—a statement of the lowest score and the highest score in a distribution. For example, a statement that the temperature on a particular day ranged from 65 degrees to

78 degrees would be a statement of the range of a distribution. You could also make a statement that the income distribution of your data ranged from $12,473 to $52,881. To report the range is to report a summary measure of a distribution. Consider the following examples of range:

Test Scores	23–98
Incomes	$15,236–$76,302
Aggression Levels	1.36–7.67
Temperature	62°–81°

The range tells you something about a distribution, but it doesn't tell you much. To have more information, you'd need a more sophisticated measure. We'll eventually explore some of the other measures, but first let's spend a little time on a central concept—the general notion of variability, or deviations from the mean.

 LEARNING CHECK

Question: What is the range?
Answer: The range is a measure of dispersion. It is a simple statement of the highest and lowest scores in a distribution.

Deviations From the Mean

Researchers are often interested in questions that have to do with variability. For example, a researcher might want to know why test scores vary, why incomes vary, why attitudes vary, and so forth. In some cases, they want to know whether or not two or more variables vary together—for example, a researcher might want to know if test scores and income levels vary together or not. Before you can even begin to answer a question like that, you first have to understand the concept of variability. To do that, you have to begin with an understanding of the notion of *deviations from the mean*.

The idea of deviation from the mean is fairly basic. It has to do with how far an individual or raw score in a distribution deviates from the mean of the distribution. To calculate the deviation of an individual score from the mean, simply subtract the mean of the distribution from the individual score. When you do this, you're determining how far a given score is from the mean.

For example, imagine a distribution with five values—a distribution with the following income data: $27,000; $32,000; $82,000; $44,000; and $52,000. As it turns out, the mean of that distribution would be $47,400. In terms of deviations from the mean, there will be five of them. An income of $27,000 deviates a certain amount from the mean of $47,400 and so does $32,000. The same is true for the values of $82,000, $44,000, and $52,000.

Table 2-7   Deviations from the Mean

Scores/Values	Deviations	
(N = 5)		
(X)	(X – Mean)	
1	1 – 3	–2
2	2 – 3	–1
3	3 – 3	0
4	4 – 3	+1
5	5 – 3	+2
		0
Mean = 3		

DEVIATIONS FROM THE MEAN

Note: The same results will occur whether you subtract the mean from each raw score or you subtract each raw score from the mean.

Each value deviates from the mean. To better understand all of this, take a look at the example shown in Table 2-7.

Regardless of how many scores there are in a distribution, there will be a deviation of each score from the mean. Consider the illustrations in Table 2-7. Focus on the relationship between each individual raw score and the mean, and how that translates into the concept of a *deviation* of each score from the mean.

Whether the individual scores in a distribution are widely dispersed or tightly clustered around the mean, the sum of the deviations from the mean will always equal 0 (subject to minor effects due to rounding). This point is important enough that it deserves an illustration. Consider a really simple distribution like the one shown in Table 2-8. Chances are that you can simply look at the first distribution and determine that the mean is equal to 3.

Assuming you've convinced yourself that the mean is equal to 3, take a close look at the distribution. Begin with the score of 1. The score of 1 deviates from the mean by –2 points (1 – 3 = –2). In other words, the score of 1 is 2 points *below* the mean (hence the negative sign). The score of 2 is –1 points from the mean (2 – 3 = –1). The score of 3 has a deviation of 0, because it equals the mean (3 – 3 = 0). Then the pattern reverses as you move to the scores that are above the mean. The score of 4 is 1 point *above* the mean (4 – 3 = 1), and the score of 5 is 2 points above the mean (5 – 3 = 2). If you were to sum all the deviations from the mean, they would equal 0. The sum of the deviations from the mean will always equal 0, because that is how the mean is mathematically defined.

As you learned earlier, the mean doesn't have to be a score that actually appears in a distribution, and the same notion applies in this instance as well.

Table 2-8 Sum of Deviations from the Mean = 0

Scores/Values	Deviations	
(X)	(X − Mean)	
1	1 − 3	−2
2	2 − 3	−1
3	3 − 3	0
4	4 − 3	+1
5	5 − 3	+2
		0
Mean = 3		

Sum of the Deviations Equals 0

Scores/Values	Deviations	
(X)	(X − Mean)	
80	80 − 90	−10
85	85 − 90	−5
90	90 − 90	0
95	95 − 90	+5
100	100 − 90	+10
		0
Mean = 90		

Sum of the Deviations Equals 0

Consider the two examples in Table 2-9. In each case, the calculated value of the mean doesn't really appear in the distribution, but the sum of the deviations from the mean still equals 0.

The principle that the sum of the deviations equals 0 holds so steadfastly that you can assure yourself of one thing: If you ever add the deviations from the mean and the total doesn't equal 0, you've made a mistake somewhere along the way. You've either calculated the deviations incorrectly, or you've calculated the mean incorrectly. As mentioned before, the only exception would be a case in which a value other than 0 resulted because of rounding procedures.

 LEARNING CHECK

Question: What are the deviations from the mean? What does the sum of the deviations from the mean always equal?

Answer: The deviations from the mean are the values obtained if the mean is subtracted from each score in a distribution. The sum of the deviations from the mean will always equal 0.

Table 2-9   Sum of Deviations from the Mean = 0

Scores/Values	Deviations	
(X)	(X – Mean)	
2	2 – 5	–3
4	4 – 5	–1
6	6 – 5	+1
8	8 – 5	+3
		0
Mean = 5		

Sum of the Deviations
Equals 0
(even when the mean is
a value that doesn't
appear in the original
distribution)

Scores/Values	Deviations	
(X)	(X – Mean)	
28	28 – 33	–5
30	30 – 33	–3
32	32 – 33	–1
34	34 – 33	+1
36	36 – 33	+3
38	38 – 33	+5
		0
Mean = 33		

Sum of the Deviations
Equals 0
(even when the mean is
a value that doesn't
appear in the original
distribution)

Assuming our goal is to get a summary measure that produces an overall picture of the deviation from or about the mean, we're obviously facing a bit of a problem. If we don't take some sort of corrective action, so to speak, we'll always end up with the same sum of deviations (a value of 0), regardless of the underlying distribution—and that tells us nothing.

The Mean Deviation

One way out of the problem would be simply to ignore the positive and negative signs we get when calculating the difference between individual scores and the mean. Indeed, that's what the *mean deviation* is all about. Before introducing you to the formula, however, let me explain the logic. I suspect it will strike you as very straightforward and remarkably similar to the calculation of the mean.

To calculate the mean deviation, here's what you do:

1. Determine the mean of the distribution.
2. Find the difference between each raw score and the mean; these are the deviations.

3. Ignore the positive or negative signs of the deviations; treat them all as though they were positive. This means you are considering only the absolute values.
4. Calculate the sum of the deviations (that is, the absolute values of the deviations).
5. Divide the sum by the number of cases or scores in the distribution.

The result is the **mean deviation.** The result gives you a nice statement of the average deviation. Indeed, the measure is sometimes referred to as the **average deviation.** The mean deviation (or average deviation) will tell you, on average, how far each score deviates from the mean. Here's the formula for the mean deviation for a set of sample scores:

$$\text{Mean Deviation} = \frac{\Sigma |X - \overline{X}|}{n}$$

Remember: The bars indicate that you are to take the absolute values; ignore positive and negative signs.

To understand how similar the mean deviation formula is to the formula for the mean, just give it a close look and think about what the formula instructs you to do. It tells you to sum something and then divide by the number of cases (the same thing that the formula for the mean instructs you to do). In the case of the formula for the mean deviation, what you are summing are absolute deviations from the mean. Take a look at the illustration in Table 2-10.

The mean deviation would be a wonderfully useful measure, were it not for one important consideration. It's based on absolute values, and absolute values are difficult to manipulate in more complex formulas. For that reason, statisticians turn elsewhere when they want a summary characteristic of the variability of a distribution. One of their choices is to look at the *variance* of a distribution.

Table 2-10 Calculation of the Mean Deviation

Scores/Values	Deviations		Absolute Values
(N = 5)			
(X)	(X – Mean)		
1	1 – 3	–2	2
2	2 – 3	–1	1
3	3 – 3	0	0
4	4 – 3	+1	1
5	5 – 3	+2	2
		0	Σ = 6
Mean = 3			

Step 1 Calculate mean.

Step 2 Calculate deviations from the mean.

Step 3 Convert deviations to absolute values.

Step 4 Sum the absolute values.

Step 5 Divide the sum by the number of cases. 6/5 = 1.20; Mean Deviation = 1.20

LEARNING CHECK

Question: What is the mean or average deviation? How does it get around the problem that the sum of the deviations from the mean always equals 0? What is its major drawback?

Answer: The mean or average deviation is a measure of dispersion. It solves the problem by using absolute values (ignoring the positive and negative signs) of the deviations from the mean. The use of the absolute values, however, makes it difficult to use in more complex mathematical operations. As a result, it is rarely used.

The Variance

Variance, as a statistical measure, attacks the problem of deviations' summing to 0 in a head-on fashion. As you know from basic math, one way to get rid of a mix of positive and negative numbers in a distribution is to square all the numbers. The result will always be a string of positive numbers. It's from that point that the calculation of distribution's variance begins. As before, we'll start with the logic.

Think back to the original goal. The idea is to get some notion of the overall variability in the scores in a distribution. We already know what to expect if we look at the extent to which individual scores deviate from the mean. We could calculate all the deviations, but they would sum to 0. If we squared the deviations, though, we would eliminate the sum-to-zero problem. Once we squared all the deviations, we could then divide by the number of cases, and we'd have a measure of the extent to which the scores vary about the mean. And that's what the **variance** is. It's the result you'd get if you calculated all the deviations from a mean, squared the deviations, summed the squared deviations, and divided by the number of cases in the distribution.

That sounds like something that's rather complicated, but it really isn't, provided you take on the problem in a step-by-step fashion. Let's consider a fairly simple distribution (see Table 2-11) and have a look at the calculation of the variance both mathematically and conceptually. Here's the step-by-step approach that we'll use:

1. Calculate each deviation and square it. Remember that you're squaring the deviations because the sum of the deviations would equal 0 if you didn't.
2. Sum all the squared deviations.
3. Divide the sum of the squared deviations by the number of cases.

Applying this approach to the scores shown in Table 2-11, you can move through the process step by step.

Table 2-11   Calculation of the Variance of a Population

Scores/Values	Deviations		Squared Deviations
(N = 5)			
(X)	(X – Mean)		
1	1 – 3	–2	4
2	2 – 3	–1	1
3	3 – 3	0	0
4	4 – 3	+1	1
5	5 – 3	+2	4
		0	Σ = 10
Mean = 3			

Sum of the squared deviations equals 10

N = 5 (treating the 5 scores as a population)

10/5 = 2

Variance = 2

Table 2-12   Calculating the Variance of a Population
(showing how values explode when they are squared)

Scores/Values	Deviations		Squared Deviations
(N = 6)			
(X)	(X – Mean)		
$21,800	21,800 – 41,300	–19,500	380,250,000
$35,600	35,600 – 41,300	–5,700	32,490,000
$52,150	52,150 – 41,300	+10,850	117,722,500
$64,250	64,250 – 41,300	+22,950	526,702,500
$32,000	32,000 – 41,300	–9,300	86,490,000
$42,000	42,000 – 41,300	+700	490,000
			Σ = 1,144,145,000
Mean = $41,300			
			1,144,145,000/6
			Variance = $190,690,833.33

I assure you the same approach will work whether your distribution has small values (for example, from 1 to 10) or much larger values (for example, a distribution of incomes in the thousands of dollars). The example in Table 2-12 illustrates that the same approach works just the same when you're dealing with larger values.

To develop a solid understanding of what the variance tells us, consider the four distributions shown in Table 2-13. In the top two distributions, the variances are the same, but the means are very different. In the bottom two distributions, the means are equal, but the variances are very different.

By now you should be developing some appreciation for the concept of variance, particularly in terms of how it can be used to compare one distribution to another. But there's still one problem with the variance as a statistical measure.

Table 2-13 Comparison of Distributions: Equal Variances and Different Means, Equal Means and Different Variances

Scores	Deviations		Squared Deviations
	(X – Mean)		
1	1 – 3	–2	4
2	2 – 3	–1	1
3	3 – 3	0	0
4	4 – 3	+1	1
5	5 – 3	+2	4
			10
Mean = 3			10/5 = 2
			Variance = 2

Scores	Deviations		Squared Deviations
	(X – Mean)		
51	51 – 53	–2	4
52	52 – 53	–1	1
53	53 – 53	0	0
54	54 – 53	+1	1
55	55 – 53	+2	4
			10
Mean = 53			10/5 = 2
			Variance = 2

Scores	Deviations		Squared Deviations
	(X – Mean)		
30	30 – 50	–20	400
40	40 – 50	–10	100
50	50 – 50	0	0
60	60 – 50	+10	100
70	70 – 50	+20	400
			1000
Mean = 50			1000/5 = 200
			Variance = 200

Scores	Deviations		Squared Deviations
	(X – Mean)		
46	46 – 50	–4	16
48	48 – 50	–2	4
50	50 – 50	0	0
52	52 – 50	+2	4
54	54 – 50	+4	16
			40
Mean = 50			40/5 = 8
			Variance = 8

The act of squaring the deviations has a way of markedly changing the magnitude of the numbers we're dealing with—something that happens anytime you square a number.

The illustration you encountered in Table 2-12 is a good example. That illustration was based on a distribution of income data, and income data necessarily involve some fairly large numbers. Inspection of that illustration reveals how quickly the original values explode in magnitude when deviations are squared.

In truth, all values have a way of exploding in magnitude when they're squared. Whether you're dealing with single-digit numbers or values in the thousands, the same process is at work. The mere act of squaring numbers can radically alter the values. In the process, you're apt to lose sight of the original scale of measurement you were working with.

Fortunately, there is a fairly easy way to bring everything back in line, so to speak. All you have to do is calculate the variance and then turn right around and take the square root. Indeed, statisticians make a habit of doing just that. Moreover, they have a specific name for the result. It is referred to as the **standard deviation.**

 LEARNING CHECK

Question: What is the variance? How does it deal with the problem that the sum of the deviations from the mean always equals 0? What is a major limitation of the variance?

Answer: The variance is a measure of dispersion. To avoid the problem of the deviations from the mean always summing to 0, the variance is based on squaring the deviations before they are summed. A major limitation of the variance is that squaring the deviations inflates the magnitude of the values in the distribution, which can cause you to lose sight of the original units of measurement.

The Standard Deviation

Before we get to the business of calculating the standard deviation, let me point out an important distinction. When we're referring to the standard deviation of a sample, we use the symbol s. When we're referring to the standard deviation of a population, however, we use the symbol σ (the lowercase symbol for the Greek letter *sigma*). Let me underscore that again. Here's the difference:

s is the standard deviation of a sample.

σ is the standard deviation of a population.

As I mentioned previously, the whole idea behind the standard deviation is to bring the squared deviations back in line, so to speak, and we do that by taking the square root of variance. In other words, the standard deviation is the square root of the variance. Looked at the other way around, the variance is simply the standard deviation squared.

Variance = Standard Deviation Squared

Square Root of the Variance = Standard Deviation

Variance is what is under the radical (square root symbol) before you take the square root when calculating the standard deviation.

 LEARNING CHECK

Question: What is the relationship between the standard deviation and the variance?

Answer: The standard deviation is the square root of the variance. The variance is the standard deviation squared.

You may have noticed that I didn't use any sort of symbol to refer to the variance when I first introduced you to the concept. As a matter of fact, I didn't even give you any sort of formula for the variance. I simply explained it to you—telling you that variance, as a measure of dispersion, is nothing more than the sum of the squared deviations from the mean, divided by the number of cases.

I avoided the use of any formula or symbols for variance for a specific reason. It had to do with how the standard deviation and variance are related to each other. As you now know, the standard deviation is simply the square root of the variance. By the same token, the standard deviation squared is equal to the variance.

Recall for a moment how we symbolize the standard deviation: s = the standard deviation of a sample, and σ = the standard deviation of a population. Since the variance is equal to the standard deviation squared, we symbolize the variance as follows:

s^2 is the variance of a sample.

σ^2 is the variance of a population.

No doubt it would have caused great confusion had I used those symbols (s^2 and σ^2) when I first introduced you to the concept of variance. Had I given you a formula for the variance, my guess is that you would have expected to see a symbol such as V—certainly not s^2 or σ^2. Recall that we had not yet mentioned the standard deviation (*s* and *σ*). Just to make certain that you now understand the link between the two—standard deviation and variance—let's summarize:

---

s = Standard Deviation of a Sample

σ = Standard Deviation of a Population

s^2 = Variance of a Sample

$σ^2$ = Variance of a Population

☑ **LEARNING CHECK**

Question: What are the symbols for the standard deviation and the variance of a sample? What are the symbols for the standard deviation and variance of a population?

Answer: For a sample, the symbol for the standard deviation is *s*, and the symbol for the variance is s^2. For a population, the symbol for the standard deviation is *σ*, and the symbol for variance is $σ^2$.

Presumably you now know what the symbols *s* and *σ* refer to—the standard deviation of a sample and a population, respectively—so we can get back to our discussion. As I mentioned before, the standard deviation is a particularly useful measure of dispersion because it has the effect of bringing squared values back into line, so to speak. You'll see the standard deviation often in the field of statistics, so you'll want to become very familiar with the concept. To help you along, consider a simple example.

Let's assume that you want to calculate the standard deviation of some data for a small class (let's say five students). Assume that you're looking at the number of times each student has been absent throughout the semester. Since you're only interested in the results for this class, the class constitutes a population. In this example, then, you're calculating the standard deviation of a population (or *σ*). You'll want to start by having a close look at the formula. Then you'll want to follow the example through in a step-by-step fashion.

$$σ = \sqrt{\frac{\sum(X - μ)^2}{N}}$$

There's no reason to let the formula throw you. It's really just a statement that tells you to calculate the variance and then take the square root of your answer. Even if you forget everything you already know about the variance, you should be able to go through the formula step by step. Think of it this way:

1. Forget the radical or square root sign for a moment, or simply think of it as a correction factor. You have to square some numbers (to get rid of the negative signs), so you're eventually going to turn around and take the square root.
2. Look at each deviation (the difference between the mean and each raw score) and square it. Once again, you're squaring the deviations because the sum of the deviations would equal 0 if you didn't.
3. Sum all the squared deviations.
4. Divide the sum of the squared deviations by the number of cases.
5. Take the square root to get back to the original scale of measurement.

Most of those steps should be familiar—after all, most of them are the same steps you used in calculating the variance.

Table 2-14 shows you the step-by-step calculations. Remember that we're calculating the standard deviation of a population. It may be very small populations (only five cases), but we're treating it as a population nonetheless. Later on, we'll deal with the standard deviation for samples.

Now let's give some thought to what the standard deviation tells us. Like the variance, the standard deviation gives us an idea of the dispersion of a distribution. It gives us an idea as to how far, in general, individual scores deviate from the mean. It gives us an overall notion as to the variability in the distribution. Moreover, it does so in a way that is free of the problems associated with the variance. Remember: The big problem with the variance is that values are magnified as a result of the squaring process.

So, what does the standard deviation really tell you about a distribution? Suppose you were told that the standard deviation for a distribution has a value of 15.5. This value of 15.5 may mean 15.5 dollars or 15.5 pounds or 15.5 test points, depending on what variable you're looking at and the nature

Table 2-14   Calculating the Standard Deviation of a Population

Scores/Values	Deviations		Squared Deviations	
(N = 5)				
(X)	(X − Mean)			
5	5 − 12	−7	49	Sum of Squared Deviations = 106
10	10 − 12	−2	4	
12	12 − 12	0	0	106/5 = 21.2 (5 is Number of Cases)
14	14 − 12	+2	4	
19	19 − 12	+7	49	Square Root of 21.2 = 4.60
			106	
Mean = 12				**Standard Deviation = 4.60**

of the data you've collected. But still it's reasonable to ask: So what? So what does the standard deviation (or variance, for that matter) really tell us? From my perspective, there are at least three answers to that question.

First, you can think of the standard deviation as a measure that tells you (sort of) how far scores or values (in general) deviate from the mean. In short, the standard deviation tracks along with the overall variability in a distribution. When there is more variability in a distribution, the standard deviation increases.

It's that last point—the notion that the value of the standard deviation increases when there is more variability in a distribution—that leads to a second interpretation or interpretative guideline regarding the standard deviation. I would also add that I believe that it's the best way to think of the standard deviation, at least at this point in your education. Simply put, you should think of the standard deviation as a relative or comparative sort of measure. In other words, it's probably best to think in terms of one standard deviation compared to another. For example, you might want to compare the standard deviation of incomes in two cities or you might want to compare the standard deviation of test scores in two classes. When you think of the standard deviation (or the variance, for that matter) as a relative or comparative measure, you begin to view it as a measure that may be very useful in situations involving more than one distribution. For example, your ultimate concern may boil down to which of the two or three or four distributions (let's say which of several sets of test scores) has the largest amount of variability. In a case like that, the standard deviation is likely to be a very useful measure.

Finally, as a third answer to the question of what the standard deviation tells us, I would tell you that it is a critical element in understanding the concept of a normal distribution or normal curve. I don't expect you to get the connection right now, particularly since there's an entire chapter devoted to the topic of the normal curve, and you've yet to encounter that chapter. For the moment, let me simply encourage you to do whatever is necessary to understand where the standard deviation fits in relationship to the variance (it is the square root of the variance—remember?). Let me also urge you to get a firm foundation in how to calculate the standard deviation. You will eventually discover that the notion of the standard deviation is a central concept.

Returning to the formula for the standard deviation (and the variance, for that matter), I should point out that different texts may present the formula in a different format—something that's quite common in the world of statistics. Sometimes it's a matter of personal preference; sometimes it's an effort to provide a formula that is more calculator-friendly. For example, consider the following two formulas for the calculation of the standard deviation for a population:

Formula for σ in This Text

A Common Alternative Formula (more suited for use with a calculator)

$$\sigma = \sqrt{\frac{\sum(X - \mu)^2}{N}}$$

$$\sigma = \sqrt{\frac{\sum X^2}{N} - \mu^2}$$

My preference for the formula presented in this text is tied to what I call its *intuitive appeal*: It strikes me as more closely representing what's apt to be going on in your mind as you think through what the concept means.

So much for abstract examples and discussions of formulas. I suspect you're getting anxious to see some direct application of all of this, so let's head in that direction. Imagine for a moment that you were in a class of 200 students taking four 100 points tests—a Math Test, a Verbal Test, a Science Test, and a Logic Test. Then assume that you received the following information about the tests: your score, the class average for each test, and the standard deviation for each test. Suppose the information came to you in a form like this:

Test	Mean	Standard Deviation	Your Score
Math	82	6	80
Verbal	75	3	75
Science	60	5	70
Logic	70	7	77

Just so you'll get in the habit of keeping matters straight in your mind, the example we're dealing with involves four populations of test scores. In each case, you have a population mean or mu (μ) and a population standard deviation (σ). Now here are the questions:

What was your best performance, relative to your classmates?

What was your worst performance? Why?

Let me suggest that you give the questions a little bit of thought before you arrive at the answers.

Assuming you've thought about it, you now have some answers in mind. But rather than just giving you the answers, let me walk you through the logic involved in deriving them.

A good place to begin is with a comparison of your individual test scores to the means. In the case of the Math Test, the mean was 82, and your score was 80. In other words, your score was actually below the mean (so that's not too good). In the case of the Verbal Test, you had a score of 75, but the mean was 75. You didn't score above or below the mean—an OK performance, but not really that great.

Now have a look at your performance on the Science Test. In that case, you had a score of 70, but the mean was 60. In other words, you scored 10 points above the mean—not bad! As a matter of fact, the standard deviation on that test was 5, so your 10 points above the mean really equates to a score that was two standard deviation units above the mean. Here's the reasoning: Each standard deviation equals 5 points; your score was 10 points above the mean; therefore, your score was two standard deviation units above the mean.

Now let's take a look at your performance on the Logic Test. The mean on that test was 70, and you had a score of 77. In other words, you scored

7 points above the mean. As it happens, the standard deviation on the test was 7 points, so your score was only one standard deviation unit above the mean.

If you want to know just how poorly you did on the Math Test, the same logic will apply. The mean on that test was 82, and your score of 80 was two points below that. Since the standard deviation on the Math Test was 6 points, your score was 2/6 or 1/3 of a standard deviation unit below the mean.

So now you have all the answers. First, your best performance (in a relative sense) was on the Science Test, even though that was your worst absolute score. Second, your worst performance turned out to be on the Math Test, even though that was your highest absolute score.

Just to demonstrate that point more completely, consider one final example. Assume for the moment that there was a fifth test thrown into the mix—let's say it's a Foreign Language Ability Test. But let's also say that unlike the other tests that were 100 point tests, let's say that the Foreign Language Ability Test was a 250 point test. In other words, scores on the Foreign Language Ability Test could range from 0 to 250. Let's also assume that the mean score on the Foreign Language Ability Test was 120 with a standard deviation of 15. Now what if your test score was a score 90—what sort of performance would that be?

If you use the same logic that you used in the other situations, you'd quickly discover that you have a new "worst performance." Your performance on the Foreign Language Ability Test equated to a score that was two standard deviations below the mean (i.e., you were 30 points below the mean; a standard deviation equals 15 points; therefore, you were two standard deviations below the mean). Before the Foreign Language Ability Test was thrown into the mix, your worst performance was on the Math Test (you were 1/3rd of a standard deviation below the mean). On the Foreign Language Ability Test, though, you were two standard deviations below the mean. Thus, your score on the Foreign Language Ability Test becomes your worst performance.

The point of the Foreign Language Ability Test example is to demonstrate something very important—it doesn't make any difference whether you're comparing tests that have the same underlying scale (e.g., test scores that can range from, let's say 0 to 100), or you're comparing all sorts of test scores—scores on a 100 point test, scores on a 250 point test, or scores on a 1500 point test, for that matter. The underlying goal is the same: Determine where a given score (in this case, your score) falls, in relationship to the mean, and express the difference in standard deviation units. To fully grasp this point, just remember what was going on in your mind as you worked through the questions—just think back to the calculations.

If you really think back to the calculations, you'll eventually arrive at a very important point—namely that all the mental calculations you went through amounted to calculating ratios. In each case, you calculated a ratio: the difference between an individual score and the mean of the distribution, expressed in terms of standard deviation units. This very important point will come up again later on, so let me urge you to take the time to really comprehend what it means to say you were calculating ratios. Once again, you were calculating a ratio that reflected the difference between the individual score and the mean of the distribution, expressed in terms of standard deviation units.

 LEARNING CHECK

Question: If you determine the difference between an individual score and the mean of a distribution, and then you divide the difference by the standard deviation of the distribution, what does the result tell you?

Answer: The answer is a statement of the distance the score is from the mean, expressed in standard deviation units.

Before we move on to the next chapter, I need to explain one last matter concerning the standard deviation—a matter I alluded to earlier. Since the standard deviation is so widely used in inferential statistics, and the business of inferential statistics involves moving from a sample to a population, it's time I introduced you to a slight difference between samples and populations when it comes to the standard deviation.

n Versus n − 1

We'll start with the notion that we generally deal with a sample in an effort to make some statement about a population (a point you encountered when we first discussed the idea of inferential statistics). It would be great if a sample standard deviation gave us a perfect reflection of the population standard deviation, but it doesn't. In fact, the accuracy of a sample standard deviation (as a reflection of the population standard deviation) is somewhat affected by the number of cases in the sample.

Here's the logic behind that last statement. Start by imagining a population distribution that has substantial variability in it—let's say the distribution of 23,000 students' ages at a large university. No doubt there would be some unusually young students in the population, just as there would be some unusually old students in the population. In other words, there would probably be a substantial amount of variability in the population. But if you selected a sample of students, there's a good chance that you wouldn't pick up all the variability that actually exists in the population. Most of your sample cases would likely come from the portion of the population that has most of the cases to begin with. In other words, it's unlikely that you'd get a lot of cases from the outer edges of the population.

If, for example, most of the students were between 20 and 25 years of age, most of the students in your sample would likely be within that age range. What you're not likely to get in your sample would be a lot of really young or really old students. You might get some, but probably not many. In other words, your sample probably wouldn't reflect all of the variability that really exists in the population. As a result, the standard deviation of your sample would likely be slightly less than the true standard deviation of the population.

Since the idea is to get a sample standard deviation that's an accurate reflection of the population standard deviation—one that can provide you with an unbiased estimate of the population's standard deviation—some adjustment is necessary. Remember: The idea in inferential statistics is to use sample statistics to estimate population parameters. If you're going to use a sample standard deviation to estimate the standard deviation of a population, you'll want a sample standard deviation that more closely reflects the true variability or spread of the population distribution.

Statisticians deal with this situation by using a small correction factor. When calculating the standard deviation of a sample (or the variance of a sample, for that matter), they change the n in the denominator to $n - 1$. This slight reduction in the denominator results in a larger standard deviation—one that better reflects the true standard deviation of the population.

 LEARNING CHECK

Question: What is the effect of using $n - 1$, as opposed to n, in the formula for calculating the standard deviation of a sample?

Answer: The effect of using $n - 1$ (as opposed to n) in the denominator is to yield a slightly larger result—one that will be a better reflection of the population standard deviation.

To better understand the reason for making this change in the formula, think about the effect of sample size: The larger your sample is, the greater the likelihood that you've picked up all the variability that is really present in the population. Imagine that first you select a sample of, let's say, 30 students. Then you select another sample, but this time you include 50 students. Each time you increase the sample size—as you work up to a larger and larger sample—you get closer and closer to having a sample standard deviation that equals the population standard deviation. What would happen if you gradually increased your sample size until you were working with a sample that was actually the entire population? You'd have the actual population standard deviation in front of you.

When you use $n - 1$ in the denominator of the formula for the standard deviation of a sample, you not only slightly increase the final answer (or value of the standard deviation), you do so in a way that is sensitive to sample size. The smaller the size of the sample, the more of an impact the adjustment will make. For example, dividing something by 2 instead of 3 will have a much greater impact than dividing something by 999 instead of 1000. In other words, the adjustment factor wouldn't have a lot of impact if you were working with a really large sample, but it would have a major impact if you were working with a really small sample.

At this point, I should tell you that different statisticians have different approaches to the use of the correction factor ($n - 1$, as opposed to just n, in the denominator). Some statisticians quit correcting when a sample size is 30 or greater; that is, they use n when the sample size reaches 30. Others require a larger sample size before they're willing to rely on n (as opposed to $n - 1$) in the denominator. The approach in this text is to always use $n - 1$ when calculating a sample standard deviation.

The issue at this point isn't when different statisticians invoke the correction factor and when they don't; the issue is why. Because the answer to that question is one that usually takes some serious thought, let me suggest that you take time out for one of those dark room moments I mentioned earlier.

First, take the time to give some serious thought to the ideas of variability and the standard deviation in general. Then take some time to think about how the standard deviation of a population is related to the standard deviation of a sample. Develop a mental picture of a population and a sample from that population. Mentally focus on why you would expect the standard deviation of the population to be slightly larger than the standard deviation of the sample. You should think about the relationship between the two long enough to fully appreciate why the correction factor is used. It all goes back to the point that the variability of a sample is going to be smaller than the variability of a population, and that's why a correction factor has to be used.

Finally, in an effort to make certain that you fully understand how to calculate the standard deviation of a sample, and the point about $n - 1$ in the denominator, let me suggest that you take a close look at Table 2-15. It's an illustration of the calculation of the standard deviation for a sample. My suggestion is that you repeat each of the calculations shown in the illustration, working each step on your own, while also paying particular attention to the next to the last step (i.e., dividing by $n - 1$ before you take the square root).

Assuming you feel comfortable about the different measures of central tendency and measures of variability (and the standard deviation, in particular), we

Table 2-15   Calculating the Standard Deviation of a Sample

Scores/Values	Deviations		Squared Deviations	
(N = 9)				
(X)	(X – Mean)			
7	(7 – 4)	3	9	Sum of Squared Deviations = 54
1	(1 – 4)	–3	9	
3	(3 – 4)	–1	1	54/8 = 6.75
5	(5 – 4)	1	1	Note that $n - 1$ or 8 is used
6	(6 – 4)	2	4	
2	(2 – 4)	–2	4	
8	(8 – 4)	4	16	
1	(1 – 4)	–3	9	
3	(3 – 4)	–1	1	Square Root of 6.75 = 2.598
			54	
Mean = 4				**Standard Deviation = 2.598**
				or round to 2.60

can move forward. Next we turn our attention to the graphic representation of data distributions—the world of graphs and curves. That's where we'll go in the next chapter.

Chapter Summary

In learning about measures of central tendency and dispersion, you've learned some of the fundamentals of data description. Moreover, you've had a brief introduction to the business of statistical notation—why, for example, different symbols are used when referring to a sample, as opposed to a population. Ideally the connection to the previous chapter hasn't been lost in the process, and you've begun to understand that it's essential to make clear whether you're discussing a sample statistic or a population parameter.

As to what you've learned about measures of central tendency, you should have digested several points. First, several measures of central tendency are available, and each one has its strength and weakness. One measure might be appropriate in one instance but illsuited for another situation. Second, you've likely picked up on the importance of the mean as measure of central tendency—a measure that finds its way into a variety of statistical procedures. For example, the mean is an essential element in calculating both the variance and the standard deviation.

On the variability or dispersion side of the ledger, you have been introduced to several different measures. Working from the simplest to the more complex, you've learned that some measures have more utility than others. You've also learned how the variance and the standard deviation are related to each other, and (ideally) you've developed a solid understanding of why both measures are in the statistical toolbox.

Finally, you have learned that there's some room for judgment and personal preference in the matter of statistical analysis. For example, you've encountered different formulas for calculating the standard deviation—one that's ideally suited for use with a calculator, and another that better reflects the logic behind the procedure. You've also learned that different statisticians have different preferences when it comes to using n versus $n - 1$ in the denominator of the formula for the sample standard deviation. These are small matters, perhaps, but they help explain why different texts present different formulas for the same statistical procedure.

Some Other Things You Should Know

At this point, you deserve to know that data and data distributions can be presented in a variety of ways. Indeed, the art of data presentation is a field in itself. The data distributions we've considered so far have been presented as ungrouped data, meaning that scores or values have been presented individually. If three 22s were present in a distribution, for example, each 22 was listed separately in the distribution. Frequently, however, statisticians find themselves working with grouped data—data presented in terms of intervals, or groups of values.

For example, a data distribution of income might be presented in terms of income intervals, showing how many people in a study had incomes between $25,000 and $29,999, how many had incomes between $30,000 and $39,999, and so on. As you might expect, statisticians have procedures to deal with such situations. An excellent treatment of the topic can be found in Moore (2000).

You should also be reminded of a point I made earlier in reference to the standard deviation (and variance, for that matter). Different formulas abound, not just for standard deviation or variance, but with respect to many other measures and procedures. It's not uncommon for two texts to approach the same topic in different ways. If a formula jumps out at you, and it's not quite the same as the presentation you've encountered here or somewhere else, don't be disheartened, threatened, or confused. Think conceptually. Think about the elements in the formula. Think about the formula in terms of its component parts, recognizing that there may be more than one way to approach some of those component parts. Sometimes the difference in presentation reflects the author's personal preference. Sometimes it's oriented toward a particular tool, such as a calculator. Whatever the reason, the fact that such differences exist is something you'll want to keep in mind, should you find yourself consulting different sources for one reason or another. The rule of thumb in this text is to focus on the formula or approach that seems to have the most intuitive appeal.

Key Terms

average deviation
bimodal distribution
central tendency
dispersion (variability)
mean
mean deviation
median

mode
mu (μ)
range
standard deviation
unimodal distribution
variance

Chapter Problems

Fill in the blanks, calculate the requested values, or otherwise supply the correct answer.

1. Three measures of central tendency are the __mean__, __median__, and __mode__.

2. The measure of central tendency that is sensitive to extreme scores is the
   Mean .

3. The most frequently represented score or response in a distribution is the
   Mode .

4. The _Median_ is a measure of central tendency that represents the midpoint of a distribution.

5. The _Range_ is a measure of _____ that is based on a statement
   of the highest and lowest scores in a distribution.

6. A distribution has 14 scores. Each score is represented only once in the distribution, with two exceptions. The score of 78, appears three times, and
   the score of 82 appears four times. What is the mode of the distribution?

7. A distribution has 32 scores. Each score appears once, with the following
   exceptions: The score of 18 appears twice, and the score of 21 appears
   twice. How would you state the mode of the distribution? _isn't one_

8. The measure of dispersion that is based upon the absolute values of the
   deviations from the mean is the _deviation score_

9. The sum of the deviations from the mean is always equal to _0_ .

10. Because the sum of the deviation from the mean always equals
    _0_ , the variance gets around the problem by _Squaring_ the
    deviations before they are summed.

11. The standard deviation is the _Square root_ of the variance.

12. In order to obtain a more accurate reflection of the standard deviation of
    a population, the standard deviation for a sample can be calculated by
    using _n_ in the denominator of the formula, as opposed to using
    _n-1_ in the formula.

Application Questions/Problems

1. Consider the following data from a sample of five cases:

   $$7 \quad 6 \quad 3 \quad 1 \quad 4$$

   a. What is the mean?
   b. What is the position of the median?
   c. What is the value of the median?
   d. What is the mean or average deviation?
   e. What is the variance?
   f. What is the standard deviation?

2. Consider the following data from a sample of eight cases:

   $$20 \quad 21 \quad 18 \quad 16 \quad 12 \quad 15 \quad 12 \quad 13$$

   a. What is the mean?
   b. What is the position of the median?

    c. What is the value of the median?

    d. What is the mode?

    e. What is the mean or average deviation?

    f. What is the variance?

    g. What is the standard deviation?

3. Consider the following data from a sample of nine cases:

$$6 \quad 1 \quad 4 \quad 3 \quad 4 \quad 1 \quad 2 \quad 9 \quad 5$$

    a. What is the mean?

    b. What is the position of the median?

    c. What is the value of the median?

    d. What is the mode?

    e. What is the mean or average deviation?

    f. What is the variance?

    g. What is the standard deviation?

4. A study based on a sample of 12 students yields the following scores on a 10-point scale of cultural diversity awareness.

$$1 \quad 4 \quad 8 \quad 7 \quad 5 \quad 2 \quad 7 \quad 2 \quad 3 \quad 7 \quad 6 \quad 4$$

    a. What is the mean?

    b. What is the median?

    c. What is the mode?

    d. What is the standard deviation?

5. An industrial psychologist investigating absenteeism of workers at a local plant collects data from a sample of 45 workers. The number of days absent (during the past year) for each worker is recorded and the variance is determined to be 9. What is the standard deviation?

6. A social psychologist is investigating leadership in small groups. Using a sample of 10 research participants and recording the number of suggestions made by each participant in a small group task experiment, the researcher obtains the following distribution:

$$1 \quad 3 \quad 2 \quad 4 \quad 6 \quad 1 \quad 1 \quad 3 \quad 7 \quad 4$$

    a. What is the mean number of suggestions for the sample?

    b. What is the standard deviation of the sample?

7. The mean score for a science exam is 72, with a standard deviation of 4. Your score on the exam is 80.

    a. How many standard deviations above the mean is your score?

    b. If you had a score of 70, how many standard deviations below the mean would your score be?

8. The mean score for a verbal exam is 65, with a standard deviation of 4. You are told that your score is two standard deviations above the mean. What is your score?

9. The mean score for a mathematics exam is 125 (on a 200 point exam), with a standard deviation of 30. You are told that your score is 1.5 standard deviations above the mean. What is your score?

3

The Shape of Distributions

Up to this point, you've been looking at distributions presented as listings of scores or values. Now it's time to expand your horizons a bit. It's time to move beyond mere listings of scores or values and into the more visual world of graphs or curves.

As we take this next step, I'll ask you to do three things. First, I'll ask you to start thinking in a more abstract fashion. Sometimes I'll ask you to think about a concrete example that relates to a specific variable, but other times I'll ask you to think about a graph or curve in a very abstract sense. Second, I'll ask you to be very flexible in your thinking. I'll ask you to move from one type of graph to another, and sometimes I'll ask you to move back and forth between the two. Finally, I'll ask you to consider distributions with a larger number of cases than you've encountered so far. There's still no need to panic, though. Remember: The emphasis remains on the conceptual nature of the material.

Before We Begin

The last chapter allowed you to string together two very important concepts—namely, the standard deviation and the mean. Now it's time you expand your thinking by visualizing distributions and how they are influenced by the mean and standard deviation. For example, imagine two groups of test scores. Imagine that they have identical means but very different standard deviations. What about the reverse situation? What about a situation in which both classes have the same standard deviation, but they have radically different means?

Simple mental exercises along those lines can be very valuable, in your conceptual understanding of statistics. When you have reached the point where you can easily visualize different distributions (if only in a generalized form), I believe you've crossed an important milestone. I'm convinced that the ability to visualize distributions, particularly one distribution compared to another, is a talent that can be nurtured and developed. I'm also convinced that it's a significant asset when it comes to learning statistics. Therefore, try to visualize the various distributions that are discussed in this chapter. If that means that you can't read through the chapter in record time, so be it. Take your time. The goals are to learn the material *and* develop your visualization skills.

The Basic Elements

We'll start with an example that should be familiar to you by now—a situation in which some students have taken a test. This time, let's say that several thousand students took the test. Moreover, let's say you were given a chart or graph depicting the distribution of the test scores—something like Figure 3-1. A quick look at the chart tells you that it represents the distribution of scores by letter

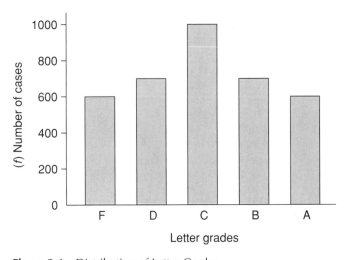

Figure 3-1 Distribution of Letter Grades

grade—the number of A's, B's, C's, and so forth. The illustration is probably very similar to many you've seen before. We refer to it as a *bar graph*.

A bar graph is particularly useful when the values or scores you want to represent fall into the category of nominal or ordinal data. Figure 3-1 is a perfect example. When the information about test scores is presented as letter grades (rather than actual test scores), you're dealing with ordinal level data; a letter grade of B is higher than a letter grade of C, but you don't really know how many points higher.

If, instead of letter grades, you had actual test scores expressed as numerical values, the measurement system would be far more refined, so to speak. That, in turn, would open the door to a more sophisticated method of illustrating the distribution of scores. Imagine for a moment that you had the actual scores for the same tests. Imagine that the measurement was very precise, with scores calculated to two decimal places (scores such as 73.28, 62.16, and 93.51). In this situation, the graph might look like the one shown in Figure 3-2.

Like the bar graph in Figure 3-1, the graph shown in Figure 3-2 is typical of what you might see in the way of data representation. Different values of the variable under consideration (in this case, test score) are shown along the baseline, and the frequency of occurrence is shown along the axis on the left side of the graph. The curve thus represents a **frequency distribution**— a table or graph that indicates how many times a value or score appears in a set of values or scores.

Instead of focusing on the specifics of the test scores presented in Figure 3-2, let's take a moment to reflect on curves or frequency distributions in general. Regardless of the specific information conveyed by the illustration, there are generally three important elements in a graph or plot of a frequency distribution.

First, there's the X-axis, or the baseline of the distribution. It reveals something about the range of values for the variable that you're considering. If you're looking at test scores, for example, the baseline or X-axis might show values ranging from 0 to 100. A frequency distribution of incomes might have a baseline with values ranging from, let's say, $15,000 to $84,000.

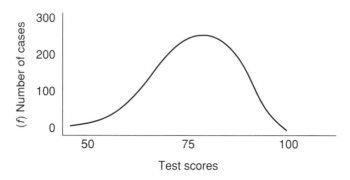

Figure 3-2 Distribution of Test Scores

Second, there's another axis—the Y-axis—usually running along the left side of the graph, with a symbol f to the side of it. The f stands for *frequency*—the number of times each value appears in the distribution, or the number of cases with a certain value (see Figure 3-3).

Now we add the third part of the graph—the curved line—as shown in Figure 3-4.

At this point, let me mention something that may strike you as obvious, but is worth mentioning nonetheless. It has to do with what is really represented by the space between the baseline and the curved line that forms the outline of the graph.

It's easy to look at a curve, such as the one shown in Figure 3-4, and forget that the area *under* the curve is actually filled with cases. Although the area under the curve may look empty, it is not. In fact, the area under the curve represents all the cases that were considered. Again, the area under the curve actually contains 100% of the cases (a point that will be important to consider later on). To understand this point, take a look at the graph shown in Figure 3-5, and think of each small dot as an individual case.

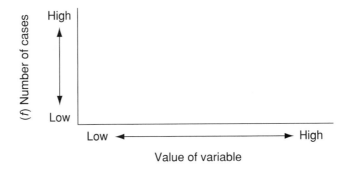

Figure 3-3 Components of a Frequency Distribution

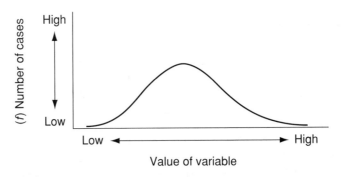

Figure 3-4 Components of a Frequency Distribution (Curve)

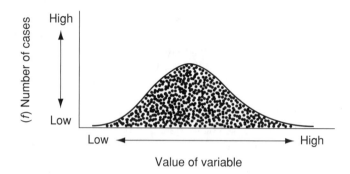

Figure 3-5 Cases/Observations Under a Curve

Remember: The area under the curve contains cases or observations! If necessary, take some time for a dark room moment at this point. Mentally visualize several different distributions. It doesn't make any difference what you think they represent. Just concentrate on the notion that cases or observations are under the curve—cases or observations stacked on top of one another (think of them as small dots, if need be, with all the dots stacked one upon the other).

 LEARNING CHECK

Question: Although it appears to be empty, what is represented by the area under a curve?

Answer: The area under the curve represents cases or observations.

Beyond the Basics: Comparisons and Conclusions

Let's now turn our attention to a question that involves some material from the previous chapter—namely, the mean and the standard deviation. Instead of thinking about the distribution of a specific variable, let's consider two distributions—Distribution A and Distribution B—in an abstract sense. These two distributions have the same mean score (50), but beyond that, they are very different. In Distribution A, the scores are widely dispersed, ranging from 10 to 90. In Distribution B, the scores are tightly clustered about the mean, ranging from 30 to 70. These two distributions are represented by the two curves shown in Figure 3-6.

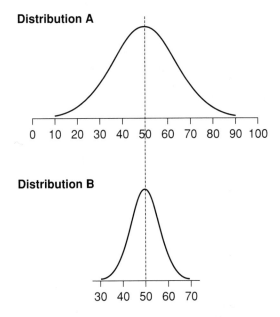

Figure 3-6   Comparison of Two Distributions
With Same Mean but Different
Standard Deviations

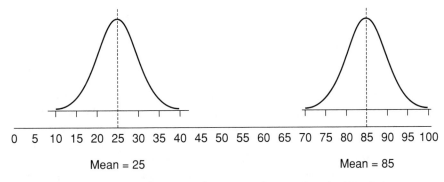

Figure 3-7   Comparison of Two Distributions With Same Standard Deviations
but Different Means

Simple visual inspection of the curves should tell you that the standard deviation of Distribution B is smaller than the standard deviation of Distribution A. The edges of the curve in Distribution B don't extend out as far as they do in Distribution A.

Now consider the examples shown in Figure 3-7. Here, the two curves represent two distributions with the same standard deviation but very different mean values.

Assuming you're getting the hang of visualizing curves in your mind, let's now consider the matter of extreme scores in a distribution. Imagine for a

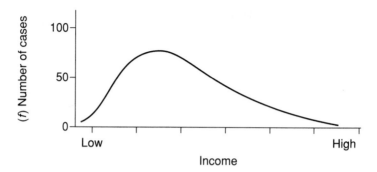

Figure 3-8   Positive Skew on Income

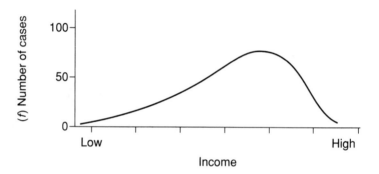

Figure 3-9   Negative Skew on Income

moment a distribution of income data—individual income information collected from a large number of people. Assume that most of the people have incomes that are close to the center of the distribution, but a few people have extremely high incomes. As you develop a mental picture, you should begin to visualize something that looks like the curve shown in Figure 3-8.

If, on the other hand, the extreme incomes were low incomes, the curve might look something like the one shown in Figure 3-9.

In statistics, we have a term for distributions like these. We refer to them as **skewed distributions.** When a distribution is skewed, it departs from *symmetry* in the sense that most of the cases are concentrated at one end of the distribution. We'll eventually have a closer look at this matter of skewness, but first let's consider some curves that lack those extremes. In other words, let's start by considering **symmetrical distributions.**

To understand the idea of symmetry (or a symmetrical distribution), imagine a situation in which you had height measurements from a large number of people. Height is a variable generally assumed to be distributed in a symmetrical fashion. Accordingly, the measurements would probably reflect roughly equal proportions of short and tall people in the sample. There might be just

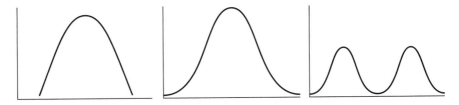

Figure 3-10   Symmetrical Curves/Distributions

a few very tall people, but, by the same token, there would be just a few very short people in the sample.

When a distribution is truly symmetrical, a line can be placed through the center of the distribution and the two halves will be mirror images. Fifty percent of the cases will be found on each side of the center line, and the shapes of the two sides of the distribution will be identical. When you think about it for just a moment, you'll realize that an infinite number of symmetrical shapes are possible. Figure 3-10 presents just a few for you to consider.

☑ **LEARNING CHECK**

Question: What is a symmetrical distribution?
Answer: A symmetrical distribution is one in which the two halves of the distribution are mirror images of each other.

Question: What is a skewed distribution?
Answer: A skewed distribution is a distribution that departs from symmetry in the sense that most of the cases are concentrated at one end of the distribution.

As I mentioned before, a curve that departs from symmetry (one that is not symmetrical) is referred to as a skewed distribution. Think back to some of the examples involving data on income. In a distribution with some extremely high incomes (relative to the other incomes in the distribution), the distribution was skewed to the right. In the case of the distribution with some extremely low incomes (relative to the other incomes in the distribution), the distribution was skewed to the left.

When a distribution is skewed to the right, we say it has a **positive skew.** When a distribution is skewed to the left, we say it has a **negative skew.** To understand why we use the terms *positive* and *negative,* just think of it this way: If you have an imaginary line of numbers with a 0 in the middle, all values to the right of 0 are positive values, and all values to the left of 0 are negative. The terms relate to the elongated portion of the curve, which statisticians refer to as the **tail of the distribution** (see Figure 3-11). If the tail of the distribution

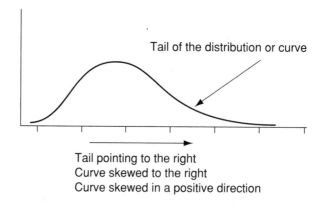

Tail of the distribution or curve

Tail pointing to the right
Curve skewed to the right
Curve skewed in a positive direction

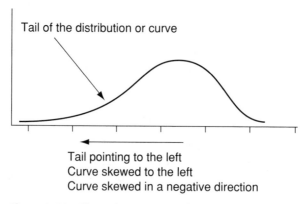

Tail of the distribution or curve

Tail pointing to the left
Curve skewed to the left
Curve skewed in a negative direction

Figure 3-11 Skewed Curves/Distributions

extends toward the right, we say that the curve has a positive skew or is skewed to the right. Conversely, a curve with a tail that extends to the left is said to be skewed to the left or negatively skewed.

I've asked you to move from skewed to symmetrical distributions and back to skewed distributions—all in an effort to get you familiar with the basic difference, and primarily so you'll develop an appreciation for symmetrical distributions. Now I'm going to ask you to make the leap again—back to symmetrical distributions—but this time, we will consider a very special case.

A Special Curve

If you paid close attention when you looked at some of the illustrations of symmetrical curves, you probably noticed that symmetrical curves can take on many different shapes. A symmetrical curve can be unimodal (one mode) or bimodal (two modes), and it can be quite flat in shape or more peaked in shape. Besides that, symmetrical curves can be very different in terms of how the curved line descends toward the baseline.

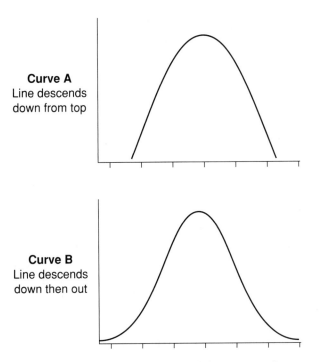

Curve A
Line descends
down from top

Curve B
Line descends
down then out

Figure 3-12 Comparison of Unimodal Symmetrical Curves

Consider, for example, Curve A in Figure 3-12. Focus on the highest point (the midpoint) of the distribution, and take note of how the line descends on either side of the midpoint. In a sense, the curved line descends out and down toward the baseline. Now focus on Curve B. Like Curve A, Curve B is a unimodal symmetrical curve (it has only one mode), but the manner in which the curved line descends toward the baseline is very different. Starting at the high point of the curve, the path of the curved line descends and then begins to turn outward. The curved line doesn't just drop to the baseline. Instead, it shows a pattern of gradual descent that moves in an outward direction.

Obviously, any number of curves could show this general pattern of descending down and then out. To statisticians, though, there's a particular type of curve that's of special interest. They refer to this very special sort of symmetrical curve as a **normal curve.**

A normal curve is symmetrical, and it descends down and then out. Moreover, the mean, median, and mode all coincide on a normal curve. But the special characteristics of a normal curve go beyond that. Indeed, a normal curve is one that conforms to a precise mathematical function. When a curve is, in fact, a normal curve, the mean and the standard deviation define the total shape of the curve. The curve may be relatively flat; it may be sharply peaked; or it may have a more moderate shape. The point is that the shape is predictable because a normal curve is defined by a precise mathematical function. Once again, the mean and the standard deviation will define the exact shape of a normal curve.

 LEARNING CHECK

Question: What type of symmetrical curve is of particular interest to statisticians?

Answer: A normal curve.

Take a close look at Figure 3-13. Starting at the top of the curve (which happens to be where the mean, median, and mode coincide), you can trace the line of the curve on one side. The line descends downward at a fairly steady rate, but the line eventually reaches a point at which it begins to turn in a more outward direction. From that point—known as the **point of inflection**—the rate of descent of the curve toward the baseline is more gradual. To appreciate this element, take the time to trace the curved line in Figure 3-13, either visually or with your index finger or a pencil. Concentrate on the point at which the curve begins to change directions—the point of inflection.

In normal curves with a small standard deviation, the curve will be fairly peaked in shape, and the degree of initial downward descent of the curve will be very noticeable. In normal curves with a larger standard deviation, the curve will be flatter, and the degree of initial downward descent of the curve will be less pronounced. Either way, the entire shape of the distribution is defined by the mean and standard deviation. Figure 3-14 shows some examples of normal curves.

Because a normal curve is one that conforms to a precise mathematical function, it's possible to know a great deal of information about the data

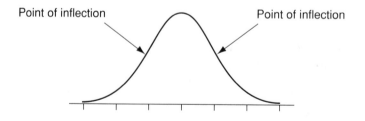

The point of inflection is the point at which the curved line begins to change direction.

Figure 3-13   Locating the Point of Inflection

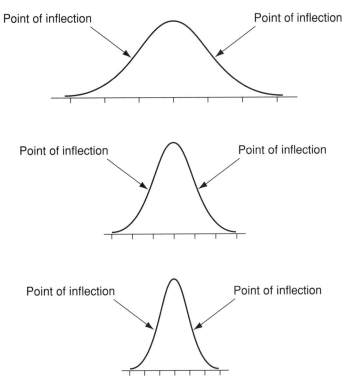

Figure 3-14 More Examples for Locating the Point of Inflection

distribution that underlies any normal curve. As a matter of fact, the point at which the curve begins to turn outward—the point of inflection—will be one standard deviation away from the mean.

For example, let's say we have a distribution of test scores, and the test scores are normally distributed. What this means is that the distribution of scores, if plotted in a graph, will form a normal curve. Now let's say that same distribution of scores has a mean of 60 and a standard deviation of 3. Since we know that the points of inflection will always be one standard deviation above and below the mean on a normal curve, we know that the points of inflection will correspond to scores of 63 and 57, respectively.

 LEARNING CHECK

Question: What is the point of inflection of a normal curve?

Answer: It is the point at which the curve begins to change direction. This point is also one standard deviation away from the mean.

As it turns out, we're in a position to know a lot more than that. For example, imagine that you're looking at a normal curve, and you mark the inflection points on both sides of the mean—the points on either side of the mean where the curve begins to change direction (even if ever so slightly). You now know that you have marked off the points that correspond to one standard deviation above and below the mean. In addition, however, if you draw lines down from the inflection points to the baseline, you will be marking off a portion of the normal curve that contains slightly more than 68% of the total cases, or 68% of the area under the curve. Why? Because that's the way a normal curve is mathematically defined.

This point is central to everything that follows, so take a close look at Figure 3-15.

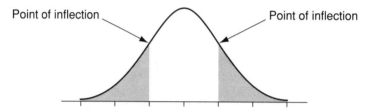

Approximately 68% of cases in a normal distribution are between one standard deviation above and below the mean.

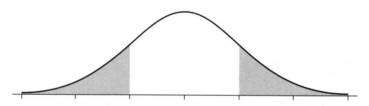

Even if the curve is relatively flat, approximately 68% of the cases will be found ±1 standard deviation from the mean.

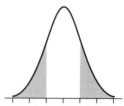

Even if the curve is relatively peaked, approximately 68% of the cases will be found ±1 standard deviation from the mean.

Figure 3-15   General Shape of a Normal Curve

If you marked off two standard deviations from the mean, you would have marked off a portion of a normal curve that contains slightly more than 95% of the total cases. And lines drawn at three standard deviations above and below a normal curve will enclose an area that contains more than 99% of the cases (see Figure 3-16). If you're still wondering why, the answer remains the same: That's how a normal curve is mathematically defined.

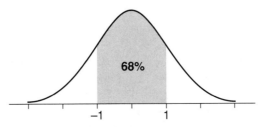

Approximately 68% of cases in a normal distribution are between one standard deviation above and below the mean.

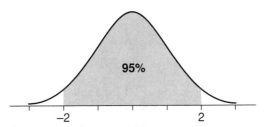

Approximately 95% of cases in a normal distribution are between two standard deviations above and below the mean.

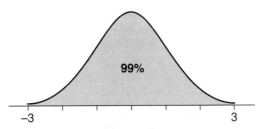

Approximately 99% of cases in a normal distribution are between three standard deviations above and below the mean.

Figure 3-16 Distribution of Cases or Area Under a Normal Curve

This information—relating standard deviations to the area under the normal curve—is so fundamental to statistical inference that statisticians often think of it as the **1-2-3 Rule.** Here it is again, just for good measure:

One standard deviation on either side of the mean of a normal curve will encompass approximately 68% of the area under the curve.

Two standard deviations on either side of the mean of a normal curve will encompass approximately 95% of the area under the curve.

Three standard deviations above and below the mean will encompass slightly more than 99% of the area under the curve.

At this point, let me suggest that you take a moment or two to digest this material. Start with an understanding that a normal curve is one that follows a precise mathematical function. Then concentrate on the notion that for any truly normal curve, there is a known area under the curve between standard deviations (for example, 68% of the area under the curve is between one standard deviation above and below the mean). Fix the critical values in your mind: ±1 standard deviation encloses approximately 68% of cases; ±2 standard deviations encompasses approximately 95%; and ±3 standard deviations encompasses slightly more than 99%.

 LEARNING CHECK

Question: What does the 1-2-3 Rule tell us?
Answer: It tells us the amount of area under the normal curve that is located between certain points (expressed in standard deviation units). Approximately 68% of the area is found between one standard deviation above and below the mean. Approximately 95% of the area is found between two standard deviations above and below the mean. Slightly more than 99% of the area is found between three standard deviations above and below the mean.

Whether you realize it or not, you're actually accumulating quite a bit of knowledge about normal curves. Indeed, if you throw in the fact that 50% of the area, or cases, under the curve are going to be found on either side of the mean, you're actually in a position to begin answering a few questions.

For example, let's say you know that some test results are normally distributed. In other words, a plot of the scores reveals a distribution that conforms to a normal curve. Let's also say that you know you scored one standard deviation above the mean. Now here's a reasonable question, given what you already know: Approximately what percentage of the test scores would be below yours? Approximately what percentage of the scores would be above yours? There's no need to hit the panic button. Just think it through.

Start with what you know about the percentage of cases (or scores) that fall between one standard deviation above and one standard deviation below the mean. You know (from what you read earlier) that approximately 68% are found between these two points. Since a normal curve is symmetrical, this means that approximately 34% of the scores will be found between the mean and one standard deviation *above* the mean. In other words, the 68% (approximately) will be equally divided between the two halves of the curve. Therefore, you will find approximately 34% of the cases (or area) between the mean and one standard deviation (either one standard deviation above or one standard deviation below). You also know (because of symmetry) that the lower half of the curve will include 50% of the cases. So, all that remains to answer the question is some simple addition:

> 50% the lower half of the curve
> \+ 34% the percentage between the mean and one standard
> ⎯⎯⎯ deviation above the mean
> 84% the percentage of cases below one standard deviation
> above the mean (therefore, aproximately 84% of
> the cases would be below your score, and approxi-
> mately 16% would be above your score)

Figure 3-17 shows the same solution in graphic form.

By now you're probably getting the idea that normal curves and distributions have an important place in the world of statistical analysis. Indeed, the idea of a normal curve is central to many statistical procedures. As a matter of fact, the notion of a normal curve or distribution is so fundamental to statistical inference that statisticians long ago developed a special case normal curve as a point of reference. We refer to it as the *standardized normal curve,* and that's our topic in Chapter 4.

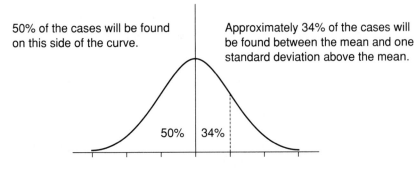

Figure 3-17 The Logic Behind the Problem Solution

Chapter Summary

In your exploration of data distributions, curves, and such, you've taken a very important step toward statistical reasoning. You took your first step in that regard as soon as you began to visualize a curve. Your ability to visualize data distributions in the form of curves is something that will come into play throughout your statistical education, so there's no such thing as too much practice at the outset.

Ideally, you've learned more than what a data distribution might look like if it were plotted or graphed. For example, you've learned about symmetrical curves, and you've learned about skewed curves. You've been introduced to the notion of a normal distribution and what normal distributions look like when they are graphed.

You've learned, for example, that a normal distribution can take on any number of different shapes (from very flat to very peaked), but the exact shape is always determined by two values—the mean and standard deviation of the underlying distribution. You've also learned that this mathematical definition of a normal curve's shape (based on the mean and standard deviation) makes the shape of a normal curve predictable.

You've learned that the points of inflection on a normal curve are the points that correspond to one standard deviation above and below the mean. And you've come to understand that, given a normal curve, a predictable amount of area (or cases) under the curve corresponds to specific points along the baseline (the 1-2-3 Rule).

As we move to the next chapter, the material that you've learned about normal curves in general will come into play in a major way. As you're about to discover, the notion of a normal distribution or normal curve is central to statistical analysis, so much so that it becomes the basis for a good amount of statistical inference.

Some Other Things You Should Know

The curves and distributions presented in this chapter were, in many instances, somewhat abstract. Sometimes actual values or scores were represented, but other times they were not. At this point, let me call your attention to a distinction that is often made in the world of numbers—namely, the distinction between discrete and continuous distributions. The difference is perhaps best illustrated by way of examples.

Consider a variable such as the number of children in a family. Respondents to a survey might answer that they had 0, 1, 2, 3, or some other number of children. The scale of measurement is clearly interval/ratio, but the only possible responses are integer values, or whole numbers. Those are considered discrete values, and a distribution based on those values is a *discrete distribution*.

Now consider a variable such as weight. Assuming that you had a very sophisticated scale, you could conceivably obtain very refined measurements— maybe so refined that ounces could be expressed to one or more decimal places. Such a system of measurement would result in what's known as a *continuous distribution*—a distribution based on such refined measurement that one value could, in effect, blend into the next.

You should take note that curves are often stylized presentations of data. A smooth curve may not be an accurate reflection of an underlying distribution based on discrete values. An accurate representation of a discrete distribution would actually be a little jagged or bumpy, because only integer values are possible, and there is no way for one integer value to blend into the next. That said, you should also know that this is really a minor point, and it doesn't reduce the overall utility of statistical analysis.

On the technology side of the ledger, you should know that a wide variety of statistical analysis software is available, all of which can reduce the task of statistical analysis to mere button pushing if you're not careful. There's no doubt that the availability of statistical software has simplified certain aspects of statistical analysis, but an overreliance on such software can work against you in the long run. There's still no substitute for fundamental brainpower when it comes to a thorough look at your data in the form of distributions and graphs before you really get started. That's why the process of visualization remains so important.

Key Terms

frequency distribution

negative skew

normal curve

1-2-3 rule

point of inflection

positive skew

skewed distribution

symmetrical distribution

tail of the distribution

Chapter Problems

Fill in the blanks, calculate the requested values, or otherwise supply the correct answer.

General Thought Questions

1. When a line can be drawn through the middle of a curve and both sides of the curve are mirror images of each other, the curve is said to be a ___normal___ curve.

2. When a curve is skewed in a positive direction, it is skewed to the ___right___; when a curve is skewed in a negative direction, it is skewed to the ___left___.

3. The points on either side of a normal curve at which the curve begins to change direction are known as the points of _____.

4. In a normal distribution, the points of inflection are located _____ standard deviation(s) above and below the mean.

5. In a normal distribution, the mean, median, and mode *equal* .

Application Questions/Problems

68% 1. In a normal distribution, and using the 1-2-3 Rule, approximately what percentage of the area under the curve is found between one standard deviation above and below the mean?

95% 2. In a normal distribution, and using the 1-2-3 Rule, approximately what percentage of the area under the curve is found between two standard deviations above and below the mean?

99% 3. In a normal distribution, and using the 1-2-3 Rule, approximately what percentage of the area under the curve is found between three standard deviations above and below the mean?

50% 4. In a normal distribution, what percentage of the area under the curve is found above the mean? What percentage of the area under the curve is found below the mean?

5. Assume that the mean of a distribution of test scores is 62 and the standard deviation is 4. Your score on the test is 70. How many standard deviations above or below the mean is your test score?

6. Assume that the mean of a distribution of test scores is 73 and the standard deviation is 5. You've been told that your test score is one standard deviation above the mean. What is your test score?

7. Assume that the mean of a distribution of test scores is 70, with a standard deviation of 5. You've been told that your score is two standard deviations above the mean. What is your test score?

8. Assume that the mean of a distribution of test scores is 200, with a standard deviation of 30. What would be the value of the score that falls two standard deviations below the mean?

9. Assume that the mean of a distribution of scores is 1250, with a standard deviation of 300. What would be the value of a score that falls one standard deviation below the mean?

4

The Normal Curve

Earlier I said there were times when it's best to approach the field of statistics without giving much thought to where you're going. This is one of those times. In fact, I'm going to ask you to take a step forward, develop a solid understanding of some information, and do all of it without one thought as to where we're headed. ·I know that's a lot to ask, but as the phrase goes: Trust me; there's a method to all of this.

We'll begin our discussion where we left off in the last chapter by asking a central question: Why all the fuss about normal curves? As it turns out, scientists long ago noticed that many phenomena are distributed in a normal fashion. In other words, the distributions of many different variables, when plotted as graphs, produce normal curves. Height and weight, for example, are frequently cited as variables that were long ago recognized as being normally distributed.

Having observed that many variables produce a normal distribution or curve, it was only natural that statisticians would focus an increasing amount of attention on normal curves. And so it was that a very special case of a normal curve was eventually formulated. This rather special case eventually came to be known as the **standardized normal curve**.

In one sense, the standardized normal curve is just another normal curve. In another sense, though, it's a very special case of a normal curve—so much so that statisticians often refer to it as the normal curve. Statisticians also use expressions such as *standardized normal distribution*. Regardless of the name—standardized normal curve, the normal curve, or standardized normal distribution—the idea is the same.

As you'll soon discover, the standardized normal curve is a theoretical curve that serves as a basis or model for comparison. It's a point of reference—a standard against which information or data can be judged. In the world of inferential statistics, you'll return to the standardized normal curve time and time again, so a solid understanding is imperative. To better understand this special curve, though, let's start by taking a look at some other normal distributions—ones you might find in the real world.

Before We Begin

Before we get started, let me ask you to think about two concepts. First, I want you to think about the concept of a percentage. Then I want you to think about the concept of a dollar. I know, that may sound very strange, but let me urge you to go along with this. There's a lesson to be learned.

Let's start with the idea of a percentage. Think about what a percentage tells you and how often you rely upon that concept when you communicate. For example, maybe someone tells you that there was a 15% drop in sales at the local grocery store last month. Another person tells you that enrollment at the local college increased by 6%. The use of a percentage to express some amount allows you to conjure up a mental image of a decrease or increase. Because a percentage represents a standard, so to speak, it's often very helpful when you want to make comparisons. For example, let's say your professor tells you that 14% of your class made a score of B, but 22% of the afternoon class made a grade of B. It really doesn't matter how many students are enrolled in each class; the percentage figures allow you to conjure up a mental image about the relative performance of students in the two classes.

In a way, you can think of a dollar in the same terms. To understand this, let me ask you to think about the concept of a dollar, but don't think of a dollar bill that's in your pocket. Instead, think about the notion of dollar as something that you rely upon as a basis for comparison. For example, let's say you've been surfing the net in search of a bargain on a television set. You find two televisions that interest you, but there's a problem. The price of one set (manufactured in Japan) is given in Japanese currency (yen), while the price of the other set (manufactured in Germany) is given in European currency (the euro). Any initial confusion you might experience is quickly erased as you begin to work your way through the situation. It's a simple matter of converting each currency (yen and euro) to dollars. Once you've done that, you're in a position to make a comparison. And that's the point. A dollar, at least in that example, isn't something tangible. Instead, it is something abstract. But a dollar, in an abstract sense, becomes essential to your ability to compare one price to the other.

Although examples about percentages and dollars might strike you as strange, they're relevant to the material that you're about to encounter. They demonstrate the importance of having a means of comparison—some sort of standard or basis that we can use as the foundation for our comparison. And that, in a nutshell, is where we're going in this chapter.

Real-World Normal Curves

Ordinary normal curves—curves like some of the ones we considered in the last chapter—are always tied to empirical or observed data. An example might be a collection of data from a drug rehabilitation program. Let's say, for example, someone gives you some summary information about the amount of time participants spend in voluntary group counseling sessions. Assume that you only know summary information, that you don't have detailed data. Let's also assume you've been told the data are normally distributed, with a mean of 14.25 hours per week and a standard deviation of 2.10 hours.

Because you know that the data reflect a normal distribution, you're in a position to figure out quite a lot, even if you don't have the actual data. For example, using some of the information you learned in the last chapter, you could quickly determine that approximately 68% of the program participants spend between 12.15 and 16.35 hours in voluntary group counseling. To refresh your memory about how you could do that, just follow the logic:

1. You know that the mean is 14.25 hours.
2. You know that the standard deviation is 2.10 hours.
3. You know that the data are distributed normally (the distribution is normal).
4. You know that 68% of the area or cases under a normal curve falls between one standard deviation above and below the mean.
5. Add one standard deviation to the mean to find the upper limit: 14.25 + 2.10 = 16.35 hours.
6. Subtract one standard deviation from the mean to find the lower limit: 14.25 – 2.10 = 12.15 hours.
7. Remembering the important point that the area under the curve really represents cases (program participants, for example), express your result as follows: Approximately 68% of the program participants spend between 12.15 and 16.35 hours per week in voluntary group counseling.

To further grasp the logic of this process, consider the illustration in Figure 4-1.

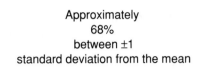

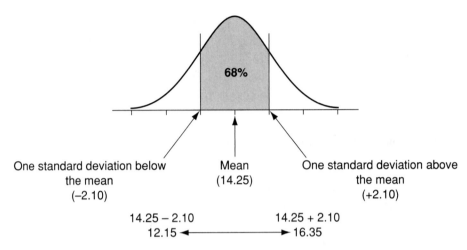

Figure 4-1   Logic Behind the Problem Solution

So much for a distribution of data concerning voluntary group counseling. You might study voluntary counseling participation, but another researcher might study the birth weights of a certain type of dog. He/she is apt to discover that the variable of birth weight (like voluntary counseling participation) is normally distributed. Of course, the values of the mean and standard deviation would be different—maybe a mean birth weight of 10.3 ounces with a standard deviation of 1.4 ounces—but the underlying logic would be the same. If you're willing to make a little leap here, you'll no doubt quickly see where we're going with all of this.

One researcher might have normally distributed data measured in hours and minutes, but the next researcher might have normally distributed data measured in pounds and ounces. Someone else might be looking at a variable that is normally distributed and expressed in dollars and cents, while another looks at normally distributed data expressed in years or portions of a year. Different researchers study different variables. It's as simple as that.

The list could go on and on—an endless array of normal distributions. The different distributions would have different means, different standard deviations, and different underlying scales of measurement (pounds, dollars, years, and so forth), but each normal distribution would conform to the same underlying relationship between the mean and standard deviation of the distribution and the shape of the curve.

The 1-2-3 Rule would always apply: Approximately 68% of the cases would be found ±1 standard deviation from the mean; approximately 95% of the cases would be found ±2 standard deviations from the mean; and more than 99% of the cases would be found ±3 standard deviations from the mean. To review the 1-2-3 Rule, see Figure 4-2.

By the same token, approximately 32% of the cases (or values) under a normal curve would be found *beyond* a value of ±1 standard deviation from the mean. (If approximately 68% of the total area falls within ±1 standard deviation, then the remaining amount—32%—must fall beyond those points.) Similarly, only about 5% of the cases (or values) under a normal curve would be

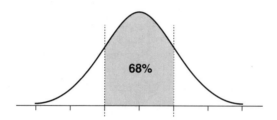

Approximately 68% of the area under a normal curve is between one standard deviation above and below the mean.

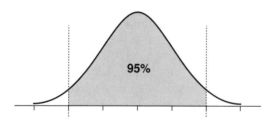

Approximately 95% of the area under a normal curve is between two standard deviations above and below the mean.

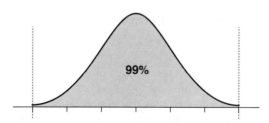

More than 99% of the area under a normal curve is between three standard deviations above and below the mean.

Figure 4-2 The 1-2-3 Rule in Review

found *beyond* a point ±2 standard deviations from the mean (100% − 95% = 5%). As for the real extremes of the curve, only about 1% of the area under the curve would be found beyond the points ±3 standard deviations from the mean (100% − 99% = 1%).

Part of what makes the 1-2-3 Rule so useful is the fact that you can use it regardless of the underlying scale of measurement. You know what percentage of scores or values will fall between or beyond certain portions of the curve, regardless of the unit of measurement in question. It doesn't make any difference whether you're dealing with pounds, ounces, dollars, years, or anything else. You know what percentage of cases will be found where—provided the curve is a normal curve. It also doesn't make any difference whether the mean and standard deviation are large numbers (let's say, thousands of dollars) or small numbers (let's say, values between 4 and 15 ounces). Assuming a normal distribution, the 1-2-3 Rule applies. The 1-2-3 Rule is useful because it is expressed in standard deviation units.

So much for normal curves that you're apt to find in real life. Now we come to the matter of the standardized normal curve—a theoretical curve. Let me urge you in advance to be open-minded as we move forward. Indeed, let me caution you not to expect any direct application right away. The applications will come in good time.

Into the Theoretical World

First and foremost, the standardized normal curve is a theoretical curve. It's a theoretical curve because it's based upon an infinite number of cases. Even if you're inclined to move right ahead with the discussion, let me suggest that you take a moment to reflect on that last point: The standardized normal curve is a theoretical curve; it is based on an infinite number of cases.

 LEARNING CHECK

Question: Why is the standardized normal curve considered a theoretical curve?

Answer: It is based on an infinite number of cases.

Here's a way to understand that point. Imagine a normal curve with a line in the middle that indicates the position of the mean. Now envision each side of the curve moving farther and farther out—the right side moving farther to the right and the left side moving farther to the left. Imagine something like the curve shown in Figure 4-3.

Because the standardized normal curve is based on an infinite number of cases, there's never an end to either side of it. As with other normal distributions, the bulk of the cases are found in the center of the distribution (clustered

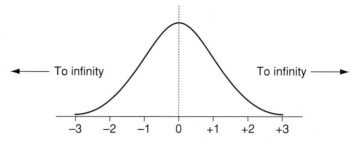

Mean, median, and mode coincide at 0; standard deviation = 1.

**The standardized normal curve is
based on an infinite number of cases.**

Figure 4-3 Theoretical Nature of the Standardized Normal Curve

around the mean), and the cases trail off from there. As the cases trail off on either side of the distribution, the curve falls ever so gradually toward the baseline. But (and this is an important *but*), the standardized normal curve never touches the baseline. Why? The standardized normal curve never touches the baseline because there are always more cases to consider. (Remember: the curve is based on an infinite number of cases.)

☑ LEARNING CHECK

Question: What is the effect of an infinite number of cases on the curve and the baseline?

Answer: The curve never touches the baseline because there are always more cases to consider.

As with any normal curve, the mean, median, and mode of the standardized normal curve share the same value; they're located at the same point. If you drew a line through the exact middle of the standardized normal curve, the line would reflect the location of the mean, median, and mode. Since that line would run through the exact middle of the curve, the two halves of the curve would be equal to each other. Just as in any normal curves that you may encounter, 50% of the area under the standardized normal curve is found to the right of the mean, and 50% is found to the left of the mean.

Now we come to the part of the discussion that explains why we refer to the standardized normal curve as *the* normal curve. To fully grasp this point, think about the example involving the drug rehabilitation program participants. In that example, the mean was 14.25 hours spent in voluntary group counseling, and the standard deviation was 2.10 hours. You might encounter another normal distribution, though, with a mean of 700 and a standard deviation of 25. At this point, it shouldn't concern you what the 700 and the 25 represent; they could be dollars or pounds or test scores or any number of other variables. The idea is to move your thinking to a more abstract level. Each distribution has a mean and a standard deviation. These values may be expressions of income amounts, test scores, number of tasks completed, growth rates, or any other variable.

In the case of the standardized normal curve, though, the mean is always equal to 0 and the standard deviation is always equal to 1. It is not the case that the mean is, let's say, 16 and the standard deviation is 2. It isn't the case that the mean is 2378 and the standard deviation is 315. You might have means and standard deviations like those in some normal distributions, but what we're considering here is the *standardized* normal curve.

Let me repeat: In the case of the standardized normal curve, the mean is equal to 0 and the standard deviation is 1. These two properties—a mean of 0 and a standard deviation of 1—are the properties that really give rise to the term *standardized*. They're also the properties that make the standardized normal curve so useful in statistical analysis.

We start with the notion that the mean is equal to 0 (see Figure 4-4). Because the mean is equal to 0, any point along the baseline of a normal curve that is above the mean is viewed as a positive value. Likewise, any value below the mean would be a negative value. As you already know, the two sides of any normal curve are equal. Therefore, the area falling between the mean and a certain distance above the mean (on the right side of the curve) is the same as the area between the mean and that same distance on the left side of the curve (below the mean).

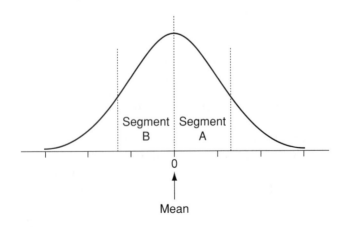

Figure 4-4   Equality of Areas on Both Sides of the
Standardized Normal Curve

In a way, the information you just digested cuts your learning in half. The only difference between the two sides of the standardized normal curve is that we refer to points along the baseline as being either positive or negative—positive for points above the mean, and negative for points below the mean. Well and good, but what am I supposed to be learning? you may ask. Patience! We'll get to that. Remember: The idea is to thoroughly digest the information.

The Table of Areas Under the Normal Curve

In a sense, it isn't the standardized normal curve itself that's so useful in statistical analysis. Rather it's the **Table of Areas Under the Normal Curve** that proves to be the really useful tool. You'll find a copy of the Table of Areas Under the Normal Curve in Appendix A, but don't look at it just yet. Instead, follow along with a little more of the discussion first.

To understand just how useful the Table of Areas Under the Normal Curve can be, think back to our previous discussion. Earlier you learned the 1-2-3 Rule, and that gave you some information about areas under a normal curve. But what about areas under the curve that fall, let's say, between the mean and 1.25 standard deviations above the mean? Or what about the area beneath the curve that is found between the mean and 2.17 standard deviations below the mean? In other words, everything is fine if you're dealing with 1, 2, or 3 standard deviations from the mean of a normal distribution, but what about other situations?

With a little bit of calculus, you could deal with all sorts of situations. You could calculate the area under the curve between two points, or the portion under the curve between the mean and any point above or below the mean. Fortunately, though, you don't have to turn to calculus. Thanks to the Table of Areas Under the Normal Curve, the work has already been done for you.

There's a chance that you're muttering something like, What work—what am I supposed to be doing? Relax; lighten up. Remember what the goal is right now—to learn some fundamental material without worrying about its direct application. Concentrate on the basic material right now; the applications will come in due time.

Before I ask you to turn to the Table of Areas Under the Normal Curve (Appendix A), let me say a word about what you're going to encounter and what you'll have to know to make proper use of the table. First, you should take time for a dark room moment to once again imagine what the standardized normal curve looks like. Imagine that you're facing a standardized normal curve. You notice the value of 0 in the middle of the baseline, along with an infinite number of hatch-marks going out to the right and to the left. Also, imagine that the area under the curve is full of cases (just as you did earlier when you were introduced to the notion that the area under the curve isn't just blank space).

Now, instead of thinking about a bunch of hatch-marks that mark points along the baseline, start thinking about the hatch-marks as something called

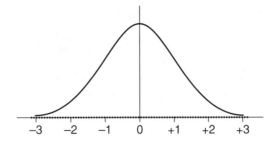

Z values along the entire baseline.

Figure 4-5   Distribution of Z Values Along the Baseline of the Standardized Normal Curve

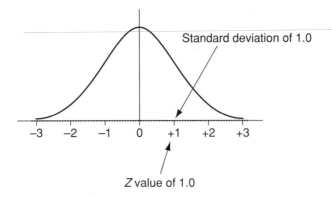

Z values are simply points along the baseline of a standardized normal curve.

Figure 4-6   Z Values as Standardized Deviations Along the Baseline of the Standardized Normal Curve

Z values. The term **Z**, or **Z score**, is the expression statisticians use to refer to points or values along the baseline of the standardized normal curve. The point at the middle of the curve has a Z value of 0; other Z values are found to the right and to the left of that zero point. The Z values on the right are considered positive Z values; the Z values on the left are considered negative Z values (see Figure 4-5).

Since the standard deviation of the standardized normal curve is equal to 1, Z values along the baseline are really expressions of standard deviations along the baseline. For example, a Z value of +2 really equals 2 standard deviation units above the mean. A Z value of −1.3 would equate to 1.3 standard deviation units below the mean. A Z value of 0 would be 0 standard deviations away from the mean because it would be equal to the mean. Consider the illustration in Figure 4-6.

Now take a look at Appendix A: Table of Areas Under the Normal Curve. It is also known as *the distribution of Z*. First, focus on the graphs in the illustration on page 308. The illustration lets you know that the table gives you information about the amount of area under the normal curve that's located between the mean and any point along the baseline of the curve. Second, focus on different columns. You'll see the symbol Z at the top of several columns. You'll also see columns marked Area Between Mean and Z.

The body of the table is filled with proportions (expressed as decimal values). These can easily be translated into percentage values by multiplying by 100. For example, the value of .4922 in the body of the table should be read as 49.22%. The percentage value of 49.22% is associated with a Z value of 2.42. How do you know that? Just have a look at the table. The value of .4922 appears next to the Z value of 2.42. The best way to understand all of this is to just jump right in and take a look at the table.

Let's say you want to find the proportion or percentage value associated with a Z value of 1.86. First you have to locate the Z value of 1.86 (see Figure 4-7). Then you look to the right of that Z value for the associated proportion. The corresponding proportion value is .4686, which translates into 46.86%. Now you ask, 46.86% of what? Here's the answer: 46.86% of the area under the normal curve is located between the mean and a Z value of 1.86. It doesn't make any difference whether it is a Z value of +1.86 or a Z value of −1.86; the associated proportion (or percentage) value is the same.

Z	Area Between Mean and Z	Z	Area Between Mean and Z	Z	Area Between Mean and Z	Z	Area Between Mean and Z
0.00	0.0000	0.50	0.1915	1.00	0.3413	1.50	0.4332
0.01	0.0040	0.51	0.1950	1.01	0.3438	1.51	0.4345
0.29	0.1141	0.79	0.2852	1.29	0.4015	1.79	0.4633
0.30	0.1179	0.80	0.2881	1.30	0.4032	1.80	0.4641
0.31	0.1217	0.81	0.2910	1.31	0.4049	1.81	0.4649
0.32	0.1255	0.82	0.2939	1.32	0.4066	1.82	0.4656
0.33	0.1293	0.83	0.2967	1.33	0.4082	1.83	0.4664
0.34	0.1331	0.84	0.2995	1.34	0.4099	1.84	0.4671
0.35	0.1368	0.85	0.3023	1.35	0.4115	1.85	0.4678
0.36	0.1406	0.86	0.3051	1.36	0.4131	**1.86**	**0.4686**
0.37	0.1443	0.87	0.3078	1.37	0.4147	1.87	0.4693
0.38	0.1480	0.88	0.3106	1.38	0.4162	1.88	0.4699
0.39	0.1517	0.89	0.3133	1.39	0.4177	1.89	0.4706

Z = 1.86

.4686 or 46.86%

Locate the *Z* value of 1.86. The corresponding value (expressed as a proportion) can be converted to a percentage by multiplying by 100. Thus, 46.86% of the area under the normal curve is located between the mean and a *Z* value of 1.86 (either +1.86 or −1.86).

Figure 4-7 A Segment of the Table of Areas Under the Normal Curve

While we're at it, let me point out a couple of things about the table.

1. What you're looking at is simply one format for presenting areas under the normal curve. Different statistics books use different formats to present the same material.

2. Pay attention to the note under the title of the table: Area Between the Mean (0) and Z. Think about what that tells you—namely, that the table gives you the amount of area under the curve that will be found between the mean and different Z values.

3. Get comfortable with how the values are expressed—as proportions in decimal format. These proportions can easily be converted to percentages. For example, the value of .4686 is the same as 46.86%.

4. You're probably better off if you immediately begin to think of the values in terms of the percentage of cases or observations between the mean and Z. In other words, each and every Z value has some percentage of cases or observations associated with it.

5. Take note of the end of the table—how it never really gets to a value of .5000 (or 50%). It goes out to a Z value of 3.9 (with an associated percentage of 49.99%), but then it ends. That's because the table is based on an infinite number of cases. Note that each time there's a unit change in the Z value (as you move further along in the table), the corresponding unit change in the associated area becomes smaller and smaller. That's because the tail of the curve is dropping closer and closer to the baseline as you move further out on the curve.

Now let's start making use of the table—first doing some things to get you familiar with the table, and then making some applications. We'll start with some problems that involve looking up a Z value and associated percentage. Always remember that the table only deals with one-half of the area under the curve. Whatever is true on one side of the curve is true on the other—right? Now consider the following questions.

Question: What is the percentage value associated with a Z value of +1.12, and how do you interpret that?

Answer: The proportion value is .3686, or 36.86%. This means that 36.86% of the area under the normal curve is found between the mean and a Z value of +1.12.

Question: What is the percentage value associated with a Z value of −1.50, and how do you interpret that?

Answer: The proportion value is .4332, or 43.32%. This means that 43.32% of the area under the normal curve is found between the mean and a Z value of −1.50.

Question: What is the percentage value associated with a Z value of +.75, and how do you interpret that?

Answer: The proportion value is .2734, or 27.34%. This means that 27.34% of the area under the normal curve is found between the mean and a *Z* value of +.75.

Question: What is the percentage value associated with a *Z* value of −2.00, and how do you interpret that?

Answer: The percentage value is .4772, or 47.72%. This means that 47.72% of the area under the normal curve is found between the mean and a *Z* value of −2.0.

Question: What is the percentage value associated with a *Z* value of +2.58, and how do you interpret that?

Answer: The proportion value is .4951, or 49.51%. This means that 49.51% of the area under the normal curve is found between the mean and a *Z* value of +2.58.

If you were able to deal with these questions successfully, we can move on to the next few questions. At this point, let me remind you again of what you already know from previous discussions: The table you're working with reflects only one side of the standardized normal curve. Now let's look at some more questions, this time concentrating on the area between two *Z* values.

Question: How much area under the curve is found between the *Z* values of +1.41 and −1.41?

Answer: 84.14% (Double 42.07% to take into account the fact that you're dealing with both sides of the curve.)

Question: How much area under the curve is found between *Z* values of +.78 and −.78?

Answer: 56.46% (Double 28.23% to take into account the fact that you're dealing with both sides of the curve.)

Question: How much area under the curve is found between *Z* values of +1.96 and −1.96?

Answer: 95% (Double 47.50% to take into account the fact that you're dealing with both sides of the curve.)

Question: How much area under the curve is found between *Z* values of +2.58 and −2.58?

Answer: 99.02% (Double 49.51% to take into account the fact that you're dealing with both sides of the curve.)

The answers to these questions were fairly straightforward because they simply required that you double a percentage value to get the right answer. You may have already gained enough knowledge about the areas under the normal curve to move forward, but I'd like to make certain that you've developed that second-nature, gut-level understanding that I mentioned earlier. To do that, I'm asking that you consider yet another round of questions.

With any questions about areas under the normal curve, it's usually a good idea to draw a rough diagram to illustrate the question that's being posed. Your

How much area under the curve is above a *Z* value of +1.44?

Answer: 7.49%.
From mean to *Z* is 42.51%. Entire half = 50%.
50 − 42.51 = 7.49.

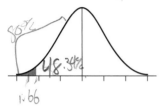

How much area under the curve is below a *Z* value of −2.13?

Answer: 1.66%.
From mean to *Z* is 48.34%. Entire half = 50%.
50 − 48.34 = 1.66.

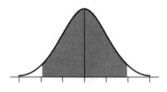

How much area under the curve is between *Z* values of ±1.96?

Answer: 95%.
From mean to *Z* is 47.50%. Consider both sides; double the value. 47.50% × 2 = 95%.

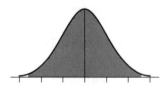

Approximately how much area under the curve is between *Z* values of ±2.58?

Answer: 99%.
From mean to *Z* is 49.51%. Consider both sides; double the value. 49.51% × 2 = Approximately 99%.

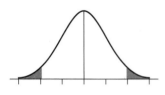

How much area falls outside of (above and below) the *Z* values of ±1.96?

Answer: 5%.
The area between *Z* values of ±1.96 is 95%. The entire area is 100%. 100% − 95% = 5% (evenly split on both sides of the curve).

How much area falls outside of (above and below) the *Z* values of ±2.58?

Answer: 1%.
The area between *Z* values of ±2.58 is 99%. The entire area is 100%. 100% − 99% = 1% (evenly split on both sides of the curve).

Figure 4-8   Problems Based on Areas Under the Standardized Normal Curve

diagram can be very unsophisticated, just as long as it allows you to put something on paper that expresses the question that's posed and what's going on in your mind when you approach the question. I should warn you to resist any urge to develop your own shortcuts based on the way a question is asked. Always take the time to think through the question. Use a diagram to convince yourself that you're approaching the question the right way.

Now take a look at the questions presented in Figure 4-8, along with the diagrams and commentary. These questions are very similar to some of those you encountered earlier. For these questions, though, focus on how helpful the diagrams are in explaining the underlying logic of the process.

By now you should have noticed that a couple of values have come up time and time again—namely, the values of 95% and approximately 99%. That wasn't by accident. As it turns out, statisticians very often speak in ways that directly or indirectly make reference to 95% or 99%. They're particularly interested in extreme values, cases, or events—the ones that lie beyond the 95% or 99% range. Another way to think of those values is to think of them as being so extreme that they're only apt to occur less than 5 times out of 100 or less than 1 time out of 100. That's why the Z values of ±1.96 and ±2.58 take on a special meaning to statisticians.

As you learned earlier, the area between Z values of ±1.96 on a normal curve or distribution will encompass 95% of the cases or values. Therefore, only 5% of the cases or values fall beyond the Z values of ±1.96 on a standardized normal curve. Similarly, the area between Z values of ±2.58 will take in slightly more than 99% of the cases or values. Therefore, less than 1% of the cases or values are beyond the Z values of ±2.58.

Those areas, the 5% and the 1%, are the areas of the extreme (unlikely) values—and those are the areas that ultimately grab the attention of statisticians. I'll have a lot more to say about that later. Right now, though, my guess is that your patience is running out and you're anxious to get to an application. Wait no longer. We'll move ahead with an example—one that may strike you as strangely familiar.

Finally, an Application

The truth of the matter is that you've already dealt with a partial application of the material you just covered. You did that earlier when you worked through the example in the last chapter involving your test scores. Think back for a moment to what that example involved. Here it is again, repeated just as it was presented earlier:

Test	Mean	Standard Deviation	Your Score
Math	82	6	80
Verbal	75	3	75
Science	60	5	70
Logic	70	7	77

By way of review, here's the situation you encountered earlier: You were part of a fairly large class (200 students); you took four tests; then I asked you some questions about your relative performance on the different tests.

An assumption was made that the distribution of scores on each test was normal. Additionally, the number of cases involved in each test was fairly large (200 cases). In situations like that—situations involving a large number of cases and distributions that are assumed to be normally distributed—you can convert raw scores to Z scores and make use of the Table of Areas Under the Normal Curve.

To understand all of this, think back to how you eventually came to view your performance on the Science Test. The mean on the Science Test was 60, with a standard deviation of 5. Your score was 70. You eventually thought it through and determined that your score was equal to two standard deviation units above the mean. Your score was 10 points above the mean; the standard deviation equaled 5 points; you divided the 10 points by 5 points (the standard deviation). As a result, you determined that your score was equal to two standard deviation units above the mean.

In essence, what you did was convert your raw score to a Z score. Had I introduced the formula for a Z score earlier, it might have caused some confusion or panic. Now the formula should make more sense. Take a look at the formula for a Z score, and think about it in terms of what was going on in your mind as you evaluated your performance on the Science Test.

$$Z = \frac{X - \mu}{\sigma}$$

Don't panic. Just think about what the symbols represent. First, you're dealing with the results of a class of students, and you're making the assumption that the class is a population. In other words, you're dealing with a population, so the mean on the Science Test is labeled μ, or mu. By the same token, the standard deviation is the standard deviation for the population (remember, we're treating the class as a population), so the standard deviation is symbolized by σ. The symbol X represents a raw score—in this case, your test score of 70.

The formula simply directs you to find the difference between a raw score and the mean, and then divide that difference by the standard deviation. For example, here's what was involved in converting your science score (raw score) to a standardized score:

$$
\begin{aligned}
Z &= \frac{X - \mu}{\sigma} \\
&= \frac{70 - 60}{5} \\
&= \frac{10}{5} \\
&= 2
\end{aligned}
$$

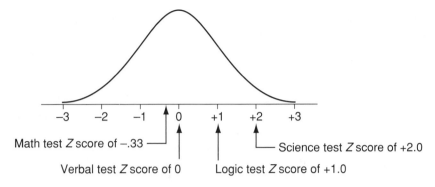

Math test *Z* score of −.33

Verbal test *Z* score of 0

Science test *Z* score of +2.0

Logic test *Z* score of +1.0

Figure 4-9 Conversion of Test Scores (Raw Scores) to *Z* Scores

When you determined that you scored two standard deviations above the mean, you were simply doing exactly what the formula directs you to do. You found the difference between your score (70) and the mean (60), and you divided that difference by the standard deviation (5). The result is a **Z ratio**. It's a ratio of the difference between a raw score and the mean, expressed in standard deviation units.

As shown in Figure 4-9, your score of 70 on the Science Test equated to a *Z* score, or *Z* ratio, of +2. By the same token, your other scores also represented *Z* scores or *Z* ratios.

In each case, you converted your test score to a *Z* score or *Z* ratio by superimposing the distribution of scores for each test onto a single standard—the standardized normal curve. The result was that you could eventually stand back and review all of your test performances in terms of what they were as *Z* scores or *Z* ratios. The results are just the same as they were when the scenario was originally presented in Chapter 2. Your best performance was on the Science Test; your worst performance was on the Math Test.

And just in case you're interested—just in case we had thrown in the Foreign Language Ability Test (like we did in Chapter 2)—it would also have its place on the illustration shown in Figure 4-9. Just to refresh your memory, think back to how the original problem was presented in Chapter 2. There were four 100 point tests to consider. After you had dealt with each of them, you were in a position to determine which was your best and worst performance. But then—at the end and after you thought the matter was settled—I asked you to consider one last scenario. I asked you to consider a situation in which you had also taken a 250 point Foreign Language Ability Test. Additionally, I told you that the mean for the test was 120 with a standard deviation of 15, and I told you that you had scored 90 on the test. If you recall what happened when we did that earlier (i.e., when we added a fifth test to the mix, but it was a 250 point test), then you recall that you had a new *worst performance*. It was the Foreign Language Ability Test score—a score that was two standard deviations below the mean. In short, if we had thrown the Foreign

Language Ability Test into the present scenario, your score on that test would find its rightful place along the baseline shown in Figure 4-9. More specifically, it would be at the point corresponding to a negative Z value—a Z of −2. The Foreign Language Ability Test score would be positioned right where it should be—right there along the baseline, just like the Z values of the other four test scores. Each test would have its own spot along the same baseline—even though four of the tests were 100 point tests and one of the tests (the Foreign Language Ability Test) was a 250 point test.

But there's got to be more to it than just that, you're likely to be saying right now. Truth be known, there is. But patience is called for right now. Remember what the goal is—namely, to develop a solid understanding of the fundamental concepts. For what it's worth, just think about all you've learned so far.

You've made your way through the fundamentals of descriptive statistics and the shapes of distributions in general. What's more, you've just had a solid introduction to the standardized normal curve, Z scores, and the Table of Areas Under the Normal Curve. In the process, you've covered quite a bit.

In learning about the standardized normal curve and The Table of Areas Under the Normal Curve, you've solidified your thinking about curves, distributions, and associated percentages of cases or probabilities of occurrence. More important, you've learned to think in the abstract—assuming you've taken the time to mentally visualize the standardized normal curve and Z scores or points along the baseline. In other words, you've learned to interpret Z scores in a fundamental way.

Let's say, for example, that someone is looking at a raw score value of 62. Then let's say that the 62 equates to a Z value of −2.13. By now, you should automatically know that a Z value of −2.13 is extreme, at least in the sense that it would be located toward the left end of a normal curve. You could look it up on the Table of Areas Under the Normal Curve and find out just how extreme it is, but you should know intuitively that it is extreme. After all, you know that a Z value of −1.96 is extreme, and a Z value of −2.13 would be even more extreme.

If you've committed just a minor amount of information to memory (in this case, the percentage associated with a Z value of ±1.96), you could say something rather important about that value of −2.13. Without even looking at the Table of Areas Under the Normal Curve, you could make the statement that a value of −2.13 is so extreme that it is likely to occur less than 5 times out of 100 (see Figure 4-10).

Besides automatically knowing the relative position of that Z value, by now you probably have a solid understanding of how the Z value of −2.13 was calculated in the first place. In other words, you understand that the process began by finding the difference between a raw score and the mean of a distribution (in this case, the difference between the mean and 62). That difference was then divided by the standard deviation of the distribution. The result was a Z ratio—a ratio of the difference between a raw score and the mean, expressed in standard deviation units.

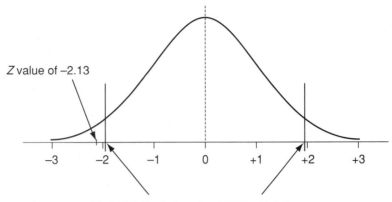

Z value of −2.13

Z of ±1.96 includes about 95% of total area.

Only about 5% of the area would be beyond *Z* values ±1.96.

In other words, only about 5% of the time would you expect to encounter a *Z* value that was more extreme than ±1.96. A *Z* value of −2.13 would be more extreme; therefore, you would expect to encounter it less than 5 times out of 100. In fact, the 5% of the area beyond a *Z* of ±1.96 would be evenly split, with 2.5% on each side of the curve. Therefore, a value of −2.13 is a value you would expect to occur less than 2.5 times out of 100.

Figure 4-10   Locating a *Z* Value of −2.13

Now here's the beauty in all of this: It doesn't make any difference whether you're studying weights, heights, incomes, levels of education, levels of aggression in prison inmates, test scores, or anything else. It doesn't make any difference whether you're dealing with values that represent dollars or years or pounds or points or anything else. A *Z* value (*Z* ratio) can serve as your standard, just so long as you're dealing with a distribution that has a fairly large number of cases and you can legitimately make the assumption that it is normally distributed.

If your distribution meets those assumptions, you're in a position to know a great deal about your distribution. Most important, you're in a position to identify the extreme values in the distribution. As I mentioned before, it's the extreme values that usually get the attention of statisticians. Indeed, it's usually an extreme result that a statistician is looking at when he/she announces that the results are *significant*.

We'll eventually get into all of that—how to determine whether or not results are statistically significant—but we've still got to cover a few remaining concepts. For that, we go to the next chapter.

Chapter Summary

This chapter was a milestone in the sense that you were introduced to one of the more theoretical but essential concepts in statistical inference—the standardized normal curve. Presumably you learned about the fundamentally theoretical nature of the standardized normal curve, and you learned how to navigate your way around it (with the use of the Table of Areas Under the Normal Curve). What's more, you moved forward on a leap of faith, learning many things about the standardized normal curve with little notion as to where the knowledge would lead.

If the approach worked, though, you eventually found out enough to make your way through some basic applications. Ideally, you moved through those applications with a certain level of intuitive understanding. If that's the way it unfolded for you, welcome to the world of statistical reasoning—you're on the right road. Yes, there are still many more applications to come. But at least you're on the right track.

Beyond that, you were introduced to the fundamental utility of the standardized normal curve—how it allows us to work with a common statistical language, so to speak. You learned that statisticians are typically interested in extreme occurrences. More important, you learned what an extreme occurrence is to a statistician.

I suspect that all of that made for a fairly full plate and a lot to digest at one sitting. Because all that follows is so dependent on what you've just covered, let me urge you to make an honest assessment of your understanding up to this point. If you think you need to reread the material a time or two, make the effort. In many respects, it's one of the keys that unlocks the door.

Some Other Things You Should Know

You deserve to know that the assumption of a normal distribution of a population (or populations, for that matter) is central to many statistical applications. You should also know that it is an assumption that isn't always met. As you might have suspected, statisticians have methods for dealing with situations in which this central assumption cannot be met, but those approaches are beyond the scope of this text. Even if you're eager to learn more about such matters, it pays to remember the old adage, first things first. Since a substantial part of inferential statistics rests on the assumption that you are working with data from a population that is normally distributed, it's essential that you thoroughly cement your understanding of the standardized normal curve.

Beyond that, you should know that there are some relatively easy ways to determine if a distribution is normally distributed—rules of thumb, so to speak, that you can rely upon as a quick alternative to more sophisticated analyses. For example, with a normal distribution, you already know that the mean, median, and mode will coincide. Were you to make a quick check of the values of the mean, median, and mode in a distribution, a substantial difference between or among the values would be an immediate signal that the distribution isn't normal. Similarly, in a normal distribution, you would expect the range divided by 6 to be very close to the value of the standard deviation. Why? You'd expect that because three standard deviations on either side of the mean should take in more than 99% of the area (or cases). Since the mean of a normal distribution would be in the middle of the distribution, you would expect three standard deviations above and below the mean to encompass something close to the total area.

So much for Some Other Things You Should Know at this point. We still have one last bit of information to cover before we really get about the business of inferential statistics, so that's where we'll turn next.

Key Terms

standardized normal curve   Z (Z score)
Table of Areas Under the Normal Curve   Z ratio

Chapter Problems

Fill in the blanks, calculate the requested values, or otherwise supply the correct answer.

General Thought Questions

1. The standardized normal curve is based upon a(n) ~~infinite~~ number of cases.

2. The mean of the normal curve is equal to _____, and the standard deviation is equal to _____.

Application Questions/Problems

1. How much area under the normal curve is between the mean and a Z value of 1.63?

2. How much area under the normal curve is between the mean and a Z value of 2.35?

3. How much area under the normal curve is between the mean and a Z value of −1.22?

4. What percentage of area (cases or observations) is above a Z value of +1.96?

5. What percentage of area (cases or observations) is below a Z value of −1.96?

6. What percentage of area (cases or observations) is above a Z value of +2.58?

(handwritten note: Same just other side of curve)

7. What percentage of area (cases or observations) is below a Z value of −2.58?

8. What percentage of area under the normal curve is above a Z value of +1.53?

9. What percentage of area under the normal curve is below a Z value of −1.12?

10. What Z value corresponds to the lowest 20% of area under the normal curve?

11. What Z value corresponds to the upper 35% of area under the normal curve?

12. What Z values correspond to the middle 60% of area under the normal curve?

5

Four Fundamental Concepts

This chapter deals with four fundamental concepts, some of which have been alluded to before. Everything we've covered up to this point is of little consequence if you gloss over the material in this chapter, so let me urge you to spend some serious time with the material you are getting ready to cover. If you have to read and reread and reread again, do that. The time spent will pay off.

First, we'll deal with the matter of random sampling. From that point, we'll take up the topic of sampling error—an essential notion that underlies the logic of inferential statistics. Then, we'll turn our attention to the idea of a sampling distribution, and more specifically, we'll look at the notion of a sampling distribution of sample means. Finally, we'll turn our attention to the Central Limit Theorem—a fundamental principle that will be important in our first major application of statistical inference.

As you go through the material, you'll likely have to take the time for a dark room moment or two—certainly more than you've had to up to this point. As I said before, don't assume that a dark room moment is beneath your intellectual dignity. Indeed, it may turn out to be a key to success when it comes to understanding the material.

Before We Begin

Let me pose two questions. First, how many times have you heard or read the expression, *random sampling*? Next, what about the expression, *sampling error,* or its cousin, so to speak, the *margin of error*? How many times have you encountered that?

My guess is you've heard phrases such as *random sampling* or *sampling error,* but you may not have a solid understanding of what each expression means. That's fine; it's not often that people have cause to think about such notions. On the other hand, those expressions are tied to some of the fundamental notions and assumptions that accompany statistical inference. From my perspective, it's virtually impossible to grasp the fundamental logic of statistical inference without some understanding of those concepts. Let me repeat: *It's virtually impossible to grasp the fundamental logic of statistical inference without some understanding of those concepts.*

Those concepts—random sampling and sampling error—are two of the concepts covered in this chapter. The other concepts—sampling distribution and the Central Limit Theorem—are no less important. I'm of the opinion that the four concepts, taken together, form the basis of a good amount of statistical inference. Therefore, it's paramount that you develop a firm understanding of each.

That said, I also know that you'll likely wonder why you have to learn each concept. Regrettably, I don't think you're going to like my answer. All I can tell you is that you're very close to entering the world of inferential statistics, and the concepts that you're about to encounter are central to opening the door.

On a positive note, you've more than earned a rest when you get through this chapter. It involves a hefty amount of material—conceptual and theoretical material that requires thinking in an abstract fashion. The chapter also makes reference to concepts that you've previously covered (for example, the standard deviation, populations, and samples). If you have any difficulty recalling what those previously introduced concepts are all about, go back to the earlier chapters to refresh your memory. A solid understanding of those concepts is essential.

Fundamental Concept #1: Random Sampling

Many statistical procedures rest on the assumption that you're working with a sample that was selected in a random fashion. The expression *random sample* is common, but it's also commonly misunderstood. Contrary to popular opinion, a random sample isn't what you get when you simply stand on the sidewalk and interview people who walk by. And a random sample isn't what you get when you use a group of students for research subjects just because they are available or accessible. To assert that you're working with a **random sample** of cases (or cases selected in a random fashion) means that you've met certain selection criteria.

First, a random sample is a sample selected in such a way that every unit or case in the population has an equal chance of being selected. There's a very important point to that requirement—namely, that you have in mind the population to which you intend to generalize. If, for example, you say that you're working with a random sample of registered voters, presumably you have in mind a population of registered voters that exists somewhere. It may be a population of registered voters throughout a city, or county, or state, or the nation. But you do have to have fixed in your mind a larger population in which you have an interest.

The second requirement is that the selection of any single case or unit can in no way affect the selection of any other unit or case. Let's say you devised a sampling plan that was based on your selecting first a Republican and then a Democrat and then a Republican and then a Democrat. If the idea of deliberately alternating back and forth in your selection of Republicans and Democrats is part of your sampling plan, you're not using a random sampling technique. Remember the criterion: The selection of one unit or case in no way affects the selection of another unit or case.

The third requirement of random sampling is that the cases or units be selected in such a way that all combinations are possible. This requirement is the one that really goes to the heart of inferential statistics, and it's the one you should key in on. The notion that all combinations are possible really means that some combinations may be highly improbable, but all combinations are possible. Indeed, British mathematician and philosopher Bertrand Russell (1955) illustrated the point with a little bit of humor. Describing a venture into a mythical hell while in a fever-induced state of delirium, Russell observed:

> There's a special department in hell for students of probability. In this department there are many typewriters and many monkeys. Every time that a monkey walks on a typewriter, it types by chance one of Shakespeare's sonnets. (p. 30)

Leaving Russell's mythical hell and returning to the more practical world of sampling, here's an illustration to consider. If you rely on a sampling technique that's truly random, and the population of registered voters is fairly evenly split between Republicans and Democrats, you'll probably end up with a sample that is roughly equally split between Republicans and Democrats. Your sample may not reflect the split between Republicans and Democrats in the population with exact precision, but it will probably be fairly close. It's very unlikely that you'll end up with a sample that is 100% Republican or 100% Democrat. Both of those outcomes (all Republicans or all Democrats) are highly improbable, but they are possible—and that's the point. If the sampling technique is truly random, all combinations are possible. For some further examples, *see* Figure 5-1.

The process of selecting cases or units in a random fashion typically begins with the identification of a **sampling frame,** or physical representation of the population. For example, your ability to make a statement about the population of registered voters in a certain county begins with your identification of a listing of all registered voters in that county. The listing, whether it exists on printed pages or in some electronic format, would constitute your sampling frame. If, on the other hand, you were interested in making a statement about all the students enrolled for six hours or more at a certain university, you would have to begin your sampling by locating some listing of all the students who met the criteria. Presumably you would get such a list from the registrar's office. That list, in turn, would serve as your sampling frame—a representation of your population.

In the case of a simple random sample, every case or unit in the sampling frame would be numbered, and then a *table of random numbers* would be used to select the individual cases for the sample. Most research methods texts have a table of random numbers included as an appendix to the book,

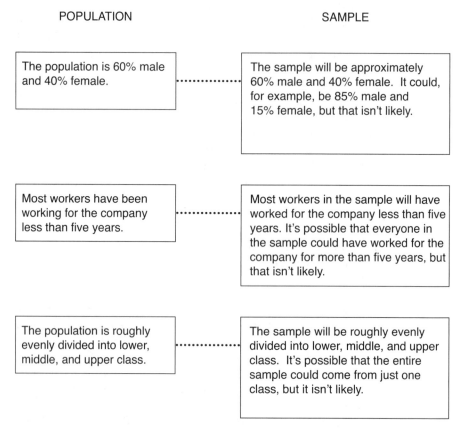

POPULATION

SAMPLE

The population is 60% male and 40% female.

The sample will be approximately 60% male and 40% female. It could, for example, be 85% male and 15% female, but that isn't likely.

Most workers have been working for the company less than five years.

Most workers in the sample will have worked for the company less than five years. It's possible that everyone in the sample could have worked for the company for more than five years, but that isn't likely.

The population is roughly evenly divided into lower, middle, and upper class.

The sample will be roughly evenly divided into lower, middle, and upper class. It's possible that the entire sample could come from just one class, but it isn't likely.

Figure 5-1   Relationship Between a Population and a Random Sample

and a quick read of the material on random sampling will provide you with a step-by-step procedure for selecting a simple random sample. In fact, most research methods texts include information on a variety of sampling designs—everything from systematic random sampling to stratified random sampling. For our purposes, though, you should simply have fixed in your mind what the term *random sampling* is all about and what is necessary if you're going to assert that you're working with a sample selected in a random fashion.

Fundamental Concept #2: Sampling Error

Assuming you've now got a grasp of what is meant by the concept of random sampling, it's time to turn to the concept of *sampling error*—something that was mentioned earlier, but only briefly. Now it's time to take a closer look. To illustrate the concept, we'll start with a simple example.

Let's say you're working as a university administrator, and you've been asked to provide an estimate of the average age of the students who are enrolled for six hours or more. Let's also say that, for all the reasons we've discussed before (factors such as time and cost), you've decided to rely on a sample to make your estimate—a random sample of 200 students from a population of 25,000 students (all enrolled for at least six hours of coursework).

The entire population of students probably includes a considerable range of ages. Some students might be extremely young—students who skipped a few years in high school because they were exceptionally bright. There may not be many students like that in the population, but there could be a noticeable number. By the same token, there might be a small but noticeable number of very old students—retirees who decided to return to school. Like the very young students, the older students would represent an extreme portion of the distribution.

The idea of sampling error comes into play with the recognition that an *infinite* number of samples are possible. You could take one sample, then another, then another (see Figure 5-2). You could continue the process time and

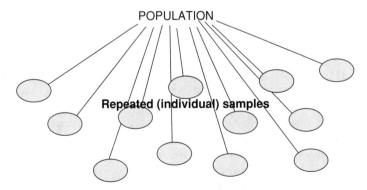

Figure 5-2   Representation of Repeated Samples from the Same Population

time again. You might not want to do something like that, but you could. And that's the point: An infinite number of samples are possible. This point is extremely important, so let me suggest here that you spend a dark room moment or two on it. Just think about the notion of taking sample after sample after sample from the same population. As ridiculous as that may seem, think about what the process would entail.

Assuming you've given some thought to the notion that an infinite number of samples is possible, let's now consider the real world. In reality, you'll have just one that you are working with. An infinite number of samples are possible, but you'll be working with only one of those samples. When it comes time to collect some information and carry out some calculation, you may think you're working with the best sample in the world (whatever that means) and that it is somehow a very special sample, but it really isn't special at all. In reality, you're working with one sample—just one out of an infinite number of samples that are possible—and your sample may or may not be an accurate reflection of the population from which it was taken.

What if, just by chance, you ended up with a sample that was somewhat overloaded with extremely young students? As you're probably aware, the chance of something like that happening may be small, but it's possible. In fact, you could end up with, let's say, 150 of the 200 cases somehow coming from the portion of the population distribution that contained the really young students. As I said, the chances are slim, but the possibility is there. By the same token, it's possible that you could end up with a random sample that was overloaded with extremely old students. Likely? No. Possible? Yes.

If your sample had an extreme overrepresentation of really young students, the sample mean age would be pulled down (the effect of extremely low values in the distribution). As a result, mean age for the sample wouldn't be a true reflection of the mean of the population (μ). Had you selected a sample that happened to have an overrepresentation of much older students, the mean of your sample would be higher than the true mean of the population. Once again, there would be a difference between your sample mean and the true mean of the population—just by chance.

You're probably starting to get the point of all this, but it's important that you understand the concept of sampling error at a level that's almost intuitive. For this reason, let me suggest that you take a serious look at the example shown in Figure 5-3. It illustrates what you might get in the way of several different sample means from one population. Even if you think you understand all of this, let me suggest that you pay attention to the specifics of the example. It takes very little effort, but it can help you understand the point in a way that will stay with you forever.

If you're starting to have a little conversation with yourself—if you're telling yourself, OK, I get it; this makes sense; of course I'd expect to see some difference—then you're on the right track as far as understanding one of the central concepts involved in statistical inference. What you've just dealt with is the concept of **sampling error**—the difference between a sample statistic and a population parameter that's just due to chance.

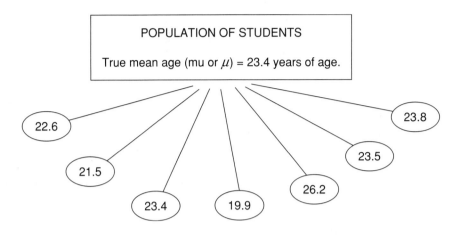

Seven samples and seven different sample means

One sample mean equals the mean of the population, but the other sample means are slightly higher or lower than the true population mean (mu or μ).

Figure 5-3 Illustration of Sampling Error

The difference could relate to a mean or a range or any other statistic. For example, a difference between the mean of the sample and the mean of the population (mu) that is just due to chance would amount to sampling error (of the mean). A chance difference between the range of the sample and the range of the population would also amount to sampling error (of the range). In both cases, we would categorize the difference as sampling error—the difference between a sample statistic and a population parameter that is due to chance.

You could be dealing with a lot of sampling error (particularly if you, by chance, came up with a rather extreme sample), or you could be dealing with only a small amount of it (if you came up with a highly representative sample). How statisticians deal with all of that is a topic for discussion down the road. For the moment, though, let's move forward to the next concept.

Fundamental Concept #3:
The Sampling Distribution of Sample Means

To begin our discussion of this concept, I'll ask you to return to our earlier example. Imagine for a moment that you're taking sample after sample after sample from the population of students. The fact that nobody except a statistician is apt to do something like that shouldn't concern you. Just imagine for a moment that you're going through the exercise—taking sample after sample after sample. Let's say that each time you take a sample you select 50 students.

Now imagine that each time you select a sample, you ask students their age and record the information. You could easily calculate the mean age of each sample—right? Of course you could. As you learned in the previous section, though, the mean age of any one of those samples is likely to be slightly different from the population mean, just by chance (or due to sampling error). Let's say you went through the process 1000 times—each time selecting 50 students, collecting information on the students' ages, and calculating the mean age for that sample. If you recorded the mean for each of the 1000 samples, you would then have what is known as a **sampling distribution of sample means.**

At this point, let me suggest that you go no further unless you're absolutely certain you have that last notion firmly fixed in your mind. Here it is again: You could take sample after sample, selecting 50 students each time. You could repeat this process until you had selected 1000 samples. If you calculated the mean of each sample, you would then have a distribution of 1000 sample means. This distribution would be known as a sampling distribution of sample means.

There's no doubt about it, that phrase is a mouthful. So let's take it apart, element by element.

The result of your exercise would be a distribution, just like any other distribution (of income, weight, height, or any other variable). Only in this case, it would be a distribution of means taken from different samples—hence the expression *distribution of sample means.* You could just as easily have a distribution of sample ranges. All you would have to do is take sample after sample after sample, record the range of each sample, and report those ranges in a distribution. Typically, though, statisticians deal with the concept of a sampling distribution of sample means, rather than a sampling distribution of sample ranges.

The expression *sampling distribution* simply means a distribution that is the result of repeated sampling. Once again, it is a rather abstract concept, and very few people would ever bother to construct a sampling distribution of anything. But here's the point: You could construct a sampling distribution if you wanted to. As a matter of fact, you could very easily construct a sampling distribution of sample means. All it would take is a little bit of time. Once you did that, you could very easily develop a graph or plot of the sampling distribution of sample means. And that brings us to the last of the fundamental concepts.

Fundamental Concept #4: The Central Limit Theorem

Imagine for a moment that you had actually constructed the sampling distribution of sample means described in the previous example. In other words, you went to the trouble of taking 1000 different samples with 50 subjects in each sample. For each sample, you calculated and recorded a mean age, and you eventually put all the mean ages into a distribution.

Now imagine that you developed a graph or plot of all of those means, producing a curve. Do you have any idea what that curve might look like? Before you answer, think about the question for just a moment. Think about how you would produce the graph or curve, and what sort of values you would be plotting. Just to help you along in your thinking, consider the following:

1. You're taking sample after sample after sample (until you have 1000 samples).
2. Each time you take a sample, you calculate a mean age for the sample (a sample mean based on 50 cases).
3. Because of sampling error, your sample mean is likely to differ from the true mean of the population.
4. Sometimes your sample mean will be less than the true mean of the population.
5. Sometimes your sample mean will be greater than the true mean of the population.

By now you should be getting a picture in your mind of all these sample means (or sample mean values)—some higher than others, some lower than others, a few really high values, a few really low values, and so forth and so on. If you're getting the idea that the distribution of sample means would graph as a normal curve, you're on the right track. Now take a look at Figure 5-4. How do we know that a sampling distribution of sample means would look like a normal curve? We know it because it's been demonstrated. The idea has been tested; the idea holds up.

As it turns out, statisticians know quite a bit about what would happen if you set out to construct a sampling distribution of sample means. What's more, they know quite a bit about how the sampling distribution of sample means would be related to the population from which the samples were drawn. As a matter of fact, this relationship—the relationship between the sampling distribution of sample means and the population from which the samples were drawn—has a name. It is known as the Central Limit Theorem. Before we deal with the Central Limit Theorem and what it says, though, let me make three more points about a sampling distribution of sample means.

First, any sampling distribution of sample means will have a mean of its own—right? To convince yourself of that, just imagine a plot or graph of all the different means you would get if you took 1000 samples and plotted the means from those 1000 samples. The plot or graph would represent an underlying distribution, and that distribution (like any distribution) would have a mean. In the case we're discussing, it would be the mean of a sampling distribution of sample means.

Second, that distribution (the sampling distribution of sample means) would, like any distribution, have a standard deviation—right? Remember: The

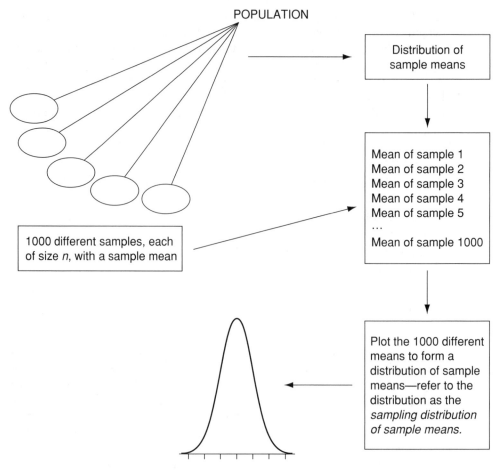

Figure 5-4   Constructing a Sampling Distribution of Sample Means

sampling distribution of sample means is, in a sense, just another distribution. All distributions have a standard deviation. In this case, we're considering a sampling distribution of sample means. It is no different. It would have a standard deviation.

Third, statisticians have a special term for the standard deviation of a sampling distribution of sample means. They refer to it as the **standard error of the mean.** That term or phrase, *standard error of the mean,* actually makes a lot of sense if you take a moment or two to think about it. It makes sense, in part, because a sampling distribution of sample means is actually a distribution of sampling error. The sampling distribution is based on a lot of means, and many of those means will actually vary from the true mean of the population. As you learned before, we refer to that chance difference between a sample mean and a population mean as *sampling error*—hence the term *error* in the expression *standard error of the mean.* Instead of saying *standard deviation of a sampling distribution of sample means,* statisticians use the expression *standard error of the mean.*

With all of that as background, let's now have a look at the Central Limit Theorem and what it tells us. First I'll present the theorem; then I'll translate.

Here is the **Central Limit Theorem:**

> If repeated random samples of size *n* are taken from a population with a mean or mu (μ) and a standard deviation (σ), the sampling distribution of sample means will have a mean equal to mu (μ) and a standard error equal to $\dfrac{\sigma}{\sqrt{n}}$. Moreover, as *n* increases, the sampling distribution will approach a normal distribution.

Now comes the translation: Imagine a population, and give some thought to the fact that this population will have a mean (mu or μ) and a standard deviation (σ). Now imagine a sampling distribution of sample means constructed from that population—a distribution of sample means, based on random sample after random sample after random sample, taken from the same population. That sampling distribution will have a mean, and it will equal the mean of the population (mu or μ). The sampling distribution of sample means will also have a standard deviation—something we refer to as the standard error of the mean. The standard error of the mean (the standard deviation of the sampling distribution of sample means) will be equal to the standard deviation of the population (σ) divided by the square root of *n* (where *n* is the number of cases in each sample).

In other words, a sampling distribution of sample means will eventually look like a normal curve (see Figure 5-5). Besides that, there's a very definite and predictable relationship between a population and a sampling distribution of sample means based on repeated samples from that population. We know that the relationship between the two is predictable because mathematicians have demonstrated that it is predictable.

It isn't the case that the mean of a sampling distribution of sample means will eventually be fairly close to or approximate the mean of the population (mu or μ). Instead, the mean of the sampling distribution of sample means will *equal* the mean of the population (mu or μ).

By the same token, it isn't the case that the standard deviation of the sampling distribution of sample means (the standard error) will sort of be related to the standard deviation of the population. Rather, the standard error will *equal* the population standard deviation (σ) divided by the square root of *n* (or the number of cases in the sample).

In the next chapter, we'll make some direct application of all of this material—but it won't do you any good to race ahead to the next chapter.

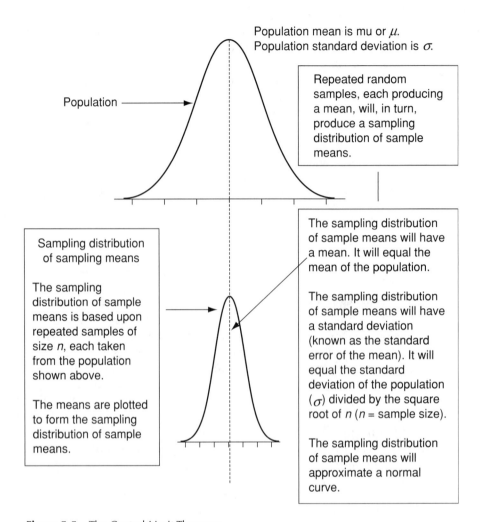

Figure 5-5   The Central Limit Theorem

Racing ahead without thoroughly understanding what we've just covered will only set you back in the long run. In fact, racing ahead will probably cause you to hit what I call the "brick wall of misunderstanding"—an experience that makes it impossible to understand all that lies ahead.

In my view, there's only one way to get over, under, around, or through the brick wall of misunderstanding, and that's to focus on the fundamental concepts until you finally understand each one of them. It won't do to tell yourself you understand when you don't. Instead, reread this entire chapter, if you have to. Read it and reread it until you understand the material at a near-intuitive level. Once you've done that, you'll be in a position to more forward.

Chapter Summary

At this point, you deserve a break. You've just been through some rather abstract and theoretical territory. If you found the material a little tough to digest at the outset, that's normal. The material is new by all reasonable standards—new concepts, new ideas, and new ways of looking at the world. New material? You bet. Difficult material? Not really. It's all a matter of thinking about each element until you have a solid understanding. As to what you just covered, it was significant.

For example, you were introduced to a technical definition of random sampling, in a way that emphasized what a random sample is and is not. You also learned that the assumption of a random sample is central to many statistical applications. Equally important, you were introduced in some detail to the concept of sampling error. Ideally, you learned that it is sampling error that prevents a direct leap from sample statistics to population parameters. Beyond all of that, you were introduced to the concept of a sampling distribution of sample means and the Central Limit Theorem. In the process, you found your way into the heart of statistical inference (at least as it relates to certain applications). A lot of material, indeed.

As we close out this chapter, let me underscore how beneficial a dark room moment might be for understanding some of the concepts that you just covered. These concepts deserve your full attention, and that's what a dark room moment is all about—a chance to bring your full attention to the question at hand.

Some Other Things You Should Know

Normally, I use this section of each chapter to point you in the direction of relevant topics left unexplored in the interest of a succinct presentation. The chapter you just read justifies a departure from that approach. Instead of pointing you to unexplored topics or directing you to additional resources, I'm going to let you in on a little secret. Here it is.

The material you just covered is, for many students, the source of the brick wall. It's the collection of concepts that ultimately separate the women from the girls and the men from the boys. My experience in teaching statistics tells me that many students say they "get it" when, in fact, they don't. The issue, of course, isn't what the students tell me; it's what they tell themselves.

The four fundamental concepts presented in this chapter will eventually be linked for you in the form of practical applications. But the logic of those applications always comes back to the fundamental concepts, and that's why they are so essential.

There's no question that some of the concepts are highly abstract. Indeed, it is this collection of concepts that always come to my mind when I stress the importance of taking time out for a dark room moment. Much material remains to be covered, so don't hamper your learning by going forward unprepared. If you need to take time out for a few dark room moments, now is the time to do it. Shore up the moments with a second or third read of the material, if necessary.

Key Terms

Central Limit Theorem	sampling error
random sample	sampling frame
sampling distribution of sample means	standard error of the mean

Chapter Problems

Fill in the blanks, calculate the requested values, or otherwise supply the correct answer.

General Thought Questions

1. In a random sample, every unit in the population has a(n) _____ chance of being selected.

2. In a random sample, the selection of any one unit _____ affect the selection of any other unit.

3. In a random sample, _____ combinations are possible.

4. When selecting a sample, the physical representation of the population is known as the _____.

5. A representative sample is one in which important characteristics in the population are mirrored in the _____.

6. The difference between a sample statistic and a population parameter that is due to chance is referred to as _____.

7. The mean of a population (μ) = 54.72, and the mean of a sample from that population ($\overline{X}$) = 54.92. Assuming the difference between the two values is due to chance, we can refer to the difference as sampling _____.

8. A sampling distribution of sample means is based on taking repeated samples (of size *n*) from the same population and plotting the _____ of the different samples.

9. According to the Central Limit Theorem, the mean of a sampling distribution of sample means will equal the _____ of the population from which the samples were drawn.

10. The standard deviation of a sampling distribution of sample means is referred to as the _____.

11. According to the Central Limit Theorem, and given a sampling distribution of sample means, the standard error of the mean will equal the _____ of the population divided by the _____ of the sample size.

12. The shape of a sampling distribution of sample means will approach the shape of a _____ curve.

Application Questions/Problems

1. A population has a mean (μ) of 24.12 and a standard deviation (σ) of 4. Assume that a sampling distribution of sample means has been constructed, based on repeated samples of $n = 100$ from this population.
   a. What would be the value of the mean of the sampling distribution?
   b. What would be the value of the standard error of the mean?

2. A population has a mean (μ) of 30 and a standard deviation (σ) of 6. Assume that a sampling distribution of sample means has been constructed, based on repeated samples of $n = 225$ from this population.
   a. What would be the value of the mean of the sampling distribution?
   b. What would be the value of the standard error of the mean?

3. A population has a mean (μ) of 120 and a standard deviation (σ) of 30. Assume that a sampling distribution of sample means has been constructed, based on repeated samples of $n = 100$ from this population.
   a. What would be the value of the mean of the sampling distribution?
   b. What would be the value of the standard error of the mean?

4. A population has a mean (μ) of 615 and a standard deviation (σ) of 90. Assume that a sampling distribution of sample means has been constructed, based on repeated samples of $n = 400$ from this population.
   a. What would be the value of the mean of the sampling distribution?
   b. What would be the value of the standard error of the mean?

5. A population has a mean (μ) of 55 and a standard deviation (σ) of 17. Assume that a sampling distribution of sample means has been constructed, based on repeated samples of $n = 100$ from this population.
   a. What would be the value of the mean of the sampling distribution?
   b. What would be the value of the standard error of the mean?

6

Confidence Intervals

In this chapter, you'll enter the world of inferential statistics. As you get started, think back over the material you've covered so far. For example, you've already learned about the mean, standard deviation, samples, populations, statistics, parameters, and sampling error. You've also been introduced to Z scores, the Table of Areas Under the Normal Curve and the Central Limit Theorem. Now it's time to bring all those elements together.

As you begin to bring the different elements together, there's a chance you'll begin taking advantage of other resources—Web sites, other texts, or additional learning aids. As before, let me encourage you to do that. Should you take that path, however, let me also remind you again about the noticeable differences that often emerge when it comes to the matter of symbolic notation. Different statisticians may use different symbols for the same concept—that's just the way it is, and there's no reason to let those little bumps in the road throw you.

Having said that, here's what lies ahead. The general application we'll cover in this chapter is known as the *construction of a confidence interval.* More specifically, we're going to deal with the construction of a confidence interval for the mean and the construction of a confidence interval for a proportion. We'll begin with the confidence interval for the mean.

Before We Begin

By now you should be adequately armed to jump into the world of statistical inference. You have the important concepts under your belt, but your patience is probably wearing thin. Therefore, there's no reason to waste too much time, except to offer up one of my favorite statistical sayings: *We really don't give a hoot about a sample, except to the extent that it tells us something about the population.* In fact, that's what the field of inferential statistics is all about—samples really aren't of interest to us, except that they provide us information that we can use to make inferences about populations. That is an extremely simple but important notion, so allow me to repeat it: *We really don't give a hoot about a sample, except to the extent that it tells us something about the population.* Simply put, you're getting ready to apply that adage. You're going to use some information gained from a sample so you can make some statements about a population.

Confidence Interval for the Mean

Let's suppose we want to estimate the mean of a population (μ) on the basis of a sample mean ($\overline{X}$). By now you should know we can't simply calculate a sample mean ($\overline{X}$) and assume that it equals the mean of the population (μ). A sample mean *might* equal the mean of the population, but we can't assume that it will. We can't do that because there's always the possibility of sampling error. Because our ultimate aim is to estimate the true value of the population mean (μ), we'll have to use a method that takes into account this possibility of sampling error.

We'll use our sample mean as the starting point for our estimate. Then we'll build a band of values, or an *interval,* around the sample mean. To do this, we'll add a certain value to our sample mean, and we'll subtract a certain value from our sample mean. When we're finished, we'll be able to assert that we believe the true mean of the population (μ) is between this value and that value. For example, we'll eventually be in a position to make a statement such as "I believe the mean age of all students at the university (μ) is somewhere between 23.4 years and 26.1 years." This statement expresses a **confidence interval for the mean** of a population based on a sample mean.

Let's think about that for a moment. This method allows us to express an interval in terms of two values. The two values are the upper and lower limits of the interval—an interval within which we *believe* the mean of the population is found. We may be right (our interval may contain the true mean of the population), or we may be wrong (our interval may not contain the true mean of the population). Even though there's some uncertainty in our estimate, we'll know the probability, or likelihood, that we've made a mistake. That's where the term *confidence* comes into play—we'll have a certain level of confidence in our estimate. What's more, we'll know, in advance, *how much* confidence we can place in our estimate.

As it turns out, there are two different approaches to the construction of confidence intervals for the mean. One approach is used when we know the value of the population standard deviation (σ), and another approach is used when we don't know the value of the population standard deviation (σ). The second approach is used more frequently, but it's the first approach that really sets the stage with the fundamental logic. For that reason, we'll begin with confidence intervals for the mean with σ known; after that, we'll turn to confidence intervals for the mean with σ unknown. Once you've mastered the logic of the first approach, the move to the second application will be easier.

 LEARNING CHECK

Question: What is a confidence interval for the mean?
Answer: It's an interval or range of values within which the true mean of the population is believed to be located.

Confidence Interval for the Mean With σ Known

We'll begin our discussion of confidence intervals with a somewhat unusual situation—one in which we're trying to estimate the mean of a population when we already know the value of σ (the standard deviation of the population). Why, you might ask yourself, would we have to estimate the mean of a population if we already know the value of the standard deviation of the population? Wouldn't we have to know the mean of the population to calculate the standard deviation? Those are certainly reasonable questions. Although situations in which you'd know the value of the standard deviation of the population are rare, they do exist.

Some researchers, for example, routinely use standardized tests to measure attitudes, aptitudes, and abilities. Personality tests, IQ tests, and college entrance exams are often treated as having a known mean and a known standard deviation for the general population (σ). The Scholastic Aptitude Test (SAT), for example, has two parts—math and verbal. Each part has been constructed or standardized in a way that yields a mean of 500 and a standard deviation of 100 for the general population of would-be college students. An example like that—one involving some sort of standardized test—is a typical one, so that's a good place to start.

An Application

Let's assume that we're working for the XYZ College Testing Prep Company— a company that provides training throughout the nation for students preparing to take the SAT college entrance examination. Part of our job is to monitor the success of the training. Let's assume we have collected information from a sample of 225 customers—225 students from throughout the nation who took our prep course—telling us how well they did on each section of the SAT. Let's say that we're only interested in the math scores right now, so that section will be our focus.

Now, let's say that the results indicate a sample mean ($\overline{X}$) of 606. In other words, the mean score on the math section for our 225 respondents was 606. The question is how to use that sample mean to estimate the mean score for all of our customers (the population). We know that we can't simply assume that the sample mean of 606 applies to our total customer base. After all, it's just one sample mean. A different sample of 225 customers might yield a different sample mean.

We can, however, use the sample mean of 606 as a starting point, and we can build a confidence interval around it. In other words, we'll start by treating the value or 606 as our best guess, so to speak. The true mean of the population (the population of our entire customer base—let's say 10,000 customers) may be above or below that value, but we'll start with the value of 606 nonetheless. After all, with random sampling on our side, our sample mean is likely to be fairly close to the value of the population mean. At the same time, though, we know that our value of 606 may not equal the true mean of the population, so we're going to build in a little cushion for our estimate. The question is, How do we establish the upper and lower values—how do we build in the cushion?

We build the cushion by adding a certain value to the sample mean and subtracting a certain value from the sample mean (don't worry right now about how much we add and subtract—we'll get to that eventually). When we add a value to the sample mean, we establish the upper limit of our confidence interval; when we subtract a value from the mean, we establish the lower limit of the confidence interval.

☑ LEARNING CHECK

Question: In general, how is a confidence interval for the mean
           constructed?

Answer: A sample mean is used as the starting point. A value
           is added to the mean and subtracted from the mean.
           The results are the upper and lower limits of the
           interval.

Given what our purpose is, along with the notion that we're going to use our sample mean as a starting point, you shouldn't be terribly confused when you look at the formula for the construction of a confidence interval. After all, it's simply a statement that you add something to your sample mean and you subtract something from your sample mean. The formula that follows isn't the complete formula, but take a look at it with an eye toward grasping the fundamental logic.

$$\text{Confidence Interval, or CI} = \text{Sample Mean} \pm Z\,(\,?\,)$$

The sample mean will be the starting point.
A value will be added to the mean and subtracted from the mean.

It's clear from the formula that we're going to be working with a sample mean $(\overline{X})$, and we'll be using a Z value, but two questions still remain: Why the Z value, and what does the question mark represent?

Reviewing Z Values

To answer those questions, let's start by reviewing something you learned earlier about Z values (see Chapter 4 if you're in any way unclear about Z values). Think back to what you learned about a Z value in relationship to the normal curve—namely, that a Z value is a point along the baseline of the normal curve. Think about the fact that Z values are expressions of standard deviation units.

To understand why this is important in the present application, let me ask you to shift gears for just a moment. We'll eventually get back to our example, but for the moment, put that aside. Instead of thinking in terms of a sample of SAT scores, assume that you're working with a large *population* of scores on some other type of test. For example, think in terms of a large number of students who took a final exam in a chemistry course. Assume the scores are normally distributed, with a mean of 75 and a standard deviation of 8.

Since the distribution is normal, 95% of the scores would fall between 1.96 standard deviations above and below the mean. That's something you learned when you learned about the normal curve and the Table of Areas Under the Normal Curve. If 95% of the cases fall between 1.96 standard deviations above and below the mean, it's easy to figure out the actual value of the scores that would encompass 95% of the cases. All you'd have to do is multiply the standard deviation of your distribution (8) times 1.96. You'd add that value (1.96 × 8) to the mean, and then you'd subtract that value from the mean. That would be the answer to the problem. Here's how the process would play out.

- Assuming that a large number of scores on a final exam are normally distributed, you'd expect 95% of the scores in your distribution to fall between ±1.96 standard deviations from the mean (that is, 1.96 standard deviations above and below the mean).
- The mean = 75
- The standard deviation = 8
- 1.96 × 8 = 15.68
- 75 – 15.68 = 59.32
- 75 + 15.68 = 90.68
- Therefore, 95% of the scores would be found between the values of 59.32 and 90.68.

To grasp the point more fully, consider these additional examples, assuming a normally distributed population in each case.

With a mean of 40 and a standard deviation of 5:
What values would encompass 95% of the scores?
Answer: 30.20 to 49.80
What values would encompass 99% of the scores?
Hint: Use a Z value of 2.58 for a 99% confidence interval.
Answer: 27.10 to 52.90

With a mean of 100 and a standard deviation of 10:
What values would encompass 95% of the scores?
Answer: 80.40 to 119.60
What values would encompass 99% of the scores?
Answer: 74.20 to 125.80

The key step in each of these examples had to do with the standard deviation of your distribution of scores. In each case, you multiplied the standard deviation by a particular Z value.

Exercises like these are interesting, and they demonstrate how useful the normal curve can be, but how does all of that come into play when we're trying to construct a confidence interval? As it turns out, we'll rely on the same sort of method. We'll calculate the value we add to and subtract from our sample mean by multiplying a Z value by an expression of standard deviation units. That brings us to the question of what Z value to use.

Z Values and the Width of the Interval

To determine the right *Z* value, we first decide how wide we want our interval to be. Statisticians routinely make a choice between a 95% confidence interval and a 99% confidence interval (Pyrczak, 1995). It's possible to construct an 80% confidence interval, or a 60% confidence interval, for that matter, but statisticians typically aim for either 95% or 99%. Without worrying right now about why they do that, just focus on the fundamental difference between the two types of intervals.

In the situation we're considering—one in which (σ) is known—a 95% confidence interval is built by using a *Z* value of 1.96 in the formula. A 99% confidence interval, in turn, is built by using a *Z* value of 2.58. By now, these should be very familiar values to you. If you're unclear as to why they should be familiar, take the time to reread Chapter 4.

 LEARNING CHECK

Question: What *Z* value is associated with a 95% confidence interval? What *Z* value is associated with a 99% confidence interval?

Answer: A *Z* value of 1.96 is used for a 95% confidence interval. A *Z* value of 2.58 is used for a 99% confidence interval.

Now we deal with the question of how to put the *Z* values such as 1.96 or 2.58 to use. In other words, what's the rest of the formula all about—the question mark (?) that follows the *Z* value? Just so it will be clear in your mind, here's the formula again:

$$\text{Confidence Interval, or CI} = \text{Sample Mean} \pm Z\,(\,?\,)$$

Typically $Z = 1.96$ or 2.58
1.96 for a 95% confidence interval
2.58 for a 99% confidence interval

Bringing in the Standard Error of the Mean

To understand what the question mark represents, take a moment or two to review what we know so far. Indulge yourself in the repetition, if necessary. The logic involved in where we've been is central to the logic of where we're going.

Returning to our example, we're attempting to estimate the mean SAT score for our total customer base of 10,000 customers, based on a sample of 225 customers. The mean math SAT score ($\overline{X}$) for the sample was 606, and we know that the SAT math section has a standard deviation (σ) of 100. It's that last bit of information ($\sigma = 100$) that allows us to approach the problem as the construction of a confidence interval with σ (the standard deviation of the population) known.

Our sample of 225 students may have produced a mean ($\overline{X}$ = 606) that equals the population mean (the mean or μ of all of our customers), but there's also a possibility it didn't. Maybe our sample mean varied just a little bit from the true population mean; maybe it varied a lot. We have no way of knowing.

The key to grasping all of this is to think back to the notion of a sampling distribution of sample means. As you know, a sampling distribution of sample means is what you would get if you took a large number of samples, calculated the mean of each sample, and plotted the means. You should also remember that most of those sample means would be located toward the center of the distribution, but some of them would be located in the outer regions—the more extreme means.

If you put our sample mean in the context of all of that, here's what you should be thinking:

> I've got a sample mean here, but I don't know where it falls in relationship to all possible sample means. A different sample could have yielded a different mean. Maybe the sample (just by chance) included mostly customers with extremely high SAT math scores, or maybe it's a sample that (just by chance) included mostly customers with extremely low scores. The probability of something like that happening is small (if a random sample was selected), but anything is possible.

In other words, there's no way to know how far the sample mean deviates from the mean (μ) of the population of 10,000 customers, if at all. In a case like that, we're left with no choice except to take into account some overall average of how far different sample means would deviate from the true population mean (μ). Of course, that's exactly what the *standard error of the mean* is—it's an overall expression of how far the various sample means deviate from the mean of the sampling distribution of sample means.

To understand this point, take some time for a dark room moment, if necessary. Just as before, imagine that you're taking an infinite number of samples, and imagine all the different means you get. Imagine a plot of all those different sample means. Most of those sample means are close to the center, but a lot of them aren't. Some deviate from the mean a little; some deviate a lot. Now begin to think about the fact that there's an overall measure of that deviation—in essence, a standard deviation for the sampling distribution. Focus on that concept—the standard deviation of a sampling distribution of sample means. Now focus on the fact that we have a special name for the standard deviation of the sampling distribution—the *standard error*. If, for some reason, that doesn't sound familiar to you, go through the dark room moment exercise again.

Assuming you're comfortable with the concept of the standard error of the mean, you can begin to think of it as analogous to what you encountered earlier in this chapter—the examples in which you were dealing with a population of scores. In those earlier situations, you multiplied the standard deviation of the distribution by 1.96 to determine the values or scores that would encompass

95% of the cases. Similarly, you multiplied the standard deviation of distribution by 2.58 if you wanted to determine the values that encompassed 99% of the cases.

In our present situation, we'll do essentially the same thing. The only change is that we'll be using the standard error instead of the standard deviation. To better understand this, take a minute or two to really focus on the illustration shown in Figure 6-1.

If you truly digested that illustration, and you realized you were looking at a sampling distribution of sample means, you noticed something very important: 95% of the *possible means* would fall between ±1.96 standard error units from the mean of the sampling distribution of sample means. By the same token, 99% of the possible means would fall between ±2.58 standard error units from the mean of the sampling distribution of sample means. None of this should surprise you. After all, the Central Limit Theorem tells us that the sampling distribution of sample means will approach the shape of a normal distribution.

Now we move toward the final stage of our solution to the problem. Remember what the task is: We want to estimate the mean math score on the SAT for our entire customer base. All we know is that the mean math SAT score for a random sample of 225 customers is 606 and that the test in question has a standard deviation (σ) of 100.

As we launch into this, let's throw in the assumption that we want to be on fairly solid ground—in other words, we want to have a substantial amount of confidence in our estimate. For this reason, we decide to construct a 99% confidence interval. For a 99% confidence interval, and taking the mean of our sample ($\bar{X} = 606$) as our starting point, we simply add 2.58 standard error units to our sample mean and subtract 2.58 standard error units from our sample mean. That will produce the interval that we're trying to construct.

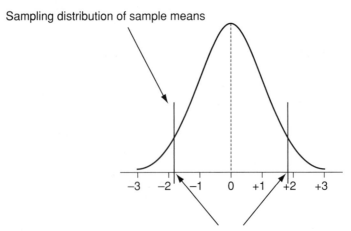

Sampling distribution of sample means

Z of ±1.96 is the same thing as ±1.96 standard error units.

Includes about 95% of the total area.

Figure 6-1   The Concept of the Standard Error of the Mean

But wait just a minute, you may be thinking. I understand that we're adding and subtracting 2.58 standard error units, but how much is a standard error unit? Indeed, that's the central question. To find the answer, all we have to do is return to the Central Limit Theorem. Think for a moment about what the Central Limit Theorem told us. Here it is once again:

If repeated random samples of size *n* are taken from a population with a mean or mu (μ) and a standard deviation (σ), the sampling distribution of sample means will have a mean equal to mu (μ) and a standard error equal to $\dfrac{\sigma}{\sqrt{n}}$. Moreover, as *n* increases, the sampling distribution will approach a normal distribution.

☑ LEARNING CHECK

Question: According to the Central Limit Theorem, what is the relationship between the standard deviation of the population (σ) and the standard error (the standard deviation of the sampling distribution of sample means)?

Answer: The standard error is equal to σ divided by the square root of the sample size.

The Relevance of the Central Limit Theorem and the Standard Error

The Central Limit Theorem tells us that the standard error of the sampling distribution (the missing value that we've been looking for) will equal the standard deviation of the population divided by the square root of our sample size. In the case we're considering here, we know that the standard deviation for the general population is 100. Thus, we divide 100 by the square root of our sample size (the square root of 225, or 15) to get the value of the standard error.

At this point, let me emphasize that what we're doing is calculating the value of the standard error. We can calculate it in a direct fashion because the Central Limit Theorem tells us how to do that. It tells us that the standard error is calculated by dividing σ by the square root of *n*:

$$\sigma_{\bar{x}} = \frac{\sigma}{\sqrt{n}}$$

Note that symbol for the standard error of the mean is $\sigma_{\bar{x}}$. Remember: We're working with a situation in which the standard deviation on the test (the math portion of the SAT) is 100 points. We obtain the standard error of the mean ($\sigma_{\bar{x}}$) by dividing σ (the standard deviation of the population, or 100) by the square root of our sample size (square root of 225, or 15):

$$\sigma_{\bar{x}} = \frac{\sigma}{\sqrt{n}}$$

$$\sigma_{\bar{x}} = \frac{100}{\sqrt{225}}$$

$$\sigma_{\bar{x}} = \frac{100}{15}$$

$$\sigma_{\bar{x}} = 6.67$$

In other words, the standard error of the mean ($\sigma_{\bar{x}}$) = 6.67.

Now that we have the standard error at hand, along with a grasp of the fundamental logic, we can appreciate the complete formula for the construction of a confidence interval with σ (the standard deviation of the population) known:

$$CI = \bar{X} \pm Z \, (\sigma_{\bar{x}}) \text{ where } (\sigma_{\bar{x}}) = \frac{\sigma}{\sqrt{n}}$$

 LEARNING CHECK

Question: How is the standard error calculated when the standard deviation of the population (σ) is known?

Answer: The standard deviation of the population (σ) is divided by the square root of the sample size (n).

All that remains to construct a 99% confidence interval is to multiply the standard error (6.67) the appropriate or associated Z value (2.58), and wrap that product around our sample mean (add it to our mean and subtract it from our mean). As it turns out, 6.67×2.58 equals 17.21. Therefore, we add 17.21 to our sample mean ($\bar{X}$ = 606) and subtract 17.21 from our sample mean to get our interval. Following through with all of that, we obtain the following:

- $606 - 17.21 = 588.79$
- $606 + 17.21 = 623.21$
- Therefore, our confidence interval is 588.79 to 623.21.
- We can estimate that the true mean math SAT score for our customer base is located between 588.79 and 623.21.

As a review of the entire process, here are all the calculations again, laid out from start to finish, in the context of the formula for the construction of a confidence interval for the mean (with σ known).

$$CI = \overline{X} \pm Z(\sigma_{\overline{x}})$$

$$CI = 606 \pm 2.58\left(\frac{\sigma}{\sqrt{n}}\right)$$

$$CI = 606 \pm 2.58\left(\frac{100}{\sqrt{225}}\right)$$

$$CI = 606 \pm 2.58\left(\frac{100}{15}\right)$$

$$CI = 606 \pm 2.58(6.67)$$

$$CI = 606 \pm 17.21$$

$$CI = 588.79 \text{ to } 623.21$$

Is it possible that we missed the mark? Is it possible that the true mean math SAT score for our 10,000 customers doesn't fall between 588.79 and 623.21? You bet it's possible. Is it probable? No, it isn't very probable. The method we used will produce an interval that contains the true mean of the population 99 times out of 100 (99% of the time). Let me repeat that: The method we used will generate an interval that contains the true mean of the population 99 times out of 100. Since I repeated that, it's obviously important, so you deserve an explanation.

Think of it this way: If the previous exercise were repeated 100 times, (100 different samples of 225 students), we'd find ourselves working with many different sample means. These different sample means would result in different final answers. We would always be wrapping the same amount around our sample mean (adding the same amount of sampling error and subtracting the same amount of sampling error), but different means would result in different final answers (different intervals). In 99 of the 100 trails, our result (our confidence interval) would contain the true mean of the population.

The method would produce an interval containing the population mean 99 times out of 100 because of what lies beneath the application—random sampling, the Central Limit Theorem, and the normal curve. Statisticians have tested the method. The method works. To fully understand this idea, take a look at the illustration shown in Figure 6-2. You'll probably find it to be very helpful.

Because the central element in all of this has to do with the method we used, let me emphasize something about the way I think an interpretation of a confidence interval should be structured. Obviously, there are different ways to make a concluding statement about a confidence interval, but here is the one that I prefer (let's assume the case involves a 99% confidence interval):

> I estimate that the true mean of the population falls somewhere between _____ and _____ (fill in the blanks with the correct values), and I have used a method that will generate a correct estimate 99 times out of 100.

In other words, the heart of your final interpretation goes back to the method that was used. You have *confidence* in the estimate because of the *method* that was used.

The Central Limit Theorem tells us that the mean of the sampling distribution of sample means will equal the mean of the population.

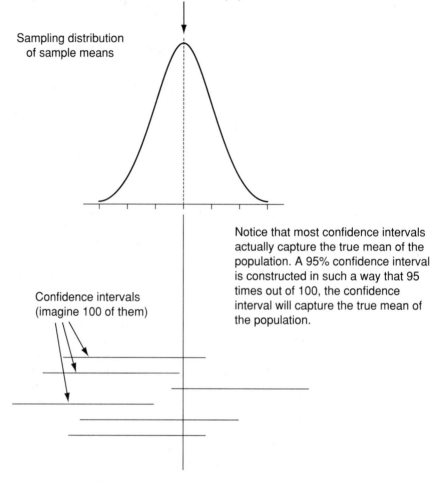

Sampling distribution of sample means

Notice that most confidence intervals actually capture the true mean of the population. A 95% confidence interval is constructed in such a way that 95 times out of 100, the confidence interval will capture the true mean of the population.

Confidence intervals (imagine 100 of them)

Figure 6-2   The Method Underlying the Construction of a Confidence Interval for the Mean (Why the Method Works)

Confidence and Interval Width

Now let's tackle a 95% confidence interval for the same problem. Everything will stay the same in the application, with one exception. In this instance, we'll multiply the standard error by 1.96 (instead of 2.58). Once again, here's the formula we'll be using:

$$CI = \overline{X} \pm Z(\sigma_{\overline{x}})$$

If we apply the same procedure we used before, changing only the Z value (using 1.96 instead of 2.58), we'll get an interval that is slightly smaller in width—something we would expect since we're multiplying the standard error by a slightly smaller value. Here is how the calculation would unfold:

$$CI = \overline{X} \pm Z(\sigma_{\overline{x}})$$

$$CI = 606 \pm 1.96\left(\frac{\sigma}{\sqrt{n}}\right)$$

$$CI = 606 \pm 1.96\left(\frac{100}{\sqrt{225}}\right)$$

$$CI = 606 \pm 1.96\left(\frac{100}{15}\right)$$

$$CI = 606 \pm 1.96(6.67)$$

$$CI = 606 \pm 13.07$$

$$CI = 592.93 \text{ to } 619.07$$

Given those calculations, the appropriate conclusion or interpretation would be as follows:

I estimate that the true mean of the population falls between 592.93 and 619.07, and I have used a method that will produce a correct estimate 95 times out of 100.

At this point, you should take note of the relationship between the level of confidence (95% versus 99%) and the width of the interval. The 95% confidence interval will, by definition, be narrower than the 99%. To convince yourself of this, compare our two sets of results:

For the 99% level of confidence, our interval is 588.79 to 623.21.

For the 95% level of confidence, our interval is 592.93 to 619.07.

In other words, all factors being equal, a 95% interval will produce a more precise estimate—an estimate that has a narrower range. By the same token, a 99% confidence interval will be wider than a 95% interval—it will produce a less precise estimate.

A word of clarification is probably in order at this point. To say that one estimate is more *precise* than another is to say that one estimate has a narrower range than the other. For example, an estimate that asserts that the mean of the population falls between 20 and 30 is a more precise estimate than one that asserts that the mean is somewhere between 10 and 40. It's particularly easy to get thrown off track on this topic, particularly if you're inclined to confuse *precision* with *accuracy*. Although the two terms can be used synonymously in some instances, the present context is not one of them.

If you want to understand the difference between the two (when thinking about confidence intervals), just consider the following statement: I estimate that the true mean age of the population of students falls somewhere between zero and a billion. That statement would obviously have a high degree of accuracy—it's very likely to be a correct statement and, therefore, accurate. We would also have a great deal of confidence in the estimate, just because of the width of the interval. The estimate reflected in that statement, however, is anything but precise—the range of the estimate is anything but narrow.

All of this is another way of saying that there is an inverse relationship between the level of confidence and precision. As our confidence increases, the precision of our estimate decreases. Alternatively, as our precision increases, our confidence decreases. For example, we could, if we wanted to, construct a 75% confidence interval. It would be a fairly narrow interval (at least compared to a 95% or 99% interval). It would be fairly narrow, and therefore rather precise, but we wouldn't have a lot of confidence in our estimate.

 LEARNING CHECK

Question: What is the relationship between the level of confidence and the precision of an estimate when constructing a confidence interval for the mean?

Answer: Level of confidence and precision are inversely related. As one increases, the other decreases.

It's also possible to affect the precision of an estimate by changing the sample size—something that should make a certain amount of intuitive sense to you if you think about it for a minute or two. Given a constant level of confidence (let's say, a 95% level), you can increase the precision of an estimate by increasing the size of the sample. The problems presented in the next section should give you an adequate demonstration of that point.

A Brief Recap

Just to make certain that you are comfortable with all of this, let me suggest that you work through the problems that follow—typical problems that call for a 95% and a 99% confidence interval. Follow the same procedure we just used.

Assume the following: $\overline{X} = 50$ $\sigma = 8$ $n = 100$
Calculate a 95% confidence interval.   Answer: 48.43 to 51.57
Calculate a 99% confidence interval.   Answer: 47.94 to 52.06

Assume the following: $\overline{X} = 50$ $\sigma = 8$ $n = 400$
Calculate a 95% confidence interval.   Answer: 49.22 to 50.78
Calculate a 99% confidence interval.   Answer: 48.97 to 51.03

Assume the following: $\overline{X} = 85$ $\sigma = 16$ $n = 25$

Calculate a 95% confidence interval.   Answer: 78.73 to 91.27

Calculate a 99% confidence interval.   Answer: 76.74 to 93.26

Assume the following: $\overline{X} = 85$ $\sigma = 16$ $n = 225$

Calculate a 95% confidence interval.   Answer: 82.90 to 87.10

Calculate a 99% confidence interval.   Answer: 82.24 to 87.76

As before, you may want to take a moment to focus on how the width of a confidence interval varies with level of confidence and how it varies with sample size.

 LEARNING CHECK

Question: What effect does increasing the size of a sample have on the width of the confidence interval and the precision of the estimate?

Answer: It decreases the width of the interval and, therefore, increases the precision of the estimate.

Confidence Interval for the Mean With σ Unknown

With the previous section as a foundation, we now take up the more typical applications of confidence interval construction—those involving an estimate of the mean of a population when the standard deviation of the population is unknown. For the most part, the logic involved is identical to what you've just encountered. There are just two hitches. I've already mentioned the first one—it has to do with the fact that you don't know the value of the population standard deviation (σ). The second hitch arises because you can't rely on the normal curve, so you can't rely on those familiar values such as 1.96 (for a 95% confidence interval) or 2.58 (for a 99% confidence interval). Rather than jumping into an application straightaway, let's take some time to really examine how the two approaches differ.

Estimating the Standard Error of the Mean

Let's start with the first hitch—the fact that you don't know the standard deviation of the population (σ). If you think back to the previous section, you were able to determine the standard error—the standard deviation of the sampling distribution of sample means—because you knew the standard deviation of the population. The Central Limit Theorem told you that all you had to do was divide the standard deviation of the population (σ) by the square root of your sample size, and the result would be standard error (the standard deviation of the sampling distribution of sample means). But now we're considering situations in which we don't know the value of the standard deviation (σ), so we can't rely on a direct calculation to get the standard error. Instead, we'll have to *estimate* it. That's the first difference in a nutshell. Remember: When you know the value of the standard deviation of the population (σ)—which you rarely do—you can make a direct calculation of the standard error of the mean. When you don't know the value of the standard deviation of the population (σ)—which is usually the case—you'll have to estimate the standard error.

 LEARNING CHECK

Question: When constructing a confidence interval for the mean, how do you approach the standard error? How does the approach differ, depending on whether you know the value of the standard deviation of the population (σ)?

Answer: If σ is known, you make a direct calculation of the value of the standard error. If σ is unknown, you have to estimate the value of the standard error.

As it turns out, there's a very reliable estimate of the standard error of the mean, and it's easy to calculate. All we have to know is the standard deviation of our sample (s) and our sample size (n). Assuming we have the standard deviation of our sample at hand, we simply divide it by the square root of our sample size. We designate the **estimate of the standard error of the mean** as $s_{\bar{x}}$. The formula for the estimate is as follows:

$$s_{\bar{x}} = \frac{s}{\sqrt{n}}$$

For example, let's say we're interested in the average expenditure per customer in a bookstore. A sample of 100 sales receipts reveals that the mean ($\bar{X}$) expenditure is $31.50 with a standard deviation (s) of $4.75. To estimate the standard error of the mean, we would simply divide the standard deviation of the sample (s = $4.75) by the square root of the sample size (n = 100).

$$s_{\bar{x}} = \frac{s}{\sqrt{n}}$$

$$s_{\bar{x}} = \frac{4.75}{\sqrt{100}}$$

$$s_{\bar{x}} = \frac{4.75}{10}$$

$$s_{\bar{x}} = .475$$

$$s_{\bar{x}} = .48$$

In other words, the standard error of the mean would be .475 (rounded to $.48).

Let me mention one minor point here. If the standard deviation of our sample was derived using the $n - 1$ correction factor discussed in Chapter 2, we will do just as I outlined above. We'll divide the sample standard deviation (s) by the square root of our sample size (n). If, on the other hand, the standard deviation of the sample (s) was obtained *without* using the $n - 1$ correction factor, we'll obtain the estimate of the standard error by dividing the sample standard deviation (s) by the square root of $n - 1$. This point is demonstrated in Table 6-1, which should help you understand why different texts approach the estimate of the standard error in different ways.

Since the approach taken throughout this book is to assume that the sample standard deviation was calculated using the $n - 1$ correction faction, all we

Table 6-1   Two Approaches to Estimating the Standard Error
of the Mean ($s_{\bar{x}}$), and an Important Note

When the sample standard deviation (s) has been calculated using $n - 1$ in the denominator, the estimate of the standard error ($s_{\bar{x}}$) is computed as follows:	When the sample standard deviation (s) has been calculated using n in the denominator, the estimate of the standard error ($s_{\bar{x}}$) is computed as follows:
$$\frac{s}{\sqrt{n}}$$	$$\frac{s}{\sqrt{n - 1}}$$

AN IMPORTANT NOTE: Just in Case You're a Little Bit Confused . . .

Always remember that different statisticians and different resources may approach the same topic in different fashions. The examples above provide a case in point. Some statisticians calculate the standard deviation of a sample using only n in the denominator when they simply want to know the sample standard deviation, but switch to $n - 1$ in the denominator when they're using the sample standard deviation as an estimate of the population standard deviation.

There's no reason to let all of this confuse you. Just remember that some of the fundamentals of statistical analysis aren't carved in stone, despite what you might have thought. If you encounter different symbols, notations, or approaches, don't let them throw you. A little bit of time and effort will, I suspect, unravel any mysteries.

had to do was divide 4.75 (the sample standard deviation, or s) by the square root of 100 (the sample size). The result was 4.75 divided by 10, or .48. That value of .48 becomes our estimate of the standard error—an estimate of the standard deviation of the sampling distribution of sample means. Just to make certain you're on the right track with all of this, consider the following examples:

Given	**Estimate of the standard error of the mean ($s_{\bar{x}}$)**
$s = 8$ $n = 100$	Answer: 0.80
$s = 20$ $n = 25$	Answer: 4.00
$s = 6$ $n = 36$	Answer: 1.00
$s = 50$ $n = 225$	Answer: 3.33

 LEARNING CHECK

Question: How do you estimate the value of the standard error of the mean ($s_{\bar{x}}$)?

Answer: The standard error of the mean is estimated by dividing the sample standard deviation (s) by the square root of the sample size ($\sqrt{n}$).

Now we turn to the second hitch—the fact that we can't rely on the normal curve or the sampling distribution of Z, with its familiar values such as 1.96 or 2.58. The why behind this problem, which can be found in a more advanced statistical text, is something you shouldn't concern yourself with at this point. What's important is what we can use as an alternative to the normal curve distribution. Instead of relying on the normal distribution and its familiar Z values, we'll rely on what's referred to as the **family of t distributions.**

The Family of t Distributions

As the expression implies, the family of t distributions is made up of several distributions. Like the normal curve, each t distribution is symmetrical, and each curve has a mean of 0, located in the middle. Positive t values, or deviation units, lie to the right of 0, and negative t values lie to the left—just like Z scores on the normal curve. But there are many different t distributions, and the exact shape of each distribution is based on sample size (n). It was William Gosset, an early-day statistician and employee of the Guinness Brewery, who developed the notion of the t distribution.

Without going into the mathematics behind Gossett's contribution, it's useful to consider what it tells us—namely, that the shape of a sampling distribution depends on the number of cases in each of the samples that make up the sampling distribution. When the number of cases is small, the distribution will be relatively flat. As the number of cases in each sample increases, however, the middle portion of the curve will begin to grow. As the middle portion of the curve grows, the curve begins to take on more height.

To understand what happens with an increase in sample size, take a look at Figure 6-3. Think of each curve as a sampling distribution of sample means. Notice how the curve begins to grow in the middle as you move from a sampling distribution based on small samples to a sampling distribution based on samples with a larger number of cases. The curves presented here are exaggerated or stylized (they're not based on the construction of actual sampling distributions), but they serve to illustrate the point.

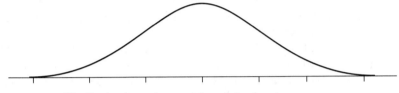

Distribution based on small sample size:
Distribution is relatively flat and the tails are elongated.

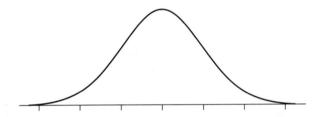

Distribution based on larger sample size:
Distribution begins to grow in the middle (and tails become shorter).

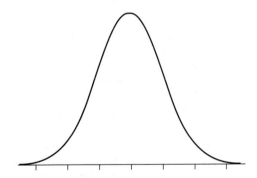

Distribution on still larger sample size:
Distribution continues to grow in the middle.
Tails become even shorter, and the distribution
begins to more closely approximate the distribution of *Z*.

Figure 6-3 Shape of *t* Distribution in Relationship to Sample Size

Assuming you've grasped the idea that the shape of the sampling distribution is a function of the size of the samples used in constructing it, we can now move on toward a more precise understanding of the specific shapes. As a first step in that direction, let me ask you to start thinking in terms of *t* values in the same way that you've thought of *Z* values. A *t* value (like a *Z* value) is just a point along the baseline of a distribution (or, more correctly, a sampling distribution). Now think back to a couple of points I mentioned earlier.

First, there are many different sampling distributions of *t,* and each one has a slightly different shape. A *t* distribution built on the basis of small samples will be flatter than one based on underlying samples that are larger. When a distribution is flat, you'll have to go out a greater distance above and below the mean to encompass a given percentage of cases or area under the curve. To better grasp this point, consider Figure 6-4 (as before, the distributions are somewhat stylized to make the point).

Remember: We're dealing with the confidence intervals for the mean when the standard deviation of the population (σ) is unknown. Since you're not going to be able to use the normal curve and its familiar values such as 1.96 or 2.58, it's time you take a look at Gossett's family of *t* distributions.

The Table for the Family of t Distributions

You'll find the family of *t* distributions presented twice—once in Appendix B and again in Appendix C. For the application we're considering here (the construction of a confidence interval for the mean), you'll be working with Appendix B. Before you turn to Appendix B, though, let me give you an overview of what you'll encounter.

First, you'll notice a column on the far left of the table. It is labeled Degrees of Freedom (*df*). The concept of *degrees of freedom* is something that comes up throughout inferential statistics and in many different applications. The exact meaning of the concept, in a sense, varies from application to application. At this point, you'll need to know a little about degrees of freedom in the context of a mean.

Here's an easy way to think of it: Given the mean of a distribution of *n* scores, *n* − 1 of the scores are free to vary. Let me give you a translation of that. Assume you have a sample of five incomes (*n* = 5) and the mean income of the sample is $26,354. In this situation, four of the incomes could be any numbers you might choose, but given a mean of $26,354, the fifth income would then be predetermined. In other words, only four of the five cases (*n* − 1) are free to vary.

Here's another example of how and why that works out. Let's say we have a sample of seven scores on a current events test with a maximum possible score of 10, and we know that the mean score is 5. With seven cases and a mean of 5, we know that the total of all the scores must equal 35. Six of the values (*n* − 1) are free to vary. Let's just make up some values—for example, 1, 2, 3, 3, 7, and 10. The total of these six values is 26. So what must the missing score be (the one that isn't free to vary)? We already know that the sum of all the

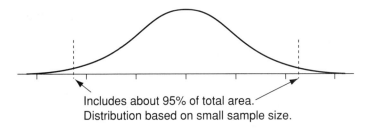

Includes about 95% of total area.
Distribution based on small sample size.

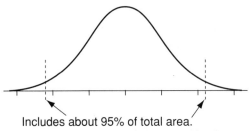

Includes about 95% of total area.
Distribution based on larger sample size.

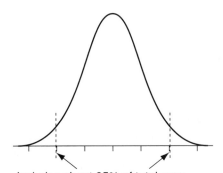

Includes about 95% of total area.
Distribution on still larger sample size.

Figure 6-4   Relationship Between Area Under the Curve
(*t* Distribution) and Sample Size

scores must equal 35 (35/7 = 5, our mean). If we have to reach a final total of 35, and these six values add up to 26, the missing score must be 35 – 26, or 9. Here is another example to illustrate the point:

Total of five scores (*n* = 5), mean = 8. Degrees of freedom (*n* – 1) = 4.

If the mean is 8 and there are five scores, the total of all scores must be 40 (40/5 = 8).

Pick any four scores (let four vary); let's say the scores are 8, 8, 10, and 10.

The total of those four scores is 36.

The total of all the scores must equal 40; therefore, the missing score has to be 4.

$8 + 8 + 10 + 10 + \mathbf{4} = 40$

The missing score—the one that is predetermined. Only four scores are free to vary; the fifth score is predetermined.

Just for good measure, here's yet another example:

Total of six scores ($n = 6$), mean = 8. Degrees of freedom ($n - 1$) = 5.

If the mean is 8 and there are six scores, the total of all scores must be 48 (48/6 = 8).

Pick any five scores (let five vary); let's say the scores are 6, 7, 7, 10, and 10.

The total of those five scores is 40.

The total of all the scores must equal 48; therefore, the missing score has to be 8.

$6 + 7 + 7 + 10 + 10 + \mathbf{8} = 48$

The missing score—the one that is predetermined. Only five scores are free to vary; the sixth score is predetermined.

All of that is what lies behind the left-hand column of the table in Appendix B. If you're attempting to construct a confidence interval of the mean, and you have a sample size of 22, you'd be working at 21 degrees of freedom ($n - 1$, or 22 – 1). If you were working with a sample of 15, you'd be working with 14 degrees of freedom ($n - 1$, or 15 – 1). And so it goes. Now let's turn our attention to another part of the table.

☑ LEARNING CHECK

Question: When using the *t* table and constructing a confidence interval for the mean (with σ unknown), how is the number of degrees of freedom computed?

Answer: The number of degrees of freedom will equal $n - 1$ (the size of the sample, minus 1).

At the top of the table, you'll see the phrase Level of Significance. Later on we'll take up the exact meaning of that phrase in greater detail. For the moment, though, I'll just ask you to make a slight mental conversion in using the table. If you want to construct a 95% confidence interval, just look at the section for the .05 (5%) level of significance. You can simply think of it this way: 1 minus the level of significance will equal the **level of confidence.** If you want to construct a 99% confidence interval, you'll go to the section for the .01 (1%) level of significance. (Remember: 1 minus the level of significance equals the level of confidence.)

Use the .05 level of significance for a 95% confidence interval (1 − .05 = .95).

Use the .01 level of significance for a 99% confidence interval (1 − .01 = .99).

Use the .20 level of significance for an 80% confidence interval (1 − .20 = .80).

Before you turn to Appendix B, let me mention one last thing about how the table has been constructed and how it differs from the Table of Areas Under the Normal Curve. Recall for a moment that the Table of Areas Under the Normal Curve was one table for one curve. What you're going to see in Appendix B is really one table for many different curves. Therefore, the Table for the Family of *t* Distributions is constructed in a different fashion.

Instead of the *Z* values that you're accustomed to seeing in the Table of Areas Under the Normal Curve, you'll see *t* values. The *t* values are directly analogous to *Z* values—you can think of the *t* values as points along the baseline of the different *t* distributions. The *t* values, however, won't be listed in columns (as was the case with the *Z* values in the Table of Areas Under the Normal Curve); instead, they will appear in the body of the table. Finally, all the different proportions (or percentages of areas under the curve) that you're accustomed to seeing in the Normal Curve Table won't appear the same way in Appendix B. As noted previously, you'll only see a few of the proportions (or percentages). What's more, the percentages that you'll see appear in an indirection fashion. The percentages values are there—for example, 80%, 90%, 95%, 99%—but they're found by looking at the column headings labeled Level of Significance (.20, .10, .05, .01). Remember: 1 minus the level of significance equals the level of confidence.

You've had enough preparation to take a serious look at Appendix B. Let me urge you to approach it the way I suggest students approach any table. Instead of simply glancing at the table and saying "OK, I've looked at it," take a few moments to thoroughly digest the material. Consider the following statements and questions as you study the table. They're designed to make you more familiar with the content of the table and how it's structured. Don't worry that you're still not making a direct application of the material. Remember what the objective is: The idea is to understand how the table is structured. Just to make sure you do, take a look at the following.

If you're going to construct a 95% confidence interval for the mean, you'll be working with values found in the .05 Level of Significance column. Remember: The confidence level is 1 minus the level of significance. Locate the appropriate column for a 95% confidence interval.

If you want a 99% confidence interval, you'll be working with values in the .01 Level of Significance column. Locate the appropriate column for a 99% confidence interval.

What about an 80% confidence interval? What column would you focus on? (Answer: .20 Level of Significance)

If you're working with a sample of 35 cases, you'll be focusing on the row associated with 34 degrees of freedom. Remember: Degrees of freedom equals the number of cases minus 1. Locate the row for 34 degrees of freedom.

What about a sample of 30 cases? What row would you focus on? (Answer: The row associated with 29 degrees of freedom)

What about a sample of 25 cases? What row would you focus on? (Answer: The row associated with 24 degrees of freedom)

 LEARNING CHECK

Question: When using the *t* table and constructing a confidence interval for the mean (with σ unknown), how do you find the level of confidence in the table? Give an example.

Answer: The level of confidence is expressed indirectly. It is equal to I minus the level of significance. For example, to work at the 95% level of confidence, use the column dedicated to the .05 level of significance (I − .05 = .95).

An Application

Assuming you feel comfortable enough to move ahead, we can now tackle an application or two. Let's say that we have a random sample of 25 retirees, and we want to estimate the average number of emails retirees send out to friends or relatives each week. Let's further assume that our sample yields a mean of 12 (12 emails per week) with a standard deviation of 3 and that we've decided to construct a 95% confidence interval for our estimate of the mean. Those are the essential ingredients we need, so now the question is how to proceed.

First, we take the sample mean of 12 as a starting point. Then, we build our cushion by adding a certain amount to the mean and subtracting a certain amount from the mean. Here's the formula we'll be working with—one that's remarkably similar to the one you encountered earlier:

$$CI = \overline{X} \pm t(s_{\overline{x}})$$

Since all we have is the sample standard deviation (the population standard deviation, or σ, is unknown), we'll be working with the t distribution, and we'll have to estimate the standard error.

The value of t we'll use is found by locating the intersection of the appropriate degrees of freedom and confidence level. In this case, we have 24 degrees of freedom ($n - 1$, or $25 - 1$), so that's the row in the table that we'll focus on. We want to construct a 95% confidence interval, so we'll focus on the .05 Level of Significance column ($1 - .05 = .95$). The point in the body of the table at which the selected row and column intersect shows the appropriate t value of 2.064 (rounded to 2.06).

We'll have to multiply the t value (2.06) by our estimate of the standard error, so the next step is to calculate the estimate. We estimate the standard error ($s_{\bar{x}}$) by dividing our sample standard deviation (s) of 3 by the square root of our sample size (the square root of 25, or 5). The result (3/5, or .60) is our estimate of the standard error.

$$s_{\bar{x}} = \frac{s}{\sqrt{n}}$$

$$s_{\bar{x}} = \frac{3}{\sqrt{25}}$$

$$s_{\bar{x}} = \frac{3}{5}$$

$$s_{\bar{x}} = 0.60$$

We now have everything we need: our sample mean as a starting point, the appropriate t value, and our estimate of the standard error. When plugged into the formula (the mean, plus and minus a little bit of cushion), here's what we get:

$$\text{CI} = \overline{X} \pm t(s_{\bar{x}})$$
$$\text{CI} = 12 \pm 2.06(0.60)$$
$$\text{CI} = 12 \pm 1.24$$
$$\text{CI} = 10.76 \text{ to } 13.24$$

We can now say we estimate that the true mean of the population falls somewhere between 10.76 and 13.24 emails per week, and we have used a method that will produce a correct estimate 95 times out of 100.

Assuming all of that made sense, let's change the problem just a bit. Let's say that we're more concerned about confidence than precision, so we want to construct a 99% interval. The steps are the same, and so are all the values, except one—the appropriate t value. In this case, we're working with a 99% confidence interval, so our t value will be 2.80. As we have seen previously, our interval will now be a little wider. Our confidence will increase (from 95% to 99%), but our precision will decrease (the interval will be wider).

$$CI = \overline{X} \pm t(s_{\overline{x}})$$
$$CI = 12 \pm 2.80(0.60)$$
$$CI = 12 \pm 1.68$$
$$CI = 10.32 \text{ to } 13.68$$

Our confidence interval now ranges from 10.32 to 13.68—an interval that's slightly wider than the one we got when we constructed a 95% confidence interval.

Assuming you're getting the idea here, let's try a few more problems that should solidify your thinking. In each case, give some thought to each element that comes into play in the problem solution.

1. Given a mean of 100, a standard deviation of 12, and $n = 16$, construct a 95% confidence interval for the mean. Answer: 93.61 to 106.39
2. Given a mean of 54, a standard deviation of 15, and $n = 25$, construct a 99% confidence interval for the mean. Answer: 45.60 to 62.40
3. Given a mean of 6500, a standard deviation of 240, and $n = 16$, construct a 95% confidence interval for the mean. Answer: 6372.20 to 6627.80

Assuming you took the time to work through those problems, let me ask you to do one more thing—something similar to what you did in the last section. Pick any one of the problems you just worked, and change it by substituting a larger sample size. For example, focus on problem 2 and change the sample size from 25 to, let's say, 100. Before you even work through the reformulated problem, give some thought to what you expect will happen to the width of the interval when you construct it on the basis of $n = 100$. Consider that this would be a substantial increase in sample size. Notice what the increase in sample size does to the width of the interval (and, therefore, what it does to the precision of the estimate).

The principle involved is the same as the one you encountered earlier. Given a constant level of confidence (let's say, 95%), you can increase the precision of an estimate (or decrease the width of the interval) by increasing your sample size. To understand the logic behind this, think of the largest sample size you could possibly have. That, of course, would be the entire population. In that case, there would be no standard error, and your estimate would exactly equal the mean of the population—the narrowest interval you could possibly have!

A Final Comment About the Interpretation of a Confidence Interval for the Mean

At this point, it's probably a good idea to return the fundamental meaning of a confidence interval for the mean. Let's take the example of a sample mean of 108 and a corresponding confidence interval that ranges from 99.64 to

116.36 (Elifson, Runyon, & Haber, 1990). In interpreting those results (or any other for that matter), it is wise to remember what a confidence interval does and does not tell us.

> In establishing the interval within which we believe the population mean falls, we have *not* established any probability that our obtained mean is correct. In other words, we cannot claim that the chances are 95 in 100 (or 99 in 100) that the population mean is 108. Our statements are valid only with respect to the interval and not with respect to any particular value of the sample mean. (Elifson et al., 1990, pp. 367–368)

Translation? A confidence interval for the mean doesn't provide you with an exact estimate of the value of the population mean. Rather, it provides you with an interval—an interval of two values—that you believe contains the true mean of the population. If you were working at a 95% level of confidence, *and you went through the exercise of constructing a confidence interval 100 times,* 95 times your result would be a confidence interval that contains the true mean of the population. Do you ever know that you've produced an interval that does, in fact, contain the true mean of the population? No. On the other hand, you do know the probability that you've produced an interval containing the population mean. It's all about probability and the method—the probability that your method has generated a correct interval estimate.

A Final Comment About Z Versus t

In practice, some statisticians use the *Z* distribution (instead of *t*), even when σ is unknown, provided they are working with a large sample. Indeed, in many texts, you'll find an application based on the use of the *Z* distribution in such cases (σ unknown, but a large sample). The easiest way to understand why it's possible to use *Z* with a large sample, even if you don't know the value of σ, is to take a close look at Appendix B again and concentrate on what happens to the *t* values as the degrees of freedom increase. To fully comprehend this point, take a moment to look at Figure 6-5.

Keeping in mind that the number of degrees of freedom is an indirect statement of sample size, you'll see something rather interesting in Figure 6-5. Once you're beyond 120 degrees of freedom (see the entry for infinity, ∞), the values of *t* and *Z* are identical. For example, if you were working with a sample of 150 cases and constructing a 95% confidence interval for the mean, it really wouldn't make any difference if you relied on the value of *t* or *Z*. Both values would be 1.96. It may be a minor point, but explanations like this can go a long way when you're trying to understand why two texts or resources approach the same topic in a slightly different fashion.

Having dealt with that minor point, we can now turn our attention to a slightly different topic. Instead of dealing with means, we'll move to the topic of proportions.

Degrees of Freedom	LEVEL OF SIGNIFICANCE					
	.20	.10	.05	.02	.01	.001
5	1.476	2.015	2.571	3.365	4.032	6.869
6	1.440	1.943	2.447	3.143	3.707	5.959
7	1.415	1.895	2.365	2.998	3.499	5.408
8	1.397	1.860	2.306	2.896	3.355	5.041
9	1.383	1.833	2.262	2.821	3.250	4.781
10	1.372	1.812	2.228	2.764	3.169	4.587
11	1.363	1.796	2.201	2.718	3.106	4.437
12	1.356	1.782	2.179	2.681	3.055	4.318
13	1.350	1.771	2.160	2.650	3.012	4.221
14	1.345	1.761	2.145	2.624	2.977	4.140
15	1.341	1.753	2.131	2.602	2.947	4.073
16	1.337	1.746	2.120	2.583	2.921	4.015
17	1.333	1.740	2.110	2.567	2.898	3.965
18	1.330	1.734	2.101	2.552	2.878	3.922
19	1.328	1.729	2.093	2.539	2.861	3.883
20	1.325	1.725	2.086	2.528	2.845	3.850
60	1.296	1.671	2.000	2.390	2.660	3.460
80	1.292	1.664	1.990	2.374	2.639	3.416
100	1.290	1.660	1.984	2.364	2.626	3.390
120	1.289	1.658	1.980	2.358	2.617	3.373
Infinity	1.282	1.645	1.960	2.327	2.576	3.291

The value of *t* equals *Z* beyond 120 degrees of freedom. Note that *t* is equal to 1.96 for a 95% confidence interval (equivalent to the *Z* value of 1.96).

Figure 6-5   What Happens to *t* Beyond 120 Degrees of Freedom

Confidence Intervals for Proportions

The application we take up now may strike you as familiar, because it's the sort of thing you're apt to encounter in everyday life—something that's very common in the fields of public opinion and market research, as well as sociology and political science.

The purpose behind a **confidence interval for a proportion** parallels that of a confidence interval for the mean. We construct a confidence interval for a proportion on the basis of information about a proportion in a sample—for example, the proportion in a sample that favors capital punishment. Our ultimate purpose, however, is to estimate the proportion (in support of capital punishment) in the population.

When someone reports the results of a political poll or a survey, he/ she frequently speaks in terms of proportions or percentages—for example,

57% responded this way and 43% responded that way, or 34 of the 60 respondents (an expression of a proportion) said this and 26 said that. To take another example, an opinion poll might report that 88% of voters in a community have a favorable attitude toward Councilman Brown. Maybe we're also told that the poll has a margin of error of ±3%. That simply means that somewhere between 85% and 91% of the voters hold a favorable attitude toward Brown (once again, an estimate expressed as an interval). In each instance, the purpose is to get an estimate of the relevant proportion in the population.

The question, of course, is how did the political pollster come up with that projection. I dare say that's a question that you've asked yourself at one time or another. As it turns out, the procedure is really quite simple, and it is based on the same logic that you encountered earlier in this chapter. The big difference is that in this instance the goal is to estimate a proportion by constructing a confidence interval for a proportion (as opposed to a mean).

 LEARNING CHECK

Question: What is the purpose behind the construction of a confidence interval for a proportion?

Answer: A confidence interval for a proportion is constructed in an effort to estimate the proportion in a population, based upon a proportion in a sample.

An Application

Let's say that Candidate Groves is running for mayor, and he's asked us to survey a random sample of 200 likely voters. He wants us to find out what proportion of the vote he can expect to receive. Let's say that our survey results indicate that 55% of the likely voters intend to vote for Groves for mayor. Given what we know about sampling error, we know that we have to take into account the fact that we're working with only one sample of 200 voters. A different sample of 200 voters would likely yield slightly different results (it's just a matter of sampling error). Given that situation, it's clear that we'll have to come up with some measure of standard error. As before, we'll eventually use that measure, along with a Z value, to develop our interval or our projection of the eventual vote. If there's a hitch in all this, it has to do with how we estimate the standard error of the proportion. We'll eventually get to all of that, but for the moment, let's review the problem under consideration, in light of our now familiar logic.

The fundamental logic in this problem will be the same as before. We've determined that 55% of the respondents said that they plan to vote for Groves, so we use that as our starting point. We'll place our observed sample proportion (or percentage) in the middle of a sampling distribution of sample proportions (not sample means, but sample proportions). Using our observed proportion as a starting point, we'll then build in a cushion, just as we did before. To build the cushion, we'll add some standard error to our observed proportion, and we'll subtract some standard error from our observed proportion. The result will be a confidence interval—just as we had in the cases involving estimates of the population mean.

For the sake of this example, let's assume that we want to construct a 95% confidence interval for the proportion. Given our sample size (n = 200), we can use the Z score associated with 95% of the area under the normal curve as one of the elements in our computation. Note how remarkably similar the formula (stated in somewhat nonmathematical terms) is to what we encountered earlier:

Confidence Interval (CI) for a proportion = observed proportion ± Z (?)

We already know that our observed proportion is .55 (the proportion intending to vote for Groves), and we know that the Z value will be 1.96 (since we're constructing a 95% confidence interval). All that remains is to determine where we get the value to substitute for the question mark. As it turns out, the value that we're looking for is the estimate of the standard error of the proportion. I should tell you in advance that the formula for the estimate of the standard error of the proportion (s_p) is a little ominous at first glance, but it's also quite straightforward if you take the time to examine it. Here it is:

$$s_p = \sqrt{\frac{P(1 - P)}{n}}$$

As complex as this formula may appear, let me assure you that it is easy to understand if you take it apart, element by element. First, the P in the formula represents the value of the observed proportion (.55, or 55% if expressed as a percentage). The value of $1 - P$, therefore, represents the remaining proportion (.45, or 45% if expressed as a percentage). In other words, $P + (1 - P)$ = 100%. As before, we'll have to consider our sample size along the way. Substituting the appropriate values for the elements in the formula, we obtain the standard error of the proportion as follows:

$$s_p = \sqrt{\frac{0.55(1 - 0.55)}{200}}$$

$$s_p = \sqrt{\frac{0.55(0.45)}{200}}$$

$$s_p = \sqrt{\frac{.2475}{200}}$$

$$s_p = \sqrt{0.0012375}$$

$$s_p = 0.035$$

Armed with the value of the estimate of standard error of the proportion (0.035), and assuming we want to construct a 95% confidence interval for the proportion, we can now complete the problem as follows:

$$CI = P \pm Z\,(s_p)$$

$$CI = 0.55 \pm 1.96 \, (0.035)$$
$$CI = 0.55 \pm 0.0686$$
$$CI = 0.4814 \text{ to } 0.6186$$
$$CI = 48.14\% \text{ to } 61.86\%$$

Thus, we're in a position to estimate that between 48.14% and 61.86% of the voters are likely to vote for Groves. As before, we could include a statement that we've used a method that generates a correct estimate 95 times out of 100.

Margin of Error

Public opinion poll results are rarely expressed in the form of an interval. Rather, the results are typically given with some reference to a **margin of error.** For example, a pollster may report that 34% approve of Proposition X, with a margin of error of ±4%. By now you should understand that the margin of error is, in effect, simply a statement of the interval width. Thinking back to the poll for Candidate Groves, we can say that the margin of error was 6.86%. After all, that was the amount that we were adding and subtracting to develop the confidence interval.

 LEARNING CHECK

Question: In a confidence interval for a proportion, what is the margin of error? Give an example.

Answer: The margin of error is an indirect statement of the width of the interval. For example, the statement that the proportion in a population is estimated at 45%, with a margin of error of ±3%, is actually a statement that the interval of the estimate ranges from 42% to 48%.

For Candidate Groves' purposes, the margin of error (55%, plus or minus 6.86%) is so large that he can't take much comfort in the poll. He might capture as much as 61.86% of the vote, but he might receive only 48.14%. For a more precise estimate (at the same level of confidence), Groves would have to request a larger sample size. For example, we could follow through the same calculations again, but with the assumption that we're working with a sample of 750 likely voters. As you'll soon discover, the width of our confidence interval (and, therefore, the margin of error) would decrease quite a bit.

First, we'll recalculate the estimate of the standard error of the proportion with our new sample size:

$$s_p = \sqrt{\frac{0.55(1 - 0.55)}{750}}$$

$$s_p = \sqrt{\frac{0.55(0.45)}{750}}$$

$$s_p = \sqrt{\frac{.2475}{750}}$$

$$s_p = \sqrt{0.00033}$$

$$s_p = 0.018$$

Then, we'll use the new estimate of the standard error of the proportion to calculate our confidence interval:

$$CI = P \pm Z\,(s_p)$$

$$CI = 0.55 \pm 1.96\,(0.018)$$

$$CI = 0.55 \pm 0.0353$$

$$CI = 0.5147 \text{ to } 0.5853$$

$$CI = 51.47\% \text{ to } 58.53\%$$

Based on a sample of 750, then, our estimate would result in a projected vote between 51.47% to 58.53%. By the same token, we could legitimately report our results as a projected vote of 55% with a margin of error of 3.53%.

 LEARNING CHECK

Question: Given a constant level of confidence, what is the effect on the margin of error of increasing the sample size when developing a confidence interval for a proportion?

Answer: Given a constant level of confidence, an increase in the size of a sample will decrease the margin of error.

As you're probably aware, pollsters commonly refer to a margin of error, but they rarely refer to the level of confidence that underlies their estimate. As a student of statistics, however, you're now aware that the two concepts are different. The two concepts are related, to be sure, but they are different in important ways. The margin of error is an indirect measure of the width of the interval, but the level of confidence actually goes to the method used in calculating the interval.

You'll find more examples of confidence intervals involving proportions at the conclusion of this chapter. They're presented in such a way that you'll be able to work through them in fairly quick fashion.

Chapter Summary

As we conclude this chapter, let's consider what you've covered. You've encountered a mountain of material. In the simplest of terms, you've entered the world of inferential statistics. You've learned how to construct confidence intervals. You've learned how to use sample characteristics (statistics) to make inferences about population characteristics (parameters).

You've learned, for example, about two basic approaches to constructing a confidence interval for the mean. You use one approach when you know the standard deviation of the population (σ) and a slightly different procedure when you don't know the standard deviation of the population (σ). You've also learned how to make a direct calculation of the standard error (when you know the value of σ) and how to estimate the standard error (when you don't know the value of σ).

Beyond all of that, you've learned how the survey results that you read or hear reported in the media are often derived—how a confidence interval for a proportion is constructed. You've also learned about margins of error and levels of confidence—how they're related, but how they are different.

Finally, and maybe most important, you've learned something about the world of inferential statistics in general. You've learned that there is no such thing as a direct leap from a sample to a population. You can't simply look at a sample mean (or a proportion, for that matter) and assume that it is equal to the true population parameter. You can use your sample value as a starting point, but you invariably have to ask yourself a central question in one form or another:

- Where did the sample value come from?
- Where did the sample value fall in relationship to all other values that might be possible?
- Where did the sample value fall along a sampling distribution of all possible values?
- What do I know about the sampling distribution, and how can I use that information to determine a reasonable estimate of the true population parameter?

Let me suggest that you take time out now for a dark room moment—one that might help you put a lot of this material into perspective. In this instance, I'm asking you to think about the construction of a confidence interval for the mean, but the same mental steps would be involved if you were constructing a confidence interval for a proportion.

Imagine that you've just surveyed a random sample of students, and you've calculated a mean age for your sample. This time I'm going to ask you to conjure up a mental image of a circle with some value in it—let's say 22.3. Treat that value as the mean age of your sample, and mentally focus on that circle with the value of 22.3 in the middle of it.

Now imagine a sampling distribution of sample means above the circle. Imagine that it looks something like a normal distribution sitting inside a cloud (since it's such a theoretical concept, the cloud image is probably appropriate). Think about what that sampling distribution represents—a distribution of all possible means, given repeated random sampling from a population. Now imagine that you're asking yourself a simple question. Where would my sample mean fall along the sampling distribution? Would it be at the upper end? Would it be at the lower end? Would it be somewhere in the middle?

Now imagine a rectangle above the sampling distribution. Imagine that the rectangle represents the population. Imagine a question mark in the middle of the rectangle—a question mark to convey the notion that you don't know what the value of the population mean is. That's as far as you have to go in this little mental exercise. Don't clutter your mind with the specifics of how you get from the circle on the bottom to the rectangle on the top. Simply take a mental step backward, and take in the entire view—circle, sampling distribution, and rectangle. Your image should look something like the one in Figure 6-6.

Imagine that you're first looking at the circle, then looking at the sampling distribution (moving through it, so to speak), and then moving to the rectangle. That's the essence of inferential statistics—from a sample, through a sampling distribution, and on to the population for a final answer or interpretation. As before, let me urge you to take the time to experience that dark room moment.

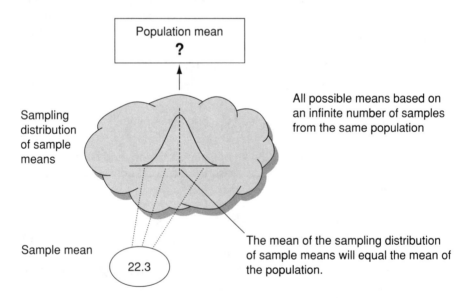

Where does the sample mean fall in relationship to all possible means?

Where does the sample mean come from in relation to all possible means that you might have obtained?

Figure 6-6 An Image of Inferential Statistics

The mental image should serve you well in the long run. What's more, it will help you prepare for our next topic—an introduction to hypothesis testing.

Some Other Things You Should Know

If there's one topic that demonstrates the matter of choice and personal preference when it comes to statistical applications, it's the topic of confidence interval construction. As I mentioned previously, some statisticians use the Z distribution (instead of t), even when σ is unknown, provided they're working with a large sample. For one statistician, though, "large" may be 60 cases; for another, it may be 100. You should always keep that in mind, particularly when you consult other resources. What may strike you as total confusion may be nothing more or less than personal preference on the part of the author.

While we're on the topic of personal preference and variation from resource to resource, you should be aware that the symbolic notation used in the field of statistical analysis is not carved in stone. For example, the notation for the estimate of the standard error used here ($s_{\bar{x}}$) is just one approach. Another text or resource may rely on a different notation (such as s_M).

Finally, you should be aware of a fundamental assumption that's involved when constructing a confidence interval for the mean with σ known. In truth, you have to make an assumption that your sample comes from a population that is equivalent to the population for which you have a known σ. Let me explain.

In the example we used at the beginning of this chapter, the assumption was made that the population of customers who had taken the SAT prep course was equivalent to the population of all students taking the SAT. We implicitly made that assumption when we took the approach that we knew the standard deviation of the population. In short, we made the assumption that our population of customers—would-be college students who enrolled in a SAT prep course—was equivalent to a population of *all* would-be college students who take the SAT. In truth, though, a population of those who enroll in a prep course may differ from the population at large in some important way (for example, maybe they are more motivated to do well, so they enroll in a prep course). For this reason, a researcher may prefer to frame the research question as though the population standard deviation (σ) were unknown, relying on a standard deviation to estimate the standard error. Once again, we're back to the matter of personal preferences.

At this point, let me encourage you to spend some time with additional resources. For example, you may want to take a look at other texts or tour the Cengage Web site www.cengage.com/psychology/caldwell. Learning to navigate your way through various approaches to the same type of question, different systems of symbolic notation, or encounters with personal preferences can provide an added boost to your overall level of statistical understanding.

Key Terms

confidence interval for the mean
confidence interval for a proportion
estimate of the standard error of
   the mean

family of *t* distributions
level of confidence
margin of error

Chapter Problems

Fill in the blanks, calculate the requested values, or otherwise supply the correct answer.

General Thought Questions

1. A confidence interval for the mean is calculated by adding and subtracting a value to and from the sample _____.

2. The purpose of constructing a confidence interval for the mean is to _____ the true value of the population mean, based upon the mean of a _____.

3. A confidence interval for the mean is an interval within which you believe the _____ of the population is located.

4. As the level of confidence increases, the precision of your estimate _____.

5. There is a(n) _____ relationship between level of confidence and precision of the estimate.

6. When constructing a confidence interval for a proportion, the margin of error is actually a reflection or statement of the _____ of the interval.

7. Whether constructing a confidence interval for a proportion or a mean, there are two ways to increase the precision of the estimate. You can _____ sample size, or you can _____ the level of confidence.

8. When constructing a confidence interval for the mean with σ known, how is the standard error of the mean calculated?

9. When constructing a confidence interval for the mean with σ unknown, how is the standard error of the mean estimated?

Application Questions/Problems: Confidence Interval for the Mean With σ Known

1. Compute the standard error of the mean, given the following values for σ (population standard deviation) and n (size of sample).
   a. $\sigma = 25\ n = 4$
   b. $\sigma = 99\ n = 49$
   c. $\sigma = 62\ n = 50$
   d. $\sigma = 75\ n = 25$

2. Given the following:

$\overline{X} = 150 \qquad \sigma = 12 \qquad n = 25$

a. Estimate the mean of the population by constructing a 95% confidence interval.

b. Estimate the mean of the population by constructing a 99% confidence interval.

3. Given the following:

$\overline{X} = 54 \qquad \sigma = 9 \qquad n = 60$

a. Estimate the mean of the population by constructing a 95% confidence interval.

b. Estimate the mean of the population by constructing a 99% confidence interval.

4. Given the following:

$\overline{X} = 75 \qquad \sigma = 5 \qquad n = 100$

a. Estimate the mean of the population by constructing a 95% confidence interval.

b. Estimate the mean of the population by constructing a 99% confidence interval.

5. Assume you've administered a worker satisfaction test to a random sample of 25 workers at your company. The test is purported to have a population standard deviation or σ of 4.50. The test results reveal a sample mean ($\overline{X}$) of 78. Based on that information, develop an estimate of the mean score for the entire population of workers, using a 95% confidence interval.

6. The mean for the verbal component of the SAT is reported as 500, with a standard deviation (σ) of 100. A sample of 400 students throughout a particular school district reveals a mean score of 498. Estimate the mean score for all the students in the district, using a 95% confidence interval?

7. The mean for the verbal component of the SAT is reported as 500, with a standard deviation (σ) of 100. A sample of 900 students throughout a particular school district reveals a mean ($\overline{X}$) score of 522. Estimate the mean score for all the students in the district, using a 95% confidence interval.

8. Repeat Problem 7 using a 99% confidence interval.

9. The mean for the math component of the New Century Achievement Test is reported as 100, with a standard deviation (σ) of 15. A sample of 400 students throughout a particular school district reveals a mean ($\overline{X}$) score of 110. Estimate the mean score for all the students in the district, using a 99% confidence interval.

Application Questions/Problems: Confidence Interval for the Mean With σ Unknown

1. Estimate the standard error of the mean, given the following values for s (sample standard deviation) and n (sample size).

a. $s = 5 \qquad\qquad n = 16$

b. $s = 12.50 \qquad n = 25$

    c. $s = 18.25$ $n = 50$
    d. $s = 35.50$ $n = 30$

2. Given the following:

    $\overline{X} = 26$ $s = 5$ $n = 30$

    a. Estimate the mean of the population by constructing a 95% confidence interval.

    b. Estimate the mean of the population by constructing a 99% confidence interval.

3. Given the following:

    $\overline{X} = 402$ $s = 110$ $n = 30$

    a. Estimate the mean of the population by constructing a 95% confidence interval.

    b. Estimate the mean of the population by constructing a 99% confidence interval.

4. Given the following:

    $\overline{X} = 80$ $s = 15$ $n = 25$

    a. Estimate the mean of the population by constructing a 95% confidence interval.

    b. Estimate the mean of the population by constructing a 99% confidence interval.

5. A sample of 25 program participants in an alcohol rehabilitation program are administered a test to measure their self-reported levels of alcohol intake prior to entering the program. Results indicate an average $(\overline{X})$ of 4.4 drinks per day for the sample of 25, with a sample standard deviation (s) of 1.75 drinks. Based on that information, develop a 95% confidence interval to provide an estimate of the mean intake level for the entire population of program participants (μ).

6. Information collected from a random sample of 29 visitors to a civic art fair indicates an average amount of money spent per person $(\overline{X})$ of $38.75, with a sample standard deviation (s) of $6.33. Based on that information, develop a 99% confidence interval to provide an estimate of the mean expenditure per person for the entire population of visitors.

7. A sample of 25 participants in a parenting skills class are administered a test to measure their skill levels on a 200 point skills test before entering the class. Results indicate that the mean $(\overline{X})$ skill level for the sample is 86, with a standard deviation (s) of 12. Based on that information, develop a 95% confidence interval to provide an estimate of the mean skill level for the entire population of program participants.

8. A sample of 25 participants in a parenting skills class are administered a test to measure their skill levels on a 200 point skills test before entering the class. Results indicate that the mean $(\overline{X})$ skill level for the sample is 101, with a standard deviation (s) of 16. Based on that information, develop a 95% confidence interval to provide an estimate of the mean skill level for the entire population of program participants.

9. Data are collected concerning the birth weights for a nation-wide sample of 30 Wimberley Terriers. Results indicate that the mean ($\overline{X}$) birth weight for the sample of pups equals 6.36 ounces, with a standard deviation (s) of 1.45 ounces. Based on that information, develop a 95% confidence interval to provide an estimate of the mean birth weight for the national population of Wimberley Terriers.

Confidence Interval Problems for a Proportion

1. In a sample of 200 freshmen at a state university, 40% report that they work at least 20 hours a week while in school. Estimate the proportion of all freshmen at the university working at least 20 hours per week. Develop your estimate on the basis of a 95% confidence interval.

2. From sample of 100 patients in a statewide drug rehabilitation program, you've determined that 20% of the patients were able to find employment within three months of entering the program. Estimate the percentage of patients throughout the program who were able to find employment within three months. Develop your estimate on the basis of a 99% confidence interval.

3. Of a sample of 200 registered voters, 32% report that they intend to vote in a school board election. Using a 95% confidence interval, estimate the percentage of all registered voters planning to vote.

4. Of a sample of 150 customers at a local bank, 15% report that they are likely to request a bank loan within the next year. Using a 99% confidence interval, estimate the percentage likely to request a loan within the population of all customers.

5. Results from a sample of 400 high school dropouts throughout the state reflect that 13% of the dropouts plan to return to school next year. Using a 99% confidence interval, estimate the percentage throughout the state planning to return to school next year.

6. An opinion poll based on a sample of 750 community residents indicates that 61% are in favor of a local civic redevelopment project. Estimate the level of support throughout the community, based on a 95% confidence interval.

7. An opinion poll based on responses from a sample of 250 community residents indicates that 61% are in favor of a local civic redevelopment project. Estimate the level of support throughout the community, based on a 95% confidence interval.

8. A poll, based upon a national sample of 1200 potential voters and focused on attitudes toward Social Security reform, indicates that 73.55% of the respondents oppose a proposal that would extend the minimum retirement age. Using a 95% confidence interval, estimate the proportion of opposition throughout the population of potential voters.

9. Repeat Problem 8 using a sample size of 750.

7

Hypothesis Testing With a Single Sample Mean

In the last chapter, you entered the world of inferential statistics when you learned how to make an inference about the population on the basis of what you knew about a sample. In this chapter, you'll find yourself using some of that same logic, but you'll go beyond a mere inference about a population value. In this chapter, you'll learn how statisticians formulate research questions, how they structure those questions, and how they put those questions to a test. In short, you'll learn about the world of *hypothesis testing*.

As we explore the world of hypothesis testing, we'll follow a path similar to the one we traveled in the last chapter. First we'll tackle hypothesis tests about a sample mean ($\overline{X}$) when we know the value of the standard deviation of the population (σ). Then we'll turn to tests about a sample mean ($\overline{X}$) when the population standard deviation (σ) is unknown. In the process, we'll make the same shift as we did before. First, we'll work with Z values and make a direct calculation of the standard error of the mean. In the second approach, we'll rely on t values and estimate the standard error of the mean.

In addition to learning about a particular statistical application, you'll learn about hypothesis testing in a general sense. In the process, you'll learn that the world of hypothesis testing has a language and a logical structure of its own. My guess is that you'll find that it's very different from anything you've ever experienced before. That's why it's a good idea to ease into the concepts gradually.

Before We Begin

To get right to the point, think about what you just covered. You dealt with confidence intervals. You dealt with concepts such as the mean, the standard deviation, and the standard error (calculated and estimated). You used those concepts when constructing confidence intervals. Now, though, we're getting ready to shift gears. Yes, we're going to rely on many of the same concepts, but our purpose will be very different. We're about to move into the world of hypothesis testing.

Before we start, let me emphasize three major points. First, hypothesis testing involves an approach to logic that may strike you as a little strange. I just ask you to remember that as you work your way through the chapter. Secondly, you need to have an objective, open mind if you really want to understand hypothesis testing. If you're inclined to hold opinions or make statements in the absence of facts, you might find the next chapter a bit bothersome. Finally, the material that you're about to encounter should probably be taken in bits and pieces. My advice is that you read about a concept or notion, think about that concept or notion, and then reread and rethink again. The concepts are important enough to warrant that sort of approach.

Setting the Stage

Researchers may want to compare a sample mean to a population mean for any number of reasons. Consider the following examples.

Let's say a researcher is about to analyze the results of a community survey, based on the responses of 50 registered voters. Assuming he/she has some knowledge about the entire population (for example, the mean age of all registered voters in the community), the researcher might start by comparing the mean age of the sample and the population, just to determine if the sample is reasonably representative of the population.

Maybe a criminologist is interested in the average sentence length handed out to first-time offenders in drug possession cases. A national study, now almost two years old, reports that the average sentence length is 23.4 months, but the criminologist wants to verify that the reported average still applies.

In yet another example, maybe a team of industrial psychologists is interested in the productivity of assembly line workers. Historical data, based on the performance of all workers over the past three years, indicate that workers will (on average) produce 193.80 units per day. The psychologists, however, believe that the level of productivity may be different for workers who've been given the option of a flextime schedule. Taking a sample of productivity records for those working on a flextime schedule, the psychologists can compare the sample mean with the historical population mean.

Those are just some of the situations appropriate for a hypothesis test involving a single sample mean. There are actually many different hypothesis-testing procedures—some involving a single sample mean, some based on two sample means, and still others that deal with three or more sample means. For the moment, though, we'll deal with the single sample situation. It's a fairly straightforward sort of application and well-suited as an introduction to the logic of hypothesis testing.

A Hypothesis as a Statement of Your Expectations: The Case of the Null Hypothesis

You've probably heard of or used the word **hypothesis** before, and you may have the notion that a hypothesis is a statement that you set out to prove. That understanding may work when it comes to writing a term paper or an essay, but it's far removed from the technical meaning of a hypothesis in a statistical sense. In truth, a statistician isn't interested so much in a hypothesis as in the **null hypothesis.**

Statisticians are forever attempting to put matters to a test, and they use a null hypothesis to set up the test. That's where we'll begin—with the notion of the null hypothesis. To be fair, though, you deserve an advance warning. You may think the logic behind the null hypothesis is totally backwards and, at times, convoluted. If that's the way it strikes you, rest assured your reaction isn't unusual. Indeed, my experience tells me that many students find the logic of hypothesis testing to be a little rough going at the outset. You may have to go over it again and again and again. What's more, you may have to take some time out for a few dark room moments along the way. Let me encourage you— do whatever you need to do. The logic of hypothesis testing is an essential element in the world of inferential statistics.

Assuming you're ready to move forward, let's take a closer look at the concept of a null hypothesis. As it turns out, the null hypothesis is a statement that can take many forms. In some cases, the null hypothesis is a statement of *no difference* or a statement of *equality*. In other cases, though, it's a statement of *no relationship*. How a null hypothesis is stated is a function of the specific research problem under consideration. In general, though, and to get on the road to understanding what the null is all about, it's probably best to begin by thinking of it as a *statement of chance*.

 LEARNING CHECK

Question: What is a null hypothesis, and how might it be expressed?

Answer: A null hypothesis is the hypothesis that is tested. It can be a statement of no difference, a statement of chance, or a statement of no relationship.

Whether you realize it or not, you're already fairly familiar with the concept of chance or probability. For example, if I asked you to tell me the probability of pulling the ace of spades out of a deck of 52 cards, you'd tell me it's 1 out of 52 (since there is only one ace of spades in the deck). If I asked you to tell me the probability of having a head turn up on the flip of a coin, you'd likely tell me it's 50%—there's a 50/50 chance of it being a head. Of course, all of this assumes an honest deck of cards, or an honest coin.

In short, all of us occasionally operate on the basis of a system of probabilities—we know what to expect in the case of chance. In fact, that's frequently the only thing we know. For example, we don't have one set of probabilities for a slightly dishonest coin and another set of probabilities for an even more dishonest coin. All we have is a set or system of probabilities based on chance.

Now, to consider yet another example of a statement of chance, think about the normal curve. It is, after all, a *probabilistic distribution;* it gives you a statement of probabilities associated with various portions of the curve. For example, there's a 99% chance, or probability, that a score in a normal distribution will fall somewhere between 2.58 standard deviations above and below the mean. By the same token, there's only a 1% chance that a score would fall *beyond* ±2.58 standard deviations from the mean.

To convince yourself of this, think about what you already know about a *Z* score of, let's say, −2.01. You already know that it would be an extremely low *Z* score (and therefore has a low probability of occurring). You know that for the following reasons:

■ The *Z* values of +1.96 and −1.96 enclose 95% of the area under the curve.

■ Therefore, only 5% of the area under the curve falls outside those values.

- Only 5 times out of 100 would you expect to get a Z value of more than +1.96 or less than –1.96.
- The extreme 5% would actually be split between the two tails of the distribution—2.5% in one tail and 2.5% in the other tail.
- Since a Z value of –2.01 is beyond the value of –1.96, you know that the probability of such a Z score occurring is fairly rare—indeed, it would have a probability of occurring less than 2.5 times out of 100 (<2.5%).

Assuming all of that made sense, let me urge you to begin thinking of extreme scores or values as nothing more or less than a score or value that has a very low probability of occurring. When a statistician views a score or value as *extreme,* it means that it has a low probability of occurrence.

 LEARNING CHECK

Question: What is an extreme score or value?
Answer: A score or value that has a low probability of occurrence.

The material you just covered is the sort of thing you'll want to keep in the back of your mind. For the moment, though, it shouldn't concern you how it relates to where we're going. In fact, you might do well to recall what I mentioned earlier—namely, that statistical analysis is sometimes best learned when you don't know where the road is leading. That said, let's take the next step along the road—in fact, a giant step. Let's jump headlong into a statistical application.

Single Sample Test With σ Known

Let's begin with a closer look at an earlier example. Assume for the moment that we're part of a team of industrial psychologists interested in how the introduction of a flextime program may have affected the productivity of assembly line workers. Instead of a set shift for every worker (such as 9:00 to 5:00), the flextime program allows each worker to select a specific shift (for example, 7:00 to 3:00, 8:00 to 4:00, or 10:00 to 6:00). Our historical information on worker productivity over the past three years shows that workers, on average, assemble 193.80 units per day, with a standard deviation of 31.55 units. Since those values are the result of complete records over the past three years, we can treat them as population values: $\mu = 193.80$ and $\sigma = 31.55$.

Let's also say that we've selected a random sample of productivity reports on 50 workers who took advantage of the flextime option. Our interest is in whether or not there's a significant difference between the productivity of flextime workers and the historical level of productivity. Calculating the mean level of productivity for our sample $(\overline{X})$, we determine that it's 202.94. There's obviously a difference between the two means (μ and $\overline{X}$). After all, the mean of the population (the population of all workers over the past three years) is 193.80 units, and the mean of the sample is 202.94 units.

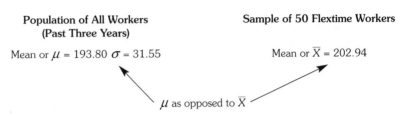

Population of All Workers
(Past Three Years)

Mean or μ = 193.80 σ = 31.55

Sample of 50 Flextime Workers

Mean or $\overline{X}$ = 202.94

μ as opposed to $\overline{X}$

A non-statistician might think about the example we're considering and say, "OK, I get it. We've compared a sample mean to a population mean to see if there's a difference. There is a difference, so that's that." With our background in statistics, however, we know there's far more to the situation than meets the eye. Once again, we're back where we've been before. We have only one sample mean in front of us—one mean out of an infinite number of sample means that are possible. The real question is whether or not our sample mean is *significantly* different from the population mean. As you'll soon discover, a significant difference is one that's so great that it has a low probability of having occurred by chance (or sampling error).

To understand all of this, let's start with the notion that we have to exercise a bit of caution. If the sample mean $(\overline{X})$ is higher or lower than the population mean (μ), we can't just jump to the conclusion that the level of productivity for flextime workers is really higher or lower than the historical mean. After all, our sample mean is just one mean, and it's subject to sampling error. So how do we determine whether the difference between the sample and population mean is noteworthy? How do we determine whether the difference is significant or just a matter of sampling error? We'll get the answers to those questions by testing a hypothesis.

 LEARNING CHECK

Question: What is a significant difference?
Answer: A significant difference is one that is so great that it has a low probability of having occurred by chance.

Refining the Null and Phrasing It the Right Way

As I mentioned before, statisticians test hypotheses by testing the *null hypothesis*. Since a null hypothesis is often a statement of equality (no difference), let's see how that plays out in the present example.

In the case we're considering here, the null hypothesis would be a statement that there's no difference between the mean of the population of flextime workers and the historical mean of the population of workers in general. At first glance, there appears to be a difference—after all, the population mean (μ) is 193.80 and the sample mean ($\overline{X}$) is 202.94—but the question really goes deeper. The real question is:

> How likely is it that we would have obtained a sample mean ($\overline{X}$) of 202.94 from a population having a mean (μ) of 193.80 and a standard deviation (σ) of 31.55?

In other words, if flextime workers are really part of the general population of workers (that is, they're not significantly different), then how likely is it that a sample of flextime workers would exhibit a sample mean of 202.94?

To answer this question, we'll eventually compare the sample mean with our expectation. If the sample mean is reasonably close to what we'd expect (based on chance or sampling error), we can attribute the difference to sampling error. If, on the other hand, the sample mean isn't reasonably close to what we might expect (based on chance or sampling error), we'll have reason to believe that the productivity of flextime workers is significantly different from the historical pattern. The question, therefore, is really whether or not a particular sample mean (whatever it might be) could reasonably come from a population with a mean (μ) of 193.80 and a standard deviation (σ) of 31.55.

Right now we're focused on the null hypothesis, and the null hypothesis is a statement of our expectation. Therefore, our null hypothesis is a statement that the mean of the population (μ) is equal to 193.80, or

$$H_0: \mu = 193.80$$

In other words, we're advancing the null hypothesis that the mean of the population of flextime workers is equal to 193.80 (the same mean as the mean of the historical population of workers). In doing so, we're also advancing the notion that the mean of the sampling distribution of sample means is equal to 193.80. Note that the null hypothesis is designated as H_0.

The Logic of the Test

Assuming you've digested all of that, let's return to the fact that we have a sample mean ($\overline{X}$) of 202.94, and we're back in familiar territory. We have to determine where our sample mean is located in terms of a distribution of many different means. The Central Limit Theorem tells us that the mean of a sampling distribution of sample means will equal the mean of the population (μ). The null hypothesis states that the mean of the population (μ) is 193.80, so (recalling what the Central Limit Theorem tells us) we would expect the mean of the sampling distribution of sample means to equal 193.80. Take a close look at Figure 7-1 to better grasp the logic underlying our approach here.

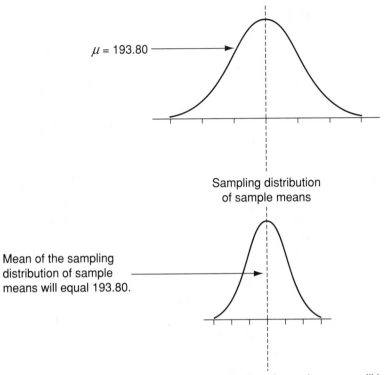

$\mu = 193.80$ ——————→

Sampling distribution
of sample means

Mean of the sampling
distribution of sample
means will equal 193.80. ——————→

The sampling distribution of sample means will have
a mean. It will equal the mean of the population.

**The central question: Where does our sample mean of 202.94 fall in relation
to all other sample means in a sampling distribution of sample means?**

Figure 7-1   What The Central Limit Theorem Tells Us and The Central Question

If you're inclined to just move ahead, without taking a serious look at Figure 7-1, let me caution against that. The illustration is there to demonstrate a basic element in the underlying logic that's in play here. Here's the logic:

- There is a known historical mean level of productivity for all workers (193.80 units per day).
- That known historical mean is treated as the mean of the population.
- We want to know if there is a difference between the level of productivity of flextime workers and the historical mean level of productivity.
- We start with the assumption that the mean for the population of flextime workers would be the same mean as the historical mean for all workers (i.e., we assume that the mean for the population of flextime workers would be 193.80 units).
- Given that assumption (and based on the Central Limit Theorem), we assume that the mean of the sampling distribution of sample means (based

on repeated samples of flextime worker records) would equal the historical mean of the population (193.80).

- We'll compare our sample mean (202.94) to the assumed mean of the sampling distribution of sample means (193.80), and we'll calculate the difference.

- We'll evaluate the difference by expressing the difference in standard error units.

- To express the difference in standard error units, we'll simply divide the difference by the standard error of the mean.

Our task is to determine where our sample mean of 202.94 would fall along a sampling distribution of different means—the many different means that we might get if we were to construct a sampling distribution of sample means. More specifically, we're going to evaluate our sample mean on the basis of a sampling distribution of sample means that has an assumed mean of 193.80. Remember: Our null hypothesis is a statement that we expect the mean of the population of flextime workers to equal 193.80. The Central Limit Theorem tells us that the mean of the sampling distribution of sample means will equal the mean of the population, so we're really working with an assumption that the mean of the sampling distribution of sample means is equal to 193.80.

If we discover that our sample mean ($\overline{X}$) of 202.94 isn't that unusual (compared to all sample means that would be possible), we can attribute the observed difference to chance (or more correctly, sampling error), and conclude that the null hypothesis is true. If, on the other hand, it appears that our sample mean is fairly extreme (in comparison to an assumed mean of 193.80), then we'd be inclined to believe that flextime workers do exhibit a significantly different level of productivity. Accordingly, we'd be inclined to reject the null hypothesis.

Now all of that represents a central notion in the matter of hypothesis testing, so let me emphasize it again. If the observed difference is relatively small, we'd be inclined to believe that the null hypothesis is true. If, however, the difference is relatively large, we'd be in a position to reject the null hypothesis. In doing so, we'd be rejecting the idea that the mean level of productivity for the flextime workers is equal to the historical level of productivity. In other words, we'd actually be suggesting that the population of flextime workers is somehow different from the population of all workers.

If that's where we end up (i.e., we reject the null hypothesis), we can say that our results are statistically significant. In other words, we can say that we found a significant difference between the two values. We'll eventually get around to learning more about how statisticians use the term *significant*. For the moment, though, let's return to the problem at hand.

Applying the Test

The central question obviously turns on the difference between the two values ($\overline{X}$ and μ) and whether the difference is extreme. Would a difference of 5.89 units per day be enough to call it extreme? What about a difference of 14.10 units per day? What if the sample mean were 212.29 units per day?

What about a mean of 239.88? Would that be different enough from the population mean to call it extreme?

As it turns out, there's a single answer to all those questions. Whether or not a sample mean represents an extreme departure from the population mean is a relative matter. It's relative in terms of how far the sample mean departs from the population mean (which is also the mean of the sampling distribution of sample means), in terms of standard deviation units.

You've learned, for example, that ±1.96 standard deviations on a normal curve (Z values of ±1.96) will take you pretty far out in the distribution or along the baseline. As a matter of fact, ±1.96 standard deviation units from the mean will take you far enough along the baseline of the distribution to encompass 95% of the area or cases. To refresh your memory on all of this, think back to what you learned in Chapter 4 about the notion of extreme scores. You ultimately learned that the real value of a Z score was found in its universal applicability. You learned that a Z score of, let's say, 2.91 (either + or – 2.91) would be extreme, whether you were referring to dollars, ounces, pounds, miles per hour, or anything else—including levels of productivity, expressed as the number of units produced per day.

It should now be clear that the central task is actually a rather simple one. All we have to do is calculate the difference between our sample mean and the population mean (which is also the mean of the sampling distribution of sample means). Then we translate that difference into a ratio that expresses the difference in standard deviation units—or more correctly, standard error of the mean units. As you learned earlier, the standard error of the mean is simply the standard deviation of the sampling distribution of sample means.

 LEARNING CHECK

Question: What is the central question surrounding a hypothesis test involving a single sample mean and a population mean?

Answer: The central question is whether the difference between the two means is extreme—whether the difference is significant.

Calculation. In the example we're considering now, we know the values of the standard deviation of the population ($\sigma = 31.55$) and the sample size ($n = 50$). Therefore, the calculation of the standard error of the mean ($\sigma_{\bar{x}}$) is straightforward. As you know from the last chapter, it's simply a matter of dividing σ (31.55) by the square root of the sample size (the square root of 50, or 7.07). Here's the formula again, just as you encountered it before, along with its calculation in the present instance:

$$\sigma_{\bar{x}} = \frac{\sigma}{\sqrt{n}}$$

Armed with the value of the standard error of the mean ($\sigma_{\bar{x}}$ = 4.46), we're now equipped to properly evaluate the difference between our sample mean and the assumed mean of the sampling distribution of sample means. First, we take note of the difference between the assumed mean (μ = 193.80) and the sample mean ($\bar{X}$ = 202.94). Subtracting the assumed mean from the sample mean, we discover that the difference equals 9.14 (i.e., the mean for the flextime workers is 9.14 units higher than the assumed mean of the population, which is also the assumed mean of the sampling distribution of sample means). From our earlier calculation, we determined that the standard error of the mean equals 4.46. To express our observed difference in terms of standard error units, we simply divide the observed difference (9.14) by the standard error of the mean (4.46). The calculation amounts to a conversion of a sample mean to a Z score, so the symbol Z now appears in the formula.

$$Z = \frac{\bar{X} - \mu}{\sigma_{\bar{x}}}$$

$$Z = \frac{202.94 - 193.80}{4.46}$$

$$Z = 2.05$$

We see that the difference of 9.14 (units produced per day) translates into a difference of 2.05 standard error units. The result (the difference divided by the standard error of the mean) is equivalent to a Z score (or a Z ratio) of +2.05. The logic behind the process we just went through may be summarized as follows:

1. Determine the difference between the two means—the sample mean minus the assumed population mean (which is also assumed to be the mean of the sampling distribution of sample means).
2. Calculate the standard error of the mean (divide the known σ by the square root of the sample size).
3. Convert the difference between the sample and population mean into a Z ratio by dividing the difference by the standard error of the mean.

Since the sampling distribution of sample means is known to approach a normal curve, we're in a position to evaluate whether or not the observed difference of 2.05 standard error units (or a Z of +2.05) is extreme. By now, you should already know the answer to that question: By most standards, a Z value of +2.05 is extreme. That's something you should already know at an intuitive level. After all, a Z value of +2.05 is more extreme than a value of +1.96, and only 5% of the sample means could be expected to fall beyond Z values of ±1.96. Since our calculated value of Z = +2.05 exceeds the value of +1.96 (see Figure 7-2), we know that it falls in a very extreme region of the curve (more specifically, a more extreme region in the upper portion of the curve). The difference is extreme enough that we'll reject our null hypothesis.

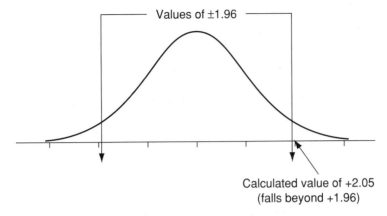

Figure 7-2   Location of Calculated Value of +2.05

Interpretation. By rejecting the null hypothesis, we're really rejecting the notion that the population of flextime workers would have a mean ($\overline{X}$) of 193.80. Accordingly, we're in a position to suggest that the productivity level of a population of flextime workers is different from the productivity level of a population of all workers (at least all workers over the past three years). But before we jump straight to that conclusion, though, let's think about how we arrived at our conclusion in the first place. Remember: It all goes back to whether an observed difference between the sample mean and a population mean is an extreme difference.

 LEARNING CHECK

Question: In the example involving the flextime workers, what does it mean to reject the null hypothesis?

Answer: To reject the null hypothesis is to reject the idea that the sample mean came from a population having a mean ($\overline{X}$) of 193.80.

Levels of Significance, Critical Values, and the Critical Region

If you think about the approach that we took, we calculated our test statistic first, and then we turned to the issue of whether or not the difference was extreme. In truth, however, statisticians actually determine what constitutes an extreme value by setting a *level of significance* before they perform any calculations. Additionally, statisticians commonly set the level of significance (also known as the alpha level or α) at the .05 or .01 level. I'll eventually give you a definition of *level of significance,* and I'll also tell you why it's set in advance. For the moment, though, let's continue with our example.

To say that we're working at the .05 level of significance, for example, is to say that we're looking for a Z value or ratio (our final answer) that is so extreme it would occur by chance only 5% of the time, or less, if the null hypothesis is true. If we discover that our calculated test statistic, or Z ratio, is equal to or more extreme than ±1.96, we can say that the value is extreme. We can say it is extreme because it's apt to occur by chance less than 5 times out of 100, assuming the null hypothesis is true. Remember: We'd expect 5% of the sample means (when converted to Z ratios) to fall at or beyond Z values of ±1.96, assuming the null is true. In fact, we'd expect a Z value equal to or greater than +1.96 only 2.5 times out of 100, and we'd expect a Z value equal to or less than −1.96 only 2.5 times out of 100 (because the extreme 5% is evenly split between the two sides of the distribution).

The same sort of reasoning would apply if we were working at the .01 level of significance. In a case like that, we'd be focused on Z values of ±2.58. Only 1% of sample means would be found at or beyond a Z value of ±2.58, assuming the null is true. One-half of the extreme 1% (.5%) would be found on one side of the distribution and one-half of the extreme 1% (.5%) would be found on the other side.

 LEARNING CHECK

Question: What levels of significance are commonly used by statisticians?

Answer: The .05 and .01 levels of significance.

To a statistician, a critical value like ±1.96 or ±2.58 is referred to as just that—the **critical value**. If our **calculated test statistic** (our result) meets or exceeds the critical value, then we can legitimately think of our observed difference as being extreme. If we can do that, we can reject the null hypothesis.

To truly appreciate the underlying logic, think back to the object of the exercise. It was to test a null hypothesis—for example, the null hypothesis that a sample mean came from a population with a certain mean value. To test the hypothesis, the difference between the sample mean and assumed mean of the sampling distribution of sample means (which is also the assumed mean of the population) was found, and the difference was evaluated. By determining a level of significance before the actual test, statisticians set the standard in advance. If the observed difference between the two means (expressed as a Z ratio) is large enough (and therefore meets the standard), the null hypothesis will be rejected. In rejecting the null hypothesis, the statistician is in a position to say that he/she has *significant* results.

In our flextime example, assuming we had predetermined our level of significance to be .05 (alpha, or α = .05), we could say we have *rejected the null hypothesis at the .05 level of significance.* The same fundamental logic underlies all hypothesis-testing situations, so let's review the process, step by step. Take a look at the summary in Table 7-1, and focus carefully on each step of the process.

What if we had selected the .01 level of significance ($\alpha = .01$) for our test? If you think back to those familiar values you first encountered in Chapter 4, you'll realize that the critical value at the .01 level of significance would be ±2.58. Those values would enclose 99% of the area or cases under the normal curve. That information, in turn, tells us that only 1% of the area or cases would be found at or beyond ±2.58. In other words, at the .01 level of significance, we'd look for a calculated test statistic (Z) that is so extreme that it is apt to occur less than 1% of the time by chance, assuming the null hypothesis is true. If our calculated test statistic (Z) was equal to or beyond the critical value of ±2.58, we could reject our null hypothesis at the .01 level of significance.

As it turned out, of course, our calculated test statistic (Z) was +2.05—a value that would not meet or go beyond a critical value of ±2.58. Our calculated value (2.05) is close to the value of 2.58, but it doesn't meet or exceed 2.58. Therefore, we would *fail to reject the null hypothesis at the .01 level of significance.* Our results may have been significant at the .05 level of significance, but our results would lead us to a different conclusion at the .01 level of significance—we would *fail to reject the null hypothesis.*

There's obviously an important lesson in all of that—namely, that whether or not our results are statistically significant is largely a matter of the level of significance that we set in advance of our hypothesis test. Significant results at one level of significance may not be significant at a different level of significance. Now you can begin to appreciate why statisticians typically set the level of significance in advance. This procedure allows them to predetermine what will be necessary for them to consider their results as *significant*—an approach that reflects the presumed objectivity of the scientific pursuit.

Table 7-1 Summary of the Hypothesis Testing Process

Formulate the null hypothesis.	H_0: $\mu = 193.80$
Determine a level of significance.	$\alpha = .05$
Identify the critical value.	±1.96
Calculate the test statistic.	$Z = \dfrac{\overline{X} - \mu}{\sigma_{\overline{x}}}$
Evaluate the test statistic in light of the critical value.	Compare calculated Z to critical value ±1.96.
Make a decision about null hypothesis.	Reject or fail to reject the null hypothesis.

Now let me say a final word about critical values. The best way to understand the critical value is to regard it as a point that marks the beginning of what's referred to as the **critical region**. The critical region, in turn, is the portion of the sampling distribution (such as the sampling distribution of Z) that contains all the values that allow you to reject a null hypothesis. For that reason, we refer to the critical region as the **region of rejection**. If our calculated test statistic (Z) is equal to or falls beyond the critical value, it has fallen into the critical region—the region that allows us to reject the null hypothesis.

 LEARNING CHECK

Question: How are the critical value and the critical region related?
Answer: The critical value is the beginning of the critical region. If our calculated test statistic meets or exceeds the critical value, thereby falling into the critical region, we are in a position to reject the null hypothesis.

At the .05 level of significance, our critical value is ±1.96. Thus, Z values of ±1.96 are the values that begin the critical regions at the .05 level of significance. Any Z value (or Z ratio) that we calculate that meets or exceeds ±1.96 is a value that falls within the critical region or the region of rejection (when working at the .05 level of significance). Similarly, ±2.58 are the values that begin the critical regions when working at the .01 level of significance. A calculated test statistic (in this case, a Z ratio) that is equal to or more extreme than ±2.58 would fall within the critical region at the .01 level of significance. *If our calculated value—our calculated test statistic—falls within the critical region, we reject the null hypothesis. If the calculated test statistic doesn't fall within the critical region, we fail to reject the null hypothesis.*

When we reject the null hypothesis, we're in a position to say that we have a *significant* finding—that's what the level of significance is all about. Another way of saying we have significant findings is to say that we have *statistically significant results*. In short, a statement that the results are significant is a statement that the calculated value of the test statistic falls within the critical region. In our flextime example, working at the .05 level of significance, we calculated a test statistic that fell within the critical region. Therefore, we rejected the null hypothesis; we had significant findings. We had reason to believe that the average productivity level of flextime workers really is different from the historical level of productivity.

But What If . . .

As we get ready to take this next step, let me urge you to first take a moment or two to think about what we've just covered. Take a moment to think about how we looked at a difference and evaluated that difference—ultimately coming to the conclusion that the difference was statistically significant at the .05 level of significance. The underlying logic and reasoning that we went through is fundamental to statistical analysis, so any time spent thinking about all of that will be well worth it.

Assuming you've reached a comfort level with the underlying reasoning, let me ask you to consider two more scenarios. Each scenario involves the same problem as before, but with some slight modifications:

> Scenario A: What if, for example, everything about the problem stayed the same (i.e., the same population mean and standard deviation, and the same number of cases in the sample), but the sample mean had been 184.51? Assuming we had worked at the .05 level of significance, what would we have concluded?

> Scenario B: What if the sample mean had been 199.53? Assuming we had worked at the .05 level of significance, what would we have concluded?

Let me suggest that you work through the problems presented in each scenario and spend some time thinking about the results.

Assuming you worked through the two problems represented by Scenarios A and B, you likely learned two very valuable lessons. Scenario A, for example, demonstrates that it's possible to end up with a negative *Z* value. Scenario B demonstrates that it's possible to end up with a difference between a sample and population mean that isn't significant (something we touched on earlier). Since those two scenarios expand the playing field in a noticeable way, let's take a closer look at each of them. As before, the assumption is made that you took the time to work through each of the scenarios.

As to a negative *Z* value under Scenario A, think about how you approached the difference between the two mean values. Assuming you used the formula presented earlier, you subtracted the mean of the population (the assumed mean of the sampling distribution of sample means) *from* the mean of the sample (see below).

$$Z = \frac{\overline{X} - \mu}{\sigma_{\overline{x}}}$$

Since the mean of the sample in Scenario A was smaller than the mean of the population, the result was a negative difference (184.51 − 193.80 = −9.29). Carrying the negative value through the remainder of the calculations in the formula, you ended up with a negative *Z* value. As it turns out, the notion of a negative *Z* value should make a certain amount of intuitive sense. After all, you're considering a negative difference—negative in the sense that the mean of the sample is lower than the assumed mean. You would still reject the null hypothesis since the *Z* value of −2.08 is more extreme than the critical value of −1.96. It's just that you'd be looking at a significant difference in which the productivity level of the flextime workers was *lower* than the historical level of productivity.

As to the particulars of Scenario B, you were working with a sample mean of 199.53. As it turned out, the difference between the sample mean and the assumed mean, when expressed in terms of standard error units, wasn't that noticeable. Indeed, it equated to a *Z* value of 1.28. Since that *Z* value (1.28) didn't meet or exceed the critical value ±1.96, you would fail to reject the null hypothesis. In other words, the sample mean was close enough to the assumed mean (at least in terms of standard error units), that it was reasonable to conclude that you could have obtained such a sample mean, just by chance. Therefore, you'd fail to reject the null hypothesis. You'd be inclined to say that there isn't a significant difference between the productivity levels of flextime workers and the historical level of productivity.

Now, just to recap the possibilities, we dealt with three different situations. In the first instance (the original problem), we found a significant difference— a difference in which the mean of the sample was higher than the historical mean of the population. In the second instance (Scenario A), we also found a significant difference—but it was a negative difference in the sense that the mean of the sample was lower than the historical mean of the population. In the third instance (Scenario B), the difference between the sample mean and the assumed mean was not significant.

But What If We're Wrong?

Now let's think about outcomes in a more general sense. Let's put aside the notion of a positive versus a negative difference and, instead, just think about two possible outcomes. One possible outcome was that we found a significant difference. In other words, we went through all of the calculations and the result was a calculated test statistic that met or exceeded the critical value. The other possibility, of course, was that we failed to find a significant difference. In other words, we went through all of the calculations and the result was a calculated test statistic that didn't meet or exceed the critical value.

As you now know, each of those outcomes would lead to a different conclusion, as follows:

If we found a significant difference, we rejected the null hypothesis.

If we didn't find a significant difference, we failed to reject the null hypothesis.

All of that is well and good, and the logic of hypothesis testing would be fairly easy to comprehend if that's all we had to consider—find a significant difference and reject the null or don't find a significant difference and fail to reject the null. There's just one problem. Regardless of the conclusion that we reached (i.e., we either rejected the null hypothesis or we failed to reject the null), we came to our conclusion on the basis of results obtained from only one sample. And it's the fact that we're relying on just one sample that's at the root of the problem, so to speak. To put the matter in the simplest of terms, it's quite possible that a different sample would have yielded different results.

As it turns out, that fact—the fact that different samples would likely yield different results—takes us another step down the road of statistical reasoning.

Type I Errors. Let's start with the assumption that the null hypothesis is true. In other words, the mean of the population of flextime workers is equal to the historical mean of all workers. Since this is fundamental to the notion of hypothesis testing, let me repeat the assumption: Assume that the null hypothesis is true. Don't ask how we know that the null hypothesis of no difference is true. Just assume that the null hypothesis is, in fact, true.

Now even if the null hypothesis is true, it's possible to obtain a sample mean that is extreme. For example, in selecting the sample of 50 productivity reports, we could, just by chance, select reports of the 50 most productive flextime workers. In a case like that, we'd eventually end up with a very high mean level of productivity for our sample of flextime workers. By the same token, we could, just by chance, select productivity reports for the 50 least productive flextime workers. In a case like that, we'd eventually end up with a very low mean level of productivity.

Now the likelihood of selecting a sample along those lines is fairly remote, but it could happen. And in either case, the point would be the same. We'd end up with an extreme mean as the result of what I like to call a *quirky* sample—a sample that doesn't really represent the population. What's more, that quirky sample would, in turn, lead to a sample mean that was quirky. Assuming that the sample mean was noticeably different from the assumed mean, we'd probably reject the null hypothesis. Unfortunately, we would have made an error.

All of that can be a confusing, so think it through again. Start with the assumption that the null is true. Then open your mind to the possibility that you could, just by chance, end up with a quirky sample. Then imagine a situation in which the quirky sample produced an extreme mean—in fact, a sample mean that was so extreme that you rejected the null hypothesis. Now think back to the fact that the null was true. You've obviously made a mistake. You've rejected the null when it was true.

To a statistician, this type of error is known as a **Type I error** (sometimes referred to as an *alpha error*). In short, a Type I error is a rejection of the null hypothesis when the null is, in fact, true. Unfortunately, we never know when we've made a Type I error. It all goes back to the notion of random sampling and the possibility of sampling error—the possibility that, just by chance, we were working with a sample that didn't really represent the population.

 LEARNING CHECK

Question: What is the definition of a Type I error?
Answer: A Type I error is the rejection of the null when, in fact, it is true.

Fine, you say. But what's the probability of making a Type I error? As it turns out, that's what the **level of significance** is all about. It's simply an expression of the probability of making a Type I or alpha error. As a matter of fact, that's why the level of significance is often referred to as the alpha level.

If you set your level of significance at .05 (often expressed as α = .05), it's simply a statement that you're willing to tolerate a 5% chance of making a Type I error (rejecting the null when it's true). Similarly, the selection of the .01 level of significance when you set up a hypothesis test is a statement that you're willing to tolerate a 1% chance of committing a Type I or alpha error.

 LEARNING CHECK

Question: What is the probability of making of a Type I error?
Answer: The probability of making a Type I error is equal to the level of significance (the alpha level).

Once again, a Type I error really derives from having selected a sample that, just by chance, doesn't really reflect reality. It results from bringing an extreme mean into the equation by accident. We know this can happen as a result of sampling error. Remember: We're always working with just one out of an infinite number of samples. When working at the .05 level of significance, for example, we can expect, just by chance, that 5 samples out of 100 would ultimately result in a rejection of the null, even though the null is true. In other words, we could go through the research exercise 100 times, each time selecting our sample and each time calculating a test statistic and each time arriving at a conclusion. In 5 of the 100 instances, though, we could end up with statistically significant results as a result of sampling error. *If we're working with one of those samples is something we can never know.* All we know is the probability that we've been working with one of those samples. All we know is the probability that we've committed a Type I or alpha error. Remember: That's what the level of significance is all about. It's the probability that we've committed a Type I error.

As we wrap up our discussion of Type I errors, let me give you a way to express your conclusion whenever you reject a null hypothesis, at least at the outset of your statistical education. It's a little more elaborate than the simple assertion *I reject the null hypothesis,* but the extra few words are important—at least in terms of helping you understand the fundamental logic involved in a hypothesis test.

Let's say, for example, that you're working at the .05 level of significance and you've found significant results. Consider the following as a way of expressing your conclusion: *I reject the null hypothesis, with the knowledge that 5 times out of 100 I could have committed a Type I error.*

I doubt that you'll see a statement like that in a scientific journal, to be sure, but rest assured of one thing—it's a statement that reflects the fundamental logic of what's involved in hypothesis testing. Remember: There's always a chance that you're working with an extreme sample (one of those quirky samples, as I like to call them). There's always a chance that you've rejected the null when, in fact, it's true.

My suggestion is that you get in the habit of phrasing your conclusion in a complete fashion at the outset of your statistical experience, at least when you find yourself in the position of rejecting a null hypothesis. Whenever you reject a null hypothesis, remind yourself that you're rejecting the null with the knowledge that there's a known probability of making a Type I error. It's the sort of thing that will constantly remind you of the logical underpinnings of the decision-making process.

So much for Type I errors. As you might suspect, there's also something known as a **Type II (or beta) error**. That's what we'll cover now.

Type II Errors. To understand what a Type II error is all about, start with the assumption that our null hypothesis is actually a false hypothesis. Returning to the flextime worker example, let's assume that the null hypothesis is false—the mean level of productivity for flextime workers *is* significantly different from the historical mean level of productivity, even though the null says that they are equal. Now even though there may be a difference (in other words, even though the null may be false) it's possible to select a sample that doesn't pick up that difference. Once again, that's something that could happen just by chance.

If we're dealing with one of those instances—an instance in which there's a significant difference, but we've failed to detect it—we've committed a Type II error. Simply put, a Type II error occurs when we fail to reject a false null hypothesis. Here's the logic again. The null hypothesis is false (i.e., there is a difference), but we didn't discover the difference. Because we didn't discover the difference, we failed to reject the null. The result is that we let the null stand. We failed to reject it. In truth, however, the null was false, and we should have rejected it. If we've failed to reject a false null hypothesis, we've committed a Type II error.

 LEARNING CHECK

Question: What is the definition of a Type II error?
Answer: It's the failure to reject the null when it is false.

At this point in your statistical education, it's not critical that you worry about how a Type II error could occur or how to determine the probability of making a Type II error. We'll deal with Type II errors in greater depth when we reach Chapter 9. At that point, we'll take a closer look at both Type I and Type II errors, and we'll also consider Type II errors in the context of power and effect size—two concepts that are particularly relevant in experimental research designs. We'll also take up the topic of alternative or research hypotheses. All of that, however, can wait. Right now the idea is to solidify your thinking on what we've just covered.

A Final Word About Phrasing Your Conclusions. As we close out this section, let me once again urge you to be very specific in how you should phrase your conclusions when testing hypotheses. After all, it makes little sense to work through a research problem, getting all of the calculations just right, only to make a mistake when state your conclusions.

If you reject a null hypothesis, I urge you to phrase your conclusion with some reference to the level of significance. For example, (and assuming you're working at the .05 level of significance), simply state that you reject the null hypothesis, with the knowledge that there is a 5% chance of having committed a Type I error. If, on the other hand, you fail to reject the null hypothesis, all you have to do is simply state that you fail to reject the null hypothesis. You don't have to state anything else. Just end the sentence right there—*I fail to reject the null hypothesis*.

On this last point (i.e., use of the phrase, *I fail to reject the null hypothesis*), I find that students often ask why they can't simply *accept* the null hypothesis. It may be my conservative nature, but here's the way I see it. A simple acceptance of the null hypothesis always strikes me as closing the door on further research. It is as though you have accepted the null, announced that the case is closed, and that is that. In saying that you *fail to reject the null,* however, it is as though you've left the door open for further research, so to speak. In that regard, I'm often reminded of the words of Popper:

> The game of science is, in principle, without end. He who decides one day that scientific statements do not call for any further test, and that they can be regarded as finally verified, retires from the game. (Popper, 1961, p. 53)

At this point, I suggest that you take a moment or two to catch your breath. Rather than plowing ahead, let me suggest that you spend a little time going over the material that we've covered so far. Concentrate on the fundamental logic first. Get familiar with all the central concepts. Once you've done that, take a step back and consider how far you've just traveled. You've learned how to conduct a hypothesis test using a single sample mean when the population standard deviation σ is known. You've also learned what it means to reject or fail to reject a null hypothesis. If you're comfortable with all of that, we can move forward to hypothesis tests using a single sample mean when the standard deviation of the population σ is unknown.

Single Sample Test With σ Unknown

Let's say that the average number of cases processed last month by social workers throughout the state is reported as 23.12 per worker. As members of the agency's management team in a regional office, we want to know how the caseworkers in the regional office compare to those throughout the state. Let's assume that we want to save time and effort, so we identify 30 caseworkers in our region and examine their work records from the previous month. The examination reveals that the workers in our sample processed a mean ($\overline{X}$) of 24.74 cases, with a standard deviation for the sample (s) equal to 4.16.

At this point, you should recognize the problem as one that's remarkably similar to those we covered in the previous section, with one minor exception. In the present example, we don't know the value of the standard deviation of the population (σ). Instead, what we have is the standard deviation for our sample (s). Nonetheless, the structure of the problem is identical to what we covered earlier. We want to determine if there is a significant difference between productivity of caseworkers throughout the state and that of the caseworkers in our region. As we move ahead with the problem, let's assume that we've decided to work at the .05 level of significance.

To deal with the fact that we don't know the value of σ, we'll make two minor changes. First, we'll rely on the family of t distributions to obtain our critical value (instead of relying on Z values). Second, we'll have to estimate the standard error of the mean (instead of calculating it in a direct fashion). By now you should recognize those as the same changes we made when we moved from the construction of a confidence interval for the mean with σ known to the construction of a confidence interval for the mean when σ is unknown.

 LEARNING CHECK

Question: In a single sample hypothesis test, what is the difference in the procedures when sigma is unknown as opposed to when sigma is known?

Answer: When sigma is unknown, the standard error of the mean is estimated and t is used. When sigma is known, the standard error of the mean is calculated in a direct fashion and Z is used.

In the material about confidence intervals, you learned quite a bit about the family of t distributions. In the same context, you also learned how to estimate the standard error of the mean. Just to refresh your memory, here's the formula we use to estimate the standard error of the mean.

$$s_{\overline{x}} = \frac{s}{\sqrt{n}}$$

Now we have everything we need to tackle the problem.

Applying the Test

The formula we'll use in this case is the same as the one we used in our previous (flextime) example, with the exception of the two minor changes

I mentioned earlier. You'll note that the formula now reflects a *t* value (as opposed to *Z*), and we use the estimate (instead of the calculated value) of the standard error of the mean.

Calculation. For the sake of clarity, let's start with the formula for estimating standard error of the mean.

$$s_{\bar{x}} = \frac{s}{\sqrt{n}}$$

$$s_{\bar{x}} = \frac{4.16}{\sqrt{30}}$$

$$s_{\bar{x}} = \frac{4.16}{5.48}$$

$$s_{\bar{x}} = 0.76$$

Now we use the formula for calculating the test statistic. Note that now we are calculating *t* instead of *Z*.

$$t = \frac{\overline{X} - \mu}{s_{\bar{x}}}$$

$$t = \frac{24.74 - 23.12}{0.76}$$

$$t = \frac{1.62}{0.76}$$

$$t = 2.13$$

As you learned in the last chapter, we'll have to take note of the relevant degrees of freedom in using the family of *t* distributions. As before, our degrees of freedom will be calculated as *n* − 1. Once we determine the appropriate number of degrees of freedom (in this case, 30 − 1 = 29), we take note of the corresponding row in Appendix B. Since we're not constructing a confidence interval, we don't have to go through any mental conversion (1 minus the level of significance) to locate the appropriate column. Instead, we can focus directly on the appropriate column—in this case, the one labeled .05 level of significance. Once we find the intersection of the appropriate degrees of freedom row (29) and the appropriate level of significance column (.05), we take note of the *t* value of 2.045, which we can round to 2.05. That *t* value—2.05— becomes our critical value. As before, it is this value that our calculated *t* value (or *t* ratio) must meet or exceed if we're to reject the null hypothesis. We now have all the information we need to come to a conclusion and interpretation.

Interpretation. With a calculated test statistic at hand (a *t* ratio of 2.13), and knowledge of the critical value at the .05 level of significance (2.05), we're in a position to formulate a conclusion and interpretation. Since our calculated *t* value exceeds the critical value, we're in a position to reject the null hypothesis. We can reject the null hypothesis with the knowledge that there is a 5% chance or probability of having made a Type I error.

Though we never know whether or not we actually committed a Type I, or alpha, error, we always know the probability of having done so. In this case, we know it is .05, or 5%. We know that because that's what the level of significance is all about—it is simply a statement of the probability of making a Type I error.

Some Variations on a Theme

Now let's consider some more examples. We can use the same situation as before, comparing the performance of the caseworkers in our region to the population of caseworkers throughout the state, but let's alter the specifics in various ways. This is one of the best ways to school yourself on the logic of hypothesis testing, from the point of setting up the hypothesis all the way through the point of conclusion and interpretation.

Let's assume that much of the problem remains the same: the same mean ($\overline{X}$ = 24.74), the same standard deviation of the sample (4.16 cases per month), and the same population mean (23.12 cases per month). As to the sample size (*n*), we'll vary that a bit. If the sample size changes, we'll have to change our estimate of the standard error of the mean, but that's easily dealt with. Finally, let's vary the level of significance. As I said before, all these variations, taken together, should give you a solid grounding in all that's involved in deriving a conclusion and interpretation of the hypothesis test.

Situation: First let's assume that we're working with a sample of 16 caseworkers instead of 30, and that everything else about the problem remains the same. How would the conclusion change, if at all?

Commentary: The change in the number of cases (*n*) results in two immediate changes. The number of degrees of freedom changes to 15 (*n* − 1 = 15), and the estimate of the standard error of the mean changes from 0.76 to 1.04. With the change in degrees of freedom, the critical value of *t* becomes 2.13. The larger estimate of the standard error of the mean results in a smaller calculated *t*—it is now 1.56. The calculated value of 1.56 does not equal or exceed the critical value of 2.13. Therefore, we would fail to reject the null hypothesis.

Situation: Let's assume that we're working with a sample of 61 caseworkers instead of 30, and that we're working at the .01 level of significance. Everything else about the problem remains the same. How would the conclusion change, if at all?

Commentary: As above, the change in the number of cases (61) results in two immediate changes. The number of degrees of freedom changes to 60 (*n* − 1 = 60), and the estimate of the standard error of the mean becomes 0.53. With degrees of freedom = 60 and our level of significance set at .01, the critical value is 2.66. The smaller estimate of the standard error of the mean results in a larger calculated *t*—it is now 3.06. The calculated value of 3.06 exceeds the critical value of 2.66. Therefore, we would reject the null hypothesis at the .01 level of significance. We reject the null with the knowledge that there's a 1% chance or probability of having made a Type I error.

Situation: Let's assume that we're working with a sample of 20 caseworkers instead of 30, and that we're working at the .01 level of significance. Everything else about the problem remains the same. How would the conclusion change, if at all?

Commentary: As above, the change in the number of cases (20) results in two immediate changes. The number of degrees of freedom changes to 19 ($n - 1 = 19$), and the estimate of the standard error of the mean becomes 0.93. With degrees of freedom = 19 and our level of significance set at .01, the critical value is 2.86. The change in the estimate of the standard error of the mean results in a change of the final calculated *t*—it is now 1.74. The calculated value of 1.74 does not meet or exceed the critical value of 2.66. Therefore, we would fail to reject the null hypothesis.

And so it goes. Different answers and different conclusions—all dependent on a couple of factors (namely, the number of cases and the level of significance).

Chapter Summary

As we bring this chapter to a close, take a moment or two to reflect again on what we've covered. As I mentioned at the outset, the chapter is as much about hypothesis testing as it is about a particular application. Indeed, if you were to get just one thing out of the chapter, I would hope it would be that—the logic of hypothesis testing.

As to the application—a single sample test—by now you should have a fairly solid understanding about how it can be used. For example, you should now know what's involved when you want to test a hypothesis involving a single sample. You should know that the underlying logic remains the same, whether σ is known or unknown. Indeed, you should know by now that the variations in the two approaches trace squarely back to the differences you encountered when constructing confidence intervals for the mean (with σ known and σ unknown).

Perhaps most important, you should have digested the fundamentals of hypothesis testing logic along the way. The new concepts—null hypothesis, critical value and critical region, level of significance, and Type I and II errors—are concepts you will encounter over and over again. Specific statistical applications will change from situation to situation, but the fundamental logic will remain the same. As I'm fond of telling my students at this point in their statistical journey, the logic of hypothesis testing is a little bit like Mozart's music—or rap music, for that matter: It's the same darned thing over and over again.

Some Other Things You Should Know

Let me bring two matters to your attention at this point. One has to do with how the logic you just encountered extends to other types of research situations. The other has to do with a possible source of confusion that you may encounter down the road.

As to the first of these matters, let me mention that the logic you encountered in this chapter extends to hypotheses involving proportions as well as means. For example, a simple procedure will allow you to determine if a proportion (or percentage value) observed in a sample differs significantly from a known or assumed proportion in a population. The procedure is directly analogous to the research situations covered in this chapter, with one exception—the focus is on proportions, rather than means. For a discussion of this procedure, consult Utts and Heckard (2002).

As to the possible confusion that may arise down the road, let me ask you to focus on the fundamental difference between the material you encountered in this chapter and the material presented in the previous chapter. My experience tells me that students often confuse the material, probably because all of the material falls into the category of inferential statistics and all the material is tied to the use of Z or t. Let me offer a simple way out of this possible confusion.

As you think about the material we covered in Chapter 6, think about the purpose of the procedures that we explored. There, we constructed confidence intervals. We didn't test hypotheses; we didn't even formulate hypotheses. We simply constructed confidence intervals. Our goal was to make statements about population parameters, based on sample statistics. We were developing estimates.

In the present chapter, however, our goal was different. In this chapter, we set out to test hypotheses. Yes, we calculated Z and we calculated t. We used the Table of Areas Under the Normal Curve and we used the table for the distribution of t (Family of t Distributions). Those are the same elements that came into play when we were constructing confidence intervals. But there was a major difference, and it had to do with our ultimate purpose. Remember: We construct a confidence interval because we want to estimate the value of a population parameter. Testing a hypothesis represents a very different goal.

Key Terms

calculated test statistic
critical region
critical value
hypothesis
level of significance

null hypothesis
region of rejection
Type I error
Type II error

Chapter Problems

Fill in the blanks, calculate the requested values, or otherwise supply the correct answer.

General Thought Questions

1. The level of significance is the probability of making a(n) _____ error.
2. Rejecting a null hypothesis when it is true represents a(n) _____ error.
3. Failing to reject a null hypothesis when it is false represents a(n) _____ error.
4. The _____ is represented by the symbol H_0.
5. The alpha level is also known as the level of _____.
6. Another name for the region of rejection is the _____.
7. If your calculated test statistic does not meet or exceed the critical value, you would _____ the null hypothesis.
8. The levels of significance most commonly used by statisticians are the _____ and ____ levels.
9. When our calculated test statistic falls within the _____, we reject the _____.

Application Questions/Problems: Hypothesis Test Based on a Single Sample $\overline{X}$ With σ Known

1. The police department of a major city reports that the mean number of auto thefts per neighborhood per year is (μ) 6.88 with a standard deviation (σ) of 1.19. As the mayor of a suburban community just outside the major city, you're curious as to how the auto theft rate in your community compares. You determine that the mean ($\overline{X}$) number of auto thefts per neighborhood per year for a random sample of 15 neighborhoods in your community is 8.13. Assume that you're working at the .05 level of significance.
   a. State an appropriate null hypothesis.
   b. What is the value of the calculated test statistic (Z)?
   c. State your conclusion.

2. Reports indicate that graduating seniors in a local high school have an average (μ) reading comprehension score of 72.55 with a standard deviation (σ) of 12.62. As an instructor in a GED program that provides alternative educational opportunities for students, you're curious how seniors in your program compare. Selecting a sample of 25 students from your program and administering the same reading comprehension test, you discover a sample mean ($\overline{X}$) of 79.53. Assume that you're working at the .05 level of significance.

a. State an appropriate null hypothesis.
b. What is the value of the calculated test statistic (Z)?
c. State your conclusion.

3. Students participating in a drug education program are given a drug awareness test at the beginning of the program. The mean score (μ) for the population of 526 students is 61, with a standard deviation (σ) of 12. As program director, you're curious as to how parents of the students perform on the drug awareness test and whether or not they are significantly different from the students. Selecting a random sample of 50 parents, you administer the test and discover a mean drug awareness score ($\overline{X}$) of 56. Assume that you're working at the .05 level of significance.
   a. State an appropriate null hypothesis.
   b. What is the value of the calculated test statistic (Z)?
   c. State your conclusion.

4. The mean (μ) educational level for adults in a community is reported as 10.45 years of school completed with a standard deviation (σ) of 3.8. Responses to a questionnaire by a sample of 40 adult community residents indicate a mean educational level ($\overline{X}$) of 11.45. Assume that you're working at the .05 level of significance.
   a. State an appropriate null hypothesis.
   b. What is the value of the calculated test statistic (Z)?
   c. State your conclusion.

5. The historical mean level of production workers at an industrial plant is shown to be 155 units produced per day, with a standard deviation of 15. Following the introduction of a new flextime worker option, a sample of productivity reports for 100 flextime workers reveals a sample mean ($\overline{X}$) of 160. Assume that you're working at the .05 level of significance.
   a. State an appropriate null hypothesis.
   b. What is the value of the calculated test statistic (Z)?
   c. State your conclusion.

6. A standardized test, designed to measure the mathematical skill level of seventh graders is said to have a mean score (μ) = 75 with a standard deviation (σ) = 10. As the principal of a private school, you're curious how seventh graders, in your school compare. Selecting a sample of 25 students from your school and administering the mathematical skill test, you discover a sample mean ($\overline{X}$) of 79. Assume that you're working at the .05 level of significance.
   a. State an appropriate null hypothesis.
   b. What is the value of the calculated test statistic (Z)?
   c. State your conclusion.

Application Questions/Problems: Hypothesis Test Based on a Single Sample Mean With σ Unknown

1. The mean (μ) level of absenteeism rate for the local school district is reported as 8.45 days per year, per student. The mean rate ($\overline{X}$) for a sample of 30 students enrolled in a vocational training program is reported as 6.79 days per year with a standard deviation (s) of 2.56 days. Assume that you're working at the .05 level of significance.
   a. State an appropriate null hypothesis.
   b. What is the value of the calculated test statistic (t)?
   c. Identify the critical value.
   d. State your conclusion.

2. The national mean (μ) absentee rate for workers working for the Old Mill Store Company is reported as 8.25 days per year. The mean rate ($\overline{X}$) for a sample of 14 workers working at your Old Mill Store franchise is reported as 7.53 days per year with a standard deviation (s) of 2.72 days. Assume that you are working at the .05 level of significance.
   a. State an appropriate null hypothesis.
   b. What is the value of the calculated test statistic (t)?
   c. Identify the critical value.
   d. State your conclusion.

3. Information collected at a local university indicates that students are working, on average (a value for μ) 15.23 hours per week while in school. Information collected from a random sample of 25 fraternity members, however, reveals a mean of 12.34 hours per week with a standard deviation (s) of 2.50 hours. Assume that you're working at the .05 level of significance.
   a. State an appropriate null hypothesis.
   b. What is the value of the calculated test statistic (t)?
   c. Identify the critical value.
   d. State your conclusion.

4. Information collected at a local university indicates that business majors enroll for an average (μ) of 10.65 credit hours per semester. As the Dean of the School of Communication, you are interested in how journalism majors compare. Taking a sample of enrollment records on 31 journalism majors, you find a mean ($\overline{X}$) credit hour enrollment of 12.22 hours, with a standard deviation (s) of 3.26. Assume that you're working at the .05 level of significance.
   a. State an appropriate null hypothesis.
   b. What is the value of the calculated test statistic (t)?
   c. Identify the critical value.
   d. State your conclusion.

5. A recent news report indicates that the mean (μ) number of years that first-time drug offenders are sentenced is 12.16. A sample of 25 court records from your county indicates a mean number of years = 11.24, with a standard deviation of 3.11. Assume that you're working at the .05 level of significance.
   a. State an appropriate null hypothesis.
   b. What is the value of the calculated test statistic (t)?
   c. Identify the critical value.
   d. State your conclusion.

6. A recent news report asserts that the weekly mean (μ) number of drinks (both mixed drinks and beer) consumed by college students is 12.56 drinks. Data from a sample of 30 students enrolled at your university indicate a weekly consumption level ($\overline{X}$) of 11.21 drinks, with a standard deviation (s) of 3.88. Assume that you're working at the .05 level of significance.
   a. State an appropriate null hypothesis.
   b. What is the value of the calculated test statistic (t)?
   c. Identify the critical value.
   d. State your conclusion.

8

Hypothesis Testing With Two Samples (Mean Difference and Difference of Means)

In this chapter, we expand on the logic we covered in the last chapter. Instead of working with single sample research questions, we'll now take up the two sample case. The applications we're going to cover are typically referred to as difference of means tests. As before, we'll be looking at information collected from samples, but our real interest will extend to the realm of two populations. You already have the background to deal with difference of means tests on a conceptual level. From the formulation of a null hypothesis, to the identification of a critical value, through the conclusion and interpretation of results, you've traveled the road of hypothesis-testing basics. What's more, you'll likely discover that the research questions involving difference of means tests are very straightforward.

The research situations that call for a difference of means test typically fall into two categories: situations involving matched or related samples, and situations involving independent samples. That's the order we'll follow in this chapter.

Before We Begin

I'm going to make a suggestion that you may or may not appreciate. I'm going to ask you to go back to the previous chapter as soon as you finish this chapter. That's right; first complete this chapter and then take another look at the previous chapter. I know that may sound strange, but there's a reason why I suggest it. I believe that many students of statistics have an easier time understanding hypothesis testing involving two samples than hypothesis testing involving one sample. As to why that might be the case, maybe it's because the idea of comparing two groups (or more correctly, two samples) is such a commonplace activity, whether it is warranted or not. At any rate, my experience tells me that it is with the two sample applications that students typically start to get comfortable with hypothesis testing. Therefore, if you struggled with the last chapter or you still don't feel on solid ground with it, let me urge you to move ahead with this chapter. Once you're through, go back to the previous chapter.

Related Samples

To say that two samples are **matched or related** in some way is to say that the cases included in the samples were not selected independently of one another. Let me give you a few examples.

Let's say we give a group of students a drug awareness test, measuring their awareness of the dangers of recreational drug use. Then we show the students a film about the dangers of recreational drug use, and we administer the test again. In this case, we will be measuring the same people twice—once before exposure to the film and again after exposure to the film. This is an example of a classic before/after test situation—a situation in which the participants are matched against themselves, so to speak. Each person is tested twice, and the focus is on any change in the test scores that occurs between the first and second tests. The two samples are obviously related to each other; they involve the same people, measured twice.

Another example might involve measuring attitudes of couples who are engaged to one another. Let's say that we're collecting information about their expectations concerning marriage, placing the males in one sample and the females in another. In this situation, the cases or people in one sample are clearly linked to the cases in the other. If the research question looked at differences between men and women in general with respect to expectations about marriage, the problem could be approached without a matched or related sample design. When the focus is on couples, however, and how the male and female members of couples differ, the question calls for a matched or related sample approach.

For a final example, consider a research situation that involves comparing the productivity of two groups of workers in different environments (such as a 5-day, 8-hour work schedule versus a 4-day, 10-hour work schedule). If research participants are selected in such a way that they are matched, for example, on the basis of age, sex, pay grade, and length of time on the job, it would be appropriate to treat the research situation as a matched sample design.

 LEARNING CHECK

Question: What are matched or related samples?
Answer: Matched or related samples are samples involving cases or subjects that share certain characteristics in common.

In all of these examples, the two samples were somehow linked on a case-by-case basis. In the first instance, a person's score on the second drug awareness test was linked back to his/her score on the first test. The focus was on any difference between the score on the first test and the score on the second. In the marital expectation scenario, a person's responses concerning expectations about marriage were linked to those of another person to whom he/she was socially tied. The focus was on any difference between the scores of the two individuals who made up a couple. In the final example, each worker in one sample was related (by matching on relevant criteria) to another worker in the other sample. To more fully grasp the structure of such research situations, consider Table 8-1.

With the basic structure of the research situation in mind, we can now turn to the logic of the matched sample test application.

The Logic of the Test

The logic in this application begins with the notion of what constitutes a difference. Let's look at the drug awareness scenario again as a starting point. Consider the set of scores presented in Table 8-2, reflecting performance on

Table 8-1 The Focus of Interest With the *t* Test for Related or Matched Samples

These differences are found by subtracting one score from the other score (score in Sample 1 from score in Sample 2, or vice versa).

Sample 1		Sample 2	Differences
Score/Value	----▸	Score/Value	d
Score/Value	----▸	Score/Value	d
Score/Value	----▸	Score/Value	d
Score/Value	----▸	Score/Value	d
Score/Value	----▸	Score/Value	d
Score/Value	----▸	Score/Value	d
Score/Value	----▸	Score/Value	d
Score/Value	----▸	Score/Value	d
Score/Value	----▸	Score/Value	d
Score/Value	----▸	Score/Value	d
			$\overline{D}$

This is the mean of the differences ($\overline{D}$).

Table 8-2 Results From Drug Awareness Test

Subject	Test 1 T_1	Test 2 T_2	Difference d
1	50	55	5
2	77	79	2
3	67	82	15
4	94	90	−4
5	64	64	0
6	77	83	6
7	85	80	−5
8	52	55	3
9	81	79	−2
10	91	91	0
11	52	61	9
12	61	77	16
13	83	83	0
14	66	70	4
15	71	75	4

$$\Sigma d = 53$$
$$\overline{D} = 53/15 = 3.53$$

the test by a sample of 15 participants in a before/after test situation. First, each of 15 participants was administered a drug awareness test, and their scores were recorded. The participants were then shown a film concerning the dangers of recreational drug use. Following exposure to the film, the 15 participants were given the drug awareness test again, and these scores were recorded, as shown in Table 8-2.

The object of our interest is the differences listed in the right-hand column of the table (column labeled Difference or d). This column includes positive differences, negative differences, and zero differences. To find the mean of those differences, we simply add up all the differences and divide by 15: 53/15 = 3.53. If we use the symbol $\bar{D}$ to indicate the mean of the differences (*ds*), then

$$\bar{D} = \frac{\Sigma d}{n}$$

$$\bar{D} = \frac{53}{15}$$

$$\bar{D} = 3.53$$

Thus, we're in a position to say that the mean of our sample differences is 3.53.

Just as we can calculate a mean of the differences, we can also calculate a standard deviation of the differences as follows:

$$s_d = \sqrt{\frac{\Sigma(d - \bar{D})^2}{n - 1}}$$

$$s_d = \sqrt{\frac{525.72}{15 - 1}}$$

$$s_d = \sqrt{37.55}$$

$$s_d = 6.13$$

Don't let those calculations throw you. The goal is to calculate a standard deviation of the differences (the *ds*). Just think back to the formula that you used before. Recall that the formula involved an $\bar{X}$ and individual X values. This application is the same, except it involves a $\bar{D}$ and individual *d* values.

Just in case you're still feeling a little lost on this matter of how to calculate the standard deviation of the differences, let me urge you to do two things. First, review the material on the standard deviation that you encountered in Chapter 2, paying attention to each element in the process and how the $n - 1$ correction factor is used. Secondly, take a look at the steps outlined in the summary, below. The summary doesn't give you every calculation along the way, but there should be enough information to clear up any confusion.

1. Find the mean of the differences (the mean of the *ds*) and designate it as $\bar{D}$.
2. Find the deviation of each *d* from $\bar{D}(d - \bar{D})$. For example:
   5 − 3.53 = 1.47
   2 − 3.53 = −1.53

15 − 3.53 = 11.47

Continue through all of the *d*s.

3. Square all of the deviations. For example:

1.47 × 1.47 = 2.16

−1.53 × −1.53 = 2.34

11.47 × 11.47 = 131.56

Continue through all of the squared $\bar{D} - d$ values (all the squared deviations).

4. Find the sum of the squared deviations (it will equal 525.72).

5. Divide the sum of the squared deviation by *n* − 1 (i.e., divide 525.72 by 14) and you have 37.55.

6. Find the square root of 37.55.

The square root of 37.55 = 6.13, so that's the answer. The standard deviation of the differences (the standard deviation of the *d*s) is symbolized by s_d. Therefore, s_d = 6.13.

Having determined that the standard deviation (s_d) of the differences (the *d* values) is 6.13, we now have quite a bit of information. We know, for example, that we have 15 observed differences and that the mean of the differences is equal to 3.53 ($\bar{D}$ = 3.53). We also know that the standard deviation of the distribution of differences is equal to 6.13. As you might have guessed, we're right back where we've been before. It's probably a good idea to take another dark room moment right now to think about the situation I'm about to describe.

Imagine that you've taken a sample of 15 people, noted their scores at Time 1 and Time 2, and calculated the differences (*d* values) between the individual scores ($T_1 - T_2$ or $T_2 - T_1$; it doesn't matter which approach you take). Now imagine that you've calculated the mean of those differences ($\bar{D}$) and you've recorded that mean. Now imagine that you repeat that process a thousand times over, each time calculating a mean and recording it.

 LEARNING CHECK

Question: In this application, how do you calculate the *d* values?

Answer: Find the difference between the two scores or values associated with a given research subject or case (e.g., difference between score at Time 1 and Time 2).

By now you should know what the next step is in your mental picture—you're plotting all of those means to create the sampling distribution of mean differences. The question, of course, boils down to the same question you've asked yourself before: Where does my observed mean difference fall along a sampling distribution of all possible mean differences? With that thought in mind, we can now turn to the null hypothesis for this application.

The Null Hypothesis

The null hypothesis in this application is simply a statement that we expect a mean difference of 0. You'll recall from the previous chapter that the null is frequently a statement of no difference, and that notion applies squarely in the present instance. Regardless of what may be operating in the back of our minds—even though we may, in truth, expect a change in scores between the first and the second test—we will test the null. And the null is a statement that we expect the mean difference to be 0. In other words, the null is a statement that we expect there to be no change. Symbolically, we can state the null hypothesis as follows:

$$H_0: \mu_{\overline{D}} = 0$$

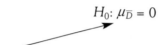

Mean of differences obtained from subtracting score at one time (T_1) from score at another time (T_2)

 LEARNING CHECK

Question: What does the statistical symbol H_0 represent?
Answer: H_0 is the symbol that represents the null hypothesis.

Combining the Logic and the Null

It's a good idea at this point to think about the big picture, in the sense that we're not really interested in what's going on with the samples (the sample at T_1 and the sample at T_2). Rather, we're interested in what's really going on with the populations (the population at T_1 and the population at T_2). We're wondering what we'd discover if we tested the entire population of students at T_1 and retested that entire population at T_2. With the null, we're making the statement that we expect the mean of any differences in the populations to be 0.

Our goal, then, is to compare our observed mean difference to an assumed mean difference of 0. Since we're assuming that the mean difference is 0, we can assume that the mean of the sampling distribution of mean differences is also equal to 0. It's the Central Limit Theorem that allows us to make that assumption. As before, we'll eventually compare our observed mean difference (3.53) to the assumed mean difference of 0, and express the magnitude of any difference between the two values in standard error units. Remember: The estimated standard error in this case will be the estimated standard deviation of a sampling distribution of mean differences (the standard deviation of the distribution you mentally constructed if you took the time for the last dark room moment I suggested).

LEARNING CHECK

Question: What is the definition of the estimate of the standard
error in the case of a *t* test for related sample means?
Answer: It is an estimate of the standard deviation of the sampling
distribution of mean differences.

The Estimate of the Standard Error of the Mean Difference

The estimate of the **standard error of the mean difference** is symbolized by
$s_{\bar{D}}$ and is calculated as follows:

$$s_{\bar{D}} = \frac{s_d}{\sqrt{n}}$$

Where s_d represents the standard deviation of the distribution of differences

You should take note of how similar the formula is to the formula for the estimate of the standard error that you encountered in Chapter 7. Assuming you
know of the standard deviation of the distribution of the *d* values (it was provided
to you or you calculated it), all you have to do is divide that value by the square
root of the sample size. The result is the estimate of the standard error of the
mean difference. In the example we're considering here, it would be as follows:

$$s_{\bar{D}} = \frac{6.13}{\sqrt{15}}$$

$$s_{\bar{D}} = \frac{6.13}{3.87}$$

$$s_{\bar{D}} = 1.58$$

   LEARNING CHECK

Question: How is the estimate of the standard error calculated in
the case of a *t* test for related sample means?
Answer: The standard deviation of the distribution of differences
(in other words, the distribution of the *d* values) is
divided by the square root of *n*.

Applying the Test

The application is now fairly straightforward. All we have to do is compare our
observed mean difference to the assumed mean difference of 0, and divide the
result by our estimate of the standard error. This procedure produces a *t* ratio,

similar to those you've encountered before. A complete formula for the calculation of the t ratio would be as follows:

$$t = \frac{\overline{D} - \mu_{\overline{D}}}{s_{\overline{D}}}$$

Since the second part of the formula ($\mu_{\overline{D}}$) is assumed to be equal to 0, we can drop that element from the formula, leaving ourselves with only the following to consider:

$$t = \frac{\overline{D}}{s_{\overline{D}}}$$

$$t = \frac{3.53}{1.58}$$

$$t = 2.23$$

Working through the calculations, we arrive at a calculated test statistic (t ratio) of 2.23. Now all that remains is to evaluate the calculated test statistic in light of the critical value—the value that our calculated test statistic must meet or exceed if we are to reject the null hypothesis.

 LEARNING CHECK

Question: What does the value of t represent in the t test for related sample means?

Answer: The t value is the calculated test statistic. It is a ratio that expresses how far the observed mean difference departs from the assumed mean difference of 0 in standard error units.

Interpreting the Results

Assuming we had set our level of significance at .05 in advance of our test, our next step is to identify the critical value and move toward a conclusion and interpretation. In a t test for related samples, the degrees of freedom will be our sample size (n) minus 1—in this case, 15 – 1, or 14. Working with 14 degrees of freedom, at the .05 level of significance, we find the critical value of t in Appendix B to be 2.15. Recall that our calculated test statistic (the t ratio) is 2.23.

Since the calculated t value exceeds the critical value, we're in a position to reject the null hypothesis. In other words, we reject the notion that there is no difference between the two populations. We reject the idea that the two populations do not differ from one another (T_1 and T_2). That, of course, is another way of saying that it appears that the two populations do differ. Exposure to the drug awareness film appears to have some effect on test scores.

In rejecting the null hypothesis at the .05 level of significance, we're acknowledging that there's always a chance that we've made a mistake. Yes, we've rejected the null—the expectation that there is no difference. It's possible, though, that there really is no difference and our observed difference was, just by chance, a very extreme case along the sampling distribution of all possible mean differences. If that's what was going on, we've made a Type I error—we've rejected the null when, in fact, it's true. As before, however, we never know whether or not we've committed a Type I error. All we know is the probability of having committed a Type I error, and that probability is our level of significance. Once again, that's why I think it's advisable at this point in your statistical education to offer an interpretation along the following lines: We reject the null with the knowledge that there's a 5% chance that we've committed a Type I error.

Later on, when you're totally comfortable with the logic of hypothesis testing, you can feel free to drop the reference to Type I errors when announcing your conclusion. Until you're comfortable, though, let me suggest you stick with a format that makes reference to the probability of making a Type I error in your conclusion. It's a good way to continually hammer home the logic of hypothesis testing.

Some Additional Examples

Just to make certain that you're on the right track with the t test for related or matched samples, give some time and thought to each of the following questions, paying particular attention to each element that goes into the calculation of the final test statistic (the t ratio).

1. Assume two matched samples, each involving 10 cases ($n = 10$) and the following information:

   Mean of the differences $(\overline{D}) = 11.65$

   Estimated standard error of the mean difference $(s_{\overline{D}}) = 3.39$

   Calculate t. Assuming a .05 level of significance ($\alpha = .05$), do you reject or fail to reject the null hypothesis?

2. Assume two related samples, each involving 10 cases ($n = 10$) and the following information:

   Mean of the differences $(\overline{D}) = 2.70$

   Estimated standard error of the mean difference $(s_{\overline{D}}) = 0.97$

   Calculate t. Assuming a .01 level of significance ($\alpha = .01$), do you reject or fail to reject the null hypothesis?

3. Assume two matched samples, each involving 14 subjects ($n = 14$) and the following information:

   Mean of the differences $(\overline{D}) = 3.42$

   Standard deviation of the differences $(s_d) = 3.46$

Recall the formula for determining the estimated standard error of the mean using n and s_d. Calculate t. Assuming a .05 level of significance ($\alpha = .05$), do you reject or fail to reject the null hypothesis?

4. Assume two matched samples each involving 19 subjects ($n = 19$) and the following information:

Mean of the differences $(\overline{D}) = 7.11$

Standard deviation of the differences $(s_d) = 13.84$

Calculate t. Assuming a .05 level of significance ($\alpha = .05$), do you reject or fail to reject the null hypothesis?

5. Assume two related samples involving the following information:

$n = 22$

$\overline{D} = 3.52$

$s_d = 5.26$

$\alpha = .05$

Discuss your results in terms of the null hypothesis.

Answers:

1. $t = 3.44$
   Reject the null hypothesis at the .05 level of significance.
2. $t = 2.78$
   Fail to reject the null hypothesis at the .01 level of significance.
3. $t = 3.68$
   Reject the null hypothesis at the .05 level of significance.
4. $t = 2.24$
   Reject the null hypothesis at the .05 level of significance.
5. $t = 3.14$
   Reject the null hypothesis at the .05 level of significance.

So much for the t test for related samples. Now we turn our attention to another application involving the t ratio with a focus on differences. In the next application, however, we encounter a very different meaning of *difference*.

Independent Samples

You've just covered the idea of sample differences (and, therefore, population differences) in one context. Now you'll encounter a different context—one with a new notion as to what constitutes a difference. While the last application is still fresh in your mind, let's turn to the next application.

Suppose that I asked you how you'd go about determining whether or not there's a difference between the drinking habits of fraternity members and nonfraternity members. My guess is that you'd probably give me a fairly good explanation. For example, you'd very likely tell me that you'd start by getting a random sample of fraternity members and a random sample of nonfraternity members. Then you might tell me that you'd get information on their drinking habits (maybe by asking them how many drinks they typically consume in a week). Maybe you'd go so far as to tell me you'd calculate the mean ($\overline{X}$) number of drinks for each sample, just so you'd have a starting point to compare the two groups. Assuming you outlined the problem that way, I'd say "Congratulations! You're on the right track." You've just outlined the basic elements in an independent sample research design.

The key notion in all of that—**independent samples**—is the idea that the sample of fraternity members is selected independently of the sample of non-members. In other words, the selection of cases for one sample in no way affects the selection of cases in the other sample. Even if we selected a single sample of students at random and then divided that sample into two groups (fraternity members and nonmembers), we would be dealing with the same principle of independence.

 LEARNING CHECK

Question: What does the phrase *independent samples* mean?
Answer: Independent samples are samples selected in such a way that the selection of cases or subjects included in one sample has no connection to or influence on the selection of cases or subjects in the other sample.

With all of that in mind, let's assume that we undertake the research you have outlined, and let's say we obtain the data regarding number of drinks per week found in Table 8-3.

The Logic of the Test

The present application allows us to compare the means of two samples with an eye toward whether or not any difference is a reflection of a true difference between the populations. So much for the central goal of the test. Now let's turn to the elements that make up the structure of the test. As a prelude, take a close look at Table 8-4.

Table 8-3   Data Regarding Drinks per Week

Fraternity	Nonfraternity
6	0
3	5
2	3
4	4
5	3
6	6
7	3
5	6
4	5
5	4
4	4
8	2
6	$n = 12$
7	$\overline{X} = 3.75$
$n = 14$	$s = 1.71$
$\overline{X} = 5.14$	
$s = 1.66$	

Study based on a sample of 14 fraternity members and a sample of 12 nonmembers

Mean of nonmembers = 3.75.

Mean of fraternity members = 5.14.

Standard deviation of nonmembers = 1.71.

Standard deviation of fraternity members = 1.66.

 LEARNING CHECK

Question: In the *t* test for difference of means for independent samples, which difference is the object of interest?

Answer: The test focuses on the difference between the mean of one sample and the mean of another sample, with an eye toward the extent to which any observed difference represents a true difference between population means.

You're already familiar with the notion of a sampling distribution of sample means when dealing with a single sample. You know, for example, that you could take sample after sample after sample, and each sample is apt to yield a slightly different sample mean. As it turns out, the same logic applies in a situation involving the difference between two samples. Returning to our example

Table 8-4 The Focus of Interest With the *t* Test for Independent Samples

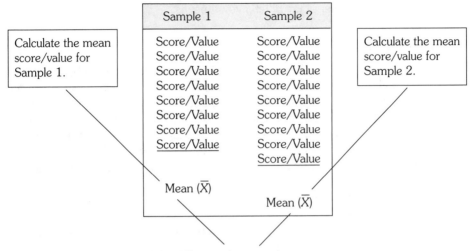

Find the difference between the two means.
The null is a statement that we expect the difference to be 0.

involving the drinking habits of fraternity members and nonmembers, consider the following:

- You could take a sample of fraternity members and a sample of nonmembers. You could calculate the mean of each sample, calculate the difference between the two means, and record that difference.
- You could then take another two samples, calculate the mean of each sample, and record the difference between those means.
- You could repeat the process over and over again—each time calculating the mean of each sample, noting any difference between the two means, and recording that difference.
- You could eventually produce a plot or distribution of all of those differences. That plot or distribution would be known as a *sampling distribution of the differences of means*.

If necessary, run that material through your mind again as a dark room moment. Take the time to mentally focus on the difference between the means that you get each time you select two samples. Focus on the fact that you're interested in the difference between the means of pairs of samples.

As you might expect, the question will ultimately come down to a matter of how extreme our observed difference between two means is in comparison to all possible differences that we might observe. It's similar to the question you've faced before—whether or not an observation is an extreme value along a sampling distribution (in this case, of the difference of means).

The Null Hypothesis

Assuming you took a careful look at Table 8-4, you noticed a central element in the logical underpinnings of the *t* test for independent samples—namely, a reference to the null hypothesis that there is no difference between the means. More specifically, the null hypothesis is a statement that there is no difference between the means of the two populations. As before, we may be looking at samples, but our interest is in what's going on with the populations from which the samples were taken. In symbolic terms, we can state the null hypothesis in two different ways:

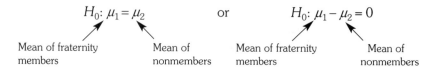

$$H_0: \mu_1 = \mu_2 \qquad \text{or} \qquad H_0: \mu_1 - \mu_2 = 0$$

Mean of fraternity members   Mean of nonmembers   Mean of fraternity members   Mean of nonmembers

Combining the Logic and the Null

Now we're back in familiar territory. If the null hypothesis is true, we'd expect the mean of the sampling distribution of the difference between means to equal 0. Moreover, we'd expect any observed difference between two sample means to be fairly close to 0. It all boils down to whether or not our observed difference is extreme.

As before, we'll assume we're working at the .05 level of significance. The question now turns on what constitutes an extreme difference and the magnitude of any observed difference, expressed in standard error units. Remember: It doesn't matter whether we're considering differences in salaries (expressed in dollars), weights (expressed in pounds or ounces), test scores (from 0 to 100), drinks per week, or anything else. It's always a question of how far our observed difference departs from the assumed difference of 0 in standard error units.

The Estimate of the Standard Error of the Difference of Means

In the previous application (the one involving related samples and the drug awareness test), the calculation of the estimate of the standard error was straightforward. We used the standard deviation of the differences as the basis for our estimate of the standard error of the mean difference. We had a distribution of differences (obtained by calculating the difference in test scores for each person), and we calculated the standard deviation of that distribution of differences. It was then a short step to divide the standard deviation by the square root of our sample size (the number of pairs of scores). The result was the estimate of the standard error of the mean difference.

The calculation of the standard error in this application (independent samples) isn't quite so straightforward. In the present case, we're no longer dealing with just one distribution (as we did in the case of the lone distribution of differences). Instead, we're dealing with two distributions. We have a distribution of scores for fraternity members and a distribution of scores for nonmembers. Thus, the estimate of the standard error becomes a bit more complex, and at times, confusing. Here's why.

Complexity and Some Possible Confusion. First, we have to consider that we're dealing with two samples. Besides that, we have to consider that we're often dealing with different sample sizes. The present situation, for example, involves 14 fraternity members but only 12 nonmembers. In other research situations, you might find yourself working with 25 cases in one sample and 45 in another.

It shouldn't take you long to realize that any measure of the variation that's present in a sample is, in part, a function of sample size. For example, you're not apt to pick up much of the variation that exists in a population if you're working with a sample of only 2 cases. A sample of 100 cases, though, will probably provide a fairly good representation of the variation. Given that, it stands to reason that our formula for the estimate of the standard error of the difference of means will be sensitive to the number of cases in each sample.

Another source of complexity (and perhaps confusion) stems from the fact that the formula begins with a consideration of the *variance* for each sample. In the previous application (involving related samples), as well as various applications in the last chapter, we used the *standard deviation* to develop our estimate of the standard error. (We simply took the standard deviation and divided it by the square root of the sample size.) In the present application, though, we'll first look at sample variances as we set out to calculate the estimate of the standard error.

The reason why we'll start with the variances traces back to the previous point—the need to take into account different sample sizes. As you probably recall, the standard deviation is the square root of the variance. Conversely, the variance is merely the standard deviation squared (s^2). Given that relationship, you might be inclined to approach the problem of different sample sizes by weighting the standard deviations of the samples—that is, multiplying the standard deviations by different values to reflect the different sample sizes.

The truth of the matter, though, is that the variance is always calculated first. We first calculate a variance, and then we take the square root of it to obtain the standard deviation. It's true that you often see statistical problems or data summaries presented with only the standard deviation given (and not the variance), but you can rest assured of one thing: The variance was calculated first.

Besides that, you should give some thought to the effect that weighting has on a variance, as opposed to a standard deviation. Let's say, for example, that we want to weight some values by a factor of 10. A *variance* of 9, for example, is equal to a *standard deviation* of 3 (the standard deviation being the square root of the variance). The variance times 10 equals 90, and the square root of 90 is 9.487. But 9.487 is hardly the same value as the standard deviation (3) times 10.

With those considerations in mind, you're in a better position to understand why the formula for the estimate of the standard error of the difference of means begins with weighted sample variances. I can assure you that the formula eventually readjusts, so to speak, into an expression of standard deviations, but it begins with a consideration of weighted variances.

All of those issues aside, the real point is what the estimate of the standard error of the difference of means allows us to do. As the standard error has done before in the other applications we've tackled, it allows us to eventually express the magnitude of the observed difference of means in a standardized way. Now let's see how it is calculated.

The Formula. The formula we'll use to estimate the **standard error of the difference of means** is as follows:

$$s_{\bar{x}_1 - \bar{x}_2} = \sqrt{\frac{(n_1 - 1)s_1^2 + (n_2 - 1)s_2^2}{n_1 + n_2 - 2} \cdot \left[\frac{1}{n_1} + \frac{1}{n_2}\right]}$$

Note: As noted previously, the formula presented for the estimate of the standard error is based on the assumption that the variance and/or standard deviation of each sample was originally calculated by using $n - 1$ in the denominator.

There's no reason to let this formula overwhelm you. Remember: A fair amount of the complexity traces back to the fact that we're initially having to deal with variances (the s^2 values), and we have two samples under consideration. Just to recap the information we have so far concerning the sample results, consider the following summary (see Table 8-3):

Fraternity members	$\bar{X}_1 = 5.14$	$n_1 = 14$	$s_1 = 1.66$
Nonmembers	$\bar{X}_2 = 3.75$	$n_2 = 12$	$s_2 = 1.71$

You'll note that the value of the standard deviation (s) is given. Recalling what we recently covered, you know that all you have to do to obtain the variance is to square the standard deviation. Thus, we determine the variance (s^2) for each of the two samples as follows:

Fraternity members	$s_1^2 = 1.66^2 = 2.76$
Nonmembers	$s_2^2 = 1.71^2 = 2.92$

Armed with the value of the variance and the number of cases for each sample, we're now in a position to develop an estimate of the standard error of the difference of means. Recalling the formula previously presented, we can calculate the estimate of the standard error as follows:

$$s_{\bar{x}_1 - \bar{x}_2} = \sqrt{\frac{(n_1 - 1)s_1^2 + (n_2 - 1)s_2^2}{n_1 + n_2 - 2} \cdot \left[\frac{1}{n_1} + \frac{1}{n_2}\right]}$$

$$s_{\bar{x}_1 - \bar{x}_2} = \sqrt{\frac{(14 - 1)2.76 + (12 - 1)2.29}{14 + 12 - 2} \cdot \left[\frac{1}{14} + \frac{1}{12}\right]}$$

$$s_{\bar{x}_1 - \bar{x}_2} = \sqrt{\frac{(13)2.76 + (11)2.92}{24}} \cdot \left[0.07 + 0.08\right]$$

$$s_{\bar{x}_1 - \bar{x}_2} = \sqrt{\frac{35.88 + 32.12}{24}} \cdot \left[0.15\right]$$

$$s_{\bar{x}_1 - \bar{x}_2} = \sqrt{\frac{68}{24}} \cdot \left[0.15\right]$$

$$s_{\bar{x}_1 - \bar{x}_2} = \sqrt{2.83\left[0.15\right]}$$

$$s_{\bar{x}_1 - \bar{x}_2} = \sqrt{0.42}$$

$$s_{\bar{x}_1 - \bar{x}_2} = 0.65$$

Applying the Test

Now we're in a position to put everything together. To do that, we'll return to the information we now have:

Fraternity members	$\overline{X}_1 = 5.14$	$n_1 = 14$	$s_1^2 = 2.76$
Nonmembers	$\overline{X}_2 = 3.75$	$n_2 = 12$	$s_2^2 = 2.92$

The estimate of the standard error of the difference of means $(s_{\bar{x}_1 - \bar{x}_2}) = .65$.

For the sake of this example, we'll assume we're working at the .05 level of significance.

Our goal is to compare any observed difference between the two means (fraternity members and nonmembers) to an assumed difference of 0, and then to convert the magnitude of any observed difference into standard error units. Accordingly, here's the way the formula looks. As before, we're converting the comparison to a t ratio—hence, the symbol t at the outset of the formula.

$$t = \frac{(\overline{X}_1 - \overline{X}_2) - 0}{s_{\bar{x}_1 - \bar{x}_2}}$$

$$t = \frac{(\overline{X}_1 - \overline{X}_2)}{s_{\bar{x}_1 - \bar{x}_2}}$$

Working our way through the formula, we obtain the following test statistic (our calculated value of t):

$$t = \frac{(5.14 - 3.75)}{0.65}$$

$$t = \frac{1.39}{0.65}$$

$$t = 2.14$$

Interpreting the Results

Now we have a calculated test statistic, t, with a value of 2.14. The question, of course, is whether it represents a significant result. In other words, does the calculated test statistic equal or exceed the critical value? To determine the answer to that question, we return to Appendix B. As before, we focus on the column for the .05 level of significance.

In the case of the t test for the difference of means, the number of degrees of freedom has to reflect the number of cases in each sample. Up to this point we've calculated the number of degrees of freedom as $n - 1$, but now we're dealing with two independent samples. Now we calculate the number of degrees of freedom for each sample, and add the two together. In other words, the number of degrees of freedom in the difference of means test is as follows:

$$(n_1 - 1) + (n_2 - 1) \qquad \text{or} \qquad (n_1 + n_2) - 2$$

In the present example, we're working with one sample of 14 cases and another sample of 12 cases. Therefore, we're working with $(14 - 1) + (12 - 1)$, or 24 degrees of freedom.

Armed with the knowledge that we're working with 24 degrees of freedom at the .05 level of significance, all that remains is to identify the critical value—found by locating the intersection of the appropriate row (degrees of freedom) and column (.05 level of significance) in Appendix B. We note that the critical value is 2.06.

We find that our calculated test statistic ($t = 2.14$) exceeds the critical value of 2.06. Therefore, we can reject the null hypothesis, with the knowledge that there is a 5% chance that we've made a Type I error. By rejecting the null hypothesis, we're rejecting the notion that the two populations (the population of fraternity members and nonmembers) are equal in terms of levels of drinking. In other words, we've found support for the assertion that the means of the two populations are, in fact, different.

Some Additional Examples

Just to increase your familiarity with the process involved in the hypothesis test for the independent samples difference of means test, consider the following problems. Additional problems are included at the end of the chapter.

1. Assume two independent samples and the following information:

Mean of Group 1 $(\overline{X}_1) = 53.92$ Mean of Group 2 $(\overline{X}_2) = 50.0$

Sample size of Group 1 $(n_1) = 11$ Sample size of Group 2 $(n_2) = 17$

Estimated standard error of the difference between means $(s_{\overline{x}_1 - \overline{x}_2}) = 2.80$

Calculate t. Assuming a .05 level of significance ($\alpha = .05$), do you reject or fail to reject the null hypothesis?

2. Assume two unrelated samples and the following information:

Mean of Group 1 ($\overline{X}_1$) = 7.39   Mean of Group 2 ($\overline{X}_2$) = 4.50

Sample size of Group 1 (n_1) = 18   Sample size of Group 2 (n_2) = 8

Estimated standard error of the difference between means $(s_{\overline{x}_1 - \overline{x}_2})$ = 0.90

Calculate t. Assuming a .01 level of significance (α = .01), do you reject or fail to reject the null hypothesis?

3. Assume two independent samples and the following information:

$$\overline{X}_1 = 24.53 \qquad n_1 = 24$$

$$\overline{X}_2 = 26.28 \qquad n_2 = 18$$

$$s_{\overline{x}_1 - \overline{x}_2} = 0.67 \qquad \alpha = .01$$

Calculate t. Do you reject or fail to reject the null hypothesis?

4. Assume two unrelated samples and the following information:

Mean of Group 1 ($\overline{X}_1$) = 6.93   Mean of Group 2 ($\overline{X}_2$) = 4.38

Variance of Group 1 (s_1^2) = 2.86   Variance of Group 2 (s_2^2) = 5.06

Sample size of Group 1 (n_1) = 14   Sample size of Group 2 (n_2) = 16

Recall the formula for calculating the estimated standard error of the difference between means using sample sizes and variances. Calculate t. Assuming a .05 level of significance (α = .05), do you reject or fail to reject the null hypothesis?

5. Assume two independent samples and the following information:

$$\overline{X}_1 = 10.81 \qquad s_1^2 = 1.85 \qquad n_1 = 15$$

$$\overline{X}_2 = 13.14 \qquad s_2^2 = 3.84 \qquad n_2 = 11$$

$$\alpha = .05$$

Calculate t. Do you reject or fail to reject the null hypothesis?

Answers:

1. t = 1.40
   Fail to reject the null hypothesis at the .05 level of significance.
2. t = 3.21
   Reject the null hypothesis at the .01 level of significance.
3. t = −2.61
   Fail to reject the null hypothesis at the .01 level of significance.
4. t = 3.49
   Reject the null hypothesis at the .05 level of significance.
5. t = −3.53
   Reject the null hypothesis at the .05 level of significance.

Chapter Summary

This chapter introduced you to one of the most commonly encountered research situations—those based on two samples. As you worked your way through the material, you discovered several important ideas and considerations that are brought to bear in two sample research situations.

First, you explored the variations in research designs as you considered related sample designs and then independent sample designs. In the process, you learned that each looks at the concept of a difference in its own way. Accordingly, you learned that different research designs call for different approaches to the calculation of the *t* ratio.

Despite those fundamental differences, you should have been aware of the central theme that is present in both research situations—namely, the basic logic of hypothesis-testing situations. By now, the rather uniform approach should be solidified in your mind. For example, you probably sense by now that the applications always begin with the formulation of a null hypothesis and selection of a level of significance. From that point, you move to the calculation of a test statistic and comparison of that test statistic to a critical value. Based on your evaluation of the test statistic in light of the critical value, you arrive at a conclusion (you either reject or fail to reject the null hypothesis).

The importance of this hypothesis-testing process and logic can't be overstated. You'll encounter the same sort of logic in most statistical test situations. The research situations will vary. The particular test that is called for will vary. But the underlying logical structure remains similar across the applications.

Some Other Things You Should Know

The difference of means test is such a widely used statistical procedure that you deserve to know a few more things about it. Toward that end, we'll consider some of the assumptions that underlie application of the difference of means test. We'll also take an abbreviated look at how to approach the test when large samples are available and what to do to test hypotheses about differences between proportions.

The *t* tests both for independent and for related or matched samples rest on the assumption that the populations in question are normally distributed. This particular assumption is of more importance with small samples and can be relaxed somewhat in situations involving large samples. There's also an assumption that the populations involved in the independent samples application have equal variances. For an excellent discussion of both of these assumptions, as well as how the assumption of equality of variance can be tested, see Gravetter and Wallnau (2000).

For the independent samples application with large samples, the appropriate test statistic is Z. Here's what that means in practical terms:

- Instead of calculating t, you would calculate Z if the combined number of cases $(n_1 + n_2)$ is greater than 100.
- The formula remains the same, except that Z replaces t at the beginning of the formula:

$$Z = \frac{(\overline{X}_1 - \overline{X}_2)}{s_{\overline{x}_1 - \overline{x}_2}}$$

- If you are calculating Z, you use the Table of Areas Under the Normal Curve (the sampling distribution of Z) to obtain the appropriate critical value. Accordingly, degrees of freedom are of no consideration.

Finally, let me call your attention to yet another two sample test situation—the difference of proportions test. Situations calling for such a test would include questions about whether the proportion of people favoring a certain candidate has changed significantly over time or whether the proportion of students favoring evening courses is significantly different among students in state universities and private universities. This test shares the same logic as the difference of means tests you've just encountered, but the focus is on proportions as opposed to means. For a discussion of the difference of proportions test, see Healy (2002).

Key Terms

independent samples
matched or related samples

standard error of the difference of means
standard error of the mean difference

Chapter Problems

Fill in the blanks, calculate the requested values, or otherwise supply the correct answer.

General Thought Questions

1. In a matched samples design (the test involving the mean difference) the number of cases in each sample must be equal. True or false?
2. In the test for the difference of means, independent sample design, the number of cases in each sample must be equal. True or false?
3. In the matched samples design (the design based on the mean difference), the sampling distribution at issue is the sampling distribution of
   _____.

4. In the independent samples design (the design based on the difference of means), the sampling distribution at issue is the sampling distribution of

_____ .

Application Questions/Problems: Matched/Related Samples Design

1. Assume you are working with the results of a research situation based on a matched sample design involving 15 participants (the same participants in a before/after test situation). The mean difference $(\overline{D}) = 14.66$, with an estimate of the standard error of the mean difference $(s_{\overline{D}}) = 5.21$. Assume that you're working at the .05 level of significance.
   a. Formulate an appropriate null hypothesis.
   b. Calculate t.
   c. Identify the critical value.
   d. State your conclusion.

2. Assume you are working with the results of a research situation based on a matched sample design involving 25 participants (the same participants in a before/after test situation). The mean difference $(\overline{D}) = 9.72$, with an estimate of the standard error of the mean difference $(s_{\overline{D}}) = 6.33$. Assume that you're working at the .05 level of significance.
   a. Formulate an appropriate null hypothesis.
   b. Calculate t.
   c. Identify the critical value.
   d. State your conclusion.

3. Thirty program participants have been given a test designed to measure their reading comprehension skill levels. Following a two-week course, designed to improve reading comprehension skills, the same participants are re-tested. The mean difference $(\overline{D}) = 5.43$, with an estimate of the standard error of the mean difference $(s_{\overline{D}}) = 2.11$. Assume that you're working at the .05 level of significance.
   a. Formulate an appropriate null hypothesis.
   b. Calculate t.
   c. Identify the critical value.
   d. State your conclusion.

4. Professor Johnson administers a 50 point test to the students in her class $(n = 29)$ at the beginning of the semester (T_1) to measure their understanding of basic sociological concepts. She administers the same test to the students at the conclusion of the semester (T_2), and records each student's T_1 and T_2 scores. She obtains the following:

   The mean of the distribution of differences $(\overline{D})$ between the students' T_1 and T_2 scores is equal to 6.57, with an estimate of the standard error of the mean difference $(s_{\overline{D}}) = 2.88$.

   Assume that you're working at the .05 level of significance.
   a. Formulate an appropriate null hypothesis.
   b. Calculate t.

    c. Identify the critical value.

    d. State your conclusion.

5. A geographer selects 30 counties from the north and 30 counties from the south, matching the two samples on the basis of urban/rural status (whether the county is inside or outside of a metropolitan area), dominant economic activity (manufacturing, retail, service, etc.), voter pattern in the last presidential election (whether the majority voted for the Republican or Democratic candidate). Focusing on the percentage of registered voters who actually voted in the last presidential election, the researcher obtains the following results:

> The mean of the distribution of differences $(\overline{D})$ between northern counties and southern counties for voter turnout is equal to 4.00%, with an estimate of the standard error of the mean difference $(s_{\overline{D}})$ = 2.35%.

Assume that you're working at the .05 level of significance.

    a. Formulate an appropriate null hypothesis.

    b. Calculate t.

    c. Identify the critical value.

    d. State your conclusion.

Application Questions/Problems: Independent Sample Design

1. Calculate t for the following research situation involving two independent samples, Sample A and Sample B. (Assume that you are subtracting the Mean of Sample B from the Mean of Sample A).

    Mean of Sample A = 12.65; n = 15

    Mean of Sample B = 10.42; n = 18

    Estimate of the standard error of the difference of means $(s_{\overline{x}_1 - \overline{x}_2})$ = .75. Assume that you're working at the .05 level of significance.

    a. Formulate an appropriate null hypothesis.

    b. Calculate t statistic.

    c. Identify the critical value.

    d. State your conclusion.

2. Consider a research situation involving two independent samples, Sample A and Sample B. (Assume that you are subtracting the Mean of Sample B from the Mean of Sample A).

    Mean of Sample A = 30.45 n = 25

    Mean of Sample B = 26.54 n = 27

    Estimate of the standard error of the difference of means $(s_{\overline{x}_1 - \overline{x}_2})$ = 2.15. Assume that you're working at the .05 level of significance.

    a. Formulate an appropriate null hypothesis.

    b. Calculate t statistic.

    c. Identify the critical value.

    d. State your conclusion.

3. Consider a research situation involving two independent samples, Sample A and Sample B. (Assume that you are subtracting the Mean of Sample B from the Mean of Sample A).

Mean of Sample A = 4.12 $n = 15$

Mean of Sample B = 6.23 $n = 13$

Estimate of the standard error of the difference of means $(s_{\bar{x}_1 - \bar{x}_2}) = 1.44$. Assume that you're working at the .05 level of significance.

  a. Formulate an appropriate null hypothesis.
  b. Calculate t statistic.
  c. Identify the critical value.
  d. State your conclusion.

4. A criminologist is interested in possible disparities between sentences given to males and females convicted in murder-for-hire cases. Selecting 14 cases involving men convicted of trying to solicit someone to kill their wives and 16 cases involving women convicted of trying to solicit someone to kill their husbands, the criminologist finds the following:

Mean length of sentence for males = 7.34 years with a standard deviation of 2.51 years

Mean length of sentence for females = 9.19 years with a standard deviation of 3.78 years

Assume that you're working at the .05 level of significance.

  a. Formulate an appropriate null hypothesis.
  b. Calculate t statistic.
  c. Identify the critical value.
  d. State your conclusion.

5. A political scientist is interested in the question of whether or not there is a difference between Republicans and Democrats when it comes to their involvement in voluntary associations. Using a 25 point scale to measure involvement in voluntary associations, and collecting information from a random sample of 22 Republicans and 17 Democrats, he/she discovers the following:

Republicans: Mean of 12.56 with a standard deviation of 3.77

Democrats: Mean of 16.43 with a standard deviation of 4.21

Assume that you're working at the .05 level of significance.

  a. Formulate an appropriate null hypothesis.
  b. Calculate t statistic.
  c. Identify the critical value.
  d. State your conclusion.

9

Beyond the Null Hypothesis

Our discussion of the null hypothesis began two chapters ago with the notion that the null hypothesis is a statement of equality (no difference) or chance. We traveled the road of hypothesis-testing logic, dealing with calculated test statistics, levels of significance, critical values, regions of rejection, and Type I and II errors. As I mentioned before, though, there is still more logic to consider, so that's where we turn now.

In doing so, however, we'll abandon the format we've relied on in the last two chapters. Instead of busying ourselves with calculations, computations, and such, we'll enter a more conceptual world. First, we'll examine the role of alternative or research hypotheses in the field of statistical analysis. That, in turn, will lead us to a discussion of the difference between one-tailed and two-tailed test situations. Finally, we'll deal with the matters of power and effect.

Before We Begin

This chapter rests on the assumption that you're familiar with the process of hypothesis testing; so much so that you have an almost intuitive understanding of the process—stating the null, selecting a level of significance, identifying the critical value, calculating the test statistic, and making a decision. There's also an assumption made that you fully understand the concept of making a Type I error.

With that as a background, we now go a bit further. For example, we'll round out your understanding of null hypotheses by giving you a look at alternative hypotheses. Also, you'll be given a chance to further your understanding of Type I errors through the discussion of Type II errors. And so it goes with this chapter. The material is highly conceptual in nature, and it deals with some of finer points of interpretation of findings.

Research or Alternative Hypotheses

To understand the concept of a research or alternative hypothesis, think about our earlier example involving exposure to a film on the dangers of recreational drug use. In that example, we tested the null hypothesis that drug awareness test scores would not change following exposure to a film on the dangers of recreational drug use. Even though we tested the null hypothesis (the expectation of no difference), it's hard to imagine that we wouldn't have expected some change or difference in the scores after exposure to the film. After all, that's what often drives our research in the first place—the expectation that we'll find a difference.

If we shift our thinking away from the null hypothesis and toward an expected difference of some sort, we can consider several alternatives. As it turns out, those alternatives are referred to as **alternative hypotheses** or **research hypotheses.** Recalling our earlier example, think about the various alternative or research hypotheses that we might have advanced:

H_1: Drug awareness test scores after exposure to the film will be higher than prior to exposure to the film.
(In other words, we expect the scores on the drug awareness test to *increase* following exposure to the film.)

H_2: Drug awareness test scores after exposure to the film will be lower than prior to exposure to the film.
(In other words, we expect the scores on the drug awareness test to *decrease* following exposure to the film.)

H_3: Drug awareness test scores before and after exposure to the film will be different or will change in some way.
(In other words, we expect the scores to *change*, but we don't know if the scores will increase or decrease.)

Each of these statements (H_1, H_2, and H_3) represents an alternative or research hypothesis. Each stands in opposition to the null hypothesis (H_0). Each statement asserts something other than the null.

 LEARNING CHECK

Question: What is an alternative or research hypothesis?

Answer: An alternative or research hypothesis is a hypothesis that stands in opposition to the null hypothesis.

Let's start with a close look at H_1 and H_2. Those are **directional hypotheses,** in the sense that they specify the nature or direction of the change or difference that we expect. H_1 is a statement that we expect the test scores to increase; H_2 is a statement that we expect the scores to decrease. H_3, on the other hand, is a **non-directional hypothesis.** It doesn't specify the direction of the expected difference; H_3 merely states that we expect to find a difference. It's still an alternative or research hypothesis, in the sense that it stands in opposition to the null, but the direction of the expected difference isn't specified.

 LEARNING CHECK

Question: What is a directional hypothesis, and what is a non-directional hypothesis?

Answer: A directional hypothesis specifies the nature or direction of a hypothesized difference. It asserts that there will be a difference or a change in a particular direction (increase or decrease). A non-directional hypothesis does not specify the nature or direction of an expected difference. It simply asserts that a difference will be present.

Up to this point we've been considering drug awareness scores, but the notion of a research or alternative hypothesis applies in a host of research situations. In one research situation, for example, we might expect alcohol consumption to be higher in one population than another. In another research situation, we might expect one group to be more productive than another. Still another research effort might find us back in a classic before/after research design, once again expecting scores to change in a particular direction. Regardless of the specifics of the research situation, it's common to approach the task with some set of expectations in place—some expectation other than the null. And that brings us back to the notion of an alternative or research hypothesis.

The research or alternative hypothesis we settle on is often a function of past research results or a particular theoretical perspective. Maybe previous research or a body of theory suggests that scores will increase or that one population will score higher than another. Maybe previous research or theoretical grounding suggests just the opposite. In some cases, previous research or theoretical statements may conflict, leaving us to expect a difference of some sort, but without any notion as to the direction of that difference.

When researchers have good reason to expect a change or difference in a particular direction, they are likely to opt for a directional alternative or research hypothesis. When there are conflicting results from previous research or contradictory suggestions from a body of theory, though, a non-directional alternative or research hypothesis is typically employed. Yes, it's still the null hypothesis that's tested, but there's also a research or alternative hypothesis in play, whether it's stated or not. In reality, it's often the research or alternative hypothesis that's driving the research in the first place. With that as a background, we can now explore the link between the alternative or research hypothesis and the topic of one-tailed and two-tailed tests.

One-Tailed and Two-Tailed Test Scenarios

In Chapters 7 and 8, we considered a variety of hypothesis-testing situations, but there was something that I neglected to tell you at the time. We approached those hypotheses as though they were *two-tailed test situations;* I just didn't bother to tell you that's what we were doing. I deliberately delayed any discussion of that for two reasons.

First, I firmly believe there's a limit to how much material anybody can absorb at once. Chapters 7 and 8 covered a lot of conceptual material, along with a hefty amount of calculations and computations. In short, you deserved a break. Second, I think it's wise to develop a solid grounding in the logic of hypothesis testing before dealing with the difference between a one-tailed and a two-tailed test. Assuming you now have a solid grasp of concepts such as the null hypothesis, calculated test statistics, and regions of rejection, we are ready to move ahead.

To illustrate the difference between the two approaches, let's take a simple example. Let's say we have a questionnaire that measures levels of religious participation (scores can range from 0 to 100). Assume we've collected scores from a sample of urban residents and a sample of rural residents and have obtained the results shown in Table 9-1.

As shown in Table 9-1, we have information from two samples (urban and rural residents), and we have a mean for each group (66.45 for the urban residents and 79.27 for the rural residents). Let's also assume that we've already calculated an estimate of the standard error (4.42). This test situation is appropriate for a difference of means test for independent samples—one in which we'd eventually calculate a t value for the difference of means. You'll recall that part of the t test procedure requires that we find the difference between the two

Table 9-1 Religious Participation Scores for Urban and Rural Residents

Urban Residents	Rural Residents
59	83
77	93
74	91
69	79
53	77
68	54
70	65
71	92
72	68
56	88
62	82

$\overline{X}$ for Urban Residents = 66.45

$\overline{X}$ for Rural Residents = 79.27

Estimate of the standard error of the difference of means = 4.42

means, which we'll eventually divide by the estimate of the standard error of the difference of means to obtain our calculated test statistic. In reality, it isn't important how we go about finding the difference. We can subtract the mean of the rural residents from the mean of the urban residents; or we can approach the problem in the opposite fashion, subtracting the mean of the urban residents from the mean of the rural residents.

In this example, the mean of the rural residents is higher than the mean of the urban residents. In this case, if we subtract the mean of the urban residents from the mean of the rural residents, we'll get a difference with a positive sign (+). If we subtract the mean of the rural residents from the mean of the urban residents, we'll get a difference with a negative sign (–). As I mentioned before, it isn't important how we go about the subtraction process, just as long as we mentally keep track of which mean was subtracted from the other and how that relates to the sign of the difference. Assuming we can do that, let's look at some different possibilities.

Testing a Non-directional Research Hypothesis

Let's start with the assumption that we really don't know what to expect. Maybe some previous research suggests rural residents would have higher participation levels, but other research suggests that urban residents would have higher participation levels. In a case like that, it would make sense to approach the problem with a non-directional alternative or research hypothesis in mind.

In terms of the actual hypothesis test, our alternative or research hypothesis is a statement that we expect to find an extreme difference—a difference that's located somewhere in the outer regions of the distribution of possible differences. Since our alternative or research hypothesis is non-directional, however, it's actually a statement that we're open to that extreme difference being found at either tail of the distribution (see Figure 9-1). It can be an extreme difference that has a positive sign (+), or it can be an extreme difference that has a negative sign (–). We're open to a difference indicating that

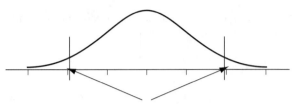

In a two-tailed test situation, we're looking for a test statistic that falls in either of the critical regions—the positive region (+) at the upper end of the distribution or the negative region (−) at the lower end of the distribution.

Figure 9-1   Critical Regions in a Two-Tailed Test Situation

rural residents have higher scores, but we're also open to a difference indicating that urban residents have higher scores. When we're working with a non-directional research hypothesis—when we're open to finding a significant difference at either end of the distribution (in the region of rejection of either tail of the distribution)—we're in a **two-tailed test scenario.**

 LEARNING CHECK

Question: What is a two-tailed test scenario, and when is it appropriate?

Answer: A two-tailed test scenario is a research situation in which the researcher is looking for an extreme difference that could be located at either end of the distribution. A two-tailed test is appropriate when the alternative or research hypothesis is non-directional.

To develop a better understanding of all of this, let's take the problem all the way from a statement of the null and a non-directional research hypothesis, along with the level of significance, through the calculation of the test statistic and interpretation of results. Consider the following information.

Null hypothesis: There is no difference between the means of rural and urban residents; the means are equal.

Research hypothesis: There is a difference between the means of rural and urban residents.

Rural residents: mean $(\overline{X}_{Rural}) = 79.27$ Sample size $(n_{Rural}) = 11$
Urban residents: mean $(\overline{X}_{Urban}) = 66.45$ Sample size $(n_{Urban}) = 11$
Difference between the means $(79.27 - 66.45) = 12.82$

Estimate of the standard error of the difference of means = 4.42
Level of significance (alpha or α) = .05

Appropriate test is the t test for difference of means.
Degrees of freedom = 20
Critical value = 2.086

Note: The critical value was obtained from Appendix B: Family of t Distributions (Two-Tailed Test). Since we don't care about the direction of any difference (we don't care if it is positive or negative), we're in a two-tailed test situation.

Following the procedures outlined in Chapter 8 (for the difference of means tests with independent samples), we calculate the test statistic (t):

$$t = \frac{\overline{X}_{Rural} - \overline{X}_{Urban}}{s_{\overline{x}_{Rural} - \overline{x}_{Urban}}}$$

$$t = \frac{12.82}{4.42}$$

$$t = 2.90$$

Given the calculated test statistic of 2.90 and the critical value (from Appendix B) of 2.086, we conclude that we should reject the null hypothesis. In rejecting the idea of no difference, we find support for our research or alternative hypothesis—that there is a difference. By now, the basics of this process should be quite familiar to you: State the null, calculate the test statistic, check the critical value, and make a decision.

What's new at this point, though, is the role of a two-tailed test in the process. We found support for the idea that there's a difference by relying on a two-tailed test scenario. We set up the research in a way that allowed us to find a significant difference in either tail of the distribution. We were looking for an extreme t value—one that was so extreme that it would fall somewhere on the most extreme 5% of the distribution. Because we were operating on the basis of a two-tailed test, the 5% was equally divided between the upper and lower tails of the distribution (2.5% in the upper tail and 2.5% in the lower tail). And that, in short, is the essence of a two-tailed test scenario. It's a situation in which an extreme score can be located at either end of the distribution (see Figure 9-2).

Testing a Directional Research Hypothesis

Now let's consider a different situation—one involving a different alternative or research hypothesis. In this instance, let's assume that we expect to discover that rural residents have *higher* religious participation scores than urban residents. Since we're now hypothesizing (in the form of the research or alternative hypothesis) that the rural residents will have higher religious participation scores than the urban residents, we are specifying the direction

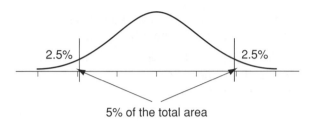

5% of the total area

Half of the total area (2.5%) is found at the upper end of the distribution, and half of the total area (2.5%) is found at the lower end of the distribution.

Figure 9-2   Allocation of the Extreme 5% of the Distribution in a Two-Tailed Test Scenario

of the expected difference. Therefore, we're relying on a *directional* research or alternative hypothesis.

As it turns out, the selection of a directional alternative or research hypothesis (as opposed to a non-directional one), results in a few changes in how we approach the test. These changes can be summarized as follows:

- The null hypothesis changes slightly. Instead of the null being a statement that we expect the two means to be equal, the null is now a statement that either the two means are equal or the mean score of the rural residents is *lower* than the mean of the urban residents. Remember, our alternative hypothesis in this case is that we expect the mean score for rural residents to be *higher* than the mean score for urban residents. Therefore, the null hypothesis (if it truly stands in opposition to the research or alternative hypothesis) is that we expect the mean score of the rural residents to be equal to or lower than the mean score of the urban residents.

- We're no longer looking for an extreme difference at either end of the distribution. Instead, we're looking for a *t* value at only one end of the curve—a *t* value that falls in only *one tail* of the distribution. Remember: We're asserting that we expect the mean score of the rural residents to be *higher* than the mean score of the urban residents. Assuming that we calculate the difference by subtracting the mean of the urban residents from the mean of the rural residents, we'll be looking for a positive difference (a difference that carries a + sign).

- Since we're only willing to accept a difference in a certain direction, we're in what is referred to as a **one-tailed test scenario.** To find our critical value, therefore, we'll use Appendix C: Family of *t* Distributions (One-Tailed Test).

- The critical value for a one-tailed test (found in Appendix C) will be different from the critical value for a two-tailed test (Appendix B).

To carry out our test, we follow the same formula as before. As a reminder, here are the same steps, repeated again:

$$t = \frac{\overline{X}_{Rural} - \overline{X}_{Urban}}{s_{\overline{x}_{Rural} - \overline{x}_{Urban}}}$$

$$t = \frac{12.82}{4.42}$$

$$t = 2.90$$

Note that our calculated t test statistic carries a positive sign because we're subtracting the mean of the urban residents from the mean of the rural residents. If we'd subtracted the mean of the rural residents from the mean of the urban residents, however, we'd have a negative t test statistic.

As noted previously, we're no longer looking for a significant t value at either extreme of the distribution of all possible t values. Instead, we're expecting it to be found in only one extreme region—in the upper end of the distribution, the area related to the positive t values. Remember: We're looking for a t value that falls in only one of the extreme regions; that's why we say we're in a one-tailed test situation.

Working at the .05 level of significance, with 20 degrees of freedom, the table for a one-tailed test (Appendix C) shows a critical value of 1.725. In this instance, the extreme 5% of the area under the curve is not divided between the two tails of the distribution. Rather, the extreme 5% is to be found *either* at the lower end of the distribution *or* at the upper end of the distribution. In other words, the extreme area in a one-tailed scenario is found on only one side of the distribution (see Figure 9-3).

Since our calculated t value is 2.90 and our critical value is 1.725, it appears that we're in good shape; we're on our way to rejecting the null hypothesis. At this point, though, we want to carefully consider the nature or direction of the difference that we found between the two means. In this case, the difference is consistent with our alternative or research hypothesis; the mean score for the rural residents was higher than the mean score for the urban residents. We're in a position to reject the null.

The entire critical region—5% of the total area under the curve—is found *either* at the lower end of the distribution *or* at the upper end of the distribution.

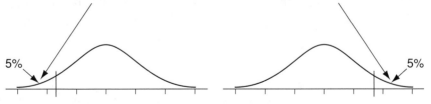

Figure 9-3 Allocation of the Extreme 5% of the Distribution in a One-Tailed Test Scenario

LEARNING CHECK

Question: What is a one-tailed test scenario, and when is it appropriate?

Answer: A one-tailed test scenario is a research situation in which the researcher is looking for an extreme difference that is located on only one side of the distribution. A one-tailed test is appropriate when the alternative or research hypothesis is directional.

In summary, we used a one-tailed test scenario, we found significant results, and the results were in the hypothesized direction (according to the alternative or research hypothesis we had advanced). If, however, we'd been working with a different alternative or research hypothesis—that urban residents would have higher participation scores than rural residents—we would have found ourselves facing a researcher's worst nightmare. We would have found a difference between the mean score of the urban and rural residents, to be sure, but the difference would have been opposite to the direction we hypothesized.

The logic involved in a one-tailed test can clearly get a little tricky, particularly when you get to the matter of whether or not the direction of the difference is consistent with the direction specified by the alternative or research hypothesis. Still, that's no reason to let it throw you. Just accept the fact that the logic is a little tricky—the sort of thing that eventually takes hold with repeated application.

Beyond that, you might also take some consolation in the fact that many researchers steadfastly avoid the use of one-tailed tests, and they do so for what they consider to be very good reason. To understand why some researchers, as a matter of course, just avoid using a one-tailed test, think back to the different critical values we encountered. When working in the two-tailed test scenario, our critical value was 2.086. In the one-tailed test situation, though, the critical value was 1.725. And that difference—the difference between the two critical values—brings us to the heart of the matter, at least in terms of how some researchers see the issue.

When you compare those values, one thing should become clear. Assuming any observed difference is consistent with the direction suggested by the alternative or research hypothesis, it's easier to achieve significant results in a one-tailed than in a two-tailed test scenario. As Gravetter and Wallnau (2002) note:

A one-tailed test allows you to reject the null hypothesis when the difference . . . is relatively small, provided the difference is in the specified direction. A two-tailed test, on the other hand, requires a relatively large difference independent of direction. (p. 189)

In simple terms, some researchers prefer to work in a situation in which the bar of proof, so to speak, is as high as reasonably possible. They shy away from the easier situations (the ones made easier by the one-tailed test scenario) and opt instead for more demanding ones—the two-tailed test scenarios. Indeed, many researchers will resort to a one-tailed test situation only under very unusual circumstances, if at all. The conclusion to all this? It's simple. Don't be terribly surprised if you never encounter a one-tailed test in the remainder of your statistical journey. It's one of the finer points of hypothesis-testing logic, but one that you should know about, nonetheless. If you do encounter a one-tailed test along the way, at least you'll know what it's all about.

That said, we can leave the present discussion. Before we close out the chapter, though, we'll consider two final concepts: power and effect. Though not routinely considered by all statisticians, these concepts are particularly relevant to the field of experimental psychology, as well as other disciplines that frequently rely on experimental research designs.

Power and Effect

We'll begin with a brief review of Type I and Type II errors. First, take a moment to think about the difference between Type I and Type II errors. Here they are, spelled out for you again:

> *Type I Error:* Rejecting the null hypothesis when it is true.
> *Type II Error:* Failing to reject a null hypothesis when it is false.

Now, instead of thinking about the errors in terms of their definitions, think about them in terms of the possibilities we encounter whenever we approach a null hypothesis. First and foremost, always remember that there are two possibilities with respect to the null hypothesis: A null hypothesis is either true, or it is false. In other words, it doesn't make any difference what our research results eventually lead us to conclude. The fact remains that the null hypothesis, in reality, is either true or false.

Given that, our test of a null hypothesis can lead to four possibilities. We can either reject or fail to reject a true null hypothesis. By the same token, we can either reject or fail to reject a false null hypothesis. Table 9-2 illustrates these four possibilities.

Since the logic involved in all of this can get a little confusing at first, let's take apart Table 9-2, cell by cell. At first you may find the explanation I'm about to give you to be a little silly, but trust me on this: A little bit of silliness at this point can serve you well. Let's start with the information on the left-hand side of the table.

Table 9-2 Logical Possibilities in the Test of a Null Hypothesis

		The Null Hypothesis Is . . .	
		True	False
Based on the Test, We Either . . .	Fail to Reject the Null	*RESEARCH OBJECTIVE*	*TYPE II ERROR*
	Reject the Null	*TYPE I ERROR*	*RESEARCH OBJECTIVE*

The left-hand side of the table represents a situation in which the null hypothesis is actually true. To fully grasp this point, pretend for a moment that we're all-knowing, and we're watching someone else undertake a research problem. Because we're all-knowing, we're in a position to know that the null hypothesis is true. Maybe the null in this case is a statement that there's no difference between the means of two populations. The point is, we know that the null is in fact true. The team of researchers who're about to test the null, however, don't know what we know. All they know is that the null says there's no difference.

Now let's say the researchers test the null hypothesis, and the test results cause them to fail to reject the null. Remember: We know that the null is true. In a case like that—we know the null is true, and the researchers have failed to reject it—we might be inclined to pat the researchers on the back: Good job! The null was true, and you failed to reject it! You reached your objective! When a null hypothesis is true, researchers want to be in a position to fail to reject it.

Now, though, let's consider a different outcome. Let's say it's still the case that the null is true, but let's say the test results led the researchers to reject the null. In other words, the researchers found an extreme difference and rejected the null. Oops! The researchers just committed a Type I error! The researchers wouldn't know it, but we would. We know that the null is true, and the researchers just rejected the null.

In summary, there are two possible outcomes when a null hypothesis is true. One outcome is desirable; the other one isn't. If researchers fail to reject a true null hypothesis, the researchers are on solid ground. If, on the other hand, the researchers reject a true null hypothesis, they have committed a Type I error. So much for null hypotheses that are true. Now let's turn to the case of a false null hypothesis.

This time, focus on the right-hand side of the table. In this case, we know (because we're all-knowing) that the null hypothesis is false. In other words, the null hypothesis says that there's no difference between two populations, but we know that there is a difference. As before, there are two possible outcomes.

Let's say a group of researchers test the null hypothesis and find a significant difference. As a result, they reject the null hypothesis. As before, we'd be inclined to pat the researchers on the back: Job well done! The null was false and you rejected it! That was a job well done in the sense that it would be consistent with another research objective. Just as researchers want to fail to reject true null hypotheses, they also want to reject false null hypotheses.

Now let's consider the other possibility. Let's say that our researchers failed to find a significant difference. We (because we're all-knowing) know there's a significant difference between the two populations, but the researchers failed to detect that difference. As a result, they failed to reject the null when, in fact, it's false. In other words, the researchers committed a Type II error.

Now all of that amounts to quite a bit of logic to digest, but digest it you must. Let me suggest that you take some time for a dark room moment to contemplate what we just covered. Imagine a situation in which you're hovering above a team of researchers and watching them work.

First, imagine a situation in which you know that the null hypothesis is true. Imagine that you know that there's no difference between two population means. Visualize the researchers failing to reject the null. Then imagine the researchers rejecting the null. Think about your reactions to what they have done.

Now imagine a situation in which you know that the null hypothesis is false. Imagine that you know that there is a difference between two population means. Visualize the researchers rejecting the null. Then imagine the researchers failing to reject the null. Think about your reactions to what they have done.

Let me suggest that you go through this visualization exercise over and over—thinking through all the possibilities time and time again, to the point that you're totally comfortable with them. Draw your own diagrams, or think up your own examples. If necessary, repeat the process to the point that you have a near-intuitive understanding of the logic. Assuming you feel comfortable with the full logic of Type I and Type II errors, we can move forward.

Remember what one of the major objectives is in the research process. If the null is false, a researcher will want to reject it. And that's where the concepts of *power* and *effect* come into play. First, we'll consider the matter of power; then we'll turn to the concept of effect.

The **power** of a statistical test is the ability of the test to reject a false null hypothesis. It's represented by the cell in the lower right-hand corner of Table 9-2. Remember: There are two possible outcomes to a statistical test when the null hypothesis is false. If we fail to reject a false null, we commit a Type II or beta (β) error. If we reject a false null hypothesis, however, we've reached our objective. Since β represents the probability of committing a Type II error, we can define the power of a test as $1 - \beta$ (or 1 minus the probability of a Type II error). To better understand all of this, consider the following example.

LEARNING CHECK

Question: What is the power of a test?
Answer: Power is the ability of a test to reject a false null
             hypothesis.

Let's say that we want to know whether or not sleep deprivation has an effect on the amount of time required to complete a task. We could approach the problem as follows:

- Assemble two groups of research participants—one sleep deprived and one not.
- Ask members of each group to complete a task.
- Record the amount of time each participant spent completing the task.
- Perform the necessary calculations—a difference of means test—and arrive at a conclusion.
- Either reject the null or fail to reject the null.

As before, this process should be very familiar to you by now. What may not be apparent to you, however, is how the concepts of power and effect are involved. In truth, the goal of the research outlined above would be to detect the effect of sleep deprivation on task completion time. In the context of research, **effect** is the change in a measurement that is attributable to a treatment condition or stimulus of some sort.

To demonstrate that sleep deprivation has an effect, we'd have to find a significant difference between the two sets of recorded times and reject the null. It stands to reason that the larger the effect, the greater the likelihood that we'd do just that. A slight difference between the means would probably result in our failing to reject the null. A large difference, though, would probably result in our rejecting the null. All factors being equal, the larger the difference between the scores, the greater the likelihood that the null will be rejected. When the null is rejected, there's support for the notion that sleep deprivation has an effect on task completion time.

Of course there's always a possibility that sleep deprivation had an effect on task completion time, but we failed to pick up on that. In other words, there's always some probability of a Type II error—the null was false, but we failed to reject it. That possibility brings us to the heart of the issue.

 LEARNING CHECK

Question: What is the definition of effect?
Answer: Effect is the change in measurement that is attributable
             to a treatment condition or stimulus of some sort.

If a treatment condition of some sort has an effect on an outcome (that is, the null hypothesis is false), we want to be in a position to detect it. We want to detect the effect and subsequently reject the null. What we don't want is a situation in which an effect is present, but we've failed to detect it.

So how might we guard against such a situation? There are certain steps that we, as researchers, can take to increase the likelihood that we'll detect or pick up on the effect of a treatment condition. There are certain things we can do at the outset of a research problem to increase the *power* of the test—the likelihood that we will reject the null hypothesis when it's false.

First, we can increase our sample size. Assuming, for example, that the design of our research has us looking for a difference of some sort between two groups of research participants, an increase in the size of the samples would increase the likelihood that we'd detect any difference between the groups that actually exists.

Second, we can opt for a one-tailed test scenario. In this case, the entire region of rejection is found at one end of the distribution, and the necessary value to reject the null hypothesis (the critical value) is reduced slightly. In turn, there is an increase in the likelihood that our results will be significant (assuming they are in the hypothesized direction).

Similarly, we can increase our level of significance (regardless of whether we were working with a one-tailed or two-tailed test scenario), and thereby increase the likelihood of rejecting the null hypothesis. Unfortunately, this option has an associated cost—namely, an increase in the probability of a Type I error.

Finally, we can, to the extent possible, strive for highly controlled research situations—for example, situations in which participants in two groups are matched on relevant variables. By matching participants on a host of variables, we reduce the possibility that any difference might be *masked* by the influence of extraneous or outside variables. In short, highly controlled research designs increase the possibility that a treatment effect will, in fact, shine through.

Chapter Summary

We've explored quite a bit of conceptual material in this chapter, so it's probably appropriate to undertake a quick review of what we've just covered and a quick check of where you should be in your statistical education. For example, by now you should be totally comfortable with the role of the null hypothesis in scientific research and how it stacks up against an alternative or research hypothesis. Similarly, you should now be comfortable with the concept of an alternative or research hypothesis and how it is incorporated into your research efforts.

With your knowledge of alternative or research hypotheses, the notions of one-tailed and two-tailed test scenarios should now make sense. Similarly, the mystery as to why there are two tables for the distribution of *t* (Appendix B and Appendix C) should now be solved. Even if you never opt to use a one-tailed test, at least you'll be familiar with the logic that's involved in the application if you see or hear reference to it.

Finally, the more in-depth exploration into the logic of Type I and Type II errors should have given you a better understanding of research objectives in the larger sense—particularly the objective of rejecting false null hypotheses. With that understanding as a base, the concepts of power and effect should have taken on some meaning.

As we close this chapter and prepare for the next, we leave the more conceptual world and return to the world of calculations, computations, critical values, and such. At the same time, though, the logical underpinnings of hypothesis testing, including much of the material we just covered, should remain part of your thinking.

Some Other Things You Should Know

Some of the material we covered in this chapter will have more relevance to some readers than to others. For example, the material on power and effect has particular relevance for those in the field of experimental psychology. These issues are typically of minimal consequence in fields such as sociology or political science, which rely on large-scale surveys (and, consequently, large sample sizes). When power and effect are of consequence, however, additional resources should be consulted. For example, excellent discussions are to be found in Dunn (2001), Hurlburt (1998), Pagano (2001), and Howell (1995).

As to one- versus two-tailed tests, you should note that there are many situations in which the choice isn't even available. For example, the ANOVA procedure we will cover in the next chapter involves a comparison of three or more means. In a case like that, only one alternative or research hypothesis is appropriate—namely, a non-directional research hypothesis stating that the means vary across the different groups. The alternative or research hypothesis is not a statement that one mean will be higher or lower than another.

Finally, you should be aware of how the logic of one-tailed and two-tailed tests is dealt with when working with Z and the Table of Areas Under the Normal Curve. Should you find yourself in that situation, you can approach the problem with the assurance that the same logic applies. For example, the table presented in this text (Appendix A) really contains one-tailed values, because it only deals with one half of the normal curve. Note that a Z value of 1.96 actually has an associated proportion of .4750 (a percentage of 47.50%). We interpret a Z value of 1.96 as encompassing 95% of the area under the normal curve, but that's because we're mentally taking into account the area between Z values of -1.96 and $+1.96$.

If we were calculating Z and working in a one-tailed test scenario at the .05 level of significance, we would want to find the Z value (the critical value) that corresponded to *either* the upper *or* lower 5% of the area. The Z value associated with the upper or lower area (but not both) is the Z value that corresponds to .4500, or 45%. That Z value turns out to be approximately 1.64.

Key Terms

alternative hypothesis	one-tailed test scenario
directional hypothesis	power
effect	research hypothesis
non-directional hypothesis	two-tailed test scenario

Chapter Problems

Fill in the blanks, calculate the requested values, or otherwise supply the correct answer.

General Thought Questions

1. A(n) _____ hypothesis is a hypothesis that stands in opposition to the null hypothesis.
2. An alternative or research hypothesis that specifies the nature or direction of a hypothesized difference is considered a _____.
3. A _____ tailed test scenario is appropriate when the alternative or research hypothesis is non-directional in nature.
4. A _____ tailed test scenario is appropriate when the alternative or research hypothesis is directional in nature.
5. A Type I error involves _____ a null hypothesis when it is _____.
6. A Type II error involves _____ a null hypothesis when it is _____.

Alternative or Research Hypotheses Application Questions/Problems

1. A researcher is examining the possibility of a difference between the grade point averages of on-campus students and commuter students.
   a. What would be an appropriate null hypothesis?
   b.–d. What alternative or research hypotheses could be advanced?
2. A criminologist is examining the possibility of a difference between the length of sentences handed out to white and non-white defendants in first-offense drug trafficking cases.
   a. What would be an appropriate null hypothesis?
   b.–d. What alternative or research hypothesis could be advanced?
3. A political scientist is examining the possibility of a difference in the levels of voter participation in rural and urban areas.
   a. What would be an appropriate null hypothesis?
   b.–d. What alternative or research hypotheses could be advanced?

4. A team of environmental geographers believe that there's no significant difference between levels of water pollution in creeks in the northern and southern parts of the state, but they still want to conduct a test to verify this belief.

   a. What would be an appropriate null hypothesis?

   b.–d. What alternative or research hypotheses could be advanced?

One-Tailed and Two-Tailed Application Questions/Problems

1. Given the information in Appendix A, identify the critical values for Z in the following situations:

   a. .05 level of significance; two-tailed test situation

   b. .05 level of significance; one-tailed test situation

   c. .01 level of significance; two-tailed test situation

   d. .01 level of significance; one-tailed test situation

2. Given the information in Appendix B and C identify the critical values for t in the following situations:

   a. 15 degrees of freedom and the .05 level of significance in a two-tailed test

   b. 21 degrees of freedom at the .05 level of significance in a one-tailed test

   c. 18 degrees of freedom at the .10 level of significance in a two-tailed test

   d. 18 degrees of freedom at the .05 level of significance in a one-tailed test

10

Analysis of Variance

The next procedure we cover is referred to as **AN**alysis **O**f **VA**riance (commonly abbreviated as **ANOVA**). More specifically, we will take up an application known as one-way ANOVA. Many statisticians think of ANOVA as an extension of the difference of means test because it's based, in part, on a comparison of sample means. At the same time, however, the procedure involves a comparison of different estimates of population variance—hence the name analysis of variance. Because ANOVA is appropriate for research involving three or more samples, it has wide applicability.

In the field of experimental psychology, for example, researchers routinely look at results from three or more samples, often referred to as *treatment groups*. One can easily imagine an educational psychologist wanting to know if students exposed to three different treatment conditions or learning environments (positive sanction, negative sanction, and sanction neutral) exhibit different test scores. Assuming the test scores are based on an interval/ratio scale of measurement, ANOVA would be an appropriate approach to the problem.

Similarly, a geographer might be interested in the growth rates of four types of cities—manufacturing centers, government centers, retail centers, and financial centers. A study along those lines would be another research problem ideally suited for ANOVA.

What makes both of these problems appropriate for ANOVA is the fact that they involve more than two groups or samples and a single variable that has been measured at the interval/ratio level of measurement. It's true that research problems like these can be approached with a series of *t* tests, and that might be your inclination if you knew nothing about ANOVA. For example, the geographer could conduct different *t* tests—comparing the growth rates of manufacturing centers with those of government centers, followed by a comparison with financial centers, and so forth—but there are inherent problems in that approach.

A study based on just four types of cities would turn into a series of six *t* tests involving all the possible comparisons. Besides the added work of six individual tests, there's the issue of Type I errors (rejection of the null hypothesis when it is true). Without going into the mathematics of the situation, the fact is that the probability of a Type I error would be magnified. Even though the probability of a Type I error on any one of the six tests would be, let's say, .05 (if that was the designated level of significance), it would increase well beyond that for the six individual tests taken together. Given that, it's no wonder that researchers commonly turn to ANOVA. In short, ANOVA allows the comparison of multiple samples in a single application. That should be apparent once you consider the logic of ANOVA.

 LEARNING CHECK

Question: ANOVA is appropriate for what types of research situations?

Answer: ANOVA is appropriate for situations involving three or more samples and a variable measured at the interval/ratio level of measurement.

Before We Begin

Up to this point, we've covered four specific hypothesis testing procedures. First there was the hypothesis test involving a single sample mean, one procedure with sigma (σ) known and then another with sigma (σ) unknown. Then we shifted to situations involving the matched and related samples, followed by situations involving two independent samples. In sum, we looked at four situations and four hypothesis testing procedures.

If you'll take the time to reflect on that—the notion that we looked at four situations and four hypothesis testing procedures—you'll likely see the repetition that occurs in the field of statistics. Just to make certain that you grasp this repetitive nature of hypothesis testing, let me urge you to think about it this way: The underlying logic remains the same; what changes is the research situation. In other words, it's the research situation or problem that dictates what procedure to use.

So, you ask, how does that relate to where we're going? The answer is pretty straight-forward. We started out with research problems involving one sample. Then we dealt with situations involving two samples. Naturally, not every research situation falls into one of those categories; it's common to encounter research situations that involve three or more samples. In a nutshell, that's where we're going in this chapter—research situations involving three or more samples.

The Logic of ANOVA

Imagine for a moment that we want to know if scores on an aptitude test actually vary for students in different types of schooling environments—home schooling, public schooling, and private schooling. This research question involves a comparison of more than two groups. Assuming that the aptitude test scores are measured at the interval/ratio level, the situation is tailor-made for an application of ANOVA. We could easily think of our study as one that asks whether or not aptitude test scores vary on the basis of school environment.

Another way to look at the question is whether or not type of school environment is a legitimate classification scheme when it comes to the matter of aptitude test scores. After all, to refer to students in terms of home, public, and private schooling is to speak in terms of a classification scheme. If aptitude test scores really do vary on the basis of school environment—if there is a significant difference between the scores in the three environments—then it's probably legitimate to speak in terms of school environments when looking at test scores. If there isn't a significant difference between the scores, however, we have to question the legitimacy of the classification scheme. In a sense, we were also dealing with the legitimacy of a classification scheme in the last chapter, particularly in reference to the test for independent sample. To suggest that two groups are different with respect to some variable is, in fact, a way of suggesting that the members of the group or cases can reasonably be classified on the basis of the variable in question. That said, let's return to the topic at hand.

To understand how all of this relates to ANOVA, consider Figure 10-1. Imagine that the three curves shown in Figure 10-1 represent the distributions of aptitude test scores for three samples—a sample of home-schooled students, a sample of public school students, and a sample of private school students.

The three distributions reflect three different means, but the means are fairly close together, and there's substantial variation in the scores within each group. Additionally, there's noticeable overlap in the distributions. The overlap exists, in part, because of those factors taken together—the fact that there's substantial variation *within* each of the distributions, coupled with minimal difference *between* the means. (Technically, the proper phrase should be *among the means* because the comparison typically involves three or more means, but in the language of ANOVA, the phrase *between the means* is used nonetheless. It's just a matter of statistical convention.)

Now consider the distributions shown in Figure 10-2. You'll note that the means of the distributions in Figure 10-2 are very different, and there's no overlap between the three curves.

A grasp of ANOVA begins with an understanding of the different patterns reflected in Figures 10-1 and 10-2. If there's more variation between groups than within groups (as suggested by the illustration in Figure 10-2), then there's support for the assertion that students in the different schooling environments are different with respect to aptitude test scores. Conversely, the illustration in Figure 10-1 would challenge the legitimacy of the classification scheme. Because the means are fairly close together in Figure 10-1, and there is a decided or noticeable overlap between the three samples (home-schooled students, public school students, and private school students), it wouldn't make much sense to speak in terms of type of schooling environment when it comes to test scores on the aptitude test.

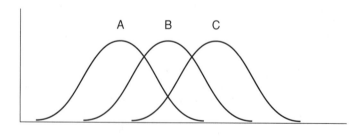

A = Home schooling
B = Public schooling
C = Private schooling

Figure 10-1   Student Performance in Three Learning Environments (Scenario #1)

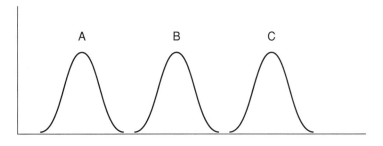

A = Home schooling
B = Public schooling
C = Private schooling

Figure 10-2   Student Performance in Three Learning Environments
(Scenario #2)

 LEARNING CHECK

Question: What are some ways to think about the purpose of
ANOVA? What does it measure?

Answer: It measures whether there's more variation between
groups than within groups. It examines the legitimacy of a
classification scheme.

From Curves to Data Distributions

So far we've been speaking in rather general terms, with vague references to
variation within groups and equally vague references to the variation between
groups. Now it's time to take a closer look at ANOVA and how it actually measures the amount of variation we're considering. In essence, ANOVA allows
us to calculate a *ratio* of the variation between groups to the variation within
groups. This ratio is referred to as the **F ratio** (named after its developer,
Sir Ronald Fisher).

At the risk of jumping ahead, let me point you in the right direction here.
Assuming that we're in search of significant results in a hypothesis-testing
situation, what we'll be looking for is more variation between the means of
several groups, relative to the variation within the groups. In short, we'll be
looking for more variation between than within. Because the F ratio is an
expression of the between-to-within ratio, we'll be looking for a large F value.
All factors being equal, the larger our F ratio, the greater the probability that
we'll reject the null hypothesis.

LEARNING CHECK

Question: What is the *F* ratio? What does it reflect?
Answer: The *F* ratio is the test statistic calculated for ANOVA.
            It is the ratio of the variation between the samples to
            the variation within the samples.

The details of how we calculate the *F* ratio is something we'll cover later. Right now, the issue is the underlying logic. So let me give you some more examples, just to get you thinking on the right track.

> A market researcher wants to determine if there's a significant difference between the response rates to five different marketing campaigns. In other words, she wants to know if there's more response rate variation *between* than *within* the different campaigns. If there's more variation in the response rates between than within the campaigns, then it's likely that response rates really do vary by type of campaign.

> A sociologist wants to determine if different types of school personnel (teachers, counselors, and coaches) vary in their abilities to recognize risk factors for youth suicide. Assuming he has some sort of interval/ratio level scale to measure risk factor awareness, the question has to do with how the scores on the scale vary by personnel classification. The researcher would have to find more variation *between* different samples (teachers, coaches, and counselors) than *within* the samples to suggest that risk factor recognition actually varies by personnel classification.

By now you should be getting the message: We'll be looking for more variation between the samples than within the samples, at least if we're going to achieve significant results. That, of course, brings us to the matter of how we measure the variation. As you might have guessed, the concept of variation relates to deviations from the mean. And that, in turn, brings us to the various means we might consider.

The Different Means

We can begin with a look at Figure 10-3, but let me warn you in advance. Figure 10-3 is rather abstract. There aren't any values or scores or data of any sort. There isn't any information about a specific research question. It's all very abstract, but it's that way for a reason. One of the best ways to sharpen your thinking about the logic of ANOVA is to think about it in purely abstract terms.

Take a few moments to look at Figure 10-3, and even replicate the illustration on a sheet of paper if you want to (just so you can add some of your

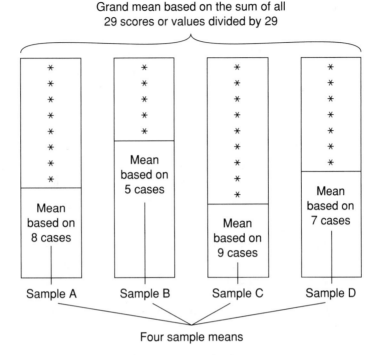

Grand mean based on the sum of all
29 scores or values divided by 29

Mean
based on
8 cases

Mean
based on
5 cases

Mean
based on
9 cases

Mean
based on
7 cases

Sample A   Sample B   Sample C   Sample D

Four sample means

Figure 10-3 The Various Means Involved in ANOVA

own notes or doodles). Figure 10-3 depicts four samples—Sample A, Sample B, Sample C, and Sample D. It doesn't make any difference at this point what those samples relate to. Each sample has its own distribution of scores or values (represented by individual asterisks).

Note that there are 8 cases in Sample A, 5 cases in Sample B, 9 cases in Sample C, and 7 cases in Sample D. Taken together, there are 4 samples and a total of 29 cases. Remember: Each case could be a person (a total of 29 persons), an organization (a total of 29 organizations), a city (a total of 29 cities), or anything else. Each asterisk represents one case—an individual score or value.

Now think about the various means we could calculate. First, there's a mean for Sample A (based on 8 cases), a mean for Sample B (based on 5 cases), a mean for Sample C (based on 9 cases), and a mean for Sample D (based on 7 cases). There are four samples, so there are four sample means.

So far we have four sample means, but there's still another mean to consider. We could, if we wanted to, calculate a **grand mean**—an overall mean based on the 29 cases. We could add all of the individual scores or values (all 29 of them) and then divide by 29. The result would be an overall or grand mean.

Note that we wouldn't calculate the grand mean by adding the 4 sample means and dividing by 4. We could do that if all the samples had the same number of cases, but that's not what we have in this example. Instead, we have 4 samples, and each sample has a different number of cases. Each sample mean, or **group**

mean, is a function, in part, of the number of cases in the sample. Therefore, we can't treat them equally (which is what we would be doing if we simply added the 4 means and divided by 4).

Take another look at Figure 10-3. Even though it's very abstract, think about what the illustration reveals—the notion of a grand mean, as well as a mean for each sample.

☑ LEARNING CHECK

Question: What two types of means come into play in ANOVA?
Answer: The grand mean and the individual sample means.

Let me suggest that you spend some time reviewing Figure 10-3 to grasp the notion of a grand mean, along with the individual sample means. The different means are highlighted in the illustration. Once you've done that, we can move to the question of variation and how we measure it.

From Different Means to Different Types of Variation

To understand the matter of variation, think back to the idea of the deviation of a score or value from a mean (a concept introduced in Chapter 3). The concept of variation typically involves the extent to which various scores in a distribution deviate from the mean of the distribution. We can easily apply the same idea to the problem we're considering here.

Let's start with the sample or group means. We'll begin with Sample A. We already know that Sample A has a mean based on the scores from eight cases, so it's easy to think in terms of how far each of the eight scores or values deviates from the mean of Sample A. For an illustration of that point, take a look at the first column in Figure 10-4.

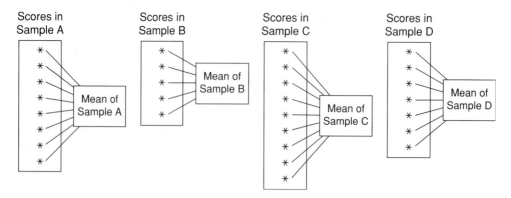

Figure 10-4   Illustration of Within-Groups Variation (Deviation of Individual Sample Scores from the Mean of the Sample)

Figure 10-4 is much the same as Figure 10-3, but with some added information. It illustrates the notion that each score or value in Sample A deviates by some amount from the mean of Sample A. Moving across to Samples B, C, and D, we encounter the same idea again and again. Each sample has a mean and individual scores or values within each sample deviate or vary from the sample mean. In other words, there is a certain amount of variation associated with each sample. This sort of deviation is what we mean by *within-groups variation.*

Now let's turn our attention to another form of variation. You'll recall from our previous discussion that we could obtain a grand mean by adding all the scores and dividing by 29 (since there are 29 cases or scores in our example). Assuming we did that, we could then calculate the difference between the mean of each sample and the grand mean—another form of variation. To get a picture of this sort of variation, take a look at Figure 10-5.

As shown in Figure 10-5, the mean of Sample A deviates a certain number of points from the grand mean, the mean of Sample B deviates a certain number of points from the grand mean, and so on. This sort of deviation is what we mean by *between-groups variation.*

Your success in understanding the ANOVA procedure will largely depend on your ability to fully comprehend these two forms of variation, so let me urge you to take a dark room moment at this point. Allow yourself to think in totally abstract terms—three samples, or seven samples, or whatever number suits you.

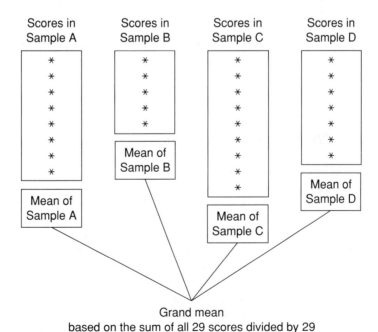

Grand mean
based on the sum of all 29 scores divided by 29

Figure 10-5 Illustration of Between-Groups Variation (Deviations of Sample Means from the Grand Mean)

Also allow yourself to think in terms of however many cases you want to have in each sample. Imagine that you've calculated a mean for each sample or group, and you've calculated a grand or overall mean. The specifics aren't important at this point. What's important is the notion of two forms of variation. First, there's the variation of scores or values from the individual sample means. Then, there's the variation of each sample mean from the grand mean.

Whenever you think about the variation of individual scores from a sample mean, remind yourself that you're thinking about *within-groups variation* (simply the variation within each sample). Whenever you think about the variation of a sample mean from the grand mean, remind yourself that you're thinking in terms of *between-groups variation* (or the variation of each sample mean from the grand mean). Repeat the process over and over with different mental images. Repeat the process until you're totally comfortable with the concepts of within-groups and between-groups variation. Assuming you've spent sufficient time thinking about those concepts, we can move on to a statement of the null hypothesis.

   LEARNING CHECK

Question: What is between-groups variation, and what is within-groups variation?

Answer: Between-groups variation is an expression of the amount of deviation of sample means from the grand mean. Within-groups variation is an expression of the amount of deviation of sample scores from sample means.

The Null Hypothesis

To understand the null hypothesis that's appropriate in the case of ANOVA, let's take up a less abstract example. Let's say, for example, that we're interested in urban unemployment and whether or not the unemployment levels in cities vary by region of the country. Let's also assume that we've used a random sampling technique to select cites in four different regions, and we've recorded the unemployment levels (measured as the percentage of the labor force currently unemployed in each city). Further, let's assume that we've calculated a group mean for each region (four means, one for each of the regions), and an overall mean (based on the unemployment levels in all the cities in our study). The null hypothesis for our study simply states that the means of the regions are equal. It can be stated symbolically as follows:

$$H_0: \mu_1 = \mu_2 = \mu_3 = \mu_4$$

In terms of the *F* ratio, recall that there has to be more variation *between* the regions than *within* the regions for the *F* ratio to be significant. It all goes back to the notion that the *F* ratio is an expression of the ratio of the variation between groups to the variation within groups; the larger the *F* ratio, the more likely it is to be significant. If all the sample means were equal, there wouldn't be any between-groups variation. That, of course, is the situation described by the null hypothesis.

We'll eventually calculate the *F* ratio (our test statistic) as a test of the null hypothesis, and we'll arrive at a conclusion. If our calculated test statistic (the *F* ratio) meets or exceeds the critical value, we'll reject the null hypothesis (with a known probability of having committed a Type I error). All of that will eventually unfold as we work through an application of ANOVA, so that's where we'll turn next.

The Application

We'll begin our application by looking at the data presented in Table 10-1. The table presents the unemployment data for cities in four regions, described in the previous scenario. The same assumptions we encountered in the difference of means test apply in this case—namely, that the unemployment levels (expressed as a percentage of the labor force) represent interval/ratio level data and that the cities were randomly selected. Following the normal convention, we want to select a level of significance in advance, so we'll set that at .05.

Take a few moments to examine the data presented in Table 10-1. First, take note that the sample sizes are different. ANOVA doesn't require the different

Table 10-1 Levels of Unemployment by Region

North	South	East	West	
3.8	4.2	8.8	4.8	
7.1	6.5	5.1	1.2	
9.6	4.4	12.7	8.0	
8.4	8.1	6.4	9.4	
5.1	7.6	9.8	3.6	
11.6	5.8	6.3	8.7	
6.2	4.0	10.2	6.5	
7.9	7.3	8.5		
9.0	5.2	11.9		
10.3	4.8	8.6		Sample mean
$\bar{X} = 7.90$	$\bar{X} = 5.79$	$\bar{X} = 8.83$	$\bar{X} = 6.03$	
$n = 10$	$n = 10$	$n = 10$	$n = 7$	Number of cases in a given sample
Grand (Overall) Mean = 7.23				

samples to be based on the same number of cases. Second, give some thought to what an informal inspection of the data suggests. The levels of unemployment appear to be relatively high in the northern region, but that's also the case in the eastern region. In contrast, the levels of unemployment in the southern and western regions appear to be somewhat lower.

Apparent differences here or there might suggest that it's reasonable to speak in terms of regional variation (at least when it comes to levels of unemployment), but the mere appearance of variation isn't enough in the world of statistical analysis. What's required is a measure of variation that is precise—and that's what the ANOVA procedure is all about. ANOVA allows us to go beyond mere visual inspection of the data and to accurately measure the ratio (*F* ratio) of between-groups variation to within-groups variation. With ANOVA applied to the problem, we'll be in a position to arrive at a conclusion grounded in measurement.

With all of that as a background, we can begin the calculation of the *F* ratio. Up to this point, I've been using the term *variation* in a very general sense. As it turns out, what we're actually going to calculate are two estimates of variance. More specifically, we're going to develop an estimate of the between-groups variance and an estimate of the within-groups variance. In other words, the *F* ratio will be an expression as follows:

$$F \text{ ratio} = \frac{\text{Estimate of between-groups variance}}{\text{Estimate of within-groups variance}}$$

The process used to develop the estimates isn't difficult, but it is a little tedious (particularly if you calculate them by hand, as opposed to relying on a computer and some statistical software). Much of the complexity can be reduced, however, if the process is broken down into its component parts:

1. Calculate what's known as the sums of squares.
2. Convert the sums of squares to estimates of variance.

The process sounds more complicated than it really is, so don't be discouraged. First, we'll approach everything in a step-by-step fashion. Second, the process is remarkably similar to one we encountered earlier, in Chapter 3, when we first encountered the concept of variance. Just as we did in Chapter 3, we'll start with a calculation of the squared deviations—what we refer to in ANOVA as the *sum of squares*.

Calculating the Within-Groups Sum of Squares (SS_W)

My preference is always to begin with the calculation of the **within-groups sum of squares (SS$_W$)**, simply because it is a bit more straightforward than the calculation of the between-groups sum of squares. We begin the process by focusing on the mean of each sample in our study. The mean unemployment level for each region is shown at the bottom of each column in Table 10-1, along with the number of cases.

First, we'll focus on the extent to which the level of unemployment for each city in a particular region deviates, or varies, from the regional mean. For example, we'll look at the extent to which the unemployment level for each city in the southern region deviates from the mean for that region, the extent to which the unemployment level for each city in the northern region deviates from the mean of that region, and so on. We will get a measure of the deviation by subtracting the regional mean from the unemployment level of each city within that region. In other words, we'll get a mathematical expression of the deviation through a simple process of subtraction.

As you learned in Chapter 3, however, the sum of the deviations from the mean always equals 0, so we'll have to square the deviations. Then we'll sum the squared deviations in each region to obtain the sum of squares for each region. In other words, each region will eventually have its own sum of squared deviations. Finally, we'll add up all the sums of squares for all the regions. This total will be the within-groups sum of squares (SS_W).

This portion of the ANOVA calculation is illustrated in Table 10-2. As you can see, the result of the within-groups sum of squares calculation is 179.29 ($SS_W = 179.29$).

I suspect you'll agree that the expression *within-groups sum of squares* is an apt phrase. After all, the process consists of calculating deviations, squaring the deviations, and summing the squared deviations across the different samples. The individual steps in the computation of the SS_W are shown below. Note how these steps correspond to the computations reflected in Table 10-2.

$$
\begin{aligned}
SS_W = {}& (3.8 - 7.90)^2 + (7.1 - 7.90)^2 + (9.6 - 7.90)^2 + (8.4 - 7.90)^2 + (5.1 - 7.90)^2 \\
&+ (11.6 - 7.90)^2 + (6.2 - 7.90)^2 + (7.9 - 7.90)^2 + (9.0 - 7.90)^2 + (10.3 - 7.90)^2 \\
&+ (4.2 - 5.79)^2 + (6.5 - 5.79)^2 + (4.4 - 5.79)^2 + (8.1 - 5.79)^2 + (7.6 - 5.79)^2 \\
&+ (5.8 - 5.79)^2 + (4.0 - 5.79)^2 + (7.3 - 5.79)^2 + (5.2 - 5.79)^2 + (4.8 - 5.79)^2 \\
&+ (8.8 - 8.83)^2 + (5.1 - 8.83)^2 + (12.7 - 8.83)^2 + (6.4 - 8.83)^2 + (9.8 - 8.83)^2 \\
&+ (6.3 - 8.83)^2 + (10.2 - 8.83)^2 + (8.5 - 8.83)^2 + (11.9 - 8.83)^2 + (8.6 - 8.83)^2 \\
&+ (4.8 - 6.03)^2 + (1.2 - 6.03)^2 + (8.0 - 6.03)^2 + (9.4 - 6.03)^2 + (3.6 - 6.03)^2 \\
&+ (8.7 - 6.03)^2 + (6.5 - 6.03)^2 \\
= {}& 51.98 + 20.39 + 53.59 + 53.33 \\
= {}& 179.29
\end{aligned}
$$

☑️ LEARNING CHECK

Question: What is the symbol for the within-groups sum of squares, and how is it calculated?

Answer: The symbol is SS_W. It is calculated by finding the deviation of each score in a sample from the sample mean, squaring the deviations, adding the squared deviations for each sample, and summing across all the samples.

Table 10-2 Calculating the Within-Groups Sum of Squares

North

X	$X - \bar{X}$	$(X - \bar{X})^2$
3.8	-4.10	16.81
7.1	-0.80	0.64
9.6	1.70	2.89
8.4	0.50	0.25
5.1	-2.80	7.84
11.6	3.70	13.69
6.2	-1.70	2.89
7.9	0.00	0.00
9.0	1.10	1.21
10.3	2.40	5.76

$\Sigma X = 79.0$

$\bar{X} = \dfrac{79.0}{10} = 7.90$

$\Sigma(X - \bar{X})^2 = 51.98$

$SS_{North} = 51.98$

South

X	$X - \bar{X}$	$(X - \bar{X})^2$
4.2	-1.59	2.53
6.5	0.71	0.50
4.4	-1.39	1.93
8.1	2.31	5.34
7.6	1.81	3.28
5.8	0.01	0.00
4.0	-1.79	3.20
7.3	1.51	2.28
5.2	-0.59	0.35
4.8	-0.99	0.98

$\Sigma X = 57.9$

$\bar{X} = \dfrac{57.9}{10} = 5.79$

$\Sigma(X - \bar{X})^2 = 20.39$

$SS_{South} = 20.39$

East

X	$X - \bar{X}$	$(X - \bar{X})^2$
8.8	-0.03	0.00
5.1	-3.73	13.91
12.7	3.87	14.98
6.4	-2.43	5.90
9.8	0.97	0.94
6.3	-2.53	6.40
10.2	1.37	1.88
8.5	-0.33	0.11
11.9	3.07	9.42
8.6	-0.23	0.05

$\Sigma X = 88.3$

$\bar{X} = \dfrac{88.3}{10} = 8.83$

$\Sigma(X - \bar{X})^2 = 53.59$

$SS_{East} = 53.59$

West

X	$X - \bar{X}$	$(X - \bar{X})^2$
4.8	-1.23	1.51
1.2	-4.83	23.33
8.0	1.97	3.88
9.4	3.37	11.36
3.6	-2.43	5.90
8.7	2.67	7.13
6.5	0.47	0.22

$\Sigma X = 42.2$

$\bar{X} = \dfrac{42.2}{7} = 6.03$

$\Sigma(X - \bar{X})^2 = 53.33$

$SS_{West} = 53.33$

$$SS_W = 51.98 + 20.39 + 53.59 + 53.33 = 179.29$$

Calculating the Between-Groups Sum of Squares (SS_B)

Now we turn to the between-groups element. The grand mean (7.23) was reported in Table 10-1, along with the mean for each region. To calculate the **between-groups sum of squares (SS_B)**, we'll follow a procedure similar to the previous one, but with a slight hitch in the process. Let me explain.

As noted previously, this part of the ANOVA procedure requires that we calculate the deviation (or, more correctly, the squared deviation) of each regional mean from the grand mean and sum those squared deviations across the regions. This will give us our between-groups sum of squares (SS_B). Unfortunately, however, it's not as straightforward as it might appear at first glance. As it turns out, we have to take into account the number of cases that went into the production of each regional mean. In other words, a regional mean based on 10 cases is one thing, but a regional mean based on, let's say, 7 cases is a different matter. Here's why.

We're going to focus on how far each regional mean departs from the grand mean, but we have to start by recognizing that the grand mean was, in part, a function of the total number of cases spread over several regions. Different regions, however, made different contributions to the grand mean. Three regions contributed 10 values or cases each, but another region (the western region) contributed only 7 values or cases. It's only appropriate, therefore, that we take into account the different contribution of each region as we move forward with our calculations. We'll do that by *weighting* our results by the number of cases in each region.

Yes, we're going to subtract the grand mean from the mean of each region to obtain a deviation. Then we're going to square that deviation. But then we're going to weight the result. We do that by multiplying the squared deviation of each region by the number of cases in the region. To better understand this weighting procedure, take a close look at Table 10-3.

As shown in Table 10-3, we subtract the grand mean from each regional mean, square the deviation, and then multiply it by the number of cases in that region. Finally, we sum across the regions to obtain the between-groups sum of squares (SS_B). Remember: We need to take into account the number of cases that were involved in the production of each sample or group mean. Therefore, we weight each group's squared deviation by the number of cases in the group. This important step is one you have to take, even if all the groups or samples have an equal number of cases.

The computations underlying the SS_B are summarized below. My suggestion is that you make a thorough study of those computations, as well as the details of Table 10-3. Once you do that, you'll be in a better position to see how we arrived at a between-groups sum of squares 60.88 ($SS_B = 60.88$).

$$
\begin{aligned}
SS_B &= 10(7.90 - 7.23)^2 + 10(5.79 - 7.23)^2 + 10(8.83 - 7.23)^2 \\
&\quad + 7(6.03 - 7.23)^2 \\
&= 4.50 + 20.70 + 25.60 + 10.08 \\
&= 60.88
\end{aligned}
$$

Table 10-3   Calculating the Between-Groups Sum of Squares

Grand Mean = 7.23

North	South
$SS_B = n(\overline{X} - \overline{X}_{Grand})^2$	$SS_B = n(\overline{X} - \overline{X}_{Grand})^2$
$= 10(7.90 - 7.23)^2$	$= 10(5.79 - 7.23)^2$
$= 10(0.67)^2$	$= 10(-1.44)^2$
$= 10(0.45)$	$= 10(2.07)$
$= 4.50$	$= 20.70$

Mean of North = 7.90   Mean of South = 5.79
$n = 10$ $n = 10$

East	West
$SS_B = n(\overline{X} - \overline{X}_{Grand})^2$	$SS_B = n(\overline{X} - \overline{X}_{Grand})^2$
$= 10(8.83 - 7.23)^2$	$= 7(6.03 - 7.23)^2$
$= 10(1.60)^2$	$= 7(-1.20)^2$
$= 10(2.56)$	$= 7(1.44)$
$= 25.60$	$= 10.08$

Mean of East = 8.83   Mean of West = 6.03
$n = 10$ $n = 7$

$$SS_B = 4.50 + 20.70 + 25.60 + 10.08 = 60.88$$

 LEARNING CHECK

Question: What is the symbol for the between-groups sum of
squares, and how is it calculated?

Answer: The symbol is SS_B. It is calculated by finding the deviation
of each sample mean from the grand mean, squaring the
deviation, weighting the squared deviation for each sample, and summing across all the samples.

Even if you feel totally comfortable with the notion of the between-groups
sum of squares concept, let me suggest that you take a short break at this point.
We've covered quite a bit. Spend a little time thinking about the sum of squares
within (SS_W) and the sum of squares between (SS_B). Concentrate on how you
calculated each, and think of these as the first important steps toward the
computation of the F ratio. Take whatever amount of time is necessary—
there's still another important step ahead.

From Sums of Squares to Estimates of Variance

Assuming you took the suggested break, our next task is to transform the two sum of squares elements (SS_B and SS_W) into estimates of variance. It's actually a simple process. All we have to do is divide each sum of squares element (SS_B and SS_W) by an appropriate number of degrees of freedom. The procedure is essentially the same as the calculation of the variance for a sample (as presented in Chapter 3). Let me urge you to review that chapter if you sense you're unsure about any of this. The estimates of variance are referred to as the **mean square between (MS_B)** and the **mean square within (MS_W)**. Just to solidify the two in your thinking, they are summarized as follows:

> MS_B = mean square between (an estimate of the between-groups variance)
>
> MS_W = mean square within (an estimate of the within-groups variance)

 LEARNING CHECK

Question: What do the mean square between and mean square within represent?

Answer: The mean square between is the estimate of the between-groups variance. The mean square within is the estimate of the within-groups variance.

Question: What are the symbols for the mean square between and mean square within?

Answer: The symbols are MS_B and MS_W, respectively.

Since the fundamental nature of the ANOVA procedure can sometimes get lost in the midst of different symbols and notations, let's take a moment to review where we've been and where we're going:

1. The goal is to calculate an F ratio.
2. The F ratio is the ratio of an estimate of the between-groups variance to an estimate of the within-groups variance.
3. These estimates are derived through a two-step process.
    a. First, we compute sums of squares (between and within).
    b. Then we transform the sums of squares to estimates of variance (known as mean squares).
4. The F ratio is derived by dividing the estimate of the between-groups variance (MS_B) by the estimate of the within-groups variance (MS_W).

Note that we haven't executed Steps 3b and 4 just yet; those will be our final steps.

Since we already have our within-groups and between-groups sums of squares, our next task is to convert the sums of squares into the mean squares, or estimates of variance. As a prelude to that, a little review of the variance is in order.

The Concept of Variance. Think back to what you learned in Chapter 3 about the variance of a distribution. Recall that the variance allowed us to get around the problem that the sum of the deviations from the mean always equals 0. You'll probably also recall how the variance was computed, both for a population and a sample. You learned that the variance for a population was computed as follows:

$$\text{Variance of a population} = \frac{\Sigma (X - \mu)^2}{N}$$

Looking carefully at the formula for the population variance, you'll note that the numerator actually amounts to the sum of squared deviations (not unlike the sum of squares we've been discussing so far), and the denominator is simply the number of cases in the population (N).

When it came to the variance of a sample, however, we introduced a slight correction factor. Instead of using N in the denominator, we used $n - 1$ (or the degrees of freedom). The denominator $n - 1$ (degrees of freedom) was used in an effort to arrive at a sample variance that would be a more accurate estimate of the population variance. If your memory is a little faulty on this point, let me suggest you take the time to review the material in Chapter 3. My guess is that it will be important to your understanding of what we encounter next.

Assuming you've taken that time, or you feel secure without the review, let's focus now on the estimates of variance that we're going to develop. First we'll develop an estimate of the between-groups variance. Then we'll develop an estimate of the within-groups variance. Both estimates are developed in much the same way.

First, the **between-groups estimate of variance** (known as the mean square between or MS_B) is derived by dividing the between-groups sum of squares (SS_B) by the appropriate number of degrees of freedom (df_B). Then the **within-groups estimate of variance** (known as the mean square within, or MS_W) is derived by dividing the within-groups sum of squares (SS_W) by the appropriate number of degrees of freedom (df_W). The process can be summarized as follows:

Between-Groups Estimate of Variance

$$\text{Mean Square Between } (MS_B) = \frac{\text{Between-Groups Sum of Squares } (SS_B)}{\text{Between-Groups Degrees of Freedom } (df_B)}$$

Within-Groups Estimate of Variance

$$\text{Mean Square Within } (MS_W) = \frac{\text{Within-Groups Sum of Squares } (SS_W)}{\text{Within-Groups Degrees of Freedom } (df_W)}$$

Obviously, we have to determine the appropriate number of degrees of freedom for each element, so that's where we'll turn now.

Degrees of Freedom. For this portion of the discussion, let's start with the between-groups sum of squares. Think back for a moment to how we computed the between-groups sum of squares (SS_B). If necessary, review the computations outlined in Table 10-3 and the associated discussion. First, we calculated the deviation of each sample mean from the grand or overall mean. Then, we squared the deviations. Next, we multiplied the squared deviation for each sample by the number of cases in each sample. Finally, we summed the squared deviations (multiplied by the number of cases in the sample) across all the samples. The result (the between-groups sum of squares) was 60.88.

The problem we're considering here involves four samples (four regions). In the language of ANOVA, the four samples represent four categories (symbolized by $k = 4$). The number of degrees of freedom associated with the between-groups estimate of variance (df_B) is $k - 1$. Since we have four categories, the **between-groups degrees of freedom** can be calculated as follows:

$$df_B = k - 1$$
$$df_B = 4 - 1$$
$$df_B = 3$$

 LEARNING CHECK

Question: How many degrees of freedom are associated with the between-groups estimate of variance (MS_B)?

Answer: The number of degrees of freedom for MS_B is $k - 1$, where k = the number of categories or samples in the study.

To obtain our between-groups estimate of variance (MS_B), we'll simply divide our between-groups sum of squares $(SS_B = 60.88)$ by the between-groups degrees of freedom $(df_B = 3)$.

$$MS_B = \frac{SS_B}{df_B}$$
$$MS_B = \frac{60.88}{3}$$
$$MS_B = 20.29$$

At this point, you should note how closely this relates to the notion of using $n - 1$ in the computation of the sample variance to obtain an unbiased estimate of the population variance.

☑ LEARNING CHECK

Question: How is the between-groups estimate of variance (MS_B) obtained?

Answer: The between-groups estimate of variance (MS_B) is obtained by dividing the between-groups sum of squares (SS_B) by the between-groups degrees of freedom (df_B).

Our next step is to develop our within-groups estimate of variance, and we'll use a similar procedure—we'll divide the within-groups sum of squares by an appropriate number of degrees of freedom. Now, of course, the question is how to determine the appropriate number of degrees of freedom for the within-groups element.

The degrees of freedom in the case of the within-groups sum of squares is a function of the total number of cases, as well as the number of samples or categories. In the present instance, we have a total of 37 cases spread over four categories. The appropriate number of degrees of freedom for the estimate of within-groups variance is equal to $n_{total} - k$, or the total number of cases minus the number of categories. With 37 cases and four categories, the **within-groups degrees of freedom** (df_W) can be calculated as follows:

$$df_W = n_{total} - k$$
$$df_W = 37 - 4$$
$$df_W = 33$$

If you take a close look at the formula for the within-groups degrees of freedom ($n_{total} - k$), you'll see that it's actually equal to the sum of the number of cases in each sample minus 1:

$$(n_1 - 1) + (n_2 - 1) + (n_3 - 1) + (n_4 - 1) = 33$$
$$(10 - 1) + (10 - 1) + (10 - 1) + (7 - 1) = 9 + 9 + 9 + 6 = 33$$

☑ LEARNING CHECK

Question: How many degrees of freedom are associated with the within-groups estimate of variance (MS_W)?

Answer: The number of degrees of freedom for MS_W is $n_{total} - k$ where n_{total} = the number of cases in the study and k = the number of categories or samples in the study.

Having determined that the appropriate number of degrees of freedom for the within-groups sum of squares is equal to 33, we can calculate the within-groups estimate of variance, or MS_W, as follows:

$$MS_W = \frac{SS_W}{df_W}$$

$$MS_W = \frac{179.29}{33}$$

$$MS_W = 5.43$$

 LEARNING CHECK

Question: How is the within-groups estimate of variance (MS_W) obtained?

Answer: The within-groups estimate of variance (MS_W) is obtained by dividing the within-groups sum of squares (SS_W) by the within-groups degrees of freedom (df_W).

We've already been through several steps, so let me suggest that you take a look at Table 10-4. This summary table outlines the important elements we've encountered along the way and gives you a look ahead toward the final step.

Calculating the F Ratio

Having developed the estimates of the between-groups variance ($MS_B = 20.29$) and within-groups variance ($MS_W = 5.43$), we're now in a position to calculate the F ratio. This ratio is obtained by dividing the between-groups estimate of variance (MS_B) by the within-groups estimate of variance (MS_W). The calculation is as follows:

$$F = \frac{MS_B}{MS_W}$$

$$F = \frac{20.29}{5.43}$$

$$F = 3.74$$

Table 10-4 Components of ANOVA

Group or Sample Means

Mean of Northern Cities	= 7.90	$n = 10$
Mean of Southern Cities	= 5.79	$n = 10$
Mean of Eastern Cities	= 8.83	$n = 10$
Mean of Western Cities	= 6.03	$n = 7$

Grand Mean = 7.23

┌── **Calculate the Sums of Squares**

Between-groups sum of squares (SS_B) = 60.88
Within-groups sum of squares (SS_W) = 179.29

┊┄┄┄┄┄┄ **Degrees of Freedom**

Between-groups degrees of freedom (df_B) = 3
Within-groups degrees of freedom (df_W) = 33

└── **Divide Sums of Squares by Appropriate Degrees of Freedom to Obtain the Estimates of Variance (the Mean Square Component)**

Between-groups estimate of variance, or mean square between (MS_B) = 20.29
Within-groups estimate of variance, or mean square within (MS_W) = 5.43

└──▶ Calculate the F Ratio $\dfrac{MS_B}{MS_W}$

 LEARNING CHECK

Question: How is the *F* ratio calculated?
Answer: The *F* ratio is calculated as follows:

$$\frac{MS_B}{MS_W}$$

So, the calculated *F* ratio (our test statistic) equals 3.74. We have a final answer—but what does it really mean? By now, you should find yourself in very familiar territory. After all, it's really just another hypothesis-testing situation.

The Interpretation

As we've already done in what probably seems like countless situations before, we find ourselves looking at a calculated test statistic—in this case, an *F* ratio. But now the question is whether or not the *F* ratio is significant. As before, the answer turns on the critical value. If our calculated test statistic (the calculated value of F) meets or exceeds the critical value, we have significant results, and we can reject the null hypothesis. If, on the other hand, our calculated test statistic falls below the critical value, we'll fail to reject the null hypothesis.

Interpretation of the F Ratio

Our next task, then, is to locate the critical value. For that information, we turn to Appendix D: Distribution of F at the .05 Level of Significance (the level of significance that we selected at the outset). Once again, to use the table we have to take into account our degrees of freedom. We know that the degrees of freedom associated with the between-groups estimate of variance is 3, and the degrees of freedom associated with the within-groups estimate of variance is 33.

If you take a close look at Appendix D, you'll note that the degrees of freedom for the between-groups variance element (the numerator in the F ratio) are listed across the top row of the table. The degrees of freedom for the within-groups variance element (the denominator in the F ratio) are listed in the first column. Once we've identified the appropriate degrees of freedom in the top row and first column, we locate the point at which the two intersect in the table. Note, however, that there is no listing for 33 degrees of freedom. At this point, you should recall our earlier rule of thumb (noted in Appendix B)—namely, find the next lower number of degrees of freedom. Therefore, you should use the value associated with 30 degrees of freedom. That value—2.92—is our appropriate critical value.

All that remains is to compare our calculated F ratio to the critical value. As it turns out, our calculated F value of 3.74 exceeds the critical value. Therefore, we reject the null hypothesis. As before, we're rejecting the null hypothesis with a known probability of having committed a Type I or alpha error (.05).

In rejecting the null hypothesis, we move a step toward suggesting that levels of unemployment in cities do vary by region. That, of course, is another way of saying it's probably legitimate to think in terms of a regional classification scheme when speaking about levels of unemployment.

Had we failed to achieve significant results, however, we would have failed to reject the null hypothesis. Since the null was a statement that the means would be equal, failing to reject the null would be tantamount to saying that there is no significant variation across the regions. In that case, it wouldn't make much sense to speak in terms of regional variation.

Whatever the final outcome of an ANOVA application, it's always important to keep in mind what the bigger picture is all about. As we've done before, we return to the central notion that what we're really interested in are populations—not samples. In this instance, our interest was in the population of all cities in the northern region, all cities in the southern region, all cities in the eastern region, and all cities in the western region. That we had sample data to work with was important in reaching our final goal, but we were ultimately interested in the larger picture.

Working at the .05 level of significance, we determined that we could reject the null hypothesis. Is it possible that the results of the sample data gave us a false picture? Yes, of course that's possible. There's always a chance that the ratio of our estimates was the result of sampling error and that the calculated F ratio isn't a reflection of what's really going on in the population. If that's what happened, then we would have made a Type I error.

As we know all too well, however, we'll never know if that was the case. That's just the way it is, and there's no getting around it (short of collecting data on all cities). We always have to live with the chance of a Type I error. On the positive side, however, we always know the probability that we've made such an error. In the case of our example, it was only 5 times out of 100.

Had we wanted to, we could have set our level of significance at .01, and that would have reduced the probability of a Type I error. In fact, that's what Appendix E is all about; it shows the Distribution of F at the .01 Level of Significance. A quick check of the appropriate critical value in Appendix E would tell us that our results were not significant at the .01 level. In other words, had we been working at the .01 level of significance, we would have failed to reject the null hypothesis. In this case, however, we were working at the .05 level of significance, and our results were significant. As a result, we were in position to reject the null hypothesis.

If you think about the ANOVA procedure for any length of time, you're apt to conclude that it only gives us a general picture regarding the null hypothesis. ANOVA allows us to determine whether or not there's a significant difference across groups or samples, but it doesn't tell us much about the specific nature of any difference. As Gravetter and Wallnau (1999, p. 338) note:

> When you reject the null hypothesis, you conclude that the means are not all the same. Although this appears to be a simple conclusion, in most cases it actually creates more questions than it answers.

To better understand that observation, think back to our interpretation of the F ratio in the problem we just considered. We found a significant F ratio, but the conclusion left the door open to further questioning. Recall how the conclusion was phrased: It is probably legitimate to think in terms of a regional classification scheme when speaking about levels of unemployment. But questions still remain as to what produced the significant F ratio in the first place. To get the answers to those questions, a statistician typically turns to post hoc testing procedures.

Post Hoc Testing

As the expression implies, post hoc testing allows us to go beyond the determination that we have a significant F ratio. As noted previously, a significant F ratio does not necessarily mean that there was a significant difference between all means when examined in terms of all possible combinations. Maybe the difference between the means of the first and second samples was so large that it had a major impact on the calculation of the between-groups variation. On the other hand, maybe it was an unusually large difference between the means of the third and fourth samples. Maybe the significant results derived from noticeable differences between *all* the means. In short, having significant results is one thing; understanding the origin of the significance is another.

Fortunately, procedures are available that allow us to peel back the findings, so to speak, and gain a better understanding of which differences of means were really responsible for the final *F* value. Tukey's Honestly Significant Difference (HSD) is such a procedure. It is considered a post hoc test, in that it's employed after significant results are found. In short, Tukey's HSD allows us to determine where the significant differences between individual means are to be found.

The HSD procedure involves the calculation of what's known as the *Q* statistic. It rests on a pair-by-pair comparison of sample means. In the example used throughout this chapter, we have four samples and, therefore, four sample means. The HSD procedure applied to our problem would involve the following six comparisons:

Mean of Sample 1	and	Mean of Sample 2
Mean of Sample 1	and	Mean of Sample 3
Mean of Sample 1	and	Mean of Sample 4
Mean of Sample 2	and	Mean of Sample 3
Mean of Sample 2	and	Mean of Sample 4
Mean of Sample 3	and	Mean of Sample 4

The calculation of *Q* is fairly straightforward. It is calculated once for each comparison, so in this case, *Q* will be calculated six times.

For each comparison, we calculate the absolute difference (the difference without regard to positive or negative sign) between the two sample means. This absolute difference becomes the numerator in the test statistic (*Q*). The denominator is partly a function of the MS_W that was calculated in the ANOVA procedure. There are actually two different ways to calculate the denominator of the *Q* statistic. One version is for situations in which the sample sizes are equal; the other version is appropriate for ANOVA applications with unequal sample sizes. The example we considered in this chapter was based on unequal sample sizes, but here are both formulas.

When All Sample Sizes Are Equal

$$Q = \frac{|\overline{X}_1 - \overline{X}_2|}{\sqrt{\dfrac{MS_W}{n}}}$$

Where $\overline{X}_1$ and $\overline{X}_2$ are any two means and *n* represents the number of cases in each sample.

When Any Two Samples Sizes Are Unequal

$$Q = \frac{|\overline{X}_1 - \overline{X}_2|}{\sqrt{\dfrac{MS_W}{\tilde{n}}}}$$

Where $\overline{X}_1$ and $\overline{X}_2$ are any two means and $\tilde{n}$ represents the harmonic mean sample size. The harmonic mean is calculated as follows:

$$\tilde{n} = \frac{k}{\dfrac{1}{n_1} + \dfrac{1}{n_2} + \dfrac{1}{n_3} + \dfrac{1}{n_4}}$$

Since our example involves unequal sample sizes, we will use the second formula for Q. We'll start by calculating the harmonic mean. Recall that the formula for the harmonic mean is as follows:

$$\tilde{n} = \frac{k}{\dfrac{1}{n_1} + \dfrac{1}{n_2} + \dfrac{1}{n_3} + \dfrac{1}{n_4}}$$

Since we have four samples (groups or categories), the harmonic mean is calculated as follows:

$$\tilde{n} = \frac{k}{\dfrac{1}{n_1} + \dfrac{1}{n_2} + \dfrac{1}{n_3} + \dfrac{1}{n_4}}$$

$$= \frac{4}{\dfrac{1}{10} + \dfrac{1}{10} + \dfrac{1}{10} + \dfrac{1}{7}}$$

$$= \frac{4}{.10 + .10 + .10 + .14}$$

$$= \frac{4}{0.44}$$

$$= 9.09$$

Armed with the value of the harmonic mean ($\tilde{n} = 9.09$), our next step is to bring in the mean square within (MS_W). Our previous ANOVA computations tell us that $MS_W = 5.43$. We now divide the MS_W (5.43) by the harmonic mean (9.09) and take the square root of the result. This gives us the denominator for our calculation of Q.

$$\text{Denominator in } Q \text{ calculation} = \sqrt{\frac{MS_W}{\tilde{n}}}$$

$$= \sqrt{\frac{5.43}{9.09}}$$

$$= \sqrt{0.60}$$

$$= 0.77$$

Having calculated the denominator for our Q statistic, we can move through the remainder of the computations with relative ease. For each comparison, it is simply a matter of finding the absolute difference between two means, treating that value as the numerator, and dividing by the denominator that we just calculated. The steps in the process are summarized in Table 10-5.

As the summary indicates, we now have six Q values, or six different calculated Q test statistics. Each calculated Q test statistic relates to a particular comparison of means. Now all that remains is to examine whether or not the Q test statistic in question is significant for each individual comparison. That brings us to the matter of the critical value for Q—the value against which we will evaluate the individual Qs that we've calculated.

Appendix F provides the critical values of Q at the .05 level of significance. (If we were working at the .01 level of significance, we would use Appendix G.) The numbers across the top of the table refer to the number of groups or samples in the ANOVA that preceded application of the HSD measure. Since our problem is based on four samples or groups (northern, southern, eastern, and western cities), our focus will be on the column labeled 4. The within-groups degrees of freedom (df_W) is something we dealt with earlier. You will recall that the appropriate number of degrees of freedom for the within-groups element was $n - k$, or the total number of cases (37) minus the number of categories or groups (4). Therefore, the number of degrees of freedom within is $37 - 4$, or 33. As before, the table has no entry for 33 degrees of freedom, but we are safe in using the row for 30 degrees of freedom. The entry associated with 30 degrees of freedom and four samples is 3.85—and that becomes our critical value.

Now all that remains is to compare the various Q values that we calculated to the critical value of Q found in Appendix F. The results are shown in Table 10-6.

Having calculated Q for each comparison and having checked each against the critical value (3.85), we determine that the only significant difference is found between the southern region and the eastern region. It is not the case

Table 10-5 Calculation of Q for Tukey's HSD

Possible Comparisons	$|\overline{X}_1 - \overline{X}_2|$	$Q = \dfrac{|\overline{X}_1 - \overline{X}_2|}{\sqrt{\dfrac{MS_W}{\tilde{n}}}}$
North and South	$|7.90 - 5.79| = 2.11$	$2.11/0.77 = 2.74$
North and East	$|7.90 - 8.83| = 0.93$	$0.93/0.77 = 1.21$
North and West	$|7.90 - 6.03| = 1.87$	$1.87/0.77 = 2.43$
South and East	$|5.79 - 8.83| = 3.04$	$3.04/0.77 = 3.95$
South and West	$|5.79 - 6.03| = 0.24$	$0.24/0.77 = 0.31$
East and West	$|8.83 - 6.03| = 2.80$	$2.80/0.77 = 3.64$

Table 10-6 Interpreting Tukey's HSD

Possible Comparisons	Q	Results
North and South	2.74	Not Significant
North and East	1.21	Not Significant
North and West	2.43	Not Significant
South and East	3.95	***Significant***
South and West	0.31	Not Significant
East and West	3.64	Not Significant

that there is a significant difference across all regions. Rather, the significant difference is found only between two regions.

A finding like that would, no doubt, send us back to the drawing board, at least when it comes to the matter of a regional classification scheme. In a real-life situation, now would be the time to consider other types of regional classifications—maybe, for example, one that rests on only three designated regions of the country.

Questions like that are for another time and place. It's time to bring our discussion of one-way ANOVA to a close. Before leaving the topic, though, it might be useful to review several points and to underscore a few things you may want to think about.

- Think about ANOVA as being appropriate in situations involving three or more samples, provided you have interval/ratio level data to work with.
- Think about the fact that ANOVA can be appropriate even if the samples have an unequal number of cases.
- Think about the F ratio as a ratio of two estimates of variance—the estimate of variance between groups and the estimate of variance within groups.
- Think about how the computation of the F ratio is essentially a two-step process—first the calculation of between and within sums of squares, and then a transformation of the sums of squares into estimates of variance.
- Think about how degrees of freedom come into play in the transformation of the sums of squares into the estimates of variance, with $k - 1$ degrees of freedom for the estimate between, and $n - k$ for the estimate within.

At the conclusion of this chapter you'll find several problems to consider. Some problems direct you to calculate the F ratio from beginning to end. Many of the problems, though, just pose questions about the component parts of the ANOVA procedure. Others give you the component parts of the ANOVA procedure; your job is to finish the calculations and provide an appropriate interpretation. My guess is that you'll find the questions sufficient to shore up your understanding of the topic.

Chapter Summary

With your introduction to ANOVA, you have been exposed to a widely used statistical procedure. Ideally, you have gained an understanding of why many statisticians think of it as an extension of the two-sample difference of means tests and why it can be thought of as a procedure that tests the legitimacy of a classification scheme. By the same token, you should have developed an understanding of why the procedure carries the name of *analysis of variance,* inasmuch as the *F* ratio is based on two estimates of variance.

As to the specific components of the ANOVA procedure, you encountered the concepts of the between- and within-groups sums of squares, as well as the between- and within-groups estimates of variance. You also developed an appreciation for the *F* ratio as an expression of the ratio of the two estimates of variance.

Beyond all of that, however, was an unstated lesson I hope you discovered along the way—namely, that the process of learning statistical applications gets easier and easier. It's true that different research situations call for different procedures. It's true that different procedures rest on different logical foundations and different calculations. But beyond that, the process of testing a null hypothesis remains fundamentally the same from application to application. State the null; set the level of significance; calculate the test statistic; compare the test statistic to a critical value; state a conclusion. As I mentioned before, you keep encountering the same process, over and over and over again.

Some Other Things You Should Know

There are still a few more things you should be aware of in connection with ANOVA. In a sense, we've just scratched the surface of ANOVA, so let me mention a few related matters.

As noted at the outset, the ANOVA procedure we considered in this chapter is technically known as one-way analysis of variance. It is referred to as one-way ANOVA because it is used in problems that deal with the relationship between one variable and another variable. For example, we dealt with an application that examined the variation in levels of unemployment (one variable) by region (the other variable).

A more complex application of ANOVA is available, however. For example, let's say we wanted to look at how levels of unemployment vary by region *and* type of city (manufacturing, retail, service, or other). In that case, we could opt for a two-way ANOVA application. The procedure is referred to as two-way ANOVA because it looks at how one variable varies on the basis of two other variables. To take another example, we might be interested in how student test scores vary by teaching method (lecture only, lecture plus discussion) and gender composition of the class (all-male classes, all-female classes, and combined male/female classes). This research question would also be suited for a two-way

ANOVA application. For an excellent discussion of the two-way ANOVA procedure, consult Pagano (2001).

Second, the ANOVA application that we just considered was based on the assumption that the samples were independent random samples. As was the case with the difference of means tests, a modified ANOVA procedure is available when the samples under consideration are matched or related. For a discussion of that application, see Dunn (2001).

Finally, the Tukey's HSD test that we considered is only one of a variety of post hoc test procedures that are available for use following an ANOVA application. The selection of one post hoc test over another is usually a function of several considerations. Discussions of various post hoc options are typically found in more advanced texts.

Key Terms

ANOVA (one-way)
between-groups degrees of freedom
between-groups estimate of variance
between-groups sum of squares (SS_B)
F ratio
grand (overall) mean

group (sample) mean
mean square between (MS_B)
mean square within (MS_W)
within-groups degrees of freedom
within-groups estimate of variance
within-groups sum of squares (SS_W)

Chapter Problems

Fill in the blanks, calculate the requested values, or otherwise supply the correct answer.

General Thought Questions

1. The calculated test statistic for ANOVA is known as the _____ ratio.
2. The F ratio is the ratio of the amount of variation _____ the groups to the amount of variation _____ the groups.
3. Explain how to calculate the within-groups sum of squares.
4. Explain how to calculate the between-groups sum of squares.
5. The between-groups sum of squares is transformed into an estimate of the between-groups variance by dividing the between-groups sum of squares by an appropriate number of _____.
6. The within-groups sum of squares is transformed into an estimate of the within-groups variance by dividing the within-groups sum of squares by an appropriate number of _____.
7. The formula for the number of degrees of freedom for the within-groups estimate of variance is _____, where n equals the total number of cases under consideration.

8. The formula for the number of degrees of freedom for the between-groups estimate of variance is _____, where k equals the number of groups or samples under consideration.

9. Another name for the between-groups estimate of variance is _____.

10. Another name for the within-groups estimate of variance is _____.

11. If you had a research problem appropriate for ANOVA and it was based on the results from three samples, what would be the null hypothesis?

Application Questions/Problems

1. Assume you had a research problem appropriate for ANOVA that was based on six samples and a total of 36 cases.
   a. How many degrees of freedom would be associated with the between-groups estimate of variance?
   b. How many degrees of freedom would be associated with the within-groups estimate of variance?

2. Assume the following:

   .05 level of significance; five samples; 21 cases; $SS_B = 26$; $SS_W = 29$
   a. Calculate the F ratio.
   b. What is the critical value?
   c. What would you conclude?

3. Assume the following:

   .05 level of significance; four samples; 30 cases; $SS_B = 80$; $SS_W = 258$
   a. Calculate the F ratio.
   b. What is the critical value?
   c. What would you conclude?

4. Assume the following:

   .05 level of significance; three samples; 27 cases $SS_B = 13$; $SS_W = 23$
   a. Calculate the F ratio.
   b. What is the critical value?
   c. What would you conclude?

5. Consider the following research data:

Sample 1	Sample 2	Sample 3
10	6	5
10	7	10
9	2	8
11	8	8
6	9	8
11	5	9
9	3	6
7	8	10
4		12
5		14
6		

a. State an appropriate null hypothesis.
b. What are the values of each category mean?
c. What is the value of the grand mean?
d. What is the value of the SS_B?
e. What is the value of the SS_W?
f. What is the value of the df_B?
g. What is the value of the df_W?
h. What is the value of the MS_W?
i. What is the value of the MS_B?
j. What is the value of F?
k. Assuming that you were working at the .05 level of significance, what would you conclude?

6. An evaluation survey, designed to measure perceived program effectiveness, was administered to a sample of 39 citizens who attended a community crime-prevention meeting. Using a scale of 0 to 10, the respondents were asked to rate the meeting in terms of effectiveness in presenting useful information. The responses were analyzed, based upon the place of residence of the respondent—northern sector, southern sector, eastern, or western sector—and the following results were found.

Northern	Southern	Eastern	Western
2	3	4	2
4	5	2	5
6	7	8	6
3	1	7	7
5	4	7	2
1	5	6	4
7	3	8	5
1	4	6	6
4		6	6
5			6
6			6

a. State an appropriate null hypothesis.
b. What are the values of each category mean?
c. What is the value of the grand mean?
d. What is the value of the SS_B?
e. What is the value of the SS_W?
f. What is the value of the df_B?
g. What is the value of the df_W?
h. What is the value of the MS_W?
i. What is the value of the MS_B?
j. What is the value of F?
k. Assuming you were working at the .05 level of significance, what would you conclude?

7. An industrial psychologist has examined the levels of absenteeism (measured in terms of days absent per year) of workers in three different work environments (morning shift, afternoon shift, and night shift). The results of the study are summarized as follows:

Day Shift	Afternoon Shift	Night Shift
3	6	5
4	4	6
3	5	4
5	4	3
7		5
$n = 5$	$n = 4$	$n = 5$

a. State an appropriate null hypothesis.
b. What are the values of each category mean?
c. What is the value of the grand mean?
d. What is the value of the SS_B?
e. What is the value of the SS_W?
f. What is the value of the df_B?
g. What is the value of the df_W?
h. What is the value of the MS_W?
i. What is the value of the MS_B?
j. What is the value of F?
k. Assuming you were working at the .05 level of significance, what would you conclude?

8. A social psychologist has been studying the relationship between group composition and level of cooperation on the part of preschool children in a task-completion exercise. Each group is observed, and the number of cooperative acts exhibited by each member of the group is recorded. Three types of groups are under study: all male, all female, and mixed (both male and female members). Results of the investigation are as follows:

All Male	All Female	Mixed Gender
4	6	3
4	9	5
3	8	6
1	4	4
3	8	7
4	8	6
$n = 6$	$n = 6$	$n = 6$

 a. State an appropriate null hypothesis.
 b. What are the values of each category mean?
 c. What is the value of the grand mean?
 d. What is the value of the SS_B?
 e. What is the value of the SS_W?
 f. What is the value of the df_B?
 g. What is the value of the df_W?
 h. What is the value of the MS_W?
 i. What is the value of the MS_B?
 j. What is the value of F?
 k. Assuming you were working at the .05 level of significance, what would you conclude?

The Chi-Square Test

Our trek through the world of hypothesis testing so far has involved procedures based on one or more means. For example, we used the t test to determine whether or not there was a significant difference between fraternity members and non-members in mean levels of alcohol consumption. We relied on the ANOVA procedure when we wanted to look at mean levels of unemployment in four regions. In each of those cases, one of the variables in the hypothesis was an interval/ratio level variable. The requirement of interval/ratio data is central to any hypothesis test involving means. The reason should be obvious: You can't calculate a mean unless you have interval/ratio data.

As you might expect, though, not all research situations involve interval-level data. Social scientists often encounter research situations in which the variables are measured at the nominal or ordinal level. The term **categorical**

data is typically used to describe information of this sort, because the data represent simple categories. Consider the following examples:

A response to a question might be *yes, no,* or *undecided.*

A response to a question might be *strongly agree, agree, disagree,* or *strongly disagree.*

A person might be classified as *Republican, Democrat,* or *Independent.*

A university might be classified as *public* or *private.*

When faced with a hypothesis-testing situation involving categorical variables (nominal or ordinal data), statisticians often turn to the chi-square test. In this chapter, we'll consider the chi-square test of independence, a procedure that is very appropriate for situations involving categorical data.

 LEARNING CHECK

Question: What does the term *categorical data* mean?
Answer: Data expressed in simple categories—nominal- or ordinal-level data.

Before We Begin

You were introduced to the notion of null hypotheses in Chapter 7, and you also learned that there were many ways to express a null hypothesis. As you moved through Chapters 7, 8, and 9, you were exposed to hypothesis testing in a variety of situations, but in most of those cases, you dealt with null hypotheses that were statements of *no difference.* In this chapter, though, you'll face something different.

First, you're going to be dealing with a different sort of data, and you won't be calculating any means. It follows, therefore, that you'll have to change your vocabulary. Instead of hypotheses about such notions as no difference between means, you'll be dealing with null hypotheses that speak in terms of no relationship or chance relationship. All of that will make more sense as we move forward. For the moment, simply prepare for a slight shift in perspective.

The Chi-Square Test of Independence

The **chi-square test of independence** is a test that allows us to determine whether or not two variables are associated in some way. For example, it allows us to answer the following sorts of questions:

Is political affiliation associated with attitude toward a certain issue?

Is gender associated with selection of an academic major?

Is place of residence associated with attitude on a certain issue?

As you explore the chi-square test of independence, you'll actually go beyond the specific test application. Indeed, you'll also learn quite a bit about how statisticians look at the association between variables in general. As always, we'll start with a look at the logic behind the test.

 LEARNING CHECK

Question: What is the chi-square test of independence?

Answer: A hypothesis-testing procedure appropriate for categorical variables. It tests whether or not there is an association between two variables.

The Logic of the Test

Let's start with a simple example. Let's assume that we've set out to determine whether or not there is any association between a person's political party affiliation (Republican, Democrat, or Independent) and how that person views a downtown redevelopment proposal (for, against, or undecided). In other words, we want to know if respondents' attitudes toward the proposal vary according to political party affiliation.

Let's assume we have asked a random sample of 180 residents to tell us about their political party affiliation (Republican, Democrat, or Independent) and how they feel about the proposal (for, against, or undecided). We can record the results in what's known as a **contingency table**. A contingency table is a classification tool that reveals the various possibilities (contingencies) in the comparison of variables. In a moment, I'll ask you to take a look at some results displayed in a contingency table. First, though, let me urge you to study carefully the various tables I ask you to consider. Don't just take a brief look and move on; take the time to carefully consider the illustrations.

Now take a look at Table 11-1. It presents two contingency tables, each reflecting a rather extreme pattern of responses, based on a sample of 180 respondents. Each table shows the possible response combinations, along with totals. Different response combinations are presented in individual cells of the table. Because the totals are presented in the margins of the table, we refer to them as **marginal totals**. In the real world, it's doubtful that we'd get such extreme patterns of responses, but we can afford to take leave of the real world for a moment or two. The goal is to develop an understanding of the chi-square test of independence and the logic that underlies it.

First, take a close look at Pattern A in Table 11-1. Think about these questions:

How many Republicans are represented in the table?

How many Democrats are represented in the table?

How many Independents are represented in the table?

Table 11-1 Two Contingency Table Patterns

Pattern A

		Political Party Affiliation			
		Republican	Democrat	Independent	Total
View of Downtown Redevelopment Proposal	For	20	20	20	60
	Against	20	20	20	60
	Undecided	20	20	20	60
	Total	60	60	60	180

Pattern B

		Political Party Affiliation			
		Republican	Democrat	Independent	Total
View of Downtown Redevelopment Proposal	For	40	10	10	60
	Against	10	40	10	60
	Undecided	10	10	40	60
	Total	60	60	60	180

Just looking at the Republicans, how are they distributed in terms of the attitude variable? Are they fairly evenly distributed, or are they more or less concentrated in a particular cell of the table? In other words, could you say it looks as though Republicans are inclined toward a particular attitude?

What about the Democrats? Are they fairly evenly distributed across the attitude variable, or are they concentrated in a particular cell? Can you associate Democrats with a particular attitude?

What about the Independents? How are they distributed?

Given what you know so far about Pattern A, does there appear to be any association between political affiliation and attitude? (The answer is no.)

The answer is no because the overall pattern of the distribution is clearly even across the cells. Republicans are just as likely to be for the proposal as they are to be against the proposal or undecided. The same is true for Democrats and Independents. In a case like that, it would be difficult to say there is a difference between Republicans, Democrats, and Independents when it comes to the distribution of attitudes toward the redevelopment proposal.

Now look at Pattern B. Think about these questions:

How many Republicans are represented in the table?

How many Democrats?

How many Independents?

Interesting—you might say to yourself—the same number of people were represented in the previous response pattern (Pattern A). But now take a look at how the overall pattern has changed.

What about the Republicans? Are they concentrated in a particular cell?

What about the Democrats? Are they more likely to be associated with a particular attitude?

When it comes to the Independents, how are they distributed in terms of the attitude variable?

What does all of that suggest? Does it appear that there's an association between the variables? (The answer is yes.)

If you study Pattern B, you'll likely conclude that there appears to be some sort of association between political affiliation and attitude. Granted, the information at hand is only based on a sample of 180 respondents, but it still appears that there's some sort of association between the two variables (political affiliation and attitude toward the redevelopment proposal).

 LEARNING CHECK

Question: What is a contingency table?

Answer: A table that presents data in terms of all combinations of two or more variables.

Before we go any further, let me reemphasize that these examples are extreme. The tables were constructed a certain way to demonstrate specific points. You *could* find results like those in the real world, but, as a rule, you're apt to find some pattern in between the two extremes. Let me explain.

First, the examples we've looked at reflect equal numbers of Republicans, Democrats, and Independents in the sample. Something like that is possible in the real world, to be sure; a community could be evenly divided among Republicans, Democrats, and Independents. More than likely, though, the actual distribution of political affiliation in a community won't be equal. Therefore, we'd expect a real-world sample to reflect the unequal distribution that actually exists in the community. Second, in a real-world instance, we'd likely get a more varied dispersion of responses over the entire table—neither completely even nor obviously concentrated in just a few cells.

That said, let me give you a general guideline to follow when looking at a contingency table: Always remember what the object of the analysis is. We want to know if the distribution of one variable seems to vary on the basis of the distribution of another variable. That, of course, is another way of saying that we want to know if there's any association between the two variables.

When there's a fairly even distribution of cases over all the cells, there's probably little, if any, association between the two variables. On the other hand, when there's a concentration of responses or cases in just a few cells, there's a greater chance that there's some sort of underlying connection between the two variables. If necessary, return to Table 11-1 to review the two patterns again. Think of Pattern A as one that reflects an even distribution of responses or cases over the table—a pattern that suggests no connection between the variables. Think of Pattern B as one that reflects a noticeable concentration of responses in just a few cells—a pattern that suggests the possibility of an association between the two variables.

The question of whether or not there's an association between two variables is something we've considered before. When we applied the difference of means test, we were actually examining the association between two variables. For example, the *t* test for the difference in alcohol consumption by fraternity members and non-members was actually a test to determine whether or not there was an association between fraternity membership status and level of alcohol consumption. When we used the ANOVA procedure to consider levels of unemployment by region, we were asking whether or not there was any association between region and unemployment level.

When it comes to the chi-square test of independence, we're asking similar types of questions. In the present example, the question is whether or not there's an association between political affiliation and attitude toward a redevelopment proposal. In other words, are the variables associated in some way, or are they *independent* of one another?

To assert that there's an association between two variables is to say that the variables are tied together in some way. In other words, there's an element of predictability in the relationship: You tell me someone's political party affiliation, and I'll tell you what the person's attitude is on the proposal. None of that, of course, has anything to do with *why* one variable seems to be tied to another or *why* you might be able to predict one variable from the other. Sometimes we're inclined to think in terms of causation—the idea that one variable *causes* the other—but I would caution you about that. As I'm fond of telling my students, causation is something that largely exists in our minds—it's a model or an explanation that we sometimes mistakenly impose on our data or results. Except in highly controlled experimental research situations, it's difficult to make legitimate claims of direct causation.

For example, some variables are associated only in the sense that they are expressions of a common concept. Consider the fact that many people who excel in the sport of football also excel in the sport of baseball. Just because people who are proficient in one sport are often proficient in the other sport doesn't mean that proficiency in one area causes proficiency in the other. In fact, both may be expressions of a common concept—namely, athletic ability. Being able to play football well probably doesn't cause someone to play baseball well (or vice versa). Instead, it's likely that people with a pronounced athletic ability tend to do well in almost any sport.

In short, the question is *whether* two variables are associated in some way—not *why* they're associated. Simply put, association doesn't necessarily imply causation. That said, we can consider the chi-square test of independence in the context of chance and a departure from chance.

A Focus on the Departure From Chance

Assuming you've gained an appreciation as to why it's a good idea to approach the notion of causality with caution, we can return to the fundamental logic behind the chi-square test of independence. To understand the logic, start with the idea that this procedure looks at the overall pattern in a contingency table and measures the extent to which the pattern reflected in the table departs from chance. To understand what this means, take another look at Pattern A in Table 11-1. One way to think about Pattern A is that it's a pattern you'd be likely to get if nothing but chance were at play. In other words, you'd be likely to get a pattern like this if the two variables were not tied together in any way.

Focus now on the marginal totals. When it comes to being a Republican, Democrat, or Independent (that is, the distribution of the political party affiliation variable), the picture reflected in Pattern A appears to be one of chance. Given the distribution of these 180 respondents, there appears to be an equal chance of being a Republican, a Democrat, or an Independent. By the same token, there appears to be an equal chance of someone's being for, against, or undecided regarding the redevelopment proposal. It seems to be mere chance whether Republicans are for, against, or undecided on the proposal. The same could be said for the Democrats and the Independents. The pattern may be extreme, but it should give you an idea of what a pattern of chance would look like in the context of a contingency table.

As you discovered before, though, Pattern B is very different. In fact, it's so different that it's reasonable to say that this response pattern represents a noticeable departure from chance. In fact, that's the meaning of the phrase *significant association*—an association that departs from chance.

In essence, that's what the chi-square test of independence is all about. It allows us to look at a pattern in a contingency table and determine whether or not the pattern we observe is one that departs from chance.

 LEARNING CHECK

Question: What does it mean to say that two variables are associated?

Answer: The pattern exhibited by the association of the two variables represents a departure from chance.

The Null Hypothesis

In the case of the chi-square test, we move away from the symbolic or mathematical statements of a null hypothesis such as those we used with the *t* test or ANOVA. For this test, there are no statements about means being equal. Instead, we move to a statement about the association between two variables.

For example, let's say we wanted to explore the association between two variables: type of community (urban, suburban, or rural) and intention to vote (whether someone plans to vote in the next election—yes, no, or undecided). An appropriate statement of the null hypothesis would be as follows:

H_0: There is no association between type of community and intention to vote.

When we use the chi-square test of independence, we test the null hypothesis by examining the results obtained from sample data. But we do so with the idea that the sample patterns are representative of population patterns. We look at the pattern in the contingency table (the observed data), but our interest really goes beyond that.

If the pattern shows little, if any, departure from what would be expected by chance, we fail to reject the null hypothesis. In other words, we fail to reject the idea of no association between the variables. If, on the other hand, the pattern reflects a significant departure from what we would expect by chance (given the marginal totals of the variables in question), we reject the null. In doing so, we are suggesting that there is, in fact, some sort of association between the two variables in the population.

The Application

As we've done before, we'll put off any discussion of the formula until we've spent a bit of time with the problem at hand. As a start, take a look at the data in Table 11-2. Once again, we have a contingency table. This time, the contingency table shows responses from 98 people to questions about their type of community and their intention to vote. Since we're beginning the application at this point, we'll assume we've set the level of significance at .05.

Table 11-2   Responses to Survey: Voter Intention by Type of Community

		Type of Community			
		Urban	Suburban	Rural	Total
Voter Intention	Yes	8	17	7	32
	No	6	8	15	29
	Undecided	19	7	11	37
	Total	33	32	33	98

Remember what a contingency table is all about and what it allows us to do. It's a mechanism that allows us to see all possible combinations of variables in a given research situation. When we look at a contingency table, the numbers we see in the various cells (with the exception of the marginal totals) are referred to as the **observed frequencies**. You've seen observed frequencies before. That's really what you saw when you looked at Pattern A and Pattern B in Table 11-1. In Table 11-2, we're looking at a different contingency table and a different pattern. The observed frequencies are simply the results that are presented in Table 11-2.

☑️ **LEARNING CHECK**

Question: In the chi-square test of independence, what are the observed frequencies?

Answer: The frequencies (results) that appear in each cell of a contingency table (excluding the marginal totals).

Table 11-2 is known as a three-by-three contingency table; it has three rows and three columns. With three rows and three columns, the table has a total of nine cells (exclusive of the cells associated with the marginal totals). The numbers in each of these nine cells are the observed frequencies or cases. Looking at the upper left-hand cell, for example, you see the number eight. The observed frequency for that cell is eight. This means that eight respondents reported that they are urban residents and that they intend to vote in the election. The concept of observed frequencies, as you've probably gathered by now, is quite straightforward. They are simply the numbers you see displayed in the contingency table. The table we're considering now has nine cells, so there are nine observed frequencies.

We turn now to the matter of **expected frequencies**. As with the observed frequencies, there will be nine expected frequencies—one for each cell. To obtain the value of the expected frequencies, though, we'll have to go through a few calculations. Let me explain.

The expected frequency for each cell is a statement of the frequency that we would expect to find, given the marginal distributions and the total number of cases in the table. More precisely, the expected frequency for a given cell is a function of the number of cases in the row in question times the number of cases in the column in question, divided by the total number of cases for the entire table. For the sake of simplicity, we can summarize the calculation as follows:

$$\text{Expected Frequency of Each Cell} = \frac{\text{Row Total} \times \text{Column Total}}{n}$$

For example, to calculate the expected frequency for the cell in the upper left-hand corner of the table (the cell that contains an observed frequency of 8), we would proceed as follows: We would multiply the row total (32) by the column total (33). Then we'd divide the product by the total number of cases in the sample ($n = 98$). The result would be 10.78. Moving to the next cell in that row (the cell with the observed frequency of 17), we would calculate the expected frequency by multiplying the row total (32) by the column total (32) and, as before, we'd divide the product by the total number of cases in the sample ($n = 98$). The result would be an expected frequency of 10.45. Calculating the expected frequencies for each cell, we'd obtain the information presented in Table 11-3. Note that there is an observed frequency (f_o) and an expected frequency (f_e) for each of the nine cells in the table.

The individual steps in the calculation of expected frequencies are shown below. Note how the individual steps correspond to the calculations presented in Table 11-3.

Upper-left f_e	$= (32 \times 33)/98 = 1056/98 = 10.78$
Upper-middle f_e	$= (32 \times 32)/98 = 1024/98 = 10.45$
Upper-right f_e	$= (32 \times 33)/98 = 1056/98 = 10.78$
Middle-left f_e	$= (29 \times 33)/98 = 957/98 = 9.77$
Middle-middle f_e	$= (29 \times 32)/98 = 928/98 = 9.47$
Middle-right f_e	$= (29 \times 33)/98 = 957/98 = 9.77$
Lower-left f_e	$= (37 \times 33)/98 = 1221/98 = 12.46$

Table 11-3 Calculation of Expected Frequencies

Cell	Observed Frequency (f_o)	Row Total	Column Total	Row Total × Column Total	Row Total × Column Total Divided by n — Expected Frequency (f_e)
Upper-left	8	32	33	1056	10.78
Upper-middle	17	32	32	1024	10.45
Upper-right	7	32	33	1056	10.78
Middle-left	6	29	33	957	9.77
Middle-middle	8	29	32	928	9.47
Middle-right	15	29	33	957	9.77
Lower-left	19	37	33	1221	12.46
Lower-middle	7	37	32	1184	12.08
Lower-right	11	37	33	1221	12.46

$$\text{Lower-middle } f_e = (37 \times 32)/98 = 1184/98 = 12.08$$
$$\text{Lower-right } f_e = (37 \times 33)/98 = 1221/98 = 12.46$$

Table 11-4 presents the observed and expected frequencies for each cell in an illustration similar to Table 11-2.

 LEARNING CHECK

Question: In the chi-square test of independence, what are the expected frequencies?

Answer: The frequencies that would be expected by chance in each cell of a contingency table, given the marginal totals.

The Formula

Given the observed frequencies, and having calculated the expected frequencies, we now have all the elements required by the formula for the chi-square test of independence. At first, the formula for chi-square (symbolized as χ^2) looks a little complicated, but keep in mind that there are really only two fundamental elements—observed frequencies and expected frequencies. Don't let

Table 11-4   Comparison of Observed and Expected Frequencies

Observed Frequencies

		Type of Community		
		Urban	Suburban	Rural
Voter Intention	Yes	8	17	7
	No	6	8	15
	Undecided	19	7	11

Expected Frequencies

		Type of Community		
		Urban	Suburban	Rural
Voter Intention	Yes	10.78	10.45	10.78
	No	9.77	9.47	9.77
	Undecided	12.46	12.08	12.46

the summation sign, the exponent, the division, or anything else throw you when you first look at the formula. The essence of the formula really has to do with the observed and expected frequencies.

$$\chi^2 = \sum \frac{(f_o - f_e)^2}{f_e}$$

Always remember what the expected frequencies represent—namely, the frequencies we'd expect if the pattern were due to chance alone (taking into account the marginal distributions of the two variables). If you examine the formula carefully, you'll note that it has to do with the *difference* between observed and expected frequencies. The formula reflects an overall summation of this difference.

Because the object of the chi-square test of independence is to determine if the pattern reflected in a contingency table departs from chance in a significant manner, it should make intuitive sense that the formula should involve a measure of the overall difference between observation and expectation (or chance). The larger the difference between the observed frequencies and the expected frequencies, the larger will be the calculated value of chi-square. With that as a background, we can now move to the specific steps in the calculation.

The Calculation

As we've done before, we'll approach the calculations in a step-by-step fashion. For the sake of review, here's the formula again, followed by the individual steps in the calculation.

$$\chi^2 = \sum \frac{(f_o - f_e)^2}{f_e}$$

$\chi^2 = (8 - 10.78)^2/10.78 + (17 - 10.45)^2/10.45 + (7 - 10.78)^2/10.78$
$\quad + (6 - 9.77)^2/9.77 + (8 - 9.47)^2/9.47 + (15 - 9.77)^2/9.77$
$\quad + (19 - 12.46)^2/12.46 + (7 - 12.08)^2/12.08 + (11 - 12.46)^2/12.46$

$\chi^2 = 7.73/10.78 + 42.90/10.45 + 14.29/10.78 + 14.21/9.77$
$\quad + 2.16/9.47 + 27.35/9.77 + 42.77/12.46 + 25.81/12.08$
$\quad + 2.13/12.46$

$\chi^2 = 0.72 + 4.11 + 1.33 + 1.45 + 0.23 + 2.80 + 3.43 + 2.14 + 0.17$

$\chi^2 = 16.38$

The formula instructs us first to find the difference between the observed and expected frequencies of each cell $(f_o - f_e)$. Those differences are then squared $(f_o - f_e)^2$. The squared difference associated with each cell is then divided by the expected frequency of the cell $(f_o - f_e)^2/f_e$. For example, beginning with the cell in the upper left-hand corner of our contingency table, we note that the observed frequency is 8 and the expected frequency (for the same cell) is calculated as 10.78. The formula directs us first to find the difference between the two values $(f_o - f_e$ or $8 - 10.78$, or -2.78). Next we square the difference, which gives us a value of 7.73. We then divide 7.73 by

Table 11-5   Calculation of Chi-Square Test of Independence Statistic

Observed Frequency	Expected Frequency	Observed Minus Expected	Observed Minus Expected Squared	Observed Minus Expected Squared and Divided by Expected
f_o	f_e	$(f_o - f_e)$	$(f_o - f_e)^2$	$\dfrac{(f_o - f_e)^2}{f_e}$
8	10.78	−2.78	7.73	0.72
17	10.45	6.55	42.90	4.11
7	10.78	−3.78	14.29	1.33
6	9.77	−3.77	14.21	1.45
8	9.47	−1.47	2.16	0.23
15	9.77	5.23	27.35	2.80
19	12.46	6.54	42.77	3.43
7	12.08	−5.08	25.81	2.14
11	12.46	−1.46	2.13	0.17
				$\Sigma = 16.38$

$$\chi^2 = \sum \frac{(f_o - f_e)^2}{f_e} = 16.38$$

the expected frequency of the cell in question (10.78). The result (7.73 divided by 10.78) is 0.72.

The same process is followed for each cell in the table—finding the difference between the observed and expected frequencies, squaring the difference, and dividing the difference by the expected frequency of the cell in question. You can follow this sequence for each cell by examining Table 11-5. Once that process is completed for each cell, the results from all the cells are summed to obtain the calculated value of the chi-square statistic. This is the statistic we'll compare to a critical value as we work our way toward a conclusion.

Conclusion and Interpretation

The calculated value of chi-square ($\chi^2 = 16.38$) is shown in the lower right corner of Table 11-5. Once again, we're right back where we've been many times before. We have a calculated test statistic ($\chi^2 = 16.38$), and now we are faced with arriving at a conclusion. As before, our conclusion will be based on a comparison of our calculated test statistic to a critical value, given a certain level of significance, and taking into account a certain number of degrees of freedom.

Appendix H is a table of critical values for the chi-square test of independence. Different levels of significance are shown across the top row of the table, and the first column lists the degrees of freedom. We set the level of significance at .05 at the beginning of our application, so we'll be working with that column. Now we come to the matter of the degrees of freedom.

The number of degrees of freedom *(df)* for the chi-square test of independence is related to the number of cells in the contingency table. More specifically, *df* is determined by multiplying the number of rows in the table, minus 1, by the number of columns in the table, minus 1. The formula is stated as follows:

$$df = (r - 1) \times (c - 1)$$

where *r* = number of rows and *c* = number of columns

Since our example involves a contingency table with three rows and three columns, the calculation is as follows:

$$df = (r - 1) \times (c - 1)$$
$$df = (3 - 1) \times (3 - 1)$$
$$df = 2 \times 2$$
$$df = 4$$

Given four degrees of freedom *(df* = 4) and the .05 level of significance, we find that the critical value is 9.49. Our calculated test statistic (our chi-square value) is 16.38. Because our calculated test statistic exceeds the critical value, we're in a position to reject the null hypothesis. In doing so, we reject the idea of no association between the two variables type of community and intention to vote.

As always, there's a known probability (in this case, a 5% chance or less) that we've rejected the null hypothesis when, in fact, it is true. In other words, there's always a chance that our sample suggested that the two variables are associated when they really aren't. The good news, of course, is that we know what the probability is—it's simply the level of significance. When all is said and done, we're on fairly safe ground in our assertion that type of community appears to be associated with intention to vote.

Having explored the chi-square test of independence, it's time for a little reflection. Think about how the various tests of significance have been presented—how you've been introduced to one test after another, yet the underlying logic of hypothesis testing remains the same.

Chapter Summary

In this chapter, we made a major transformation. We moved from consideration of interval data and the calculation of means to the world of categorical data and the analysis of contingency tables. In doing so, we broadened our understanding of the types of situations that are suitable for statistical analysis.

Equally important, we examined the matter of chance, particularly as it relates to the portrayal of research results presented in a contingency table. In doing so, we began to think in terms of both chance and a departure from chance. Moreover, we learned to think of a departure from chance as a suggestion that two variables are associated with each other.

Finally, we looked at what it really means to assert that two variables are associated. With a word of caution, we explored the idea of causation, noting that causation—the idea that a given measurement or response on one variable somehow *causes* a given measurement or response on another variable—can be a tricky matter. In the process, you should have gained some understanding of a larger issue—one that goes beyond the specifics of any particular statistical procedure. In short, you should have gained even more understanding of the logic of scientific research.

Some Other Things You Should Know

The chi-square test of independence is widely used, but it is subject to certain limitations. For example, problems can arise when the number of cases is small, relative to the number of cells in a table. In short, the idea behind the chi-square test of independence is to analyze the pattern of a distribution, but it's difficult to see a pattern when there are just a few cases spread over a lot of cells.

There are two ways to deal with this problem. The table can be restructured so that it has a smaller number of cells—something you could accomplish by combining categories for either or both variables. That approach, however, should always be accompanied by sound justification. It's not something you should do just for the sake of statistical analysis. A more acceptable approach, if possible, is to simply increase the size of the sample. By increasing the sample size, you end up with more cases available to distribute over the same number of cells. That, in turn, increases the likelihood that a pattern of association will emerge (assuming there's a true pattern of association between the variables in the population).

In some cases, certain correction factors are suggested when working with the chi-square test of independence. For example, a 2×2 contingency table typically calls for the use of the Yate's correction for continuity. This involves decreasing the difference between the observed and expected frequencies by .5 for each cell. Similar corrections are often used when the expected frequency in any cell (of any contingency table, not just 2×2 tables) is less than 5.

Finally, you should be aware that the chi-square test of independence only indicates whether or not there is an association between variables. It doesn't say anything about the *strength* of the association. In other words, the test can point to an association or link between two variables, but it says nothing about how strong that association or link might be. To explore the matter of association strength, a separate procedure (a measure of association application) is required. For a wide-ranging discussion of some of the more commonly used measures of association, see Healy (2002).

Key Terms

categorical data
chi-square test of independence
contingency table

expected frequency
marginal totals
observed frequency

Chapter Problems

Fill in the blanks, calculate the requested values, or otherwise supply the correct answer.

General Thought Questions

1. A _____ table is a classification tool that reveals the various possibilities in the comparison of variables.

2. Information obtained on variables measured at the nominal or ordinal level is said to be _____ data.

3. _____ frequencies are the frequencies presented in the cells of a table.

4. The _____ frequency is the frequency that would be expected to occur in a particular cell, based upon chance and the marginal distributions.

5. The equation for expected frequency for the chi-square test of independence is _____.

6. The equation for degrees of freedom for the chi-square test of independence is _____.

7. There are _____ cells in a 2×2 contingency table.

8. There are _____ cells in a 3×4 contingency table.

9. A 4×6 contingency table has _____ degrees of freedom.

10. A 3×5 contingency table has _____ degrees of freedom.

Application Questions/Problems

1. A chi-square test of independence value of $\chi^2 = 9.26$ is calculated from data in a 3×3 contingency table. Assuming a .05 level of significance, identify the critical value and state your conclusion about the null hypothesis.

2. A chi-square test of independence value of $\chi^2 = 24.05$ is calculated from data in a 4 × 5 contingency table. Assuming a .05 level of significance, identify the critical value and state your conclusion about the null hypothesis.

3. A chi-square test of independence value of $\chi^2 = 4.28$ is calculated from data in a 2 × 2 contingency table. Assuming a .05 level of significance, identify the critical value and state your conclusion about the null hypothesis.

4. A chi-square test of independence value of $\chi^2 = 12.26$ is calculated from data in a 3 × 3 contingency table. Assuming a .05 level of significance, identify the critical value and state your conclusion about the null hypothesis.

5. A chi-square test of independence value of $\chi^2 = 6.15$ is calculated from data in a 4 × 5 contingency table. Assuming a .05 level of significance, identify the critical value and state your conclusion about the null hypothesis.

6. You are interested in whether there is any association between gender and academic major. Questioning 75 students, you obtain the following results:

		Academic Major				
		Business	Science	Liberal Arts	Other	Total
Gender	Female	10	9	9	7	35
	Male	12	11	10	7	40
	Total	22	20	19	14	75

   a. How many degrees of freedom are involved?
   b. What is the calculated value of χ^2?
   c. Assuming the .05 level of significance, what would you conclude?

7. You are interested in whether there is any association between attitude (favorable, unfavorable, or undecided) toward Candidate Busk and place of residence (urban, suburban, or rural). Questioning 95 potential voters, you obtain the following results:

		Attitude Toward Candidate			
		Favorable	Unfavorable	Undecided	Total
Place of Residence	Rural	19	7	8	34
	Suburban	9	14	6	29
	Urban	6	8	18	32
	Total	34	29	32	95

    a. How many degrees of freedom are involved?
    b. What is the calculated value of χ^2?
    c. Assuming the .05 level of significance, what would you conclude?

8. You are interested in whether there is any association between gender and perception of movie plots. You show a movie that contains both action and love themes to a group of 70 research participants. You ask each participant to categorize the plot as either love, action, or both. Consider the following table of results:

		Perception of Movie Plot			
		Love	Action	Both	Total
Gender	Female	7	12	15	34
	Male	9	11	16	36
	Total	16	23	31	70

    a. How many degrees of freedom are involved?
    b. What is the calculated value of χ^2?
    c. Assuming the .05 level of significance, what would you conclude?

12

Correlation and Regression

In the last chapter, we looked at the idea of the association between two categorical variables. In doing so, we explored the idea of two variables being tied to one another by something other than chance. In this chapter, we extend our understanding of the idea of association as we take up two procedures appropriate for situations involving two interval/ratio level variables. First, we'll examine Pearson's r, or simple correlation analysis. Following that, we'll explore a related procedure known as regression analysis. As a prelude to both, we'll explore the use of scatter plots as a means to visually represent the association between two variables.

Before We Begin

As you encounter this twelfth and final chapter, I'm going to ask you to explore some additional dimensions related to relationships. First, you're going to be introduced to the notions of the strength and direction of relationships. In doing so, you'll deal with the question of how closely tied one variable is to the other, as well as how the variables vary together, so to speak. You'll also be dealing with the matter of prediction—the idea that if you know something about the way two variables are related, you're then in a position to make predictions. For example, if you have some knowledge as to the strength and direction of the relationship between two variables, X and Y, it is possible to make a prediction about the likely value of Y, given a certain value of X.

All of that may strike you as a little bit abstract as we begin this chapter, but I can assure you that you're already familiar with a lot of concepts that you're going to encounter. Means, standard deviations, and Z scores are about to reenter the picture. If you think you're a little rusty on some of those concepts, particularly standard deviations or Z scores, take a little time to reread previous material on the topics. The review will serve you well.

Scatter Plots

A **scatter plot** is an extremely useful tool when it comes to looking at the association between two variables. In short, a scatter plot allows us to simultaneously view the values of two variables on a case-by-case basis. A typical example used to illustrate the utility of a scatter plot is one involving the association between height and weight. Table 12-1 shows a hypothetical distribution of values of those variables (height and weight) for 20 cases.

A visual representation of the same data in the form of a scatter plot is shown in Figure 12-1. Height measurement values are shown along the horizontal or X-axis of the graph; weight measurement values are shown along the vertical or Y-axis of the graph. Focusing on case number 1, shown in the lower left corner of the scatter plot, we can interpret the point as reflecting a person (case) with a height of 59 inches (or 4' 11") and a weight of 92 pounds. Each of the 20 points can be interpreted in the same fashion—a reflection of the values of two variables (height and weight) for a given case.

Note that the scales along the X- and Y-axes are different. The variable of height is expressed in inches, but the variable of weight is expressed in pounds. As you learned earlier when you encountered Z scores, though, the fact that the scales are based on different units of measurement is not a deterrent to statistical analysis. Indeed, correlation analysis is a technique that is perfectly suited for such situations. All of that in good time, though. For the moment, let's take a closer look at scatter plots and what they can tell us.

Table 12-1   Height/Weight Data for 20 Cases
(Young Adult Females): Raw Scores

Case	Height (Inches)	Weight (Pounds)
1	59	92
2	61	105
3	61	100
4	62	107
5	62	114
6	63	112
7	63	120
8	63	130
9	64	132
10	64	137
11	65	132
12	65	138
13	65	120
14	66	136
15	66	132
16	67	140
17	67	143
18	68	139
19	68	134
20	69	153

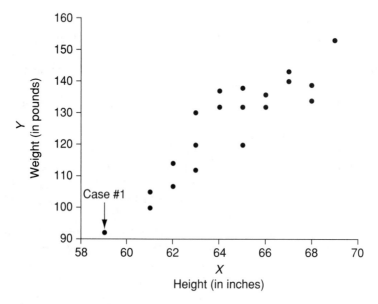

Figure 12-1   Height/Weight Data for 20 Cases (Young Adult Females):
Scatter Plot

Linear Associations: Direction and Strength

When two variables (Variable *X* and Variable *Y*) are associated, they can be associated in several ways. A scatter plot can provide a graphic and concise statement as to the general relationship or association between two variables. In short, a scatter plot tells us something about the *direction* and *strength* of association. To better grasp the variety of relationships or associations that are possible, take a look at Figures 12-2 through 12-5. These illustrations reflect data on two variables—Variable *X* and Variable *Y*. As you consider the illustrations, don't worry about what the *X* and *Y* variables represent or how they might be measured. Just look at each axis as a scale that has low to high values. Treat the illustrations as abstract representations; focus on the general trends or associations that may or may not be reflected in the scatter plots.

One of the first observations we might make about the illustrations in Figure 12-2 is that they reflect *linear* patterns of association. To suggest that an association between two variables is linear is to suggest that the pattern could be described as approximating a straight line. Looking at both illustrations in Figure 12-2, however, we note that **linear associations** can take different forms.

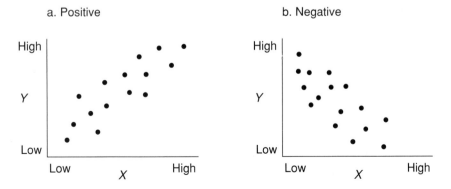

Figure 12-2 Moderate Positive (Direct) and Negative (Inverse) Associations

Direction of Association. Figure 12-2a depicts what we refer to as a **positive** or **direct association**. To say that two variables are related or associated in a positive or direct fashion is to say that they track together; it means that a high value on Variable X is generally associated with a high value on Variable Y, and a low value on Variable X is generally associated with a low value of Variable Y. If, however, the variables are related in a negative or inverse fashion, an opposite pattern appears (see Figure 12-2b). In a **negative** or **inverse association**, high values on Variable X are associated with low values on Variable Y, and low values on Variable X are associated with high values on Variable Y. In short, the variables track in opposite directions.

☑ LEARNING CHECK

Question: What is a positive or direct association?
Answer: It's an association in which the variables track together. As one variable increases in value, the other variable increases in value. As one variable decreases in value, the other variable decreases in value.

Question: What is a negative or inverse association?
Answer: It's an association in which the variables track in opposite directions. As one variable increases in value, the other variable decreases in value. As one variable decreases in value, the other variable increases in value.

Strength of Association. Figure 12-3 presents similar patterns, but with one important difference. There is less dispersion of the points in the plots (when compared to the patterns shown in Figure 12-2), and the general trend (either positive or negative) is more easily detected. In that sense, the illustrations in Figure 12-3 reflect associations that are stronger than those represented in Figure 12-2.

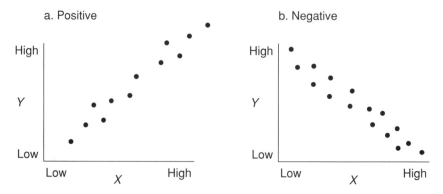

Figure 12-3 Stronger Positive and Negative Associations

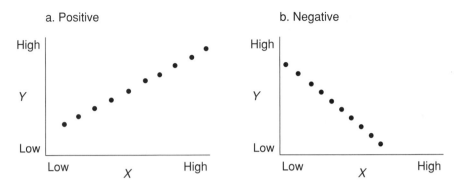

Figure 12-4 Perfect Positive and Negative Associations

Now take a look at Figure 12-4. Note that the association between the variables is shown as being even stronger. Indeed, the points in the scatter plots appear to be aligned in a straight line. Although such associations are rare in the real world, we could characterize the relationships shown in Figure 12-4 as **perfect associations**. They're perfect in the sense that the value on one variable could serve as a perfect or precise predictor of the value on the other variable.

As noted above, we rarely encounter perfect associations in the world of social science research. Even so, the idea of a perfect relationship is useful, because it helps us understand what is meant by **strength of association**. In many respects, the strength of an association is just an expression of how close we might be to being able to predict the value on one variable from knowledge of the value on another variable. Some associations are stronger than others in the sense that they come closer than others to the notion of perfect predictability.

 LEARNING CHECK

Question: What is meant by the term *strength of association?*
Answer: It's an expression of the extent to which the value of one variable can be predicted on the basis of the value of another variable.

Other Types of Association

Finally, take a look at Figure 12-5. In Figure 12-5a, the points in the scatter plot are widely dispersed, and there isn't any discernable pattern. For all practical purposes, the relationship or association is *non-existent*. In the case of Figure 12-5b, a clear pattern is evident, but it's a **curvilinear association** (as opposed to the more linear relationships depicted in the previous illustrations). As the values of Variable X increase, the values of Variable Y also increase— up to a point. Eventually, however, the pattern begins to flatten and then reverses; as the values on Variable X increase, the values on Variable Y decrease. In short, a curvilinear association is one that is best described by a curved line.

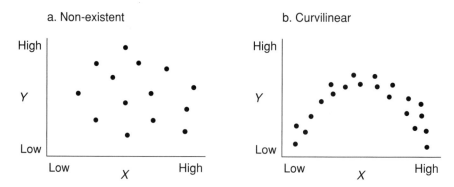

Figure 12-5 Non-existent and Curvilinear Associations

✅ **LEARNING CHECK**

Question: In terms of a scatter plot, what is a curvilinear relationship?
Answer: It's a scatter plot in which the general pattern of the plot conforms to a curved line.

Question: In terms of a scatter plot, what does it mean to say that an association is non-existent?
Answer: It's a scatter plot in which there is no apparent association or pattern.

By now, you should be getting the picture. The association between two variables can take many forms. It can be positive, negative, weak, or strong. It can also be linear, curvilinear, or non-existent.

It's clear that a scatter plot can be a helpful tool in statistical analysis. It provides a visual statement about the general nature of an association and does so in a concise format. Statisticians, however, generally want something more exact—some sort of quantitative expression about the nature of associations—and for that they turn to correlation analysis.

Correlation Analysis

Correlation analysis is a technique developed by Karl Pearson; thus, it's often referred to as **Pearson's r**. The popularity of Pearson's r stems from what it tells us about the direction and strength of association between two variables. When Pearson's r is calculated, the result will be a value that ranges from −1.0 to +1.0, depending on the direction and strength of association. Without going into the mathematics of the calculation just yet, let's take a closer look at what it means to say that the value of r has a known range between −1.0 and +1.0.

LEARNING CHECK

Question: What is Pearson's r?
Answer: It's a measure of the strength and direction of association between two variables.

Question: What is the range of r?
Answer: The value of r can range from −1.0 to +1.0.

Assuming that the two variables under investigation are related in a linear fashion (as opposed to a curvilinear fashion), the sign and value of r will tell us quite a lot about the relationship. A positive sign signals a positive or direct association; a negative sign signals a negative or inverse association. The closer the value is to +1.0 or −1.0, the stronger the association is between the two variables. An r value of +1.0 would indicate a perfect positive or direct association between the variables; an r value of −1.0 would indicate a perfect negative or inverse association between the variables. As I mentioned before, a perfect association, whether positive or negative, is one in which there would be perfect predictability. Knowledge of the value of one variable would allow us to make an exact prediction of the value of the other variable.

 LEARNING CHECK

Question: If the value of r has a positive sign, what does that mean?
Answer: It means that the variables are associated in a positive or direct fashion.

Question: If the value of r has a negative sign, what does that mean?
Answer: It means that the variables are associated in a negative or inverse fashion.

Keep in mind that none of this necessarily indicates causation. Just because two variables appear to be closely associated with one another, it doesn't necessarily mean that one variable *causes* the other variable. Remember some of the points we covered in the last chapter. Recall that outside of highly controlled experimental research, it's virtually impossible to legitimately infer causality. Also keep in mind that what may look like a case of causality may be nothing more than the fact that two variables are expressions of a common concept. That said, we move on to our discussion of Pearson's r, or simple correlation analysis.

Two Variables: X and Y

Our discussion of scatter plots and Pearson's r has thus far revolved around the notion of two variables, usually referred to as Variable *X* and Variable *Y*.

We could have used the symbols Variable 1 and Variable 2, or almost any other designation, but as a matter of convention, we typically speak in terms of Variable *X* and Variable *Y*. Those notations appear time and time again in our discussions, so some additional commentary is warranted.

When researchers speak in terms of Variable *X* and Variable *Y*, they commonly propose some logical connection between the two. For example, the *X* variable is commonly regarded as the **independent variable**, and the *Y* variable is commonly regarded as the **dependent variable**. In the language of research, an independent variable is a variable that's presumed to influence another variable. The dependent variable, in turn, is the variable that's presumed to be influenced by another variable.

For example, it's common to assert that there's a connection between a person's level of education and level of income. Educational level would be treated as the independent variable, and level of income would be regarded as the dependent variable. In other words, education (independent) is thought to exert an influence on income (dependent).

 LEARNING CHECK

Question: What's the definition of an independent variable?
Answer: It's the variable that's presumed to influence another
              variable.

Question: What's the definition of a dependent variable?
Answer: It's the variable that's presumed to be influenced
              by another variable.

Once again, it's important to remember that the notion of one variable exerting an influence on another is not the same thing as pure causality. For example, it's easy to understand how one's level of education would have some connection to one's level of income, but it's difficult to imagine that education is the only variable that determines income. A person's level of education might be one influence on level of income, but that's hardly the same thing as saying level of education causes a person's level of income.

Although researchers rely on simple logic when it comes to identifying the independent and dependent variables, not all research situations are clear-cut. Consider the association between the level of unemployment in a community and the level of in-migration. The level of unemployment in a community may influence the amount of in-migration, but continued in-migration is likely to affect the level of unemployment. Job opportunities (expressed in low levels of unemployment) could attract significant numbers of job seekers, to the point that the level of unemployment is pushed upward. Much like the relationship between the temperature in a room and a thermostat, each variable has a way of affecting the other. Such relationships are said to be *reciprocal*—relationships or associations in which each variable is presumed to exert an influence on the other.

LEARNING CHECK

Question: What is a reciprocal relationship?
Answer: A reciprocal relationship is one in which each variable is presumed to exert an influence on the other variable.

Given that, it's probably best to expand your thinking about Variable X and Variable Y as follows: When you can reasonably assign a variable's place in a logical sequence of events, it's reasonable to think in terms of Variable X as the independent variable and Variable Y as the dependent variable. When you can't make a reasonable assignment of place in a logical sequence of events, just think of Variable X and Variable Y as two variables—plain and simple, without regard for causality, logical sequencing, or anything else.

Later on, we'll deal with Variable X as the variable that you'd use to *predict* Variable Y, but all of that can wait until our discussion of regression. For the present, we'll continue with our discussion of simple correlation analysis as a measure of the association between Variable X and Variable Y. As before, we'll start with the logic.

The Logic of Correlation

In truth, correlation analysis takes many forms (such as multiple correlation or partial correlation); the one we're considering here is referred to as *simple correlation*. In short, simple correlation analysis allows us to measure the association between two interval/ratio level variables (assuming that the two variables, if associated, are associated in a linear fashion). The logic of correlation analysis traces back to the notion of Z scores (something you encountered in Chapter 2). You'll want to review the material in Chapter 2 if you think you're not quite up to speed on the topic. Assuming you feel comfortable with the concept, however, we can move to the topic of Z scores and what they allow us to do in the context of correlation analysis.

Earlier you learned how to transform a raw score into a Z score by finding the difference between a raw score and the mean of a distribution and dividing that difference by the standard deviation of the distribution. Just to refresh your memory on this point, consider the formula for a Z transformation and recall what it allows you to do. Z transformations allow you to convert the scores on different scales to a single scale based on Z scores (or points along the baseline of the normal curve).

$$Z = \frac{\text{Raw Score} - \text{Mean}}{\text{Standard Deviation}}$$

For example, look back at Figure 12-1. Note that the values along the horizontal and vertical axes are expressed in different scales or units of measurement: inches along the horizontal axis and pounds along the vertical axis. When we consider the raw scores of the points represented in the scatter plot, then, we are dealing with two different scales. The two sets of scores will be on the same scale, though, if they're transformed into Z scores. The same is true for any number of situations.

For example, student aptitude test scores (SAT scores) and grade point averages (GPAs), when expressed as raw scores, are based on very different underlying scales, but the raw scores can easily be transformed into Z scores to create a single scale of comparison. Data on education (expressed as the number of school years completed) and income (expressed in dollars) can share a common scale when transformed into Z scores. The list goes on. All we need is the mean and standard deviation of each distribution. It's a simple transformation: Subtract the mean from each raw score in the distribution, and divide each difference by the standard deviation.

Decades ago, Pearson discovered something very interesting about distributions of Z scores. In short, he discovered that it's possible to transform two distributions of raw scores (expressed as pairs of scores or values) into Z scores, perform some very minor calculations, and end up with a statistic that will always range between −1.0 and +1.0. What Pearson discovered became the basis for the computation of r.

In developing the correlation procedure, Pearson found that two distributions of closely associated Z scores that tracked together in a positive (direct) fashion would result in an r value approaching +1.0. He also discovered that two distributions of Z scores that were closely associated in a negative (inverse) direction would result in an r value approaching −1.0. All that's necessary is a couple of minor calculations, once the raw scores have been converted to Z scores. This brings us to the formula for r, so that's where we'll turn next.

The Formula for Pearson's r

Because the computational formula for r includes the steps necessary to convert raw scores to Z scores, it has a way of appearing extremely complex. Assuming you know the basis of Pearson's r (namely, the conversion of raw scores into Z scores), though, you're in a position to rely on a more *conceptual* formula—one I suspect you'll find very simple to follow. The heart of the more conceptual approach has to do with what we refer to as the *cross products of the Z scores.* That sounds like a mouthful until it's explained, so let's start with a look at the data presented in Table 12-2.

Table 12-2 shows pairs of values or scores associated with 10 cases. Columns 2 and 4 show the raw score distributions for the two variables, X and Y. The means and standard deviations of the raw score distributions are given at the bottom of the table. Columns 3 and 5 show the Z scores or transformations based on the associated raw scores. (Recall that these are calculated by subtracting the mean from each raw score and dividing by the standard deviation.) Case number 1, for example, has a raw score X value of 20 (shown in Column 2) and a Z score (Z_X) value of −1.49 (shown in Column 3). The raw score Y value for case number 1 is 105 (shown in Column 4), and the Z score (Z_Y) value of −1.57 (shown in Column 5).

The cross products are obtained by multiplying each Z_X value (the entry in Column 3) by the associated Z_Y value (the entry in Column 5). The results of the

Table 12-2 Cross Product Calculations for X and Y Variables
(Positive Association)

(1) Case	(2) X	(3) Z_X	(4) Y	(5) Z_Y	(6) $Z_X \cdot Z_Y$
1	20	−1.49	105	−1.57	2.34
2	25	−1.16	126	−0.84	0.97
3	30	−0.83	122	−0.98	0.81
4	35	−0.50	130	−0.70	0.35
5	40	−0.17	155	0.17	−0.03
6	45	0.17	159	0.31	0.05
7	50	0.50	153	0.10	0.05
8	55	0.83	184	1.18	0.98
9	60	1.16	177	0.94	1.09
10	65	1.49	190	1.39	2.07

Sum of Cross Products = 8.68

Mean of X = 42.50
Standard Deviation of X = 15.14

Mean of Y = 150.10
Standard Deviation of Y = 28.65

cross product multiplication are shown in Column 6 ($Z_X \cdot Z_Y$). Earlier I mentioned that the cross products of the Z scores lie at the heart of correlation analysis.

Now that you know how to derive the cross products, it's time to encounter the formula for the calculation of r. My guess is that you'll find it to be rather straightforward.

$$r = \frac{\sum(Z_X \cdot Z_Y)}{n - 1}$$

As in Table 12-2, the symbol Z_X denotes the Z scores for the X variable, and Z_Y denotes the Z scores for the Y variable. All you need to do is sum the cross products and divide the sum by the number of paired cases minus 1. The result is our calculated value of r. For the data presented in Table 12-2, the calculation is as follows:

$$r = \frac{\sum(Z_X \cdot Z_Y)}{n - 1}$$

$$r = \frac{8.68}{9}$$

$$r = +0.96$$

Note that we use $n - 1$ in the denominator of the formula. You should be aware, though, that some presentations of the formula rely on n alone. The difference in the two approaches traces back to the manner in which the standard deviation for each distribution was calculated (recall that the standard deviation is a necessary ingredient for the calculation of a Z score). As you may recall from Chapter 2, the choice of using $n - 1$ versus n in the denominator when

Table 12-3 Cross Product Calculations for X and Y Variables
(Negative Association)

(1) Case	(2) X	(3) Z_X	(4) Y	(5) Z_Y	(6) $Z_X \bullet Z_Y$
1	20	−1.49	190	1.39	−2.07
2	25	−1.16	177	0.94	−1.09
3	30	−0.83	184	1.18	−0.98
4	35	−0.50	153	0.10	−0.05
5	40	−0.17	159	0.31	−0.05
6	45	0.17	155	0.17	0.03
7	50	0.50	130	−0.70	−0.35
8	55	0.83	122	−0.98	−0.81
9	60	1.16	126	−0.84	−0.97
10	65	1.49	105	−1.57	−2.34

Sum of Cross Products = −8.68

Mean of X = 42.50
Standard Deviation of X = 15.14

Mean of Y = 150.10
Standard Deviation of Y = 28.65

calculating the standard deviation of a sample is somewhat discretionary. The assumption in this text is that $n − 1$ was used in the calculation of the standard deviations of Variable X and Variable Y.

Just to make certain that you're on track with the notion of cross products and how they're used to develop a value for r, consider the data presented in Table 12-3—another example similar to the one you encountered in Table 12-2. In the case of Table 12-3, however, you'll note that as the raw scores (and the corresponding Z scores) for Variable X increase, those for Variable Y decrease, indicating a negative association. As expected, the resulting r value reflects the negative or inverse direction of the relationship:

$$r = \frac{\Sigma(Z_X \bullet Z_Y)}{n - 1}$$

$$r = \frac{-8.68}{9}$$

$$r = -0.96$$

 LEARNING CHECK

Question: In the context of Pearson's r, what is a cross product; that is, how is a cross product computed?

Answer: A cross product is the result of multiplying a Z_X score by a Z_Y score. To obtain the Z_X and Z_Y scores, individual X and Y scores must first be converted to Z scores.

Earlier I mentioned that the computational formula for r can be rather threatening if you don't know what it really represents. Now you know, however, that the calculation (based on the cross products of Z scores) is actually quite straightforward. Still, you deserve to have a look at a typical computational formula for r—if only to convince yourself that the business of statistical analysis isn't always as complex as it might appear. The formula that follows, for example, is typical of how a computational formula for r might be presented:

$$r = \frac{n\Sigma XY - (\Sigma X)(\Sigma Y)}{\sqrt{\left[n\Sigma X^2 - (\Sigma X)^2\right]\left[n\Sigma Y^2 - (\Sigma Y)^2\right]}}$$

Such a formula can be very handy if you're using a calculator to compute the value of r. Given the increasing use of computers and statistical software, however, the real issue is likely to be whether or not you have a solid understanding of what lies behind a procedure and how to interpret the results. In the case of Pearson's r, my guess is that the conceptual formula, based on the cross product calculations, gives you a better understanding of what's really involved in the calculation.

Application

We've covered the necessary information to move forward with a typical research application, so let's begin with the example presented in Table 12-4. Assume that information has been collected from a sample of 20 people on two different variables: level of education (the number of school years completed) and number of memberships in voluntary associations (clubs and organizations). We'll treat the education variable as the X or independent variable; the variable related to the number of memberships will be treated as the Y or dependent variable. The raw scores are shown as Variable X and Variable Y.

A quick examination of the data suggests that there's likely to be a positive association between the two variables. After all, the general pattern is one in which high levels of education are associated with a high number of association memberships. By the same token, low levels of education are generally associated with low numbers of memberships. The question, of course, is just how strong the association is. Rather than relying on the more complex computational formula, we'll move forward on the basis of the conceptual formula outlined earlier. Recall that we'll be working toward developing a value for r as a function of the cross products.

The first step is the conversion of the raw score distributions into Z score distributions. The mean and standard deviation (which are necessary ingredients in the conversion of raw scores to Z scores) are given at the bottom of the table. The Z score transformations, along with the cross products, are listed

Table 12-4 Raw Data and Cross Product Calculations for Educational Level and Association Memberships

Case	X Educational Level	Y Association Memberships	Z_X	Z_Y	$Z_X \bullet Z_Y$
1	10	5	−0.16	0.51	−0.08
2	11	3	0.09	−0.56	−0.05
3	16	6	1.32	1.04	1.37
4	7	4	−0.90	−0.03	0.03
5	6	2	−1.15	−1.09	1.25
6	7	0	−0.90	−2.15	1.94
7	11	3	0.09	−0.56	−0.05
8	20	4	2.31	−0.03	−0.07
9	14	5	0.83	0.51	0.42
10	11	5	0.09	0.51	0.05
11	6	4	−1.15	−0.03	0.03
12	7	4	−0.90	−0.03	0.03
13	9	4	−0.41	−0.03	0.01
14	7	2	−0.90	−1.09	0.98
15	10	6	−0.16	1.04	−0.17
16	16	6	1.32	1.04	1.37
17	17	7	1.57	1.57	2.46
18	11	7	0.09	1.57	0.14
19	10	2	−0.16	−1.09	0.17
20	7	2	−0.90	−1.09	0.98

Sum of Cross Products = 10.81

Mean of X = 10.65
Standard Deviation of X = 4.04

Mean of Y = 4.05
Standard Deviation of Y = 1.88

in the appropriate columns. The sum of the cross products (10.81) is shown at the bottom of the last column.

Recall that all we have to do now to obtain the value of r is divide the sum of the cross products by $n - 1$. Thus, we can calculate the value as follows:

$$r = \frac{\sum(Z_X \bullet Z_Y)}{n - 1}$$

$$r = \frac{10.81}{19}$$

$$r = +0.57$$

Interpretation

We now have a calculated *r* value of +0.57, but there's still the question of how we should interpret it. Statisticians actually use the information provided by the *r* value in two ways.

The value of *r* is referred to as the **correlation coefficient**. The sign (+ or −) in front of the *r* value indicates whether the association is positive (direct) or negative (inverse). The absolute value of *r* (the magnitude, without respect to the sign) is a measure of the strength of the relationship. The closer the value gets to 1.0 (either +1.0 or −1.0), the stronger the association.

☑ LEARNING CHECK

Question: What does the sign of the correlation coefficient tell us?
Answer: The sign of the correlation coefficient tells us the direction of the association (either positive or negative).

Question: What does the magnitude of the correlation coefficient tell us?
Answer: The magnitude of the correlation coefficient tells us the strength of the association.

As a rule, correlation coefficients, whether positive or negative, are interpreted as follows (Salkind, 2000):

.0 to .2   No relationship to very weak association
.2 to .4   Weak association
.4 to .6   Moderate association
.6 to .8   Strong association
.8 to 1.0   Very strong to perfect association

Although the value of *r* is important in its own right, the real utility of the measure is found in its squared value. When *r* is squared (to become r^2), it's referred to as the **coefficient of determination**. It's the coefficient of determination that's so meaningful in statistical analysis. Let me explain.

A quick look at the data tells us that each variable reflects some variation. People's level of education varies, and the number of associations to which they belong also varies. The question is, how much of the variation in one variable can be attributed to variation in the other variable? As it turns out, that's what the coefficient of determination is all about.

In other words, the coefficient of determination (r^2) is a measure of the explained variance—the amount of variation in one variable that is attributable to variation in the other variable. Having obtained a positive *r* value, we know that the association between the variables is in a positive direction. The coefficient of determination, though, allows us to go well beyond that in our statement about the relationship.

☑ LEARNING CHECK

Question: What is the coefficient of determination, and how is it symbolized?

Answer: The coefficient of determination is the amount of variation in one variable that is attributable to variation in another variable. It is symbolized as r^2.

Remember: The coefficient of determination is simply the value of r squared (r^2). The r^2 value is transformed into a percentage value as follows: $r^2 \times 100$. For example, starting with our r value of $+0.57$, we can derive the coefficient of determination as follows:

$$r = +0.57$$
$$r^2 = 0.325$$
$$r^2 \times 100 = 32.5\%$$

Interpretation: 32.5% of the variation in number of memberships is attributable to variation in level of education.

The interpretation of r^2 is really quite telling. In this example, it tells us that variation in level of education explains 32.5% of the variation in the number of memberships in voluntary organizations. In everyday terms, it allows us to make more quantitatively based statements about why some people have more memberships and some people have fewer memberships. It's certainly true that some portion of the variation remains unexplained or is not explained by the independent variable (in this case, 67.5%), but the information provided by the coefficient of determination tells us quite a bit about the relationship at hand.

That said, let me caution you about something. When working with Pearson's r, always bear in mind that the real interpretive power is found in the coefficient of determination. Accordingly, you should remind yourself that what might appear at first glance to be a strong association (an r value approaching ±1.0) has a way of decreasing in magnitude when the value is squared. For example, an r value of -0.70 might seem to be quite strong. When the value is squared, however, we find ourselves looking at an r^2 value of 0.49.

Finally, it's important to remember that r^2 is considered to be a symmetrical measure. That means that the interpretation of r^2 works both ways. We can think of r^2 as indicating the amount of variation in Y that is attributable to variation in X, or we can think of it as the amount of variation in X that is attributable to variation in Y.

Assuming you've digested the matter of r and r^2, there's one more element to consider—namely, the matter of a hypothesis test. So far in this chapter, our attention has been directed toward the question of the strength and direction of the association between two variables. We've yet to deal with the matter of a hypothesis test for the significance of r. That's where we'll turn now.

An Additional Step: Testing the Null

It's one thing to measure the apparent strength of association between two variables based on a pattern that's reflected in sample data. It's quite another matter, though, to deal with the question of whether or not the sample reflects what's occurring in the larger population. To deal with this second question—whether or not the pattern reflects the larger population—we turn to a hypothesis-testing procedure. In short, we test the significance of r.

As always, we'll start by stating an appropriate null hypothesis, and we'll select a level of significance in advance. Because our interest is in the question of whether or not the observed association departs from chance (the assumption of no association), we can express the null hypothesis as follows:

$$H_0: r = 0$$

Following the normal procedure of selecting a level of significance in advance, we'll set the level of significance at .05. It's possible to test the null hypothesis using t, but we can also simply compare the calculated value of r (the calculated test statistic) to a table of critical values such as the one in Appendix I. In short, the table shown in Appendix I takes all the work out of the process.

 LEARNING CHECK

Question: When testing the significance of r, what is the null hypothesis?

Answer: The null hypothesis is a statement that $r = 0$.

As with other tables of critical values you've used, Appendix I presents critical values on the basis of the appropriate number of degrees of freedom and level of significance. When looking at Appendix I, note that the critical values of r are presented without regard to the sign that may be associated with the r value (+ or −). For example, a critical value of 0.43 actually represents a critical value of +0.43 *or* −0.43.

In testing the significance of r, the number of degrees of freedom is defined as $n - 2$, where n equals the number of cases or paired observations under consideration. For example, the r value we just calculated was based on observations for 20 people or cases. Thus, the appropriate number of degrees of freedom is equal to 20 – 2, or 18. The degrees of freedom are listed in the first column of Appendix I.

 LEARNING CHECK

Question: How do you determine the number of degrees of freedom when testing the significance of *r*?

Answer: The number of degrees of freedom is equal to the number of cases or paired observations minus 2 (*n* – 2).

Levels of significance are listed across the top of the table; we're working at the .05 level. Locating the column for the .05 level of significance and the row for 18 degrees of freedom, we note that the point of intersection reveals a critical value of 0.444. Comparing our calculated test statistic of 0.57 to this critical value, we determine that the calculated test statistic exceeds the critical value. Therefore, we reject the null hypothesis (with a .05 probability of making a Type I error).

Let me suggest you take a couple of moments to carefully examine the critical values in Appendix I, particularly the way they vary according to the number of degrees of freedom. For example, the critical value (at the .05 level of significance) for 28 degrees of freedom is shown as 0.361. In other words, when working with a sample of 30 cases (degrees of freedom = 28), it would take a calculated value of *r* (either + or –) equal to or greater than 0.361 to reject the null. When working with a sample of 10 cases, however (degrees of freedom = 8), it would take a calculated *r* value (+ or –) equal to or greater than 0.632 to reject the null hypothesis. This point should make intuitive sense to you by now. In terms of what it might take to convince you that there's an association between two variables, you'd probably demand more extreme evidence (a larger *r* value), so to speak, if you were working with a very small sample, as opposed to a larger sample.

Conclusion and Interpretation

A test of the null hypothesis gives us an important foundation for our results from a correlation analysis. It's one thing to determine that there appears to be a strong (positive or negative) association between two variables based on sample data, but there's still the issue of whether or not the pattern in the sample data reflects a similar pattern in the population. And that, of course, is much the same question that we've dealt with in other hypothesis-testing procedures.

The issue always comes back to the notion that the sample data, in one way or another, could be extreme—sample information that doesn't really mirror the population in question. Since the critical values of *r* are so dependent on sample size, a test for the significance of *r* (the test of the null hypothesis that *r* = 0) is really a second but very important step in correlation analysis.

Assuming a noteworthy value of *r* is obtained, it should always be viewed in the context of whether or not it's significant.

In retrospect, it's *easy* to see why Pearson's *r* is such a popular statistical measure. The simple multiplication (cross products) of the *Z* scores, divided by *n* − 1, produces an *r* value, and that *r* value, in turn, tells us something about the strength and direction of the association between two variables. We also know that squaring the value of *r* will produce the coefficient of determination (r^2)—a measure of the extent to which the variation in one variable is attributable to variation in the other variable. We also know that there is a simple procedure available to test the significance of *r*, assuming that the presumed association between two variables is strong enough to capture our attention.

By most standards, all of that would be quite enough benefit from one simple measure. As it turns out, though, the fun has just begun, so to speak. Armed with the value of *r*, along with the means and standard deviations of the raw scores in two distributions, we're actually in a position to make certain predictions. More specifically, we can make predictions about a *Y* value on the basis of a known or assumed *X* value. How we go about that falls under the topic of **regression analysis**, and that's what we take up next.

Regression Analysis

A central element in the calculation of *r* was the conversion of distributions of raw scores into distributions of *Z* scores. Indeed, it was the conversion of raw scores into *Z* scores that allowed us to look at the association between two variables originally measured on very different scales (for example, height measured in inches and weight measured in pounds).

In the case of regression analysis, we find ourselves working with results of the correlation analysis, but we also return to our distribution of raw scores. We go back to our raw scores because the aim of regression analysis is the prediction of one value from another. In a sense, you can think of regression analysis as a technique that allows you to use existing data to predict future values. To better understand all of that, let's turn to an example.

An Application

Let's say a university administrator is concerned about the number of graduate students who enter the university but fail to complete their degrees. Let's assume the administrator's goal is to get a better handle on the association between a student's performance on the GRE (the Graduate Record Examination, a standardized graduate school admission test) and graduate school GPA (grade point average in graduate school). Knowing something about the association between these two variables might put the administrator in a better position to predict the future performance of an applicant.

Let's assume the administrator has selected a random sample of 10 student files for analysis (including students who completed a graduate degree and those who dropped out or were dismissed). The stage is now set for a detailed analysis of the data presented in Table 12-5.

Following the convention outlined earlier, we designate the student GRE score as the independent or X variable and the GPA score as the dependent or Y variable. The X variable (the GRE score) is measured as the combined score on the quantitative and verbal portions of the test. Because each portion of the test has a score range from 200 to 800, a combined score could range from 400 to 1600. The Y variable (GPA) is measured on a scale that ranges from 0.00 to 4.00. Note that the mean and standard deviation for each distribution are given at the bottom of the table. Also shown are the calculated values of r (+0.92) and r^2 (0.85, or 85%).

A scatter plot of the data from Table 12-5 is shown in Figure 12-6. As we might have expected, the general pattern suggests a positive association between the two variables. As GRE scores increase, so do GPAs. The pattern, however, is far from perfect. By no means are the points in the scatter plot aligned in a straight line.

With a little imagination, we might conceive of a line that could pass through the distribution represented by the points—a line that reflects the general trend in the pattern of cases. But an imaginary line that was eyeballed, so to speak, might not be too useful. After all, different people are apt to come up with different imaginary lines, and some lines would more accurately represent the data than others. There's one line—a very precise line—however, that best fits

Table 12-5   Data for 10 Cases (GRE scores and GPAs)

	X	Y	Z_X	Z_Y	$Z_X \bullet Z_Y$
Case	GRE Score	GPA			
1	1378	3.55	1.01	0.72	0.73
2	956	2.65	−0.86	−0.86	0.74
3	1222	3.54	0.32	0.70	0.22
4	830	2.24	−1.42	−1.58	2.24
5	991	3.00	−0.71	−0.25	0.18
6	1300	3.77	0.67	1.11	0.74
7	1521	4.00	1.65	1.51	2.49
8	899	2.62	−1.11	−0.91	1.01
9	1254	3.07	0.46	−0.12	−0.06
10	1149	2.94	0.00	−0.35	0.00

Sum of Cross Products = 8.29

Mean of X = 1150
Standard Deviation of X = 225.20

Mean of Y = 3.14
Standard Deviation of Y = 0.57

r = +0.92
r^2 = 0.85 (85%)

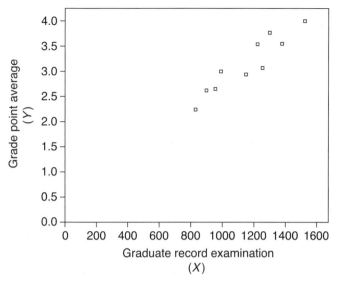

Figure 12-6 GRE and GPA Values

the data. It is known, appropriately enough, as the **line of best fit**. This line, also called the **regression line**, allows us to predict the value of Y on the basis of the value of X. To understand how all of that is done, let's take a look first at the logic behind the line and then at the equation for the line.

The Logic of Prediction and the Line of Best Fit

Returning to our example involving GRE scores and GPAs, recall that we already have the value of Pearson's r (the correlation coefficient) as +0.92 (see Table 12-5). Let's assume we have tested the null hypothesis at the .05 level of significance and found that we could reject the idea of no association between the variables. Armed with this information, we are ready to take the next step—attempting to predict an applicant's future success (measured in terms of GPA) on the basis of the applicant's GRE score.

Had we discovered that the association between the two variables was perfect, we would have obtained an r value of +1.0. Had we discovered a perfect association, we could have produced a scatter plot and easily drawn a straight line through the points. It would have been a rather simple task because in a scatter plot based on a perfect association, all the points would be aligned in a straight line. In a case like that, it would be easy to make a prediction about future success. All we'd have to do is locate a person's GRE score along the X-axis, draw a line up to the line passing through the cases, and then draw a line over to the axis representing future GPA values. The predicted GPA value would simply be the GPA associated with a given GRE score.

Unfortunately, however, we didn't find a perfect association between the GRE scores and future GPAs. Our *r* and r^2 values were high, but they certainly fell short of indicating a perfect association between the two variables. Thus, the prediction of students' future performance based on their GRE scores becomes a bit more problematic. As you're about to discover, however, the prediction may be a bit more problematic, but it's possible nonetheless. It begins with the same notion we've dealt with before—namely, the idea of a straight line passing through the distribution of points in a scatter plot.

As it turns out, we can mathematically determine the path of a straight line that best fits a scatter plot—one that passes through the various points in such a way that the line best represents the overall pattern of association between the values. It is the line that passes through the points in such a way that the squared distances of the points (cases) from the line (taken collectively) are at a minimum. In a sense, that's what the term *regression analysis* is all about. The term refers to the various elements involved in producing the line of best fit and making predictions based on that line.

Because the regression line (or line of best fit) is the line that passes through the distribution in such a manner that the squared distances of the points to the line is at a minimum, it's also often referred to as the **least squares line**. The regression line (or line of best fit or least squares line) for the data we're considering is shown in Figure 12-7. This is the same scatter plot as the one shown in Figure 12-6, but the regression line has been added. Let me suggest that you take a few moments to study the scatter plot, along with its associated line of best fit.

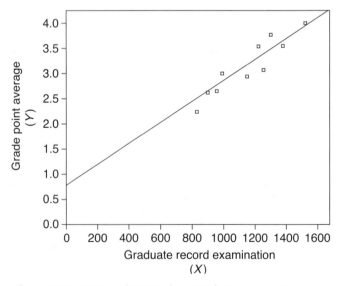

Figure 12-7   GRE and GPA Values (With Regression Line)

And that brings us back to the central purpose of regression analysis. Assuming we knew something about the regression line—assuming we knew the path of the line—it would be a simple matter to predict the value of one variable on the basis of the value of the other variable. In other words, given a value of X, we should be able to predict the value of Y. That, in short, is what regression analysis allows us to do. Given this ultimate goal, we now turn to the equation and related formulas.

 LEARNING CHECK

Question: What is the line of best fit? What are some other terms for the same line?

Answer: The line of best fit is the line that passes through the points in a scatter plot in such a way that it provides the best representation of the overall association between the variables. This is also known as the regression line or the least squares line.

The Regression Equation

Remember what our task is: We want to predict students' future performance (GPA) on the basis of their GRE scores. To do this, we'll rely on the **regression equation**—an equation that describes the least squares line (or line of best fit). The regression equation is defined as follows:

$$Y' = a + bX$$

The elements of the formula are as follows:

- Y' is a value that we're attempting to predict (in this case, a particular GPA); the symbol is read as **Y-prime**. The term Y' stands for a predicted value, as opposed to an actual value.
- X is a value that we are given (in this case, an applicant's GRE score).
- a is the point where the regression line (the line of best fit) crosses the Y-axis of a scatter plot. This is known as the Y-intercept (the point at which the line *intercepts* the Y-axis).
- b represents the slope of the regression line (the amount of change in Y that is associated with a unit change in X).

Assuming we can come up with the values of a and b (referred to as *constants*), we can predict a future GPA on the basis of a GRE score. Since the relationship between the two variables is less than perfect, we approach the analysis with the knowledge that our prediction will likely be less than perfect as well. On the other hand, it's safe to say that the use of the regression equation puts us in a position to make a very educated guess, even though it is apt to be less than perfect.

Returning to the elements in the equation, it's clear that now we need to know the values for a and b (the constants). Down the road, once we have a and b, we can substitute values for X to make predictions about Y values (or, more correctly, the Y' values). But first we have to have the values of a and b.

Calculation of the b Term (the Slope of the Line). As noted previously, the **b term in the regression equation ($Y' = a + bX$)**, is the slope of the line—that is, the amount of change in Y that accompanies a unit change in X. In our present example, the slope tells us the increase in a student's GPA that is expected to occur with a one-point increase in a student's GRE score.

Since we're interested in actual scores on the GRE and actual GPA values, we return to our raw scores for this portion of our analysis. The transformed Z scores came into play when we calculated the correlation coefficient, and the correlation coefficient comes into play in the regression procedure. But we have to deal with the raw scores to get an accurate picture of the unit changes that are going on in each distribution (that is, how a change in GRE score is accompanied by a change in GPA).

The situation is rendered far more comprehensible if we think in terms of standard deviation units—a change of a certain number of standard deviation units in one variable accompanied by a change of a certain number of standard deviation units in the other variable. As it turns out, this idea lies at the heart of the computation of the b term in the regression equation. In fact, the b term is simply an expression of the ratio of the standard deviation of the Y variable (s_Y) to the standard deviation of the X variable (s_X), taking into account the strength of association (the value of r) between the two variables.

We already have the standard deviation for each distribution of raw scores. Those, along with the means of each distribution, were shown in Table 12-5 as follows:

$$\overline{X} = 1150 \qquad s_X = 225.20$$
$$\overline{Y} = 3.14 \qquad s_Y = 0.57$$

The next step is to express the relationship between the two standard deviations as follows: s_Y/s_X. The final step in the calculation of the b term is to multiply the ratio by the correlation coefficient (r). Note that we'll multiply the ratio by the value of r, not the value of r^2. The various steps for the calculation of the b term can be summarized as follows:

$$b = r\left(\frac{s_Y}{s_X}\right)$$
$$b = 0.92\left(\frac{0.57}{225.20}\right)$$
$$b = 0.002$$

The real meaning of the *b* term, or slope of the line, doesn't come to the forefront until we have calculated the Y-intercept (the *a* term). Therefore, we'll turn to that calculation next.

Calculation of the *a* Term (the Y-Intercept). The *a* term in the regression equation (*Y′* = *a* + *bX*) was previously defined as the point where the regression line (the line of best fit in a scatter plot) crosses the Y-axis. It is mathematically defined as follows:

$$a = \overline{Y} - b\overline{X}$$

or the mean of Y, minus the slope (*b*) times the mean of X

It should make intuitive sense to you that the regression line will, in some way, reflect the means of both distributions. It's true that there is a certain amount of variation in the GRE scores, but there is also an average GRE score (a mean for the distribution of GRE scores). By the same token, there's a certain amount of variation in the GPAs, but there's also an average GPA (a mean for the distribution of GPAs). In essence, the formula for the calculation of the Y-intercept (the *a* term) takes into account both means—the mean of X (the GRE scores) and the mean of Y (the GPAs). By the same token, it should make intuitive sense that the formula would also take into account the slope of the line (the *b* term), inasmuch as the slope of the line will, in part, influence where the line crosses the Y-axis.

The means for our raw score distributions (GRE and GPA raw scores) were given in Table 12-5 as 1150 and 3.14, respectively. Using that information, along with our calculated *b* term (for the slope of the line, equal to .002), we can easily determine the *a* term (the Y-intercept) as follows:

$$a = \overline{Y} - b\overline{X}$$
$$a = 3.14 - b(1150)$$
$$a = 3.14 - 0.002(1150)$$
$$a = 3.14 - 2.30$$
$$a = 0.84$$

Making a Prediction. To make a prediction (to calculate a *Y′*), all that's necessary is to return to the formula for the regression equation: *Y′* = *a* + *bX*. For example, let's say we are reviewing an application for admission to graduate school, and the student's GRE score equals 1000. Since we now know the values of *a* and *b*, it's a simple matter to make the prediction. Using the regression equation, the prediction would move forward as follows:

$$Y' = a + bX$$
$$Y' = 0.84 + b(1000)$$
$$Y' = 0.84 + 0.002(1000)$$
$$Y' = 0.84 + 2.00$$
$$Y' = 2.84$$

Given a GRE score of 1000, we predict the student will achieve a GPA of 2.84. Does this mean that we know, without question, that the student will ultimately achieve a GPA of 2.84? No, we can't make a prediction like that with total certainty. The regression line would only yield a perfect prediction if we were dealing with an underlying perfect association. On the other hand, the regression procedure (with its line of best fit and associated equation) does give us a decided advantage over a pure guess. Yes, it may amount to a guess, but it's an educated guess.

Additionally, you should note that the prediction, in this case, would be a prediction of Y' on the basis of a value of X. In statistical jargon, we say that we have regressed Y on X. Unlike the correlation procedure that produces a symmetrical measure (one that will produce the same result regardless of which variable is designated as X and which is designated as Y), the results of a regression analysis are very much a function of how you designate the variables. Some thoughtful consideration of how the constants are determined should convince you of why that is the case.

Now, what about our prediction that a GRE score of 1000 will result in a GPA of 2.84? You may have a few doubts about all this. True, the regression equation allows us to make an educated guess. But, you may well ask, just how "educated" is that guess likely to be.

The Standard Error of the Estimate

If you think back to what you learned earlier when you learned how to estimate the mean of a population or a proportion—when you learned how to construct confidence intervals—you probably sense where this is going. You're probably already thinking about the fact that your estimate (your prediction, as it were) is subject to a certain amount of error. If that's where your thinking has taken you, let me congratulate you—you're definitely on the right track.

Remember: Any prediction you make (short of one based on a perfect association or an r value of ± 1.0) will be subject to some amount of error. In regression terms, this overall expression of potential error in an estimate of Y' is referred to as the **standard error of the estimate** (s_e). Conceptually, it's an overall measure of the extent to which the predicted Y' values deviate from the actual Y values. Since the standard error of the estimate is an overall measure of deviation (deviation between the predicted and actual values of Y), you can think of it as a type of standard deviation.

The formula for the calculation of the standard error of the estimate is as follows:

$$s_e = \sqrt{\frac{\Sigma(Y - Y')^2}{n - 2}}$$

Note that this formula is remarkably similar to the formula for the standard deviation that you first encountered in Chapter 2. First, it involves the summation of deviations—in this case, the deviations between the predicted values (the Y' values) and the actual values (the Y values). Next, the sum of the deviations is divided by $n - 2$, to yield the error variance. The final step merely involves taking the square root of the error variance.

If we return to our example involving the GRE scores and the GPAs, we could calculate the standard error of the estimate (s_e) according to the steps outlined in Table 12-6. Assuming we carried out these calculations, we'd eventually discover that the standard error of the estimate is equal to 0.22. We'd then be in a position to make a more grounded statement about a predicted value.

For example, we could think back to the 1-2-3 Rule that we encountered earlier and easily make use of it in connection with our prediction. As you'll recall, we learned from the 1-2-3 Rule that approximately 95% of the cases under a normal distribution will be found ±2 standard deviations from the mean.

Table 12-6 Calculation of the Standard Error of the Estimate

Case	X	Y	Y'	$(Y - Y')$	$(Y - Y')^2$
1	1378	3.55	3.60	−0.05	0.00
2	956	2.65	2.75	−0.10	0.01
3	1222	3.54	3.28	0.26	0.07
4	830	2.24	2.50	−0.26	0.07
5	991	3.00	2.82	0.18	0.03
6	1300	3.77	3.44	0.33	0.11
7	1521	4.00	3.88	0.12	0.01
8	899	2.62	2.64	−0.02	0.00
9	1254	3.07	3.35	−0.28	0.08
10	1149	2.94	3.14	−0.20	0.04

$$\sum(Y - Y')^2 = 0.42$$

Calculation of Standard Error of the Estimate

$$s_e = \sqrt{\frac{\sum\left(Y - Y'\right)^2}{n - 2}}$$

$$s_e = \sqrt{\frac{0.42}{8}}$$

$$s_e = \sqrt{0.05}$$

$$s_e = 0.22$$

Our predicted GPA (based on a GRE score of 1000) is 2.84, and we know that the standard error of the estimate (which is really a standard deviation) is equal to 0.22. Suppose we subtract two standard error units from our predicted value and add two standard error units to our predicted value:

$$2.84 - 2(0.22) = 2.40$$
$$2.84 + 2(0.22) = 3.28$$

We're now back in somewhat familiar territory. Indeed, we're in a position to estimate that a GRE score of 1000 will be associated with a GPA that ranges between 2.40 and 3.28 and that we have used a method that will generate a correct estimate approximately 95 times out of 100.

Can we be 100% certain about our estimate? No, we can't be 100% certain that our estimate is correct. On the other hand, our estimate amounts to a very educated guess. And, as a friend of mine is fond of saying, an educated guess always beats a shot in the dark.

At the conclusion of this chapter, you'll find a variety of questions and problems, all designed to enhance your understanding of both correlation and regression. As in previous chapters, you'll find an emphasis on conceptual as opposed to computational elements, but you'll have a chance to sharpen your skills on both fronts. Let me suggest that you give the required time to the question/problem section. Correlation and regression are part of the statistical shelf of staples, so to speak. A solid understanding of the concepts will serve you well.

Chapter Summary

In this chapter, you were introduced to the topics of correlation and regression analysis, two of the more popular statistical procedures. Along the way, you extended your understanding of the notion of a relationship or association between variables as you added the concepts of strength and direction to your storehouse of knowledge. You were introduced to the notions of the correlation coefficient and the coefficient of determination—two concepts that allow us to say quite a lot about the association between two variables. What's more, you learned that it's an easy matter to test a null hypothesis involving a correlation coefficient.

In your exploration of regression analysis, you learned about the regression line and the regression equation. You also learned that it's possible to predict the value of one variable, given the value of another variable (provided the variables are associated in a linear pattern). You also learned, however, that such a prediction will not be perfect (unless, of course, the underlying association between the variables is perfect).

In short, you learned quite a lot. However, a full exploration of correlation and regression analysis is impossible in just a few pages. For this reason, I urge you to pay close attention to the next section ("Some Other Things You Should Know"). Think of it as an invitation to further exploration into the world of statistical analysis.

Some Other Things You Should Know

In many ways, a complete chapter on the topics of correlation and regression could approach a near limitless length. We've only scratched the surface in this presentation—touching on the very basic principles involved in the most fundamental applications. The topics of correlation and regression are so substantial that entire texts (often of considerable length) have been devoted to them. It's always difficult to draw the line when it comes to the matter of an introductory voyage into the world of statistics, and just how much should be given over to the topics of correlation and regression is a case in point.

More advanced texts, for example, often deal with the techniques of multiple and partial correlation. Similarly, other texts may present material on more advanced regression techniques. For example, see Ramsey and Shafer (2002) for an excellent treatment, should you want to explore the more advanced procedures.

As to the material presented here, there are still a few things you should take into consideration before you launch into a simple correlation or regression analysis. With the widespread availability of computer-based statistical software, correlation or regression analysis can be tempting, particularly if you're faced with a mountain of data that's crying out for analysis. On the other hand, certain assumptions should be met before embarking on the procedures, and you should always approach your interpretation of results with some caution.

As to the fundamental assumptions that underlie simple correlation analysis, you're already aware that the procedure rests on the availability of interval/ratio level data—two variables, each expressed in terms of an interval/ratio scale of measurement. Moreover, there is an assumption that each variable under consideration is normally distributed and that the variances of each distribution are roughly equal.

As to the caution that should be exercised in the interpretation of results, keep in mind that a prediction made on the basis of regression analysis is always subject to error. Just as the estimate of a population mean or proportion is always accompanied by some margin of error, the same applies in the case of a prediction of Y' on the basis of the regression equation.

Finally, you should always remember that your analysis, more than likely, will involve sample data, and with that go certain limitations and assumptions. Now, however, you're armed to deal with them. *Welcome to the world of statistical analysis!*

Key Terms

a term in the regression equation
  ($Y' = a + bX$)
b term in the regression equation
  ($Y' = a + bX$)
coefficient of determination
correlation
correlation coefficient
curvilinear association
dependent variable
independent variable
least squares line
line of best fit

linear association
negative (inverse) association
Pearson's *r*
perfect association
positive (direct) association
regression analysis
regression equation
regression line
scatter plot
standard error of the estimate
strength of association
Y prime (Y')

Chapter Problems

Fill in the blanks, calculate the requested values, or otherwise supply the correct answer.

General Thought Questions

1. An *r* value of _____ would be interpreted as a perfect negative association.

2. An *r* value of _____ would be interpreted as a perfect positive association.

3. The value of *r* has a range from _____ to _____.

4. An *r* value of 0 would be interpreted as _____ association.

5. A _____ is a visual representation of the values of two variables on a case-by-case basis.

6. The _____ coefficient, or *r*, reveals the strength and direction of an association between two variables.

7. The coefficient of _____, or r^2, tells the amount of variation in one variable that is associated with or explained by variation in the other variable.

8. The regression line is the _____ of best _____; it is also referred to as the ____ squares line.

9. The equation for the regression line is Y' = _____.

10. In the regression equation, _____ is the value that we are attempting to predict.

11. In the regression equation, _____ is the Y-intercept or the point where the regression line crosses the Y-axis.

12. In the regression equation, _____ represents the slope of the regression line.

Application Questions/Problems

1. Consider the following set of data:

Case	X	Y
1	3	4
2	5	7
3	8	7
4	2	2
5	6	5
6	5	4
7	5	5
8	7	8
9	9	8
10	10	9
11	12	10
12	8	7
13	3	2

   a. What is the value of the mean of X?
   b. What is the value of the standard deviation of X?
   c. What is the value of the mean of Y?
   d. What is the value of the standard deviation of Y?
   e. What is the value of the sum of the cross-products?
   f. What is the value of r?

2. Consider the following set of data:

Case	X	Y
1	8	39
2	10	42
3	9	51
4	10	59
5	12	84
6	12	38
7	8	48
8	9	59
9	12	63
10	10	77

   a. What is the value of the mean of X?
   b. What is the value of the standard deviation of X?
   c. What is the value of the mean of Y?
   d. What is the value of the standard deviation of Y?
   e. What is the value of the sum of the cross-products?
   f. What is the value of r?

3. Two variables, Variable X and Variable Y, are the focus of a study. The study involves 14 research participants. The sum of the cross products $(Z_X \cdot Z_Y)$ for the 14 cases is -11.62.
   a. Calculate and interpret r.

   b. Calculate and interpret r^2.
   c. Assuming you were to test the significance of *r* at the .05 level of significance, state an appropriate null hypothesis. What would you conclude?

4. Two variables, Variable *X* and Variable *Y*, are the focus of a study. The study involves 50 research participants. The sum of the cross products $(Z_X \cdot Z_Y)$ for the 50 cases is 15.66.
   a. Calculate and interpret *r*.
   b. Calculate and interpret r^2.
   c. Assuming you were to test the significance of *r* at the .05 level of significance, state an appropriate null hypothesis. What would you conclude?

5. Two variables, Variable *X* and Variable *Y*, are the focus of a study. The study involves 25 research participants. The sum of the cross products $(Z_X \cdot Z_Y)$ for the 25 cases is 21.58.
   a. Calculate and interpret *r*.
   b. Calculate and interpret r^2.
   c. Assuming you were to test the significance of *r* at the .05 level of significance, state an appropriate null hypothesis. What would you conclude?

6. A researcher discovers the following information about the association between Variable *X* and Variable *Y*:

   Mean of *X* = 50.49   Standard deviation of *X* = 12.83

   Mean of *Y* = 18.30   Standard deviation of *Y* = 4.11

   r = −0.71

   Calculate *a* and *b* in the regression equation $(Y' = a + bX)$.

7. A researcher discovers the following information about the association between Variable *X* and Variable *Y*:

   Mean of *X* = 20   Standard deviation of *X* = 6

   Mean of *Y* = 100   Standard deviation of *Y* = 30

   r = +0.83

   Calculate *a* and *b* in the regression equation $(Y' = a + bX)$.

8. Assume you've collected information from 6 students as to how many hours they work each week and their grade point averages (GPAs). The information is shown below.

Student	X Hrs. Worked	Y GPA	Z_X	Z_Y	$Z_X \cdot Z_Y$
1	10	3.80	−0.66	0.76	−0.50
2	20	3.44	0.00	0.14	0.00
3	40	2.50	1.32	−1.48	−1.95
4	35	2.81	0.99	−0.95	−0.94
5	0	4.00	−1.32	1.10	−1.45
6	15	3.62	−0.33	0.45	−0.15

Mean of X = 20   Standard deviation of X = 15.17

Mean of Y = 3.36   Standard deviation of Y = 0.58

Note that the two variables, or number of hours worked each week (X) and GPA (Y), have already been transformed into Z scores.

a. Calculate and interpret r.
b. Calculate and interpret r^2.
c. Calculate a and b in the regression equation (Y' = $a + bX$).

9. Assume you've collected information from customers at a local bookstore. More specifically, for 10 customers, you have the following information on their levels of education and expenditures on book purchases.

Mean of X = 13   Standard deviation of X = 3.46

Mean of Y = 15.70   Standard deviation of Y = 15.28

Note that the two variables, years of education (X) and dollar amount of expenditure (Y), have already been transformed into Z scores

	X Yrs. Education	Y $ Expenditure	Z_X	Z_Y	$Z_X \cdot Z_Y$
1	13	5	0.00	−0.70	0.00
2	17	45	1.16	1.92	2.23
3	9	0	−1.16	−1.03	1.19
4	11	18	−0.58	0.15	−0.09
5	15	25	0.58	0.61	0.35
6	8	4	−1.45	−0.77	1.12
7	13	10	0.00	−0.37	0.00
8	18	35	1.45	1.26	1.83
9	16	15	0.87	−0.05	−0.04
10	10	0	−0.87	−1.03	0.90

a. Calculate and interpret r.
b. Calculate and interpret r^2.
c. Calculate a and b in the regression equation (Y' = $a + bX$).
d. Calculate the standard error of the estimate.

10. Using the information that you developed in your responses to Question 9 (related to level of education and expenditures at a book store), predict the amount of expenditure for someone with 20 years of education.

Appendixes

Appendix A

Table of Areas Under the Normal Curve (Distribution of Z)

Z	Area Between Mean and Z	Z	Area Between Mean and Z	Z	Area Between Mean and Z	Z	Area Between Mean and Z
0.00	0.0000	0.50	0.1915	1.00	0.3413	1.50	0.4332
0.01	0.0040	0.51	0.1950	1.01	0.3438	1.51	0.4345
0.02	0.0080	0.52	0.1985	1.02	0.3461	1.52	0.4357
0.03	0.0120	0.53	0.2019	1.03	0.3485	1.53	0.4370
0.04	0.0160	0.54	0.2054	1.04	0.3508	1.54	0.4382
0.05	0.0199	0.55	0.2088	1.05	0.3531	1.55	0.4394
0.06	0.0239	0.56	0.2123	1.06	0.3554	1.56	0.4406
0.07	0.0279	0.57	0.2157	1.07	0.3577	1.57	0.4418
0.08	0.0319	0.58	0.2190	1.08	0.3599	1.58	0.4429
0.09	0.0359	0.59	0.2224	1.09	0.3621	1.59	0.4441
0.10	0.0398	0.60	0.2257	1.10	0.3643	1.60	0.4452
0.11	0.0438	0.61	0.2291	1.11	0.3665	1.61	0.4463
0.12	0.0478	0.62	0.2324	1.12	0.3686	1.62	0.4474
0.13	0.0517	0.63	0.2357	1.13	0.3708	1.63	0.4484
0.14	0.0557	0.64	0.2389	1.14	0.3729	1.64	0.4495
0.15	0.0596	0.65	0.2422	1.15	0.3749	1.65	0.4505
0.16	0.0636	0.66	0.2454	1.16	0.3770	1.66	0.4515
0.17	0.0675	0.67	0.2486	1.17	0.3790	1.67	0.4525
0.18	0.0714	0.68	0.2517	1.18	0.3810	1.68	0.4535
0.19	0.0753	0.69	0.2549	1.19	0.3830	1.69	0.4545
0.20	0.0793	0.70	0.2580	1.20	0.3849	1.70	0.4554
0.21	0.0832	0.71	0.2611	1.21	0.3869	1.71	0.4564
0.22	0.0871	0.72	0.2642	1.22	0.3888	1.72	0.4573
0.23	0.0910	0.73	0.2673	1.23	0.3907	1.73	0.4582
0.24	0.0948	0.74	0.2704	1.24	0.3925	1.74	0.4591
0.25	0.0987	0.75	0.2734	1.25	0.3944	1.75	0.4599
0.26	0.1026	0.76	0.2764	1.26	0.3962	1.76	0.4608
0.27	0.1064	0.77	0.2794	1.27	0.3980	1.77	0.4616
0.28	0.1103	0.78	0.2823	1.28	0.3997	1.78	0.4625
0.29	0.1141	0.79	0.2852	1.29	0.4015	1.79	0.4633
0.30	0.1179	0.80	0.2881	1.30	0.4032	1.80	0.4641
0.31	0.1217	0.81	0.2910	1.31	0.4049	1.81	0.4649
0.32	0.1255	0.82	0.2939	1.32	0.4066	1.82	0.4656
0.33	0.1293	0.83	0.2967	1.33	0.4082	1.83	0.4664
0.34	0.1331	0.84	0.2995	1.34	0.4099	1.84	0.4671
0.35	0.1368	0.85	0.3023	1.35	0.4115	1.85	0.4678
0.36	0.1406	0.86	0.3051	1.36	0.4131	1.86	0.4686
0.37	0.1443	0.87	0.3078	1.37	0.4147	1.87	0.4693
0.38	0.1480	0.88	0.3106	1.38	0.4162	1.88	0.4699
0.39	0.1517	0.89	0.3133	1.39	0.4177	1.89	0.4706
0.40	0.1554	0.90	0.3159	1.40	0.4192	1.90	0.4713
0.41	0.1591	0.91	0.3186	1.41	0.4207	1.91	0.4719
0.42	0.1628	0.92	0.3212	1.42	0.4222	1.92	0.4726
0.43	0.1664	0.93	0.3238	1.43	0.4236	1.93	0.4732
0.44	0.1700	0.94	0.3264	1.44	0.4251	1.94	0.4738
0.45	0.1736	0.95	0.3289	1.45	0.4265	1.95	0.4744
0.46	0.1772	0.96	0.3315	1.46	0.4279	1.96	0.4750
0.47	0.1808	0.97	0.3340	1.47	0.4292	1.97	0.4756
0.48	0.1844	0.98	0.3365	1.48	0.4306	1.98	0.4761
0.49	0.1879	0.99	0.3389	1.49	0.4319	1.99	0.4767

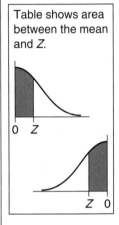

Table shows area between the mean and Z.

(continued)

Table *(continued)*

Z	Area Between Mean and Z	Z	Area Between Mean and Z	Z	Area Between Mean and Z	Z	Area Between Mean and Z
2.00	0.4772	2.50	0.4938	3.00	0.4987	3.50	0.4998
2.01	0.4778	2.51	0.4940	3.01	0.4987	3.60	0.4998
2.02	0.4783	2.52	0.4941	3.02	0.4987	3.70	0.4999
2.03	0.4788	2.53	0.4943	3.03	0.4988	3.80	0.4999
2.04	0.4793	2.54	0.4945	3.04	0.4988	3.90	0.4999
2.05	0.4798	2.55	0.4946	3.05	0.4989		
2.06	0.4803	2.56	0.4948	3.06	0.4989		
2.07	0.4808	2.57	0.4949	3.07	0.4989		
2.08	0.4812	2.58	0.4951	3.08	0.4990		
2.09	0.4817	2.59	0.4952	3.09	0.4990		
2.10	0.4821	2.60	0.4953	3.10	0.4990		
2.11	0.4826	2.61	0.4955	3.11	0.4991		
2.12	0.4830	2.62	0.4956	3.12	0.4991		
2.13	0.4834	2.63	0.4957	3.13	0.4991		
2.14	0.4838	2.64	0.4959	3.14	0.4992		
2.15	0.4842	2.65	0.4960	3.15	0.4992		
2.16	0.4846	2.66	0.4961	3.16	0.4992		
2.17	0.4850	2.67	0.4962	3.17	0.4992		
2.18	0.4854	2.68	0.4963	3.18	0.4993		
2.19	0.4857	2.69	0.4964	3.19	0.4993		
2.20	0.4861	2.70	0.4965	3.20	0.4993		
2.21	0.4864	2.71	0.4966	3.21	0.4993		
2.22	0.4868	2.72	0.4967	3.22	0.4994		
2.23	0.4871	2.73	0.4968	3.23	0.4994		
2.24	0.4875	2.74	0.4969	3.24	0.4994		
2.25	0.4878	2.75	0.4970	3.25	0.4994		
2.26	0.4881	2.76	0.4971	3.26	0.4994		
2.27	0.4884	2.77	0.4972	3.27	0.4995		
2.28	0.4887	2.78	0.4973	3.28	0.4995		
2.29	0.4890	2.79	0.4974	3.29	0.4995		
2.30	0.4893	2.80	0.4974	3.30	0.4995		
2.31	0.4896	2.81	0.4975	3.31	0.4995		
2.32	0.4898	2.82	0.4976	3.32	0.4995		
2.33	0.4901	2.83	0.4977	3.33	0.4996		
2.34	0.4904	2.84	0.4977	3.34	0.4996		
2.35	0.4906	2.85	0.4978	3.35	0.4996		
2.36	0.4909	2.86	0.4979	3.36	0.4996		
2.37	0.4911	2.87	0.4979	3.37	0.4996		
2.38	0.4913	2.88	0.4980	3.38	0.4996		
2.39	0.4916	2.89	0.4981	3.39	0.4997		
2.40	0.4918	2.90	0.4981	3.40	0.4997		
2.41	0.4920	2.91	0.4982	3.41	0.4997		
2.42	0.4922	2.92	0.4982	3.42	0.4997		
2.43	0.4925	2.93	0.4983	3.43	0.4997		
2.44	0.4927	2.94	0.4984	3.44	0.4997		
2.45	0.4929	2.95	0.4984	3.45	0.4997		
2.46	0.4931	2.96	0.4985	3.46	0.4997		
2.47	0.4932	2.97	0.4985	3.47	0.4997		
2.48	0.4934	2.98	0.4986	3.48	0.4997		
2.49	0.4936	2.99	0.4986	3.49	0.4998		

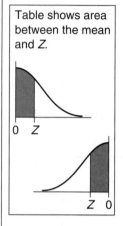

Table shows area between the mean and Z.

Source: Adapted from tables constructed by Victor Bissonnette, Berry College, retrieved from http://facultyweb.berry.edu/vbissonette/tables/tables.html. Used with permission.

Appendix B

Family of t Distributions (Two-Tailed Test)

Degrees of Freedom (df)	LEVEL OF SIGNIFICANCE					
	.20	.10	.05	.02	.01	.001
5	1.476	2.015	2.571	3.365	4.032	6.869
6	1.440	1.943	2.447	3.143	3.707	5.959
7	1.415	1.895	2.365	2.998	3.499	5.408
8	1.397	1.860	2.306	2.896	3.355	5.041
9	1.383	1.833	2.262	2.821	3.250	4.781
10	1.372	1.812	2.228	2.764	3.169	4.587
11	1.363	1.796	2.201	2.718	3.106	4.437
12	1.356	1.782	2.179	2.681	3.055	4.318
13	1.350	1.771	2.160	2.650	3.012	4.221
14	1.345	1.761	2.145	2.624	2.977	4.140
15	1.341	1.753	2.131	2.602	2.947	4.073
16	1.337	1.746	2.120	2.583	2.921	4.015
17	1.333	1.740	2.110	2.567	2.898	3.965
18	1.330	1.734	2.101	2.552	2.878	3.922
19	1.328	1.729	2.093	2.539	2.861	3.883
20	1.325	1.725	2.086	2.528	2.845	3.850
21	1.323	1.721	2.080	2.518	2.831	3.819
22	1.321	1.717	2.074	2.508	2.819	3.792
23	1.319	1.714	2.069	2.500	2.807	3.768
24	1.318	1.711	2.064	2.492	2.797	3.745
25	1.316	1.708	2.060	2.485	2.787	3.725
26	1.315	1.706	2.056	2.479	2.779	3.707
27	1.314	1.703	2.052	2.473	2.771	3.690
28	1.313	1.701	2.048	2.467	2.763	3.674
29	1.311	1.699	2.045	2.462	2.756	3.659
30	1.310	1.697	2.042	2.457	2.750	3.646
40	1.303	1.684	2.021	2.423	2.704	3.551
50	1.299	1.676	2.009	2.403	2.678	3.496
60	1.296	1.671	2.000	2.390	2.660	3.460
80	1.292	1.664	1.990	2.374	2.639	3.416
100	1.290	1.660	1.984	2.364	2.626	3.390
120	1.289	1.658	1.980	2.358	2.617	3.373
∞	1.282	1.645	1.960	2.327	2.576	3.291

Note: If looking for a certain number of degrees of freedom (df) that does not appear in the table (for example, $df = 75$), use the next lower entry (for example, use $df = 60$).

Source: Adapted from tables constructed by Victor Bissonnette, Berry College, retrieved from http://facultyweb.berry.edu/vbissonette/tables/tables.html. Used with permission.

Appendix C

Family of t Distributions (One-Tailed Test)

Degrees of Freedom (df)	LEVEL OF SIGNIFICANCE					
	.10	.05	.025	.01	.005	.0005
5	1.476	2.015	2.571	3.365	4.032	6.869
6	1.440	1.943	2.447	3.143	3.707	5.959
7	1.415	1.895	2.365	2.998	3.499	5.408
8	1.397	1.860	2.306	2.896	3.355	5.041
9	1.383	1.833	2.262	2.821	3.250	4.781
10	1.372	1.812	2.228	2.764	3.169	4.587
11	1.363	1.796	2.201	2.718	3.106	4.437
12	1.356	1.782	2.179	2.681	3.055	4.318
13	1.350	1.771	2.160	2.650	3.012	4.221
14	1.345	1.761	2.145	2.624	2.977	4.140
15	1.341	1.753	2.131	2.602	2.947	4.073
16	1.337	1.746	2.120	2.583	2.921	4.015
17	1.333	1.740	2.110	2.567	2.898	3.965
18	1.330	1.734	2.101	2.552	2.878	3.922
19	1.328	1.729	2.093	2.539	2.861	3.883
20	1.325	1.725	2.086	2.528	2.845	3.850
21	1.323	1.721	2.080	2.518	2.831	3.819
22	1.321	1.717	2.074	2.508	2.819	3.792
23	1.319	1.714	2.069	2.500	2.807	3.768
24	1.318	1.711	2.064	2.492	2.797	3.745
25	1.316	1.708	2.060	2.485	2.787	3.725
26	1.315	1.706	2.056	2.479	2.779	3.707
27	1.314	1.703	2.052	2.473	2.771	3.690
28	1.313	1.701	2.048	2.467	2.763	3.674
29	1.311	1.699	2.045	2.462	2.756	3.659
30	1.310	1.697	2.042	2.457	2.750	3.646
40	1.303	1.684	2.021	2.423	2.704	3.551
50	1.299	1.676	2.009	2.403	2.678	3.496
60	1.296	1.671	2.000	2.390	2.660	3.460
80	1.292	1.664	1.990	2.374	2.639	3.416
100	1.290	1.660	1.984	2.364	2.626	3.390
120	1.289	1.658	1.980	2.358	2.617	3.373
∞	1.282	1.645	1.960	2.327	2.576	3.291

Source: Adapted from tables constructed by Victor Bissonnette, Berry College, retrieved from http://facultyweb.berry.edu/vbissonette/tables/tables.html. Used with permission.

Appendix D

Distribution of F (.05 Level of Significance)

df_W	df_B								
	1	2	3	4	5	6	7	8	12
5	6.61	5.79	5.41	5.19	5.05	4.95	4.88	4.82	4.68
6	5.99	5.14	4.76	4.53	4.39	4.28	4.21	4.15	4.00
7	5.59	4.74	4.35	4.12	3.97	3.87	3.79	3.73	3.57
8	5.32	4.46	4.07	3.84	3.69	3.58	3.50	3.44	3.28
9	5.12	4.26	3.86	3.63	3.48	3.37	3.29	3.23	3.07
10	4.96	4.10	3.71	3.48	3.33	3.22	3.14	3.07	2.91
11	4.84	3.98	3.59	3.36	3.20	3.09	3.01	2.95	2.79
12	4.75	3.89	3.49	3.26	3.11	3.00	2.91	2.85	2.69
13	4.67	3.81	3.41	3.18	3.03	2.92	2.83	2.77	2.60
14	4.60	3.74	3.34	3.11	2.96	2.85	2.76	2.70	2.53
15	4.54	3.68	3.29	3.06	2.90	2.79	2.71	2.64	2.48
16	4.49	3.63	3.24	3.01	2.85	2.74	2.66	2.59	2.42
17	4.45	3.59	3.20	2.96	2.81	2.70	2.61	2.55	2.38
18	4.41	3.55	3.16	2.93	2.77	2.66	2.58	2.51	2.34
19	4.38	3.52	3.13	2.90	2.74	2.63	2.54	2.48	2.31
20	4.35	3.49	3.10	2.87	2.71	2.60	2.51	2.45	2.28
21	4.32	3.47	3.07	2.84	2.68	2.57	2.49	2.42	2.25
22	4.30	3.44	3.05	2.82	2.66	2.55	2.46	2.40	2.23
23	4.28	3.42	3.03	2.80	2.64	2.53	2.44	2.37	2.20
24	4.26	3.40	3.01	2.78	2.62	2.51	2.42	2.36	2.18
25	4.24	3.39	2.99	2.76	2.60	2.49	2.40	2.34	2.16
26	4.23	3.37	2.98	2.74	2.59	2.47	2.39	2.32	2.15
27	4.21	3.35	2.96	2.73	2.57	2.46	2.37	2.31	2.13
28	4.20	3.34	2.95	2.71	2.56	2.45	2.36	2.29	2.12
29	4.18	3.33	2.93	2.70	2.55	2.43	2.35	2.28	2.10
30	4.17	3.32	2.92	2.69	2.53	2.42	2.33	2.27	2.09
40	4.08	3.23	2.84	2.61	2.45	2.34	2.25	2.18	2.00
60	4.00	3.15	2.76	2.53	2.37	2.25	2.17	2.10	1.92
80	3.96	3.11	2.72	2.49	2.33	2.21	2.13	2.06	1.88
100	3.94	3.09	2.70	2.46	2.31	2.19	2.10	2.03	1.85
120	3.92	3.07	2.68	2.45	2.29	2.18	2.09	2.02	1.83
∞	3.84	3.00	2.61	2.37	2.22	2.10	2.01	1.94	1.75

Source: Adapted from tables constructed by Victor Bissonnette, Berry College, retrieved from http://facultyweb.berry.edu/vbissonette/tables/tables.html. Used with permission.

Appendix E

Distribution of F (.01 Level of Significance)

df_W	\multicolumn{9}{c}{df_B}
	1	2	3	4	5	6	7	8	12
5	16.26	13.27	12.06	11.39	10.97	10.67	10.46	10.29	9.89
6	13.75	10.92	9.78	9.15	8.75	8.47	8.26	8.10	7.72
7	12.25	9.55	8.45	7.85	7.46	7.19	6.99	6.84	6.47
8	11.26	8.65	7.59	7.01	6.63	6.37	6.18	6.03	5.67
9	10.56	8.02	6.99	6.42	6.06	5.80	5.61	5.47	5.11
10	10.04	7.56	6.55	5.99	5.64	5.39	5.20	5.06	4.71
11	9.65	7.21	6.22	5.67	5.32	5.07	4.89	4.74	4.40
12	9.33	6.93	5.95	5.41	5.06	4.82	4.64	4.50	4.16
13	9.07	6.70	5.74	5.21	4.86	4.62	4.44	4.30	3.96
14	8.86	6.51	5.56	5.04	4.69	4.46	4.28	4.14	3.80
15	8.68	6.36	5.42	4.89	4.56	4.32	4.14	4.00	3.67
16	8.53	6.23	5.29	4.77	4.44	4.20	4.03	3.89	3.55
17	8.40	6.11	5.18	4.67	4.34	4.10	3.93	3.79	3.46
18	8.29	6.01	5.09	4.58	4.25	4.01	3.84	3.71	3.37
19	8.18	5.93	5.01	4.50	4.17	3.94	3.77	3.63	3.30
20	8.10	5.85	4.94	4.43	4.10	3.87	3.70	3.56	3.23
21	8.02	5.78	4.87	4.37	4.04	3.81	3.64	3.51	3.17
22	7.95	5.72	4.82	4.31	3.99	3.76	3.59	3.45	3.12
23	7.88	5.66	4.76	4.26	3.94	3.71	3.54	3.41	3.07
24	7.82	5.61	4.72	4.22	3.90	3.67	3.50	3.36	3.03
25	7.77	5.57	4.68	4.18	3.85	3.63	3.46	3.32	2.99
26	7.72	5.53	4.64	4.14	3.82	3.59	3.42	3.29	2.96
27	7.68	5.49	4.60	4.11	3.78	3.56	3.39	3.26	2.93
28	7.64	5.45	4.57	4.07	3.75	3.53	3.36	3.23	2.90
29	7.60	5.42	4.54	4.04	3.73	3.50	3.33	3.20	2.87
30	7.56	5.39	4.51	4.02	3.70	3.47	3.30	3.17	2.84
40	7.31	5.18	4.31	3.83	3.51	3.29	3.12	2.99	2.66
60	7.08	4.98	4.13	3.65	3.34	3.12	2.95	2.82	2.50
80	6.96	4.88	4.04	3.56	3.26	3.04	2.87	2.74	2.42
100	6.90	4.82	3.98	3.51	3.21	2.99	2.82	2.69	2.37
120	6.85	4.79	3.95	3.48	3.17	2.96	2.79	2.66	2.34
∞	6.64	4.61	3.78	3.32	3.02	2.80	2.64	2.51	2.19

Source: Adapted from tables constructed by Victor Bissonnette, Berry College, retrieved from http://facultyweb.berry.edu/vbissonnette/tables/tables.html. Used with permission.

Appendix F

Distribution of Q (.05 Level of Significance)

df_w	\multicolumn{8}{c}{k (number of groups)}							
	3	4	5	6	7	8	9	10
5	4.60	5.22	5.67	6.03	6.33	6.58	6.80	6.99
6	4.34	4.90	5.30	5.63	5.90	6.12	6.32	6.49
7	4.16	4.68	5.06	5.36	5.61	5.82	6.00	6.16
8	4.04	4.53	4.89	5.17	5.40	5.60	5.77	5.92
9	3.95	4.41	4.76	5.02	5.24	5.43	5.59	5.74
10	3.88	4.33	4.65	4.91	5.12	5.30	5.46	5.60
11	3.82	4.26	4.57	4.82	5.03	5.20	5.35	5.49
12	3.77	4.20	4.51	4.75	4.95	5.12	5.27	5.39
13	3.73	4.15	4.45	4.69	4.88	5.05	5.19	5.32
14	3.70	4.11	4.41	4.64	4.83	4.99	5.13	5.25
15	3.67	4.08	4.37	4.59	4.78	4.94	5.08	5.20
16	3.65	4.05	4.33	4.56	4.74	4.90	5.03	5.15
17	3.63	4.02	4.30	4.52	4.70	4.86	4.99	5.11
18	3.61	4.00	4.28	4.49	4.67	4.82	4.96	5.07
19	3.59	3.98	4.25	4.47	4.65	4.79	4.92	5.04
20	3.58	3.96	4.23	4.45	4.62	4.77	4.90	5.01
24	3.53	3.90	4.17	4.37	4.54	4.68	4.81	4.92
30	3.49	3.85	4.10	4.30	4.46	4.60	4.72	4.82
40	3.44	3.79	4.04	4.23	4.39	4.52	4.63	4.73
60	3.40	3.74	3.98	4.16	4.31	4.44	4.55	4.65
120	3.36	3.68	3.92	4.10	4.24	4.36	4.47	4.56
∞	3.31	3.63	3.86	4.03	4.17	4.29	4.39	4.47

Source: Adapted from Table VIII in Jay Devore and Roxy Peck, *Statistics: The Exploration and Analysis of Data* (4th ed.), Brooks/Cole, 2001.

Appendix G

Distribution of Q (.01 Level of Significance)

	k (number of groups)							
df_W	3	4	5	6	7	8	9	10
5	4.60	5.22	5.67	6.03	6.33	6.58	6.80	6.99
6	6.33	7.03	7.56	7.97	8.32	8.61	8.87	9.10
7	5.92	6.54	7.01	7.37	7.68	7.94	8.17	8.37
8	5.64	6.20	6.62	6.96	7.24	7.47	7.68	7.86
9	5.43	5.96	6.35	6.66	6.91	7.13	7.33	7.49
10	5.27	5.77	6.14	6.43	6.67	6.87	7.05	7.21
11	5.15	5.62	5.97	6.25	6.48	6.67	6.84	6.99
12	5.05	5.50	5.84	6.10	6.32	6.51	6.67	6.81
13	4.96	5.40	5.73	5.98	6.19	6.37	6.53	6.67
14	4.89	5.32	5.63	5.88	6.08	6.26	6.41	6.54
15	4.84	5.25	5.56	5.80	5.99	6.16	6.31	6.44
16	4.79	5.19	5.49	5.72	5.92	6.08	6.22	6.35
17	4.74	5.14	5.43	5.66	5.85	6.01	6.15	6.27
18	4.70	5.09	5.38	5.60	5.79	5.94	6.08	6.20
19	4.67	5.05	5.33	5.55	5.73	5.89	6.02	6.14
20	4.64	5.02	5.29	5.51	5.69	5.84	5.97	6.09
24	4.55	4.91	5.17	5.37	5.54	5.69	5.81	5.92
30	4.45	4.80	5.05	5.24	5.40	5.54	5.65	5.76
40	4.37	4.70	4.93	5.11	5.26	5.39	5.50	5.60
60	4.28	4.59	4.82	4.99	5.13	5.25	5.36	5.45
120	4.20	4.50	4.71	4.87	5.01	5.12	5.21	5.30
∞	4.12	4.40	4.60	4.76	4.88	4.99	5.08	5.16

Source: Adapted from Table VIII in Jay Devore and Roxy Peck, *Statistics: The Exploration and Analysis of Data* (4th ed.), Brooks/Cole, 2001.

Appendix H

Critical Values for Chi-Square (χ^2)

Degrees of Freedom (df)	LEVEL OF SIGNIFICANCE		
	.10	.05	.01
1	2.706	3.841	6.635
2	4.605	5.991	9.210
3	6.251	7.815	11.345
4	7.779	9.488	13.277
5	9.236	11.070	15.086
6	10.645	12.592	16.812
7	12.017	14.067	18.475
8	13.362	15.507	20.090
9	14.684	16.919	21.666
10	15.987	18.307	23.209
11	17.275	19.675	24.725
12	18.549	21.026	26.217
13	19.812	22.362	27.688
14	21.064	23.685	29.141
15	22.307	24.996	30.578
16	23.542	26.296	32.000
17	24.769	27.587	33.409
18	25.989	28.869	34.805
19	27.204	30.144	36.191
20	28.412	31.410	37.566
21	29.615	32.671	38.932
22	30.813	33.924	40.289
23	32.007	35.172	41.638
24	33.196	36.415	42.980
25	34.382	37.652	44.314

Source: Adapted from tables constructed by Victor Bissonnette, Berry College, retrieved from http://facultyweb.berry.edu/vbissonette/tables/tables.html. Used with permission.

Appendix I

Critical Values of r (Correlation Coefficient)

Degrees of Freedom (df)	LEVEL OF SIGNIFICANCE				
	0.20	0.10	0.05	0.01	0.001
3	0.687	0.805	0.878	0.959	0.991
4	0.608	0.729	0.811	0.917	0.974
5	0.551	0.669	0.754	0.875	0.951
6	0.507	0.621	0.707	0.834	0.925
7	0.472	0.582	0.666	0.798	0.898
8	0.443	0.549	0.632	0.765	0.872
9	0.419	0.521	0.602	0.735	0.847
10	0.398	0.497	0.576	0.708	0.823
11	0.380	0.476	0.553	0.684	0.801
12	0.365	0.458	0.532	0.661	0.780
13	0.351	0.441	0.514	0.641	0.760
14	0.338	0.426	0.497	0.623	0.742
15	0.327	0.412	0.482	0.606	0.725
16	0.317	0.400	0.468	0.590	0.708
17	0.308	0.389	0.456	0.575	0.693
18	0.299	0.378	0.444	0.561	0.679
19	0.291	0.369	0.433	0.549	0.665
20	0.284	0.360	0.423	0.537	0.652
21	0.277	0.352	0.413	0.526	0.640
22	0.271	0.344	0.404	0.515	0.629
23	0.265	0.337	0.396	0.505	0.618
24	0.260	0.330	0.388	0.496	0.607
25	0.255	0.323	0.381	0.487	0.597
26	0.250	0.317	0.374	0.479	0.588
27	0.245	0.311	0.367	0.471	0.579
28	0.241	0.306	0.361	0.463	0.570
29	0.237	0.301	0.355	0.456	0.562
30	0.233	0.296	0.349	0.449	0.554
35	0.216	0.275	0.325	0.418	0.519
40	0.202	0.257	0.304	0.393	0.490
45	0.190	0.243	0.288	0.372	0.465
50	0.181	0.231	0.273	0.354	0.443
60	0.165	0.211	0.250	0.325	0.408
70	0.153	0.195	0.232	0.302	0.380
80	0.143	0.183	0.217	0.283	0.357
90	0.135	0.173	0.205	0.267	0.338

Source: Adapted from tables constructed by Victor Bissonnette, Berry College, retrieved from http://facultyweb.berry.edu/vbissonette/tables/tables.html. Used with permission.

Appendix J

Data Sets and Computer-Based Data Analysis

We'll begin with a definition of a data set, a concept introduced early on in this text. By way of review, a data set may be defined as a bundle or collection of information about one or more variables, typically assembled for the purpose of analysis. It may be that you've collected data on 750 customers, 4500 students, 312 cities, or any other population of interest. Your data set may be very limited (consisting of a small number of cases and variables) or it may be extensive (consisting of hundreds of variables associated with thousands of cases). Despite the variation in size and content, most data sets share certain commonalities in terms of their basic structure. As it turns out, some knowledge about data set structure—even minimal knowledge—can be of substantial benefit to your statistical education in at least two ways.

First, most students who spend any amount of time dealing with statistical applications will eventually find themselves working in a computer-based analytical environment. For example, many statistics courses include an introduction to the use of computers in statistical analysis. Indeed, many statistics courses are structured as two semester courses, with the first semester being devoted to the basics of statistical analysis and the second being devoted to the use of computers in statistical analysis. For other students, the introduction to the use of computers in statistical analysis comes later, maybe in the form of a graduate course or in the world of work. It suffices to say that modern-day statistical analysis is typically undertaken with the assistance of a computer and some rather sophisticated software. In that sense, it's just a practical matter; if you're going to conduct a serious statistical analysis, you'll probably find yourself working with a computer.

The second reason why you should know something about the structure of data sets has to do with the overall learning process. As it turns out, some basic knowledge about the structure of data sets can serve to jump-start your statistical education. At a minimum, it can cause you to starting thinking in terms of cases, variables, and levels of measurement. If you're armed at the outset with a solid understanding of those concepts, your probability of success tends to increase substantially.

With those as reasons enough to take a look at this matter of data set structure, we begin our brief look at the basics of data set structure and the use of computers in statistical analysis. Along the way, you'll discover some good news, along with a few words of caution.

It Usually Starts with Rows and Columns

In the simplest of terms, computer-based data sets are all about rows and columns. As a rule, each case or observation takes one row in the overall format, and different columns are devoted to different variables. There are many different statistical analysis programs on the market, but most share this *row and column* format approach. For example, SPSS and SAS are two widely used software programs. While there are differences between them, both rely upon the same general data structure format. Rows are devoted to individual cases or observations; columns are devoted to the different variables. When the underlying software program directs the computer to look at the data, it's directing the system to look at all of the cases or observations in a structured format. What's more, it's telling the system the name that you've assigned to each variable and where each variable will be found. It's really the first step. Specific instructions about what analysis to perform or what type of report to print are matters that come later. What always comes first is the data entry process—the process of entering the information into the computer and letting the computer know the fundamentals about how the data set is structured. To better understand this point, let's take a look at a hypothetical data set.

Imagine for a moment that you had data on 25 different cities. More specifically, let's say that you had the following information on each city:

Name of the city

Total population in 1990

Total population in 2000

Ranking in terms of sales tax revenues collected during 2000 (ranking from 1 to 25)

Median family income in 2000

% of adult population having a college degree

Region of the nation in which the city is located (i.e., north, south, east, or west)

While it's true that a data set with only 25 cases might be small enough to cause you to think about making use of the old fashioned paper/pencil approach, you'd probably want to turn to a computer-based system, at least in the real world. Not only are computer-based systems widely available (and typically at a rather reasonable cost), the matter of data entry is very straightforward. What's more, it's also likely that in the real world you might find yourself working with a much larger number of cases and variables—something that's no problem for the more popular software systems. The SPSS and SAS systems, for example, can easily handle thousands of cases and hundreds of variables.

All of that, though, has to do with capabilities. The issue at hand has to do with how the data set would be structured. Figure J-1 provides an illustration of the general layout that you'd see on a computer terminal screen if you had entered the data described above (i.e., the data on the 25 cities). If you've never really worked with a computer-based statistical analysis program, let me urge you to take a careful look at the illustration. Focus on the overall structure—each row devoted to a single case or observation and each column devoted to a specific variable.

Even if you've taken a close look at Figure J-1, let me ask you to take another look with an eye toward some specific points.

City	1990 Population	2000 Population	Sales Tax Revenue Ranking for 2000	Median Family Income ($)	Adults with College Degree (%)	Region
Arthurville	21,500	32,841	15	31,863	16.51	1
O'Dell Park	15,602	17,611	21	21,336	21.34	1
Lunnville	5282	6328	16	53,119	33.11	3
Bandiville	10,853	12,260	17	42,781	26.81	2
		Continue with data entry through entire data set				
Woodville	31,338	42,132	7	39,388	17.26	4
Lake Grinstead	18,665	21,893	61	41,990	11.59	3
Klepferville	7033	8622	5	39,338	21.53	1
Groves City	24,817	31,992	9	52,167	28.85	4

Figure J-1   Example of Data Set Structure for a Data Set Involving Demographic Data for a Sample of 25 Cities

First, look at the entire illustration with the thought in mind that it could just as easily involve thousands of cases and hundreds of variables (a point that I made earlier in a discussion of the near-limitless capacity of many software packages). Imagine that you could scroll down the terminal screen, with cases appearing, one after another, in a near-endless stream. Similarly, imagine that you're moving across the screen and even more variables begin to appear (e.g., maybe you had 125 different variables in your study). Imagine that additional columns start to appear, again in a near-endless stream.

Secondly, take note of the fact that a row of data constitutes information about a case. For example, the first row of data has information about Arthurville. The second row of data has information about O'Dell Park. And so it goes. One row, one case; another row, another case; all the way through until the last community, Groves City.

Now take a look at the very top of the illustration—the area that is shaded in the illustration. Those are the names that have been given to the different variables. What you should understand at this point is that most statistical analysis packages have great flexibility in this area. For many of the software packages, for example, you can assign very short names to each variable— short names that you'll use when you issue commands to the system (e.g., when you tell the system to compute the mean and standard deviation for the variable of Pop 90). The real flexibility is found in the fact that many of the packages ultimately allow you to assign very detailed, elongated labels to each variable name. In other words, most programs allow you to expand the short name to provide a far more descriptive name or label. As a rule, the expanded names or labels don't come into play until you actually conduct some sort of analysis. When the analysis is complete and the results appear on the screen or on the printer, you'll see the elongated names or labels appear. For example, you may refer to the variable known as Pop 90 when you're issuing instructions to the system, but the results that appear (after you've completed your analysis) will use the expression Population in 1990 Census (if that's the elongated name or label that you've assigned).

In a sense, the business of assigning elongated names or labels is something that occurs in the background, so to speak. Your real focus is on entering and working with the cases and variables that you see on the screen and doing so on the basis of the short variable names that you assigned at the outset. But that's just one of the background elements. Here are just a few other things that are likely to occur in the background:

> *Each variable is identified in terms of its level of measurement (e.g., nominal, ordinal, interval/ratio).*
>
> *Each variable is identified as either numeric or alphanumeric— numeric variables being variables expressed in numbers and alphanumeric variables being variables expressed in numbers, alphabetic characters, or both).*
>
> *The system has been told how to recognize missing information or deal with cases in which some of the information is incomplete.*
>
> *The system understands the coding system that you're using (e.g., if you use the letter N to stand for North, the system will understand that and will print out results accordingly).*

The list of capabilities could go on and on and on. Suffice it to say that contemporary statistical analysis software packages are extremely sophisticated—so much so that a good amount of time can be spent in exploring the capacities of a single package. What's important at this point, though, is just the basic structure of the data set, and that is something that is fairly uniform across the various packages. Just remember the basic rule of thumb: Cases are in rows; variables are in columns.

If you've never dealt with a data set that was structured for use with a computer program, let me offer the following as a suggested exercise. Simply conjure up a study of some sort—a research project that you might like to conduct. It could be a study of students enrolled at a university, customers at a local store of some sort, prime-time television programs, newspaper editorials, court records, or anything else that might cross your mind. Once you've settled on a topic of interest, imagine that you're going to collect information on, let's say, 20 cases (i.e., 20 students, 20 customers, 20 television programs, etc.). Also imagine that you'll be collecting information on specific variables. For example, maybe your goal is to collect information on the age, sex, place of residence, grade point average, and academic major of each student in your sample. Once you have the basics of your study design in your mind, imagine the way the data would look on a computer screen, assuming that you entered the data into a computer-based data set. If you've had experience working with data sets, the exercise may strike you as rather simplistic. If the world of data sets is something very new to you, though, I suspect you're likely to find the exercise to be a very valuable one.

Assuming that you now have some basic understanding of data-set structure, let me offer a few comments about the day-to-day reliance upon computers for statistical analysis. This is where the mixed message comes into the discussion.

Good News; Words of Caution; It's Up to You

Regardless of when you might get directly involved in computer-based data analysis, my guess is that you'll be a little amazed at the capabilities of most statistical analysis software packages. I've already alluded to the rather extraordinary number of cases and variables that most packages can handle, but that's just the start of it. The truly amazing element is the speed at which the data are manipulated and calculations are performed. Extremely sophisticated analyses can be carried out in split seconds and with the highest levels of accuracy. Just to take one example, imagine that you wanted to calculate a simple average (the mean, as it's referred to in statistical parlance), but you wanted to calculate that average for 127 different variables with a sample involving 38,294 cases. All you have to do is type in a couple of commands, tell the system to go to work, and your results will appear in the blink of an eye.

All of that should be very good news for anyone who's venturing into the world of statistical analysis for the first time. If that's where you are—if you're just beginning your first systematic study of statistical analysis—you might do well to always remember that the sophisticated software is, for the most part, readily available. In doing so, you can take comfort in the fact that you could most likely rely upon some very user-friendly software to do part of the job for you. Consequently, your mind should be freed up a bit for more important matters—important matters such as selecting the appropriate statistical procedures and interpreting the results. Just to set your mind at ease, let me repeat: You can take comfort in the fact that serious statistical analysis is typically done with the assistance of a computer. The days of pencils, paper, and tedious calculations are over. On the other hand, you're never free of the responsibility of knowing how to select and interpret the appropriate statistical procedure.

All of that, of course, returns us to a point raised earlier—namely the importance of developing a solid understanding of the underlying conceptual elements involved in statistical analysis. Statistical calculations represent only one part of the equation, so to speak. The other part—indeed, the most important part—has to do with the logical and conceptual basis of statistical analysis. Simply put, you can always rely upon statistical software to carry out complex calculations, but selecting the appropriate procedure and interpreting the results is something that falls to you.

As to what that means when you're working your way through this or any other text, let me offer the following approach. You should always be careful in your calculations. You should strive for precision. But you should never look at a statistical task with a focus on how long it might take you to work your way through the problem. If there are highly tedious steps involved in a particular procedure, just accept the fact that it's part of the process and there's little you can do except work your way through it. Don't let some temporary frustration about tedious procedures block your understanding of the underlying logic or conceptual basis. In the final analysis, it's your understanding of the underlying logic and conceptual basis that will pay off.

In short, it's probably a good idea to remind yourself every now and then that you could, if push came to shove, rely upon computer-based data analysis for almost any sort of statistical analysis. In doing so, you're apt to lower your stress level, at least to some degree. But when you do that, you'd be well served to keep your mind focused on the more important issues—logic and concepts.

Appendix K

Some of the More Common Formulas Used in the Text

$$\mu = \frac{\Sigma X}{N} \qquad \textit{Mean of a population}$$

$$\overline{X} = \frac{\Sigma X}{n} \qquad \textit{Mean of a sample}$$

$$\sigma^2 = \frac{\Sigma (X - \mu)^2}{N} \qquad \textit{Variance of a population}$$

$$s^2 = \frac{\Sigma (X - \overline{X})^2}{n - 1} \qquad \textit{Variance of a sample}$$

$$\sigma = \sqrt{\frac{\Sigma (X - \mu)^2}{N}} \qquad \textit{Standard deviation of a population}$$

$$s = \sqrt{\frac{\Sigma (X - \overline{X})^2}{n - 1}} \qquad \textit{Standard deviation of a sample}$$

$$\sigma_{\overline{X}} = \frac{\sigma}{\sqrt{n}} \qquad \textit{Standard error of the mean}$$

$$s_{\overline{X}} = \frac{s}{\sqrt{n}} \qquad \textit{Estimate of the standard error of the mean}$$

$$S_p = \sqrt{\frac{P(1 - P)}{n}} \qquad \textit{Estimate of the standard error of the proportion}$$

$$\text{CI} = \overline{X} \pm Z(\sigma_{\overline{X}}) \qquad \textit{Confidence interval for the mean (σ known)}$$

$$\text{CI} = \overline{X} \pm t(s_{\overline{x}}) \qquad \textit{Confidence interval for the mean (σ unknown)}$$

$$\text{CI} = P \pm Z(s_P) \qquad \textit{Confidence interval for the proportion}$$

$$\overline{D} = \frac{\Sigma d}{n} \qquad \textit{Mean difference}$$

$$s_d = \sqrt{\frac{\Sigma (d - \overline{D})^2}{n - 1}} \qquad \textit{Standard deviation of the differences}$$

$$s_{\overline{D}} = \frac{s_d}{\sqrt{n}} \qquad \textit{Estimate of the standard error of the mean difference}$$

$$s_{\overline{X}1-\overline{X}2} = \sqrt{\frac{(n_1 - 1)s_1^2 + (n_2 - 1)s_2^2}{n_1 + n_2 - 2} \cdot \left[\frac{1}{n_1} + \frac{1}{n_2}\right]}$$

Estimate of the standard error of the difference between means

$$Z = \frac{X - \mu}{\sigma}$$

Conversion of a raw score in a population to a Z score

$$Z = \frac{X - \overline{X}}{s}$$

Conversion of a raw score in a sample to a Z score

$$Z = \frac{\overline{X} - \mu}{\sigma_{\overline{X}}}$$

Single sample test involving a mean with σ known

$$t = \frac{\overline{X} - \mu}{S_{\overline{X}}}$$

Single sample test involving a mean with σ unknown

$$t = \frac{\overline{D}}{S_{\overline{D}}}$$

Two sample test involving mean difference (matched or related samples)

$$t = \frac{\overline{X}_1 - \overline{X}_2}{S_{\overline{X}1-\overline{X}2}}$$

Two sample test involving difference between means (independent samples)

$$F = \frac{MS_B}{MS_W}$$

F ratio for Analysis of Variance

$$MS_B = \frac{SS_B}{df_B}$$

Mean square between

$$MS_W = \frac{SS_W}{df_W}$$

Mean square within

$$\chi^2 = \sum\left[\frac{(f_0 - f_e)^2}{f_e}\right]$$

Chi-Square Test

$$r = \frac{\sum(Z_X \cdot Z_Y)}{n - 1}$$

Correlation Coefficient

Answers to Chapter Problems

CHAPTER 1

1. Academic major; test performance
2. Gender; attitude toward abortion
3. Nominal
4. Ordinal
5. Interval or interval/ratio
6. Nominal
7. Ratio
8. Ordinal
9. 500; 23,419
10. Sample; population
11. Statistics; parameters
12. Descriptive; inferential

CHAPTER 2

General Thought Questions

1. Mean, median, and mode
2. Mean
3. Mode
4. Median
5. Range; dispersion
6. 82
7. Bi-modal distribution; the modes are 18 and 21
8. Mean deviation or average deviation
9. 0
10. 0; squaring
11. Square root
12. $n - 1$; n

Application Questions/Problems

1. a. 4.2; b. 3rd score; c. 4; d. 1.84; e. 5.70; f. 2.39

2. a. 15.88; b. 4.5th score; c. 15.5; d. 12; e. 2.88; f. 12.41; g. 3.52
3. a. 3.89; b. 5th score; c. 4; d. 1 and 4; e. 1.90; f. 6.61; g. 2.57
4. a. 4.67; b. 4.50; c. 7; d. 2.35
5. 3
6. a. 3.20; b. 2.10
7. a. 2; b. .50
8. 73
9. 170

CHAPTER 3

General Thought Questions

1. Symmetrical
2. Right; left
3. Inflection
4. 1
5. Coincide (or are equal)

Application Questions/Problems

1. 68%
2. 95%
3. 99%
4. 50%; 50%
5. 2
6. 78
7. 80
8. 140
9. 950

CHAPTER 4

General Thought Questions

1. Infinite
2. 0; 1

Application Questions/Problems

1. 44.84%
2. 49.06%
3. 38.88%
4. 2.5%
5. 2.5%
6. .5%
7. .5%
8. 6.30%
9. 13.14%
10. approximately −.84
11. approximately .39
12. approximately ±.84

CHAPTER 5

General Thought Questions

1. Equal
2. Does not
3. All
4. Sampling frame
5. Sample
6. Sampling error
7. Error
8. Means
9. Mean
10. Standard error of the mean
11. Standard deviation; square root
12. Normal

Application Questions/Problems

1. 24.12; .40
2. 30; .40
3. 120; 3
4. 615; 4.50
5. 55; 1.70

CHAPTER 6

General Thought Questions

1. Mean
2. Estimate; sample
3. Mean
4. Decreases
5. Inverse
6. Width
7. Increase; decrease

8. σ divided by the square root of n
9. s divided by the square root of n

Application Questions/Problems: Confidence Interval for the Mean With σ Known

1. a. 12.50; b. 14.14; c. 8.77; 15.00
2. a. 145.30–154.70;
   b. 143.81–156.19
3. a. 51.73–56.27; b. 51.01–56.99
4. a. 74.02–75.98; b. 73.71–76.29
5. 76.24–79.76
6. 488.20–507.80
7. 515.47–528.53
8. 513.41–530.59
9. 108.06–111.94

Application Questions/Problems: Confidence Interval for the Mean With σ Unknown

1. a. 1.25; b. 2.50; c. 2.58; d. 6.48
2. a. 24.14–27.86; b. 23.49–28.51
3. a. 360.96–443.04;
   b. 346.69–457.31
4. a. 73.81–86.19;
   b. 71.61–88.39
5. 3.68–5.12
6. \$35.52–\$41.98
7. 81.05–90.95
8. 94.40–107.60
9. 5.83 ounces–6.89 ounces

Application Questions/Problems: Confidence Interval for the Proportion

1. 33.22%–46.78%
2. 9.68%–30.32%
3. 25.51%–38.49%
4. 7.47%–22.53%
5. 8.67%–17.33%
6. 57.51%–64.49%
7. 54.96%–67.04%
8. 71.06%–76.04%
9. 70.39%–76.71%

CHAPTER 7

General Thought Questions

1. Type I
2. Type I
3. Type II
4. Null hypothesis

5. Level of significance
6. Critical region
7. Fail to reject
8. .05 and .01
9. Region of rejection or critical region; null hypothesis

Application Questions/Problems: Hypothesis Involving a Single Sample Mean With σ Known

1. H_0: μ = 6.88; b; Z = 4.03;
Reject the null at the .05 level.
2. H_0: μ = 72.55; b; Z = 2.77;
Reject the null at the .05 level.
3. H_0: μ = 61; b; Z = −2.94;
Reject the null at the .05 level.
4. H_0: μ = 10.45; b; Z = 1.67;
Fail to reject the null at the .05 level.
5. H_0: μ = 155; b; Z = 3.33;
Reject the null at the .05 level.
6. H_0: μ = 75; b; Z = 2.00;
Reject the null at the .05 level.

Application Questions/Problems: Hypothesis Test Involving a Single Sample Mean With σ Unknown

1. H_0: μ = 8.45; b; t = −3.53;
Critical value = 2.045;
Reject the null at the .05 level.
2. H_0: μ = 8.25; b; t = −.99;
Critical value = 2.160;
Fail to reject the null at the .05 level.
3. H_0: μ = 15.23; b; t = −5.78; Critical value = 2.064; Reject the null hypothesis at the .05 level.
4. H_0: μ = 10.65; b; t = 2.66; Critical value = 2.042; Reject the null hypothesis at the .05 level.
5. H_0: μ = 12.16; b; t = −1.48; Critical value = 2.064; Fail to reject the null hypothesis at the .05 level.
6. H_0: μ = 12.56; b; t = −1.90; Critical value = 2.045; Fail to reject the null hypothesis at the .05 level.

CHAPTER 8

General Thought Questions

1. True
2. False

3. Mean differences
4. The difference between means

Application Questions/Problems: Matched/Related Samples Design

1. a. H_0: $\mu_{\bar{D}}$ = 0; **b.** t = 2.81; **c.** Critical value = 2.145; **d.** Reject the null at .05 level.
2. a. H_0: $\mu_{\bar{D}}$ = 0; **b.** t = 1.54; **c.** Critical value = 2.064; **d.** Fail to reject the null at .05 level.
3. a. H_0: $\mu_{\bar{D}}$ = 0; **b.** t = 2.57; **c.** Critical value = 2.045; **d.** Reject the null at .05 level.
4. a. H_0: $\mu_{\bar{D}}$ = 0; **b.** t = 2.28; **c.** Critical value = 2.048; **d.** Reject the null at .05 level.
5. a. H_0: $\mu_{\bar{D}}$ = 0; **b.** t = 1.70; **c.** Critical value = 2.045; **d.** Fail to reject the null at .05 level.

Application Questions/Problems: Independent Samples Design

1. a. H_0: $\mu_1 - \mu_2$ = 0; **b.** t = 2.97; **c.** Critical value = 2.042; **d.** Reject the null at .05 level.
2. a. H_0: $\mu_1 - \mu_2$ = 0; **b.** t = 1.82; **c.** Critical value = 2.009; **d.** Fail to reject the null at .05 level.
3. a. H_0: $\mu_1 - \mu_2$ = 0; **b.** t = −1.47; **c.** Critical value = 2.056; **d.** Fail to reject the null at .05 level.
4. a. H_0: $\mu_1 - \mu_2$ = 0; **b.** t = −1.58; **c.** Critical value = 2.048; **d.** Fail to reject the null at .05 level.
5. a. H_0: $\mu_1 - \mu_2$ = 0; **b.** t = −2.93; **c.** Critical value = 2.042 (use critical value for 30 degrees of freedom); **d.** Reject the null at .05 level.

CHAPTER 9

General Thought Questions

1. Alternative or research
2. Directional hypothesis
3. Two-tailed
4. One-tailed
5. Rejecting; true
6. Failing to reject; false

Application Questions/Problems: Alternative or Research Hypotheses

1. **a.** H_0: There is no significant difference between on-campus and commuter students with respect to grade point average.

   b. H_1: There is a significant difference between on-campus and commuter students with respect to grade point average.

   c. H_2: On-campus students have a significantly higher grade point average than commuter students.

   d. H_3: Commuter students have a significantly higher grade point average than on-campus students.

2. **a.** H_0: There is no significant difference in length of sentences handed out to white and non-white defendants in first-offense drug trafficking cases.

   b. H_1: In first-offense drug trafficking cases, the length of sentence handed out to non-white defendants is significantly different than the length of sentence handed out to white defendants.

   c. H_2: In first-offense drug trafficking cases, the length of sentence handed out to non-white defendants is significantly higher than the length of sentence handed out to white defendants.

   d. H_3: In first-offense drug trafficking cases, the length of sentence handed out to white defendants is significantly higher than the length of sentence handed out to non-white defendants.

3. **a.** H_0: There is no significant difference between rural and urban areas in terms of levels of voter participation.

   b. H_1: There is a significant difference between rural and urban areas in terms of levels of voter participation.

   c. H_2: The level of voter participation is significantly higher in rural areas than it is in urban areas.

   d. H_3: The level of voter participation is significantly higher in urban areas than it is in rural areas.

4. **a.** H_0: There is no significant difference between the levels of water pollution in creeks in the southern part of the state and levels of water pollution in creeks in the northern part of the state.

   b. H_1: There is a significant difference between the levels of water pollution in creeks in the southern part of the state and levels of water pollution in creeks in the northern part of the state.

   c. H_2: Levels of water pollution in creeks in the southern part of the state are significantly higher than levels of water pollution in creeks in the northern part of the state.

   d. H_3: Levels of water pollution in creeks in the northern part of the state are significantly higher than levels of water pollution in creeks in the southern part of the state.

Application Questions/Problems: One-tailed and Two-tailed Critical Values

1. **a.** 1.96; **b.** 1.64; **c.** 2.58; **d.** 2.33
2. **a.** 2.131; **b.** 1.721; **c.** 1.74; **d.** 1.734

CHAPTER 10

General Thought Questions

1. F
2. Between; within
3. Find the difference or deviation between each score and the mean of each category; square the deviations; add the squared deviations; sum the squared deviations across all categories.
4. Find the difference or deviation between each category mean and the grand mean; square the deviations; multiply the squared deviations in each category by the number of cases in the category; sum across all categories.
5. Degrees of freedom
6. Degrees of freedom
7. $n - k$
8. $k - 1$
9. Mean square between
10. Mean square within
11. $\mu_1 = \mu_2 = \mu_3$

Application Questions/Problems

1. **a.** 5; **b.** 30
2. **a.** 3.59; **b.** 3.01; **c.** Reject the null at the .05 level.

3. a. 2.69; **b.** 2.98; **c.** Fail to reject the null at the .05 level.

4. a. 6.77; **b.** 3.40; **c.** Reject the null at the .05 level.

5. a. $\mu_1 = \mu_2 = \mu_3$; **b.** Sample 1 = 8.00, Sample 2 = 6.00, Sample 3 = 9.00; **c.** 7.79; **d.** 40.64; **e.** 170.00; **f.** 2; **g.** 26; **h.** 6.54; **i.** 20.32; **j.** 3.11; **k.** Fail to reject the null at the .05 level.

6. a. $\mu_1 = \mu_2 = \mu_3 = \mu_4$; **b.** Northern = 4.00, Southern = 4.00, Eastern = 6.00, Western = 5.00; **c.** 4.74; **d.** 25.43; **e.** 122.00; **f.** 3; **g.** 35; **h.** 3.49; **i.** 8.48; **j.** 2.43; **k.** Fail to reject the null at the .05 level.

7. a. $\mu_1 = \mu_2 = \mu_3$; **b.** Day Shift = 4.40, Afternoon Shift = 4.75, Night Shift = 4.60; **c.** 4.57; **d.** .27; **e.** 19.14; **f.** 2; **g.** 11; **h.** 1.74; **i.** .14; **j.** .08; **k.** Fail to reject the null at the .05 level.

8. a. $\mu_1 = \mu_2 = \mu_3$; **b.** Male = 3.17, Female = 7.17, Mixed Gender = 5.17; **c.** 5.17; **d.** 48; **e.** 34.52; **f.** 2; **g.** 15; **h.** 2.30; **i.** 24; **j.** 10.43; **k.** Reject the null at the .05 level.

CHAPTER 11

General Thought Questions

1. Contingency
2. Categorical
3. Observed
4. Expected
5. (row total × column total)/n
6. $(r - 1) \times (c - 1)$
7. 4
8. 12
9. 15
10. 8

Application Questions/Problems

1. 9.488; Fail to reject the null hypothesis at the .05 level.
2. 21.026; Reject the null hypothesis at the .05 level.
3. 3.841; Reject the null hypothesis at the .05 level.
4. 9.488; Reject the null hypothesis at the .05 level.
5. 21.026; Fail to reject the null hypothesis at the .05 level.

6. a. 3 degrees of freedom; **b.** .10; Fail to reject the null at the .05 level.

7. a. 4 degrees of freedom; **b.** 18.35; Reject the null at the .05 level.

8. a. 2 degrees of freedom; **b.** .27; Fail to reject the null at the .05 level.

CHAPTER 12

General Thought Questions

1. −1.00
2. +1.00
3. −1.00 to +1.00
4. No association
5. Scatter plot
6. Correlation
7. Determination
8. Line of best fit; least squares line
9. $a + bx$
10. Y'
11. a
12. b

Application Questions/Problems

1. a. 6.38; **b.** 2.96; **c.** 6; **d.** 2.55; **e.** 11.11; **f.** .93

2. a. 10.00; **b.** 1.56; **c.** 56.00; **d.** 15.60; **e.** 3.53; **f.** .39

3. a. −.89; This is a strong, negative relationship; **b.** .79; 79% of the variation in Y is attributable to variation in X; **c.** $r = 0$; Reject the null at the .05 level

4. a. .39; This is a weak, positive relationship; **b.** .10; 10% of the variation in Y is attributable to variation in X; **c.** $r = 0$; Reject the null at the .05 level

5. a. .90; This is a strong, positive relationship; **b.** .81; 81% of the variation in Y is attributable to variation in X; **c.** $r = 0$; Reject the null at the .05 level

6. $a = 29.91$ and $b = -.23$

7. $a = 17$ and $b = 4.15$

8. a. −.998; This is a strong, negative relationship; **b.** .996; 99.6% of the variation in Y is attributable to variation in X; **c.** $a = 4.12$ and $b = -.04$

9. a. .83; This is a strong, positive relationship; **b.** .69; 69% of the variation in Y is attributable to variation in X; **c.** $a = -\$32.01$ and $b = 3.67$

10. $41.39

Glossary

1-2-3 Rule A statement of how much area under the normal curve is found between ±1, ±2, and ±3 standard deviations from the mean.

a term in the regression equation ($Y' = a + bX$) The Y-intercept; the point at which the regression line crosses the Y-axis.

alternative hypothesis A hypothesis that stands in opposition to the null hypothesis. It may be directional or nondirectional.

ANOVA (analysis of variance, one-way) A test to determine if there is a significant difference among three or more groups or samples.

average deviation See *mean deviation*.

b term in the regression equation ($Y' = a + bX$) The slope of the regression line; the change in Y that accompanies a unit change in X.

between-groups degrees of freedom The number of degrees of freedom associated with the estimate of between-groups variance; equivalent to the number of groups minus 1.

between-groups estimate of variance See *mean square between*.

between-groups sum of squares The sum of the squared deviation of each sample mean from the grand mean, weighted by the number of cases in each sample, and summed across all samples.

bimodal distribution A distribution with two modes.

calculated test statistic The result of a hypothesis-testing procedure; the value that is compared to a critical value when testing the null hypothesis.

categorical data Information obtained on variables measured at the nominal or ordinal level; responses that can be classified into categories.

Central Limit Theorem A statement about the relationship between a population and a sampling distribution based on that population. The Central Limit Theorem is stated as follows:

> If repeated random samples of size n are taken from a population with a mean or mu (μ) and a standard deviation (σ), the sampling distribution of sample means will have a mean equal to mu (μ) and a standard error equal to $\dfrac{\sigma}{\sqrt{n}}$. Moreover, as n increases the sampling distribution will approach a normal distribution.

central tendency The center or typicality of a distribution. The three most common measures of central tendency are the *mean, median,* and *mode*.

chi-square test of independence A test to determine whether there is an association between two categorical variables.

333

coefficient of determination The value of r^2; a measure of the amount of variation in Y that is attributable to variation in X.

confidence interval for a proportion A statement of two values (or an interval) within which you believe the true proportion of the population is found.

confidence interval for the mean A statement of two values (or an interval) within which you believe the true mean of the population (μ or mu) is found.

contingency table A classification tool that reveals the various possibilities (contingencies) in the comparison of variables; a table that presents data in terms of all combinations of two or more variables.

correlation A procedure designed to determine the strength and direction of an association between two interval/ratio level variables. Also known as Pearson's r.

correlation coefficient The value of r; a measure of the strength and direction of an association between two interval/ratio level variables. The value of r can range from -1.0 to $+1.0$.

critical region The portion of a sampling distribution that contains all the values that allow you to reject the null hypothesis. If the calculated test statistic (e.g., Z or t) falls within the critical region, the null can be rejected.

critical value The point on a sampling distribution that marks the beginning of the critical region; the value that is used as a point of comparison when making a decision about a null hypothesis. If the calculated test statistic (e.g., Z or t) meets or exceeds the critical value, the null hypothesis can be rejected.

curvilinear association An association between two variables that would, if represented in a scatter plot, conform to a general pattern of a curved line.

data Information.

data distribution A listing of the values or responses associated with a particular variable in a data set.

data point The individual pieces of information in a data set.

data set The collection or bundle of information relative to specific variables.

dependent variable The variable that's presumed to be influenced by another variable.

descriptive statistics Statistical procedures used to summarize or describe data.

directional hypothesis An alternative or research hypothesis that specifies the nature or direction of a hypothesized difference. It asserts that there will be a difference or a change in a particular direction (increase or decrease).

dispersion (variability) The extent to which the scores in a distribution are spread around the mean value or throughout the distribution. The two most commonly used measures of dispersion are the *variance* and the *standard deviation*.

effect The change in a measurement that is attributable to a treatment condition or stimulus of some sort.

estimate of the standard error of the mean An estimate of the standard deviation of the sampling distribution of sample means; a function of the standard deviation of a sample.

expected frequency The frequency that would be expected to occur in a particular cell, given the marginal distributions and the total number of cases in the table.

F ratio The ratio of the between-groups estimate of variance to the within-groups estimate of variance. The F ratio is frequently referred to as the ratio of the mean square between to the mean square within.

family of t distributions A series of sampling distributions (of the t statistic) developed by Gossett. The shape of any one distribution is a function of sample size (or degrees of freedom, equal to $n - 1$).

frequency distribution A table or graph that indicates how many times a value or score appears in a set of values or scores.

grand (overall) mean The mean that would result if the values of all cases in an ANOVA application were added and the sum divided by the total number of cases.

group (sample) mean The mean of an individual sample in an ANOVA application.

hypothesis A statement of expectations. See also *null hypothesis* and *alternative hypothesis*.

independent samples Samples selected in such a manner that the selection of any case in no way affects the selection of any other case.

independent variable The variable that's presumed to influence another variable.

inferential statistics Statistical procedures used to make statements or inferences about a population, based on sample statistics.

interval level of measurement A system of measurement based on an underlying scale of equal intervals. See also *interval/ratio level of measurement* and *ratio level of measurement*.

interval/ratio level of measurement Since there is no practical difference between the interval and ratio levels of measurement when it comes to statistical analysis, the terms are often combined to refer to any scale of measurement that is either interval or ratio.

least squares line See *line of best fit.*

level of confidence The amount of confidence that can be placed in an estimate derived from the construction of a confidence interval. Level of confidence is mathematically defined as 1 minus the level of significance. The level of confidence is a statement of the percentage of times (99%, 95%, etc.) one would obtain a correct confidence interval if one repeatedly constructed confidence intervals for repeated samples from the same population.

level of significance The probability of making a Type I error.

linear association An association between two variables that would, if represented in a scatter plot, conform to a general pattern of a straight line.

line of best fit The line that passes through a scatter plot in such a way that the square of the distance from each point in the plot to the line is at a minimum. Also known as the *regression line* or the *least squares line.*

margin of error A term used to express the width of a confidence interval for a proportion.

marginal totals The row and column totals that are presented in the margins of a table.

matched or related samples Samples selected in such a manner that cases included in one sample are somehow related or matched to cases in another sample. In some instances, the matching is achieved by using the same subjects tested in two situations (for example, in a before/after test situation). In other instances, the matching is achieved by matching subjects or cases on the basis of relevant criteria.

mean The most widely used measure of central tendency. The mean is calculated by summing all the scores in a distribution and dividing the sum by the total number of cases in the distribution.

mean deviation An infrequently used measure of dispersion based, in part, on the absolute deviations from the mean of the distribution. Also known as the *average deviation.*

mean square between The between-groups estimate of variance; calculated by dividing the between-groups sum of squares by the between-groups degrees of freedom.

mean square within The within-groups estimate of variance; calculated by dividing the within-groups sum of squares by the within-groups degrees of freedom.

median The score that divides a distribution in half; the midpoint of a distribution, or the point above and below which one-half of the scores or values are located. The formula for the median is a positional formula; it will tell you the position of the median in the distribution, not its value.

mode The response or value that appears most frequently in a distribution. The mode is the only measure of central tendency that is appropriate for nominal level data.

mu (μ) The mean of a population.

negative (inverse) association A pattern of association in which the variables track in opposite directions; as one variable increases in value, the other variable decreases in value.

negative skew The shape of a distribution that includes some extremely low scores or values. A distribution is said to have a negative skew if the tail of the distribution points toward the left.

nominal level of measurement The simplest level of measurement; a system of measurement based on categories that are mutually exclusive and collectively exhaustive.

non-directional hypothesis An alternative or research hypothesis that does not specify the nature or direction of a hypothesized difference. It simply asserts that a difference will be present.

normal curve A unimodal, symmetrial curve that is mathematically defined on the basis of the mean and standard deviation of an underlying distribution.

null hypothesis A statement of equality; a statement of no difference; a statement of chance. In the case of a hypothesis test involving a single sample mean (that is compared to a known population mean), the null is typically a statement of the value of the population mean.

observed frequency The result or frequency presented in each cell of a contingency table.

one-tailed test situation A research situation in which the researcher is looking for an extreme difference that is located on only one side of the distribution.

ordinal level of measurement A level of measurement that presumes the notion of order (greater than and lesser than).

parameter A characteristic of a population. Compare *statistic*.

Pearson's r See *correlation*.

perfect association A pattern of association between variables in which there is perfect predictability; knowledge of the value of one variable allows a precise prediction of the value of the other variable.

point of inflection The point at which a normal curve begins to change direction. It is one standard deviation above or below the mean of the underlying distribution.

population All possible cases; sometimes referred to as the *universe*. It is often thought of as the total collection of cases that you're interested in.

positive (direct) association A pattern of association in which the variables track in the same direction; as one variable increases in value, the other variable increases in value.

positive skew The shape of a distribution that includes some extremely high scores or values. A distribution is said to have a positive skew if the tail of the distribution points toward the right.

power The ability of a test to reject a false null hypothesis.

random sample A sample selected in such a way that every unit has an equal chance of being selected, and the selection of any one unit in no way affects the selection of any other unit. In a random sample, all combinations are possible.

range A statement of the difference between the highest and lowest scores or values in a distribution. As a measure of dispersion or variability, the range is simple to calculate, but it doesn't say much about the distribution.

ratio level of measurement A level of measurement that has all the properties of the interval level of measurement, plus the presence (or possibility) of a true or legitimate zero (0) point. See *interval/ratio level of measurement*.

region of rejection See *critical region*.

regression analysis A technique that allows the use of existing data to predict future values.

regression equation The equation that describes the path of the line of best fit. The regression equation is used to predict a value of Y (referred to as Y' or Y-prime) on the basis of an X value ($Y' = a + bX$).

regression line See *line of best fit*.

research hypothesis See *alternative hypothesis*.

sample A portion of a population.

sampling distribution of sample means The result you would get if you took repeated samples from a given population, calculated the mean for each sample, and plotted the sample means.

sampling error The difference between a sample statistic and a population parameter that is due to chance.

sampling frame A physical representation of the population; a listing of all the elements in a population.

scatter plot A visual representation of the values of two variables on a case-by-case basis.

skewed distribution A distribution that departs from symmetry, in the sense that most of the cases are concentrated at one end of the distribution.

standard deviation A widely used measure of dispersion or variability. The standard deviation is the square root of the variance.

standard error of the difference of means The standard deviation of a sampling distribution of the difference between two sample means. The sampling distribution, in this case, would be the result of repeated sampling—each time taking two samples, calculating the mean of each sample, calculating the difference between the means, and recording/plotting the differences. The standard error would be the standard deviation of the sampling distribution.

standard error of the estimate An overall measure of the difference between actual and predicted values of Y.

standard error of the mean The standard deviation of a sampling distribution of sample means.

standard error of the mean difference The standard deviation of a sampling distribution of mean differences between scores reflected in two samples. The sampling distribution, in this case, would be the result of repeated sampling—each time looking at two related samples, and focusing on the difference between the individual scores in each sample. The individual differences would be treated as forming a distribution, and that distribution has a mean. The repeated samplings would result in repeated mean differences. The recording/plotting of those mean differences would constitute the sampling distribution. The standard error would be the standard deviation of the sampling distribution.

standardized normal curve A unimodal, symmetrical, theoretical distribution based on an infinite number of cases, having a mean of 0 and a standard deviation of 1.

statistic A characteristic of a sample. Compare *parameter*.

strength of association The extent to which the value of one variable can be predicted on the basis of the value of another variable.

symmetrical distribution A distribution in which the two halves are mirror images of each other.

table of areas under the normal curve A table of values that tell you what proportion of the area under the normal curve is found between the mean and any Z value.

tail of the distribution In a skewed distribution, the elongated portion of the curve.

two-tailed test scenario A research situation in which the researcher is looking for an extreme difference that could be located at either end of the distribution.

Type I error Rejection of the null hypothesis when the null is true.

Type II error Failure to reject the null hypothesis when the null is false.

unimodal distribution A distribution with only one mode.

universe See *population*.

variable Anything that can take on different quantities or qualities; anything that can vary.

variance A widely used measure of dispersion or variability. The variance is equal to the standard deviation squared.

within-groups degrees of freedom The number of degrees of freedom associated with the within-groups estimate of variance; equivalent to the number of cases minus the number of groups.

within-groups estimate of variance See *mean square within*.

within-groups sum of squares The sum of the squared deviations of each score from its sample mean, summed across all samples.

Y prime (Y′) The Y value that you are attempting to predict, based on a given value for X and the regression equation.

Z (Z score) A point along the baseline of a standardized normal curve.

Z ratio The result of finding the difference between a raw score and a mean, and dividing the difference by the standard deviation. This procedure converts a raw score into a Z score.

References

Cuzzort, R. P., & Vrettos, J. S. (1996). *The elementary forms of statistical reason*. New York: St. Martin's.

Dunn, D. S. (2001). *Statistics and data analysis for the behavioral sciences*. New York: McGraw-Hill.

Elifson, K. W., Runyon, R. P., & Haber, A. (1990). *Fundamentals of social statistics* (2nd ed.). New York: McGraw-Hill.

Gravetter, F. J., & Wallnau, L. B. (1999). *Essentials of statistics for the behavioral sciences* (3rd ed.). Pacific Grove, CA: Brooks/Cole.

Gravetter, F. J., & Wallnau, L. B. (2000). *Statistics for the behavioral sciences* (5th ed.). Belmont, CA: Wadsworth.

Gravetter, F. J., & Wallnau, L. B. (2002). *Essentials of statistics for the behavioral sciences* (4th ed.). Pacific Grove, CA: Wadsworth.

Healy, J. F. (2002). *Statistics: A tool for social research* (6th ed.). Belmont, CA: Wadsworth.

Howell, D. C. (1995). *Fundamental statistics for the behavioral sciences* (3rd ed.). Belmont, CA: Duxbury.

Hurlburt, R. T. (1998). *Comprehending behavioral statistics* (2nd ed.). Pacific Grove, CA: Brooks/Cole.

Kachigan, S. K. (1991). *Multivariate statistical analysis: A conceptual introduction* (2nd ed.). New York: Radius.

Moore, D. S. (2000). *The basic practice of statistics* (2nd ed.). New York: W. H. Freeman.

Pagano, R. R. (2001). *Understanding statistics in the behavioral sciences* (6th ed.). Belmont, CA: Wadsworth.

Popper, K. R. (1961). *The logic of scientific discovery*. New York: Science Editions.

Pryczak, F. (1995). *Making sense of statistics: A conceptual overview*. Los Angeles, CA: Pryczak Publishing.

Ramsey, F. L., & Schafer, D. W. (2002). *The statistical sleuth: A course in methods of data analysis* (2nd ed.). Pacific Grove, CA: Duxbury.

Russell, B. (1955). *Nightmares of eminent persons, and other stories*. New York: Simon & Schuster.

Salkind, N. J. (2000). *Statistics for people who think they hate statistics*. Thousand Oaks, CA: Sage.

Utts, J. M., & Heckard, R. F. (2002). *Mind on statistics*. Pacific Grove, CA: Duxbury.

Index